The Faith of the Early Church:

An Ancient Apologetic

for the New Evangelization

Nicholas L. Gregoris, S.T.D.

New Hope Publications
P.O. Box 10
New Hope, KY 40052 USA
270-325-3061
www.newhopepublications.org
Ask for stock #3292.

ISBN 978-1-892875-64-8

Cover design by Vanessa Hurst
Printed in the United States of America

TABLE OF CONTENTS

FOREWORD

This book is a compilation of articles originally written for the *The Catholic Response*, a bi-monthly Catholic publication.

Now revised and updated, the purpose of this book is to deepen the reader's understanding of the apostolic roots of the Catholic Faith. On the wings of reason and faith we seek to rise to the contemplation of timeless, indeed eternal truths. These truths are firmly rooted in Sacred Scripture, Sacred Tradition and the Magisterium. We endeavor to present these truths in such a way that the contemporary person appreciates them not as relics of the past but as his or her own patrimony for the present and the future.

In a word, the truths of the Catholic Faith constitute the Church's heritage. All peoples are invited to appreciate the inestimable value of the fullness of the Gospel message, for it is indeed "the pearl of great price."

Here we should mention certain features of the book. The ample footnotes are not meant as a distraction to the reader, but serve to flesh out, clarify and enrich the book's content. Particular attention is given to the definition of key theological terms and concepts. Due to the complexity of certain topics, it was thought best to define such terms and concepts in footnotes for immediate reference rather than in a separate glossary.

The artwork found throughout is also meant as a pedagogical tool. At the end of the book are other tools, such as a list of suggested further reading. At the conclusion of several chapters is included an *Excursus* for anyone interested in gleaning information germane to the topic of a given chapter though not essential.

The book is divided into seven main sections:

1. Chapters One and Two form a general introduction to the Fathers of the Church, as well as to the early heresies and schisms to which they ardently responded.

2. Chapters Three to Nine focus on the contributions of the first seven Ecumenical Councils that established a firm doctrinal and devotional foundation for the united Church of the first Christian millennium.

3. Chapters Ten to Twenty-One seek to unpack the thought of select Fathers, situating each Father in chronological order, with particular attention paid to his cultural and historical background.

4. Chapter Twenty-Two deals with the formation of the Catholic Canon of the Bible, highlighting too its relation to the Jewish, Eastern Orthodox and Protestant Canons.

5. Chapters Twenty-Three to Twenty-Six are focused on early key Christian writings and their portrayal of the four marks of the Church (one, holy, catholic and apostolic) and her unique role in human history as the universal sacrament of salvation.

6. Chapters Twenty-Seven to Thirty continue to explore early Christian writings on certain essential Catholic doctrines, namely atonement for sin, the Petrine primacy, episcopal authority and ecclesial communion and charity.

7. Chapter Thirty-One serves as the capstone for the entire book, much as Chapter Eight on "Mary in the Mystery of Christ and the Church" served as the capstone of the Second Vatican Council's Dogmatic Constitution on the Church, *Lumen Gentium*. This chapter is focused on Patristic Marian doctrine and devotion, including two of the most venerable Marian prayers in our Christian patrimony: the *Sub Tuum Praesidium* and the "Akathist" Hymn.

Hopefully, this book will be useful for Catholic school teachers and students, indeed for anyone interested in what the early Christians believed and practiced. The reader is challenged to discover or perhaps rediscover how the teachings of the early Church correspond faithfully to the Deposit of Catholic and Apostolic Faith as we are called to know, believe and live it today.

As we continue to engage in the "New Evangelization" in the Third Christian Millennium, we should be mindful of Saint Peter's exhortation: "Always be prepared to make a defense to anyone who calls you to account for the hope that is in you, yet do it with gentleness and reverence" (1 Peter 3:15).

Nicholas L. Gregoris, S.T.D.

ABBREVIATIONS

General:

d. (died)

c. or ca. ("circa," "around" or "about")

B.C. ("Before Christ")

A.D. ("Anno Domini," "In the Year of the Lord")

Cf. or cfr. ("confer," "refer to")

f or ff. (see the following verses)

passim (a quote that continues "here and there," but not consecutively on the pages indicated)

St. (Saint)

Sts. (Saints)

Aram (Aramaic)

Heb (Hebrew)

Gr (Greek)

Lat (Latin)

OT (Old Testament)

NT (New Testament)

CCC (Catechism of the Catholic Church)

PG (Patrologia Greca)

PL (Patrologia Latina)

Abbreviations of the Books of the Bible

Old Testament

Gen (Genesis)

Ex (Exodus)

Lev (Leviticus)

Num (Numbers)

Deut (Deuteronomy)

Jos (Joshua)

Jgs (Judges)

Ru (Ruth)

1 Sam (First Samuel)

2 Sam (Second Samuel)

1 Kgs (First Kings)

2 Kgs (Second Kings)

1 Chr (First Chronicles)

2 Chr (Second Chronicles)

Ezr (Ezra)

Neh (Nehemiah)

Tob (Tobit)

Jdt (Judith)

Est (Esther)

1 Mac (First Maccabees)

2 Mac (Second Maccabees)

Jb (Job)

Ps (Psalms)

Prov (Proverbs)

Eccl (Ecclesiastes)

Sg (Song of Songs)

Wis (Wisdom)

Sir (Sirach)

Is (Isaiah)

Jer (Jeremiah)

Lam (Lamentations)

Bar (Baruch)

Ez (Ezechiel)

Dan (Daniel)

Hos (Hosea)

Jl (Joel)

Am (Amos)

Ob (Obadiah)

Jon (Jonah)

Mi (Micah)

Na (Nahum)

Hab (Habakkuk)

Zep (Zephaniah)

Hag (Haggiah)

Zec (Zechariah)

Mal (Malachi)

New Testament

Mt (Matthew)

Mk (Mark)

Lk (Luke)

Jn (John)

Acts (Acts of the Apostles)

Rom (Romans)

1 Cor (First Corinthians)

2 Cor (Second Corinthians)

Gal (Galatians)

Eph (Ephesians)

Phil (Philippians)

Col (Colossians)

1 Thes (First Thessalonians)

2 Thes (Second Thessalonians)

1 Tim (First Timothy)

2 Tim (Second Timothy)

Ti (Titus)

Phlm (Philemon)

Heb (Hebrews)

Jas (James)

1 Pt (First Peter)

2 Pt (Second Peter)

1 Jn (First John)

2 Jn (Second John)

3 Jn (Third John)

Ju (Jude)

Rev (Revelation)

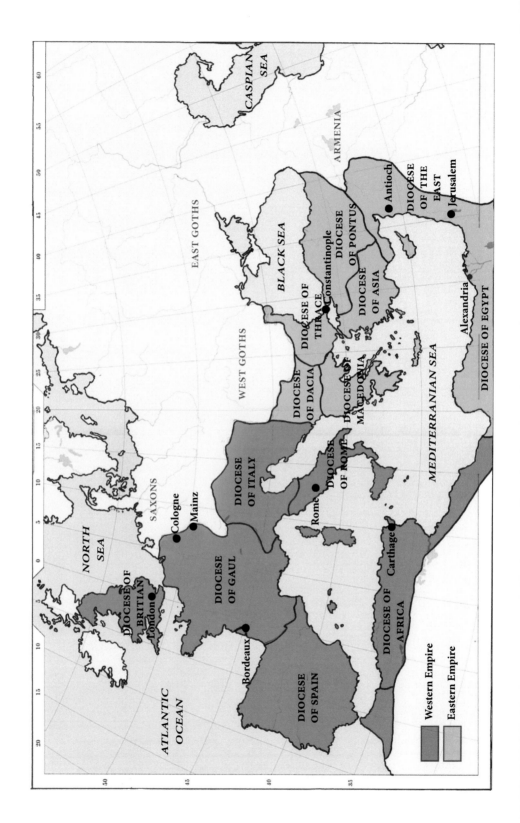

PART I

Chapters One and Two form a general introduction to the Fathers of the Church, as well as to the early heresies and schisms to which they ardently responded.

CHAPTER ONE:
FAITH OF OUR FATHERS

Do the Fathers of the Church[1] really know best? Who are the Fathers of the Church? The Fathers were, first of all, the teachers of Christian antiquity. They were a motley crew, whose provenance stretched from Spain to Syria. The Fathers were men of varying temperaments, some quite fiery, like Jerome and John Chrysostom.

Jerome (340-420), Priest and Doctor of the Church, received an excellent classical education at Rome. He was baptized at the age of twenty-five and ordained a priest at the age of thirty-eight. He traveled frequently to Asia Minor and the Holy Land where he encountered many famous and learned Eastern Fathers of the Church. For a time, he lived as a hermit in Chalcis (Syria) where he engaged a rabbi to teach him Hebrew.

Jerome served the Church in Constantinople and in Rome as personal secretary to Pope Damasus who commissioned him to translate the Bible into Latin (*Editio Vulgata* or "Vulgate") from the original Hebrew and Greek languages.[2]

---

[1] Cf. Gerald O'Collins, S.J., Edward S. Farrugia, S.J., *A Concise Dictionary of Theology* [Revised and Expanded Edition] (Paulist Press, 2000), 89: "**Fathers of the Church.** A popular title for certain early Christians who wrote in Greek, Latin, Syriac, and Armenian, and whose doctrine and personal holiness won general approval in the Church. 'Each in a different way and to a different degree,' they remain 'classics of Christian culture' (1989 *Instruction on the Fathers* by the Congregation for Catholic Education). In theological controversy it became customary to appeal to the Eastern and Western Fathers, their unanimous consent being considered a decisive argument. In the West the era of the Church Fathers is understood to have ended with St. Isidore of Seville (ca. 560-636), in the East with St. John of Damascus (ca. 675-ca.749)."

[2] Cf. James s, *History of the Catholic Church: From the Apostolic Era to the Third Millennium* (Ignatius Press, 2012), 79: "Jerome, in his hermitage at Bethlehem, devoted himself to translating the whole Bible into Latin, a translation called the *Vulgate* ("people's book") because at the time Latin was the spoken language of most people in the West. Prior to Jerome, Christians outside Palestine mainly relied for their knowledge of the Old Testament on the Septuagint, which had been written in Greek. Jerome, however, translated directly from the Hebrew. Use of the Bible was facilitated by the invention of the book—pages of manageable size bound together so as to allow them to be turned over one by one, replacing long

Jerome eventually returned to Palestine maintaining the discipleship of certain noble Roman matrons who had abandoned their wealthy lifestyles in order to consecrate their lives in poverty, chastity and obedience (the three evangelical counsels). Jerome served as their spiritual father and encouraged them, for example, through his personal letters, to model their lives of consecrated virginity on those of Christ and the Blessed Virgin Mary.

Jerome established a monastery in Bethlehem, living in a cave underneath what, during the time of the Emperor Justinian, became the Basilica of the Nativity in Bethlehem (Hebrew: "house of bread") that is still extant. Notice the connection between Jesus' birthplace and the mystery of the Holy Eucharist.

The low door leading into the Basilica is nicknamed "the door of humility." Although originally constructed to keep men from entering the church astride their horses, theologically the door has come to signify the need to humble oneself in imitation of God who became a baby and who was adored by humble shepherds and wise men.

Jerome is the patron saint of biblical scholars. Perhaps his most quoted line is: "Ignorance of Scripture is ignorance of Christ." In art Jerome is often depicted as a cardinal (although the office did not exist during his lifetime), perhaps because of Jerome's close association with Pope Damasus.

Furthermore, one will often notice that Jerome is depicted with a lion. Legend has it that while Jerome was lecturing one day on the Scriptures a lion came into his classroom. While everyone was afraid, Jerome was not. Realizing the lion was injured, he removed a thorn from its paw. The grateful lion decided to become Jerome's pet. Saint Jerome's liturgical memorial is September 30.

John Chrysostom (c. 350-407) is venerated as a Bishop and Doctor of the Church. Chrysostom is not a proper surname; it was his nickname in Greek (which means "golden-tongued"), afforded Saint John because he was a renowned preacher.[3] He was born at Antioch, becoming a hermit[4] and then

unwieldy scrolls that had to be laboriously unrolled. Gradually, the Greek word for a book (*biblia*) came to have only one meaning, the Bible."

3   Cf. Hitchcock, *History of the Catholic Church*, 61: "St. John Chrysostom [...] excoriated the people of his city, especially the rich, for their injustices and their neglect of the needy. (He antagonized people by his bluntness and was soon deposed) [....]." See also, 62-63: "Chrysostom uttered a modern-sounding complaint in one of his sermons, expressing exasperation that, as often as he reminded his hearers of the need to increase their donations, it did no good."

4   As a monk, St. John Chrysostom dwelt in the desert. The Greek word for desert is *heremos*, hence the word "hermit."

a monk at Antioch. He was installed as Archbishop of Constantinople by the Emperor Arcadius (395-408) in 398 and ended his days in exile. The Divine Liturgy of Saint John Chrysostom is popularly ascribed to his authorship. It is one of the most significant liturgies used in the Eastern Orthodox and Byzantine Catholic traditions. Saint John Chrysostom's liturgical memorial is September 13.

A Father's character, philosophical prowess and theological acumen also depended in part on his occupational and educational background. Some were farmers, others lawyers and rhetoricians, still others biblical exegetes and apologists.

The Fathers did not always see eye-to-eye on all issues, but as Blessed John Henry Newman[5] was quick to point out, no single Father of the Church at any given time speaks for the Universal Church. Rather, Blessed Newman proposed that we read each individual Father or group of Fathers in perspective of the Apostolic Tradition as a whole. Russell instructs us in this regard:

> Does one have to agree with everything that a Father of the Church says? The witness of any one Father is occasionally of great weight for doctrine when taken singly, if he is teaching a subject on which he is recognised by the Church as an especial authority. Examples are Saint Augustine on the Blessed Trinity and Saint Athanasius on the divinity of the Son. But the authority of single Fathers in itself is not infallible.[6]

---

[5] John Henry Newman lived from 1801 to 1890. He was born in London and died in Birmingham, England. He was educated at Trinity College, Oxford, and flourished as a Fellow of Oriel College. He eventually helped spearhead, with the collaboration of fellow intellectuals like Edward Bouverie Pusey, John Keble and Ambrose Saint John, "The Oxford Movement" that sought to bring the Anglican Church back to its Catholic historical and theological roots. He was an ordained clergyman of the Church of England, serving as Rector of the University Church of Saint Mary at Oxford. On October 9, 1845, Newman was received into full communion with the Catholic Church by Blessed Dominic of the Mother of God (Barberi), an Italian Passionist. His writings are voluminous, including sermons, theological treatises, poems, letters and diaries. He was ordained a Catholic priest in Rome, having studied at the College of the Propagation of the Faith (*Propaganda Fidei*) for one year. Returning from Rome, Newman introduced into England the Congregation of the Oratory that was originally founded at Rome by Saint Philip Neri in the sixteenth century. In 1879, Pope Leo XIII created Newman a Cardinal-Deacon, assigning him the titular Church of San Giorgio in Velabro (Rome). Thus, Pope Leo helped vindicate Newman's reputation as an outstanding churchman. In 2010, Pope Benedict XVI beatified Newman in England. His relics are kept at the Oratory Church in Birmingham. Blessed Newman's liturgical memorial is October 9.

[6] Cf. Claire Russell, *Glimpses of the Fathers of the Church: Selections from the Writings of the Fathers of the Church*, (Scepter Press, 1994), XV.

We should note that the Fathers are commonly divided linguistically into two main groups, namely Latin and Greek, even though Fathers of the Church whose mother tongue was Syriac or Coptic, for example, are listed in separate categories. We know that we do not always possess the original text of a given Father of the Church, so that, for instance, only fragments of the Greek texts of Saint Irenaeus of Lyons remain, while the bulk of his writing has come down to us in Latin manuscripts.

Robert Louis Wilken offers some distinguishing characteristics that set the Fathers of the Church apart from the *hoi polloi* of the early Church:

> Early Christian thought is biblical, and one of the lasting accom-
> plishments of the patristic[7] period was to forge a way of thinking,
> scriptural in language and inspiration, that gave to the Church and
> to Western Civilization a unified and coherent interpretation of the
> Bible as a whole [...]. Christian thinking is anchored in the church's
> life, sustained by such devotional practices as the daily recitation of
> the Psalms, and nurtured by the liturgy, in particular by the regular
> celebration of the Eucharist.[8]

The Fathers have been officially recognized by the Church[9] as men who passed on through their orthodox teaching, preaching, sacramental celebrations, holiness of life, and, in some instances, through their unbroken hierarchical communion as successors of the Apostles,[10] the one, holy, catholic and apostolic Faith.

---

[7]   Cf. O'Collins, Farrugia, *A Concise Dictionary of Theology*, 194: "**Patristics.** (Lat. 'Study of the Fathers'). The study of the theology of the Church Fathers. This term has often been used inaccurately as a synonmy for *patrology* [...]. **Patrology.** (Gr. 'Study of the Fathers'). A term coined in the seventeenth century for the study of the Fathers of the Church. A 1989 instruction on the study of the Church Fathers (issued by the Vatican's Congregation for Catholic Education) distinguishes *patrology*, the historical and literary study of the Church Fathers, from *patristics*, the study of their theological thought."

[8]   Cf. Robert Louis Wilken, *The Spirit of Early Christian Thought: Seeking the Face of God* (Yale University Press, 2003), XVII-XVIII *passim*.

[9]   The Second Vatican Council treats of the Fathers of the Church in the following documents: *Dei Verbum*, 8; *Optatam Totius*, 16; *Ad Gentes*, 22; *Presbyterorum Ordinis*, 19. Furthermore, the Catechism of the Catholic Church cites individual Fathers more than three hundred times. The Fathers are also mentioned collectively on numerous occasions. St. Augustine is the most quoted of the Fathers of the Church in the Catechism, cited almost ninety times. After St. Augustine, St. Irenaeus of Lyons is the most popular, cited over thirty times. Cf. Mike Aquilina, *The Fathers of the Church: An Introduction to the First Christian Thinkers* (Our Sunday Visitor, Inc., 1994), 49.

[10]   However, non-bishops are also included in this illustrious list of the Fathers of the Church like St. Ephrem the Syrian (c. 306-373) who was a deacon. His liturgical memorial is June 9.

Vincent of Lérins developed four criteria for determining how a man could be rightfully considered a Father of the Church: 1) orthodox teaching; 2) holiness of life; 3) universal Church approval; 4) antiquity. Saint Vincent formulated a principle that serves as a barometer of the teachings of the Fathers of the Church: *quod ubique, quod semper, quod a omnibus creditum est.* In other words, their teachings had to correspond to what is believed everywhere, always and by all.[11]

St. Paul Preaching at Athens *by Raphael, 1515.*

These criteria or principles are commonly referred to as the Vincentian Canon. Russell comments on how Saint Vincent of Lérins contributed to forming an identity-kit for the Fathers of the Church:

---

[11] Cf. O'Collins, Farrugia, A Concise Dictionary of Theology, 62f: "**Development of Doctrine.** Growth in the Church's teachings since the apostolic age. Authentic development requires identity-in-change between the new teaching and the original Deposit of Faith or revelation that reached its climax with Christ. St. Vincent of Lérins (d. before 450) compared doctrinal development identity-in-change between a child and the same person as an adult. When completing *An Essay on the Development of Christian Doctrine* (1845), John Henry Newman (1801-1890) became a Catholic. He criticized St. Vincent's canon of ubiquity, universality, and unanimity, '*quod ubique, quod semper, quod ab omnibus creditum est*' (Lat. 'what is believed everywhere, always, and by all') as too abstract and elaborated seven notes or tests for distinguishing between faithful development and corruption. In grappling with the issue of development much depends on one's view of revelation, understanding, and interpretation."

Saint Vincent of Lérins writing in a famous document, *Commonitorium*,[12] in 434, offers an accurate description. The Fathers of the Church are those alone who, though in diverse times and places yet persevering in the communion and faith of the one Catholic Church, have been approved teachers. Modern theologians reach the same conclusion by requiring a Father of the Church to be of orthodox doctrine and learning, living a saintly life and being of certain antiquity. The criteria by which one can judge whether an ecclesiastical writer is a Father or not, are: citation by a general council, reference in the public Acts of the Pope addressed to the Church, inclusion in the Roman martyrology as *sanctitas et doctrina insignis*,[13] public reading in the Churches in the early centuries and citation with praise (as an authority to the Faith) by one of the more celebrated Fathers.[14]

Categorizing the Fathers

We commonly distinguish the Fathers as:

1. Apostolic—living in the first and second generations subsequent to the Apostles;[15]

2. Pre-Nicene—living during the time leading up to the First Ecumenical Council of Nicaea in A.D. 325;[16]

---

[12] From Latin, "a book of warnings" or "book of admonitions."

[13] "holiness and outstanding teaching."

[14] Russell, *Glimpses of the Fathers of the Church*, XIV.

[15] Cf. Benedict XVI, *The Fathers* (Our Sunday Visitor, Inc., 2008), 7.

[16] Jaroslav Pelikan explains the historical background of using A.D. as an abbreviation: "But in the sixth century a Scythian monk, living in Rome, Dionysius Exiguus ('Little Denis'), proposed a new system of reckoning. It was to be named not for the pagan myth of the founding of Rome by Romulus and Remus, nor for the persecutor Diocletian, but for the Incarnation of Jesus Christ, specifically for the day of the Annunciation to the Virgin Mary by the Angel Gabriel, 25 March, in the year 753 A.U.C. [*Ab Urbe Condita*, 'From the Founding of the City of Rome']. For reasons that seem still to be somewhat obscure, Dionysius Exiguus miscalculated by four to seven years, producing the anomaly by which it is sometimes said that Jesus was born in 4 B.C. Such trifles aside, however, Dionysius' identification of 'the Christian era' gradually established itself, even though the process of establishing it required many centuries, and is now universal. Henceforth the dates of history and biography are marked as A.D. and B.C., according to 'the years of Our Lord.' Even the life of an Antichrist is dated by the dates of Christ; biographers of his enemies have to be written this way, so that we speak of Nero as having died in A.D. 68 and of Stalin as having died in A.D. 1953. In this sense at any rate, and not only in this sense, everyone is compelled to acknowledge that because of Jesus of Nazareth history will never be the same" (*Jesus Through the Centuries: His Place in the History of Culture*, Yale University Press, 1987, 33).

3. Nicene—working to develop the Council of Nicaea during the fourth century;

4. Post-Nicene—closing the Patristic era in the time after Nicaea until the middle of the eighth century.[17]

5. Some scholars include Bernard of Clairvaux[18] among the Fathers of the Church. However, most theologians agree that John Damascene (645-ca.749) is the last of the Eastern Fathers, while Isidore of Seville (556-636) or Bede the Venerable[19] would be considered the last of the Western Fathers.

---

[17] Cf. Aquilina, *The Fathers of the Church*, 14. Aquilina uses a felicitous phrase in reference to the fourth century A.D., "a golden age of doctrinal expression."

[18] Bernard of Clairvaux (c. 1090-1153), Abbot and Doctor of the Church, was nicknamed *Doctor Mellifluus* (Honey-Tongued) on account of his attractive preaching. He refounded the Cistercian Order at Cîteaux (France) and founded nearly seventy monasteries from Spain to Syria, from Sicily to Sweden. At the behest of Pope Urban II, Bernard preached the Second Crusade. He wrote numerous commentaries on Sacred Scripture, his most famous being his commentary on the Song of Songs. Bernard interprets the Song of Songs as a human-divine love poem. It describes not only the human love between a man and a woman but also in mystical, spiritual and transcendent terms the love of God for His chosen people, Israel; the love of Christ for His spotless bride, the Church; the love of God desirous of intimacy with the soul of the baptized believer; the love of God for the Virgin Mary as His mystical spouse in the mystery of the Incarnation. One of his ascetical principles was: "Love is the greatest force of the spiritual life." Bernard is lauded in Dante's *Divine Comedy* (*Paradise* 31: 52-69, 94-142; 32: 151; 33:1-54). Saint Bernard's liturgical memorial is August 20.

[19] Bede the Venerable (673-735), Priest and Doctor of the Church, was a Benedictine monk of Jarrow (England). He wrote an impressive Ecclesiastical History of the English Peoples. He helped introduce the notion of dating events from the time of Jesus' birth (A.D.). Saint Bede's liturgical memorial is May 25.

Excursus: Doctors of the Church

Who are Doctors of the Church?[20] In order for a person to qualify for the title he or she must be a canonized saint and then officially recognized by the Pope as having been an outstanding teacher and moral exemplar of the catholic and apostolic Faith.

Not all Fathers of the Church are Doctors of the Church. In fact, two Fathers of the Church, namely Origen of Alexandria and Tertullian of Carthage, probably would not qualify for the title.

Origen was condemned (posthumously!) for having speculated that hell was not an eternal state of being and that God in His infinite mercy would save Satan and the fallen angels at the end of time.[21]

Tertullian, on the other hand, joined a schismatic sect of moral rigorists

---

[20] Cf. O'Collins, Farrugia, *A Concise Dictionary of Theology*: "**Doctor of the Church.** A title given to certain saints for their outstanding, orthodox teaching. From the eighth century the West recognized four such doctors: Pope Gregory the Great (ca. 540-604), Ambrose of Milan (ca. 339-397), Augustine of Hippo (354-430) and Jerome (ca. 342-420). A century later in the East, Basil the Great (ca. 330-379), Gregory of Nazianzus (328-389), and John Chrysostom (ca. 347-407) came to be known as the three hierarchs and ecumenical teachers. Then Athanasius of Alexandria (ca. 296-373) was added, so as to have four Eastern doctors paralleling four Western doctors. Pope Benedict XIV (1675-1758) elaborated the norms for qualifying as a doctor of the Church, above all, eminence of doctrine and sanctity of life. The last Eastern saint to become a doctor was St. Ephraem the Syrian (ca. 307-373), who was so proclaimed in 1920 by Benedict XV (pope 1914-1921). In 1970 Pope Paul VI put two women saints on the list of doctors of the Church: Catherine of Siena (ca. 1347-1380) and Teresa of Avila (1515-1582). In 1997 Pope John Paul II added St. Thérèse of Lisieux (1873-1897), bringing the number of doctors to thirty-three." The reader should note that on October 7, 2012, Pope Benedict XVI added two Doctors of the Church: St. John of Avila (1500-1569) and St. Hildegard von Bingen (1098-1179). In 2015, Pope Francis added St. Gregory of Narek (ca. 950-1003).

[21] Cf. O'Collins, Farrugia, *A Concise Dictionary of Theology*, 183: "**Origenism.** The doctrines and school of thought inspired by Origen of Alexandria (ca. 183-ca. 254). He developed a biblical hermeneutic in terms of the literal, moral and allegorical senses of Scripture. As the first great systematic theologian of Christianity, he stressed images (with sensible reality symbolizing the invisible spiritual world) and our deification through grace. His liking for allegory and, much more, his theses about the ultimate sacrifice of all (*apocatastasis*), the preexistence of human souls (including Christ's) and an apparent subordination of the Son to the Father met with repeated criticism and opposition. Eventually Emperor Justinian I had Origenism condemned at a synod in 543 and then at the Second Council of Constantinople in 553. Nevertheless, it is still not clear how far Origen himself was at fault, how far he was simply exploring a variety of views, and how far false views were ascribed to him after his death. It is difficult to decide, since his works were to a large extent destroyed. Any fair judgment on Origen should also take into account such Fathers of the Church who greatly admired him, including St. Athanasius of Alexandria (ca. 290-373), St. Basil the Great (ca. 330-379), and St. Gregory of Nazianzus (329-389)."

and religious fanatics known as the Montanists (see Excursus on Montanism) toward the end of his brilliant literary career, dying outside full communion with the Catholic Church. Perhaps, then, to avoid confusion, it might be more prudent to refer to Origen and Tertullian as early Christian writers. Russell explains:

> Thus even Tertullian and Origen (whose works while they were faithful sons of the Church are of great value), when they erred in later life are reminders that if something new or unheard of is introduced beyond or against the saints, then it pertains not to religion but to temptation.[22]

What is Heresy?[23]

Our English word "heresy" derives from the Greek word *haeresis*, "to pick" or "to choose." Sadly, we come to know this precise meaning in our own times when we discover so-called "Cafeteria Catholics," even conspicuously ranking among our civil and political leadership.

A heretic, therefore, is a person who picks and chooses those doctrines of the Church he or she finds acceptable, while rejecting other doctrines deemed unsuitable.

Perhaps the basis of a heretical choice is to appease men rather than God, to be politically correct rather than conform to objective standards of truth, goodness and beauty. Other times, people fall into heresy because their beliefs are centered on secularism and moral relativism rather than on Gospel truths. With this frame of mind, a person begins to sacrifice genuine love of God and neighbor for popular recognition, political gain, ambition, money and power. Other people are deliberately heretical in order to suit their immoral lifestyles and wayward ideologies, persisting in intransigent opposition to the teachings of Christ and His Church.

Heresy creates a false dichotomy between the mind and the heart, reason and faith, free will and divine grace, the soul and the body. These dichotomies not only endanger the salvation of the individual who espouses them, but likewise threaten the integrity of the oneness and holiness of the catholic and apostolic Church.

---

[22] Russell, *Glimpses of the Church Fathers*, XV.

[23] Cf. O'Collins, Farrugia, *A Concise Dictionary of Theology*, 103: "**Heresy.** (Gr. 'choice'). In the NT a sectarian group (Acts 5:7) or a disruptive faction and opinion (1 Corinthians 11:19; Galatians 5:20; 2 Peter 2:1). Heresy came to mean a baptized person's willful and persistent dissent from orthodox doctrines of faith. At times the challenge of heresy has encouraged the solemn definition of Church teaching."

For this reason, the Church must safeguard her integrity and the salvation of her children throughout the centuries by reiterating the timeless truths of the Gospel, most especially when heresies and schismatic sects arise to tear asunder the seamless garment of the divine Deposit of Faith.

What are Schism and Apostasy?

Our English word "schism" derives from the Greek word *schisma*, meaning "a tearing apart" (a "sundering" of ecclesial communion).

"Apostasy" stems from the Greek, meaning "to stand away from," and denotes a baptized Christian's renunciation of his or her Christian beliefs.

Excursus: Montanism[24]

Patrick Verbraken explains who the Montanists were and why their theology was so heterodox:

> A pagan priest in Phrygia, Montanus, was converted to the Christian Faith. But in 172 he felt himself suddenly gripped by ecstasy and prophetic urges. He announced the approach of the Second Coming of the Lord and the imminent descent upon the earth of the heavenly Jerusalem, which would end the era of the Son (just as the Incarnation of the Son had ended the era of the Father) and would inaugurate that of the Spirit. Two prophetesses[25] contributed to assuring for him an

---

[24] Cf. O'Collins, Farrugia, *A Concise Dictionary of Theology*, 166: "**Montanism.** An enthusiastic revival movement initiated by Montanus, a converted pagan priest, in second-century Phrygia (in modern-day Turkey), that won many adherents, including even Tertullian (ca. 160-ca. 220). Announcing the consummation of the world, Montanus saw the activities of ecstatic prophets and prophetesses (such as his associates Priscilla and Maximilla) as signs of the end. Ascetic in its demands, the movement forbade remarriage after the death of one's partner and imposed severe rules of fasting. Montanus came to regard himself as the incarnation of the Holy Spirit. The movement's contempt for institutional structures, expressed by its free-lance way of administering the sacraments, met with church condemnation."

[25] The names of these prophetesses were Priscilla and Maximilla. A noted discrepancy is that in some works on Montanism the name Priscilla appears as Prisca. Cf. Jonathan Hill, *Zondervan Handbook to the History of Christianity* (Lion Publishing PLC, 2006), 63-64: "One important movement was Montanism, which was founded in the second half of the second century by a Phrygian named Montanus. Shortly after becoming a Christian, Montanus believed he was given a new revelation, which appointed him as the leader of the church in its final days before the reappearance of Christ. His main disciples were two prophetesses Prisca and Maximilla, who spoke with what their followers believed was the voice of the Holy Spirit. The movement's followers therefore called it the "New Prophecy"; "Montanism," like many labels of this period was applied by their opponents. The Montanists did not preach any particular doctrines that anyone objected to, but other Christians were disturbed by the ecstatic, wild demonstrations that accompanied the prophecies. They were

audience among the electrified people. They rushed in a crowd to the plain of Pepuza (the holy city of the Montanists, 200 km. east of Ephesus, a little like a Moslem[26] Mecca), to prepare themselves for these great events by a very austere common life where the religious effervescence and the sudden enthusiasms became intense (there are many similarities between the Montanists and Wesley's Methodists of the eighteenth century). Montanism numbered many communities of followers in the East (the entire city of Thyatire),[27] and also in the West (at Lyons, Rome, Carthage); it survived until the eighth century. Montanus separated himself from the doctrine of the Church in placing prophecy above the hierarchy. For him, anyone who felt himself sent by the Spirit to prepare his reign on earth was freed from any obligation to bishops, who were only the successors of the Apostles of Christ whose reign was practically over.[28]

---

not always happy about the prominence of women in the movement, either. Most of the Montantist prophecies were concerned with morality, and they taught a very strict way of living. They were harsher than most Christians to those who failed to live up to the standard, and they denied that post-baptismal sin could be forgiven at all. Many people were attracted by the movement and it spread beyond Anatolia where it originated, to the whole empire. It proved especially popular in Africa. Here, as elsewhere, it developed an ecclesiastical structure of its own, with its own priests and bishops working as rivals to the mainstream ones. Mystical rites were celebrated in secret, apparently based on standard Christian ones but also on imitating the ecstatic trances of the prophetesses. Thus, the movement began to resemble the pagan mystery religions. The death of Montanus and his prophetesses, and the non-reappearance of Christ, did not harm the movement's vitality, and it was still in existence—as a minor, secretive cult—in the sixth century."

[26] Alternate spelling: Muslim.

[27] Alternate spelling and more commonly used is Thyatira. Thyatira was one of the seven churches mentioned in the Book of Revelation. Cf. Revelation 2:18-29.

[28] Patrick Verbraken, *The Beginnings of the Church: The First Christian Centuries*, (Paulist Press/Deus Books, 1968), 63.

CHAPTER TWO:
EARLY HERESIES AND SCHISMS

Gnosticism[1]

Already in the first century A.D., we discover how the Apostle John strove to defend the Church against the onslaught of primitive forms of nascent Gnosticism—a very complex system of thought with multiple variations on a basic theme.[2]

Gnosticism derives from the Greek word *gnosis,* meaning "knowledge." The adjective "Gnostic" describes an individual or group that claims to have "secret knowledge" concerning doctrinal beliefs and devotional practices that go above and beyond the sacred Deposit of Divine Revelation.

This so-called "secret knowledge," to which one could only have access by belonging to a particular Gnostic sect, was not only comprised of notions contradictory to Sacred Scripture and Sacred Tradition but also of teachings that were self-contradictory. For the most part, entrance into these Gnostic sects occurred by means of secret rites of initiation.

Henry Chadwick reflects on what he terms the *phenomenon of Gnosticism*:

> Gnosticism was (and still is) a theosophy with many ingredients. Occultism and oriental mysticism became fused with astrology, magic and cabbalistic elements from Jewish tradition, a pessimistic reading of Plato's doctrine that man's true home does not lie in this

---

[1] Cf. O'Collins, Farrugia, *A Concise Dictionary of Theology*, 96f: "**Gnosticism.** A dualistic movement that clearly emerged in the second century. It drew on Jewish, Christian, and pagan sources and presented salvation as spiritual elements being freed from an evil material environment. Christian Gnostics denied Christ's real Incarnation and the *salus carnis* (Lat. 'salvation of the flesh') He effected. They rejected (or modified) the Tradition and Scriptures of mainline Christianity, claiming a privileged knowledge (of God and our human destiny) from secret traditions and revelations. Orthodox Christian writers, especially St. Irenaeus (ca. 130-ca.200), provide much information about Gnosticism. Extensive direct knowledge of the movement became available after 1945 when fifty-two separate Gnostic tractates from the fourth century A.D., written in Coptic, were found at Nag Hammadi (Egypt)."

[2] Cf. Hitchcock, *History of the Catholic Church*, 36-39.

bodily realm, above all the catalyst of the Christian understanding of redemption in Christ. A dualism[3] of spirit and matter, mind and body, was joined with a powerful determinism or predestinarianism: the Gnostics (or "people in the know") are the elect, their souls fragments of the divine, heeding liberation from matter and the power of the planets. The huge majority of humanity are earthly clods for whom no hope may be entertained.[4]

Gnostic Dualism[5]

Gnosticism was dualistic at its core, having a Platonic philosophical base that envisioned the soul as imprisoned in the body. It pitted matter against spirit, body against soul, creating the belief that material realities were inherently evil and only spiritual ones inherently good. Chadwick notes the dire consequences of Gnostic Dualism:

> In antiquity the Gnostic separation of spirit from matter had consequences for two prominent features of mainstream Christianity. The Gnostics could not believe that in Christ the eternal God could have polluted himself by taking on flesh and enduring the Crucifixion; in the First Epistle of John this denial is directly combated. Secondly (and relatedly) the Gnostics tended to deny significance to the Sacraments of Baptism and Eucharist.[6]

---

[3] Cf. O'Collins, Farrugia, A Concise Dictionary of Theology, 68: "**Dualism.** Any interpretation of reality that explains everything through two quite independent primordial principles. An example of dualism in philosophy is that of René Descartes (1596-1650), who interpreted the universe in terms of two irreducible principles, mind and matter (even though he held that God ultimately created both). Radical theological dualism normally proposes two antagonistic deities, a good one and an evil one, as did the Manichaeans and some Gnostics in the early Church and, in the Middle Ages, the Albigensians and the Cathars in the West and Bogomils in the East. Christianity acknowledges a qualified dualism (between soul and body, above all, between God and the created universe), but proclaims that in Christ all things are reconciled to God (2 Corinthians 5:18-20)."

[4] Henry Chadwick, "The Early Christian Community," in *The Oxford History of Christianity* [ed. John McManners] (Oxford University Press, 1993), 28.

[5] Cf. Hitchcock, *History of the Catholic Church*, 36f: "Gnosticism is the name given to a variety of movements, most of them pagan but some ostensibly Jewish or Christian. At stake, was the most fundamental of all the teachings of the Judaeo-Christian faith—that one God created the universe and rules over it. Gnosticism, by contrast, was fundamentally dualist, positing two equal gods, ruling two wholly separate realms of the universe—spiritual and material, light and dark, good and evil. It promised redemption not from sin but from Fate—from history itself—teaching that men, composed of souls and bodies that are ultimately incompatible, are trapped between two realms because of some primordial catastrophe. Salvation consists in freeing the soul from the prison of the body, achieved through the acquisition of secret knowledge (*gnosis*)."

[6] Chadwick, "The Early Christian Community," in *The Oxford History of Christianity*, 29.

Aquilina concurs with Chadwick's judgment and explores reasons for the moral decrepitude of Gnostic Dualism:

> [Gnostics'] loathing of the body and creation led different sects to different conclusions about the moral life. Some concluded that, because all flesh was evil, the actions performed in the body did not matter, so everything was permitted: sexual license, theft, even murder. These Gnostics saw the commandments as arbitrary prohibitions imposed by a despotic creator. Others, however, concluded that, because all flesh was evil, the body's every desire must be severely repressed, and this led them to ascetical extremes: beyond celibacy and temperance to self-castration, rigorous fasting, and even suicide.[7]

Gnostic-dualists, who pitted matter against spirit, considered the material world inherently evil, and therefore beyond redemption. For these Gnostics, the immaterial, good God, not wishing to "dirty his hands," chose to create the material world through an evil god or demiurge, who is sometimes identified with Jesus. Jesus is therefore considered an inferior emanation of the Father-God and not fully God Himself, but only seeming or appearing to be God.

The consequences of these Gnostic heresies are really devastating, especially when their implications for man's salvation are considered. The true essence of the Christian religion, "the mystery of piety" (Latin: *mysterium pietatis*)[8] refers to the mystery of the Lord's Incarnation and Paschal Mystery, His Passion, Death and Resurrection.

These mysteries, which constitute our redemption in Christ Jesus, the Second Person of the Blessed Trinity and the Divine Word Incarnate, were eviscerated by the Gnostics. The Gnostics equated the doctrine of the real enfleshment of God with the "mystery of iniquity" (Latin: *mysterium iniquitatis*).

Contrary to Gnostic doctrine, the Church's soteriology[9] makes clear that it was precisely in order to overcome the "mystery of iniquity" that Our Lord's condescension and "self-emptying" (Greek: *kenosis*)[10] in the Incarnation and Paschal Mystery took place in the fullness of time.

---

[7]　Aquilina, *The Fathers of the Church*, 40.

[8]　Cf. 1 Timothy 3:16.

[9]　Soteriology, from the Greek words, *soter* (savior) and *logos* (word), refers to the branch of theology that studies the mysteries of our salvation.

[10]　*Kenosis* or "self-emptying," is an expression found in the writings of St. Paul. Cf. Philippians 2:5-11; Ephesians 1:13-14; Colossians 1:15-20. These texts were most likely liturgical hymns of the early Christians incorporated into St. Paul's writings.

Gnostic Docetism[11]

The Greek verb *dokein* means "to appear" or "to seem." The Gnostics denied the authentic reality of Our Lord's Sacred Humanity in the mystery of His Incarnation, reducing it to a mere "appearance." The Docetics or Docetists were Gnostics claiming that the true God, who is pure spirit, could never have meddled directly with the creation of a corrupt material universe, let alone substantially united a corrupt human nature to His divine essence in the Incarnation.

Hence, the Docetics generally posited the need for an emanation of a lesser god or other intermediary forces.[12]

For these Gnostics, Jesus was sent by the Father for the purpose of redeeming or rescuing the sparks of divine light, which got trapped in the material world.

The Apostle John was so aghast at the early versions of Gnostic Docetism that he considered their adherents to be "antichrists." Why "antichrists"? To qualify for the ominous title of "antichrist" in the Epistles of John meant that a person opposed the mystery of the Incarnation, espousing a position that flew in the face of the truth revealed by Jesus about Himself and taught by His Church.

Simply put, if the Second Person of the Blessed Trinity was not both truly God and truly Man, then we have been deceived, and we have not been saved from our sins.

Saint John "the Divine Theologian"[13] in emphasizing the realism of the incarnational principle at the heart of the Christian religion shuns any form of Gnosticism when he confesses:

> That which was from the beginning, which we have heard, which we have seen with our eyes, which we have looked upon and touched with our hands, concerning the word of life — the life was made

---

[11] Cf. O'Collins, Farrugia, *A Concise Dictionary of Theology*, 65f: "**Docetism.** (Gr. 'appearance'). The early heresy which held that the Son of God merely seemed to be a human being. Christ's bodily reality was considered heavenly or else a body only in appearance, with someone else, such as Simon of Cyrene, suffering in his place. Against Docetic views, which were already rejected in the NT (1 John 4:1-3; 2 John 7), the Church taught that Christ took from Mary a genuine body like ours and suffered in a really human way."

[12] These "intermediary forces" were sometimes referred to as "demiurges," or "aeons."

[13] In the Eastern tradition only three saints have the privileged title "Theologian" attached to their name: Saint John the Evangelist is known as "The Divine Theologian"; Saint Gregory of Nazianzus as "The Theologian"; and Saint Symeon as "The New Theologian." Saint Gregory Nazianzus was also called "The Christian Demosthenes."

An early Christian depiction of the Good Shepherd in the Museo Pio Cristiano.
Source: Sailko, Wikimedia.

manifest, and we see it, and testify to it, and proclaim to you the eternal life which was with the Father and was made manifest to us — that which we have seen and heard we proclaim also to you, so that you may have fellowship with us; and our fellowship is with the Father and with His Son Jesus Christ. And we are writing this that our joy may complete.[14]

Again, John the Beloved takes aim at Gnostics with this admonition to the early Christian community:

Beloved, do not believe every spirit, but test the spirits to see whether they are of God; for many false prophets have gone out into the world. By this you know the Spirit of God: every spirit that confesses that Jesus Christ has come in the flesh is of God, and every spirit which does not confess Jesus is not of God. This is the spirit of the anti-Christ, of which you heard that it was coming, and now it is in the world already.[15]

The orthodox position of sacred authors, like John, against the Gnostics would be advanced in most notable fashion by Fathers of the Church: Irenaeus

---

[14] 1 John 1:1-4.
[15] 1 John 4: 1-3.

of Lyons, Justin Martyr, Tertullian of Carthage, Origen of Alexandria, Clement of Alexandria, Athanasius of Alexandria, John Chrysostom, Gregory of Nazianzen,[16] Jerome, Ambrose of Milan and Augustine of Hippo.

Gnostic Docetics asserted that Jesus only appeared to die on the cross, while what was claimed to be His Resurrection was only a carefully plotted act of resuscitation.[17]

Heterodox Christians probably were among the first Christians, and perhaps the only Christians, to "evangelize" Mohammad in the Arabian Desert. As a result, the Koran (Qu'ran) offers evidence of a distorted understanding of Jesus Christ. Hill notes:

> [...] it seems that the Christianity of the Arabian Peninsula may
> have influenced Muhammad.[18] There was a tradition that he had a
> Monophysite teacher called Sergius Bahira. Moreover, there are simi-
> larities between early Islam and early Jewish Christianity. It may be
> that some Jewish Christians, cast out by the mainstream Church in
> the Roman Empire, retreated to Arabia, where they never developed
> the doctrines of Jesus' divinity or the Trinity. A common title for
> Muhammad himself was "seal of the prophets," a term he is said to

---

[16] Gregory of Nazianzus (330-390), Bishop and Doctor of the Church. "Nazianzen" or "Nazianzus" derives from the Greek word Nazianzenos. Saint Gregory's place of birth was Arianzum in Cappadocia. He later became the Bishop of Nazianzus, a city not far from Arianzum. Gregory is also honored with the title "the Theologian" because of his tremendous intellectual prowess and oratorical skills. Gregory was a life-long friend and correspondent of Saint Basil of Caesarea or "Basil the Great." When Basil the Great died, Gregory of Nazianzus wrote a letter of condolence to Basil's brother, Saint Gregory of Nyssa. Collectively, these Fathers of the Church are known as the "Cappadocian Fathers" because of their association primarily with this region of Turkey. In 380, after much dispute, the Emperor Theodosius I had Gregory Nazianzen enthroned as Archbishop of Constantinople. Saint Gregory of Nazianzus shares a liturgical memorial with Saint Basil the Great (c. 330-379) which is celebrated on January 2 in the Roman calendar.

[17] Cf. Hitchcock, *History of the Catholic Church*, 37: "Gnosticism required the rejection of the Old Testament, since the all-good God could not have created the material universe, which is the realm of a second, perhaps lesser, divinity. Gnostics also reinterpreted Jesus Himself, whom they could not accept as a real man who once lived on earth. Thus they tended to approach the New Testament in a wholly 'spiritual' way, as composed mainly of allegories of the soul in its relationship to God. Their denial of history, including the New Testament accounts of Jesus' life (He could not really have died), allowed them to 'transcend' particular beliefs and to soar into the realm of the mystical imagination. Various early books written under Gnostic auspices—the 'gospels' of Judas, Thomas, and Philip as well as stories about Mary Magdalen—differed substantially from the four Gospels and sometimes contradicted them. All were written much later than the New Testament."

[18] Alternate spelling: Mohammad.

have used himself. But the earliest known appearance of this phrase is Christian: it was used by Tertullian to describe Christ.[19]

Valentinus

Another noteworthy example of early Gnosticism was the system of Valentinus,[20] who professed belief in a *pleroma* of *aeons*, that is, a "fullness" or multitude of intermediary powers or demiurges used by the transcendent God to create the material world. Hill singles out Valentinus as an example of Gnostic belief based on bizarre mythological notions:

> Valentinus, an extremely influential Gnostic who lived in the first half of the second century, believed that the spiritual world contained thirty-one deities, arranged in a hierarchy from the highest God of all, "Bythos" or "Depth," ranging down to "Sophia" or "Wisdom." Sophia rebelled, dissatisfied with her position at the bottom of the divine scale; she was restored, but her "Passion" was purged from her and cast out. Out of this Passion emerged matter and the Demiurge, who, unaware of the spiritual world, believed himself to be God, and made the physical world. This ignorant Creator was the "God" of the Old Testament, a different being from the loving Father of the New Testament [...]. We are created out of imperfect "Passion," cast out of Heaven — and so we are flawed, but we still retain a spark of our heavenly origins. Gnostics such as Valentinus believed that salvation consisted of escaping from the evil, physical world and returning that spiritual spark to the divine realm. This could only happen after death, but many Gnostics believed that they could start the process now by living ascetic, austere lives, involving themselves with matter as little as possible. Others reasoned that, if the material world is evil, it doesn't really matter what you do with it, and so they lived as libertines with no moral rules at all [...]. Valentinus believed that only some people have the spiritual spark and the chance of salvation, and so only they could be taught these doctrines.[21]

---

[19] Cf. Hill, *History of Christianity*, 120.

[20] Cf. O'Collins, Farrugia, *A Concise Dictionary of Theology*, 280f: "**Valentinians.** Followers of Valentinus, who founded one of the most important Gnostic sects in the second century. He seems to have been born in Egypt and to have led the Gnostics in Alexandria before leaving for Rome around 135. He stayed there for about twenty years, and at one point apparently hoped to become Bishop of Rome. He taught a complicated system of aeons, which originally formed the *pleroma*. Later, through *syzigies* (Syriac 'coupling' 'marrying'), Sophia, a female goddess and of the lowest aeons, gave birth to the demiurge or creator of the universe, identified with the (evil) God of the OT. This system was vigorously challenged by St. Irenaeus of Lyons (ca. 130-ca. 200)."

[21] Hill, *History of Christianity*, 64-65 *passim*.

Marcionism[22]

Marcionism, which scholars now generally agree does not quite fit into the category of Gnosticism, bears further explanation.

Patrick Verbraken sizes up Marcion:

> During the second century the Church had a formidable enemy in the person of Marcion. Son of the Bishop of Sinope[23] on the Black Sea, excommunicated by his father, Marcion came to Rome in 139, where his violently anti-Jewish speeches led to a second excommunication in July 144; he then organized a new Church, that of the Marcionites, which spread quickly and reached its highest peak in the east in the fifth century. A man of action rather than a theologian, Marcion saw it as his duty to fight both against the unreasonable demands of the Judaeo-Christians and against the learned lucubrations of the Gnostics, but by his excessive simplification he fell into the opposite errors. For him the Old Testament was to be rejected in its entirety, and the New was to be rigorously expurgated (only the Gospel of Saint Luke and some of Saint Paul's Epistles, that to the Galatians especially, found favour in his eyes). His work entitled *The Antitheses* opposed systematically the God of the old dispensation (jealous and revengeful Yahweh) to the God of the new (the Father of all Mercies); the promised Messiah (hard, warlike), to Christ Jesus (friend of the unfortunate, loving); and the Synagogue (blinded by the letter which kills) and even the Church (successor of the Synagogue).[24]

Marcion held a dualistic notion of Divine Revelation. This is evident in the fact that he invented an artificial contrast between the God of the Old Testament and the God of the New Testament. Marcion, therefore, posited the notion of a false rivalry between the Old Testament's "God of the Law" and the New Testament's "God of Love."[25]

Consequently, the Nicene Creed contains the following statement about the Holy Spirit, *who has spoken through the prophets.* This was intended, at least in part, to answer the heresy of Marcionism that rejected the Old Testament as the inspired Word of God.

---

[22] Cf. O'Collins, Farrugia, *A Concise Dictionary of Theology*, 150.
[23] Pontus in Asia Minor.
[24] Verbraken, *The Beginnings of the Early Church*, 62-63.
[25] Cf. Hitchcock, *History of the Catholic Church*, 37f.

Chadwick takes Marcion to task:

> The Gnostic critique and rejection of the Creator God of the Old Testament was taken to extremes by Marcion in the first half of the second century. He and his followers listed moral contradictions between the Old and New Testaments, and abominated allegory as a sophisticated device for evading difficulty. But the apostolic writings themselves had been corrupted, he thought, by unknown persons determined to keep Christianity Jewish, preserving the new wine of Jesus in old bottles. Marcion felt that even the Apostles themselves had seriously misunderstood the intentions of their Master by failing to see how utterly new His message was. He therefore set out to produce a corrected text first of the letters of Saint Paul his hero, then of the Gospel of Paul's companion Luke (the other Gospels being scrapped), which he thought the work of Paul himself in its original form. Marcion's principle of exclusion gave sharp impetus to the early Church's need to define which books did or did not rank as authoritative documents to which appeal could be made.[26]

Adoptionism[27]

Another heresy fought by the early Church was Adoptionism, propounded by Paul of Samosata. A synod at Antioch held in A.D. 286 condemned his position that the man Jesus of Nazareth was not the Son of God by nature but only by the grace of "adoption."[28] The orthodox position, however, is that *we* (not Jesus!) become the adoptive sons of God by the grace of Baptism. Thus, according to Galatians 4:4-7, we become *filii in Filio* (sons in the Son). In other words, we become by grace what Jesus is by nature. Adoptionism conflates the two realities, denying Jesus His divine sonship from all eternity.

Ebionism[29]

In the early Church there existed a heretical group known as the Ebionites. They derived their name from the Hebrew (Aramaic) word *ebion*, meaning "poor one," since they practiced extreme poverty; they were also vegetarians. The Ebionites

---

[26] Chadwick, "The Early Christian Community," in *The Oxford History of Christianity*, 30-31.

[27] Cf. O'Collins, Farrugia, *A Concise Dictionary of Theology*, 4.

[28] Cf. CCC, 465.

[29] Cf. O'Collins, Farrugia, *A Concise Dictionary of Theology*, 71: "**Ebionites.** (Heb. 'poor men'). An ascetic group of Jewish Christians in the first and second centuries who considered Jesus to be the human son of Mary and Joseph, a mere man on whom the Spirit descended at Baptism. They stressed adherence to the Law of Moses, and for this reason rejected St. Paul."

are mentioned in Origen's famous apologetical work, *Contra Celsum* (Against Celsus*).*

The Ebionites were Jewish Christians who denied the full divinity of Jesus Christ in an attempt to safeguard a strict form of monotheism, the unity and unicity of God.

Hill discusses the Ebionites in the context of other schismatic and heretical sects in early Christianity:

Although the Montanists agreed with other Christians in doctrine, many groups did not. One major disagreement was over the nature of Jesus. Was He human, God or something else? The Docetists, who denied Jesus' true humanity, were still around, and they were joined by their opposite number, the Ebionites. These people were condemned primarily because they regarded Jesus simply as a human being and nothing more, but there seems to have been more to them than that. Their name comes from the Aramaic for "poor"—those to whom Jesus had promised the Kingdom of God. Judging by the fragments that remain of their writings, the Ebionites regarded themselves as Jews who believed in Jesus. Before Jesus, Judaism had revolved around sacrifices in the Temple; now, they believed, it was to revolve around obeying the Law in the light of the teaching of Jesus. They seemed to regard Paul—and the Gentile form of Christianity which he founded—as a heretical movement. Here, then, we have what seems to be a group descended from the "original" Jewish Christians, increasingly marginalized by "mainstream" Gentile Christianity. It existed mainly on the eastern fringes of the Empire, around Jerusalem and perhaps in Persia; and very little is known of it. The Ebionites were still around in the fourth century, but as far as most Christians were concerned, they were a minor, heretical sect.[30]

---

[30] Hill, *History of Christianity*, 64.

Modalism[31]

Heretics known as Modalists, many of whom were followers of Sabellius in the third century, claimed that the three Persons of the "Trinity" only constituted three different "modes" of existence for the one God, but not three co-equally divine Persons. Another Modalist was Noetus of Smyrna. Hubert Cunliffe-Jones explains:

> Noetus of Smyrna, according to the treatise against him by Hippolytus of Rome, Tertullian's contemporary, began from a literal interpretation of the Johannine text, "I and the Father are one." This meant that the one true God, the Father, was incarnate as Jesus Christ, and was the subject of human experiences. To Noetus this was far from shocking. "What have I done wrong," he protested, "in glorifying the one only God, who was born and suffered and died?" He was anxious to de-personalize the biblical term "Word." If God is one without distinctions, then His Word must be a spoken word; to allege the "Word" is "Son" would be strange. When Saint John speaks of the Word in the fourth Gospel, it must be borne in mind that there, and in the Apocalypse, he uses the term allegorically.[32]

Donatism[33]

Norbert Brox outlines the Donatist schism:

> Following the line of strict African church discipline, some bishops, including a certain Donatus, held the consecration of the Bishop Caecilian in Carthage to be invalid because there had been a so-called

---

[31] O'Collins, Farrugia, *A Concise Dictionary of Theology*, 162: "**Modalism.** (Lat. 'aspect, facet'). The heresy that so stressed the divine unity as to assert that Father, Son and Spirit are only distinctions made by the human mind and are not so personally distinct. They are only three manifestations or ways in which the one God is revealed and acts in creation and redemption. Starting in Asia Minor with Noetus (ca. 200), the heresy was propagated in the West by Praxeas (ca. 200), Sabellius (early third century), Photinus (fourth century), and to a certain degree, by Marcellus of Ancyra (Ankara)."

[32] Hubert Cunliffe-Jones, *A History of Christian Doctrine* (T & T Clark LTD, 1997), 54.

[33] Cf. O'Collins, Farrugia, *A Concise Dictionary of Theology*, 67. "**Donatism.** A schism that arose ca. 311 over the episcopal consecration of Caecilian of Carthage by a bishop (Felix of Aptunga) who was accused of being a traitor during the persecution of the Emperor Diocletian. The dissenting bishops chose instead Majorinus, later succeeded by Donatus—hence the name of the schism. The Donatists seem to have denied the validity of the sacraments administered by unworthy ministers, and to have required the rebaptism of Christians who lapsed back into sin. St. Augustine of Hippo (354-430) strongly opposed the Donatists; a conference organized at Carthage in 411 weakened them, and they finally disappeared when the Saracens destroyed the church in North Africa."

traditor codicum[34] among the consecrating bishops, namely a bishop who had weakened in persecution and handed over sacred writings or vessels to the authorities. The dogmatic issue was the dependence of the validity and effectiveness of a sacrament on the moral quality of the one bestowing it. The Church split again over this dispute: alongside the Catholic Church the Donatist church (Donatism) came into being; in Augustine's day (fourth/fifth century) it was still the larger of the two [...]. The two controversies over Novatianism and Donatism brought enduring clarification to both theology and church practice. Novatian rigorism was opposed by a conviction that the bishop had authority in matters of penance in the Church and by the merciful attitude of the community; but the tolerance of the confessors was thought to trivialize sin (apostasy). Against the Donatist objections the Church maintained that the sacrament is independent of the one who administers it, which protects the recipient from an intolerable insecurity. The two schisms cost the Church much effort, substance and credibility. They belong to the history of the confrontation between Church and State as consequences of the persecution of Christians.[35]

Manichaeism[36]

Gnostic heretics arose in the third century, known as the Manicheans. Manicheans derived their origin from "Manes" or "Mani," the sect's founder who lived from ca. A.D. 216 to A.D. 276. Joseph Kelly characterizes Manes as:

> a Persian dualist who described a cosmic struggle between two deities, one good and one evil. In his system, there was little room for free will.[37]

---

34 From Latin: "one who hands over (the liturgical) books."

35 Norbert Brox, *A Concise History of the Early Church* (The Continuum Publishing Company, 1996) 45-46 *passim*.

36 Cf. O'Collins, Farrugia, *A Concise Dictionary of Theology*, 149f: "**Manichaeism.** The doctrine of Mani, born in Persia ca. A.D. 215 and skinned alive by order of the Persian emperor in 275. Borrowing elements from Zoroastrianism, Buddhism, Gnosticism, and Christianity, Mani saw himself as following OT prophets, Zarathustra, Buddha, and Jesus to free the sparks of light in human beings and so deliver them from matter and darkness. A strict asceticism and vigorous missionary activity spread his teaching to India, China, Italy, North Africa, and other parts of the Roman Empire. For nine years prior to his conversion St. Augustine of Hippo (354-430) subscribed to Manichaeism. *Manichee* was often used synonymously with *heretic*, especially in the context of similar dualistic movements."

37 Joseph F. Kelly, *The World of the Early Christians: Message of the Early Church* [Volume One] (The Liturgical Press, 1997), 206.

Kelly adds:

> Augustine had a life-long fascination with evil, and in his youth
> belonged to a Manichee group. But eventually his brilliance showed
> him that Manichaeism offered no real solution to the problem of
> evil but only a cosmic myth that avoided the myriad particulars of
> the problem.[38]

The Manicheans went to extremes by adopting a strict form of vegetarianism,
occasionally even condemning sexual intercourse and matrimony, especially
since they viewed these latter activities as the products of the evil god of matter,
forever at enmity with the good god of the spirit.

Henry Chadwick comments on the long-term effects of the Manichean
heresy:

> Only one second-century sect — the Mandeans of Iraq — remains
> alive today. But the version of Gnostic mythology and practice
> propagated by the third-century heretic, Mani (from Mesopotamia),
> enjoyed a millennium of diffusion from Cadiz to China: one text
> from a Christian writer of late fourth-century Spain, Priscillian of
> Avila, first becomes intelligible in the light of a Manichee catechism
> of AD 800 extant in Chinese. In one form or another Gnosticism
> has permanently remained an underground concomitant of the
> Church. The Church soon constructed fences against it.[39]

Pelagianism[40]

Kelly contrasts Manichaeism and Pelagianism in relation to a triumphant
Saint Augustine:

> Virtually opposed to the Manichees were the Pelagians, who were
> given that name by Augustine, who in turn took it from Pelagius (ca.
> 350-ca. 420). He was a British monk who believed that humans could

---

[38] Kelly, *The World of the Early Christians*, 206.
[39] Chadwick, "The Early Christian Community," in *The Oxford History of Christianity*, 29.
[40] Cf. O'Collins, Farrugia, *A Concise Dictionary of Theology*, 195: "**Pelagianism.** A heresy concerning grace initiated by Pelagius (lived ca. 400), a monk from Britain or Ireland, who, first
in Rome and then in North Africa, taught that human beings can achieve salvation through
their own sustained efforts. Original Sin amounted to no more than Adam's bad example,
which did not harm interiorly his descendants and, in particular, left intact the natural use
of free will. Reducing grace to the good example of Christ, Pelagius encouraged a strongly
ascetical life and the emergence of a church for the morally elite. His disciples, Celestius
(fifth century) and Julian of Eclanum (ca. 386-454), developed Pelagianism as a system.
Strongly opposed by St. Augustine of Hippo (354-430), this heresy was condemned by two
councils in North Africa, then in 431 by the Council of Ephesus."

discipline their free wills so firmly that they could be saved without grace. Although Pelagius said that this was rare, Augustine felt that his teaching threatened divine grace, and, in a series of books as well as many comments in his biblical exegesis, he attacked Pelagius; but, in so doing, he ended up by arguing for divine predestination and the salvation of the elect to whom God gave grace and whom Augustine considered to be rather few. He may have produced "a frightening conception of God," but it was one that dominated much subsequent theology, especially in the Reformation. Western Christianity, as history knows it, would be inconceivable without Augustine.[41]

Excursus: Neo-Gnosticism

Neo-Gnosticism persists in our contemporary society camouflaged, for example, by the New Age Movement, secular materialism, and relativistic slogans such as, "As long it feels good and I'm not hurting anyone, then I should be able to do with my body whatever I want." The use of such slogans is, at best, misguided and, at worst, insidiously evil. Such slogans encapsulate a type of *dictatorship of relativism*, as Benedict XVI identified it.

Many people in our society seem indoctrinated when, in the name of personal freedom, they support intrinsically evil acts, such as those that separate the unitive and the procreative purposes of sexual intercourse. Such individuals are inclined to fall down a slippery slope from engaging in fornication and using artificial contraception to procuring abortions, advocating infanticide and promoting euthanasia, among other evils.

Consequently, we owe a great deal of gratitude to Fathers of the Church for expending so much time and energy in combatting Gnosticism and the other heresies that we have considered.

Excursus: Albigensianism[42]

We owe a debt of gratitude to the preaching of Saint Dominic of Guzman[43]

---

41 Kelly, *The World of the Early Christians*, 206.
42 Cf. O'Collins, Farrugia, *A Concise Dictionary of Theology*, 5: "**Albigensianism.** A medieval heresy named after its center, Albi, in southern France. It understood redemption as the soul's liberation from the flesh, dismissed matter as evil, and hence rejected Christ's Incarnation, sacraments, and the resurrection of the body. Its adherents were divided into the perfect, who did not marry and lived an extremely austere existence, and ordinary believers, who led normal lives until they came to be in danger of death. In 1215 the heresy was condemned at the Fourth Lateran Council."
43 Dominic of Guzman (c. 1170-1221), Priest. In the thirteenth century, Dominic founded the mendicant "Order of Preachers," more commonly referred to as "the Dominicans," which is both a play on the saintly founder's name (Latin word *Dominicus*, "belonging to the

who effectively wiped out the Albigensian (Catharist)[44] heresy which was rampant in southern France in the thirteenth century, and to those in the Church who combated a puritanical heresy spawned in the seventeenth century, known as Jansenism.[45]

The reader should not pass over the fact that certain heresies rear their ugly heads at almost regular intervals in the Church.[46]

The Five Ancient Patriarchates[47]

Before proceeding in our discussion of Early Church Fathers, it is opportune to mention here that in the ancient Church there were five patriarchal sees (dioceses headed by patriarchs):

Lord") as well as a play on the Latin words: *Domini* (of the Lord) and *Canes* (dogs, hounds). A story is told that Dominic's mother had a dream that she carried in her womb a black and white spotted dog which carried in its mouth a burning torch to illumine the world. Hence, such a hound is often depicted at Dominic's feet for indeed through his preaching and teaching he fulfilled his mother's dream. Also, the colors of the Dominican habit, black and white, may be associated with the fulfillment of this dream not only through the successful preaching of Dominic against the Albigenisians but also through the Order's dogged pursuit of the truth in charity, bringing the light of the Gospel to the world since they were founded in 1215. *Veritas*, the Latin word for "truth," is the Order's motto not to mention that of Harvard University. Another motto is *contemplata aliis tradere*, meaning: "the things you have contemplated hand on to others." The Dominicans were among the best and brightest teachers (e.g., Thomas Aquinas) in the first European universities (e.g., Paris, Naples). One of Dominic's epithets in the Dominican Rite is *novus athleta Domini*, "the new athlete of the Lord," paying homage to his unique role in Christian evangelization during the Middle Ages, a period also known as "The Age of Faith." The liturgical memorial of Saint Dominic is August 8.

[44] The Cathars derived their name from the Greek word, *catharos*, meaning "pure one." Cf. O'Collins, Farrugia, *A Concise Dictionary of Theology*, 36.

[45] Cf. O'Collins, Farrugia, *A Concise Dictionary of Theology*, 124f: "**Jansenism.** A theological and spiritual movement, characterized by moral rigidity and pessimism about the human condition. It is named after Cornelius Otto Jansen (1585-1638), who in 1636 was consecrated bishop of Ypres, Belgium. With his friend Jean Duvergier de Hauranne, abbot of Saint-Cyran (1581-1643), Jansen wanted to encourage a true reformation of Catholic doctrine and morals. Since Protestantism frequently appealed to St. Augustine of Hippo (354-430), Jansen thoroughly studied his writings, especially those directed against Pelagius. In his posthumous *Augustinus* (1640), among other points Jansen argued that God's grace irresistibly determines our free choices and that without special grace we cannot keep the commandments. Five propositions from Jansen's *Augustinus* were officially condemned in 1653, and in 1690. Despite their stress on the power of God's grace, Jansenists preached and practiced a strict morality and a scrupulous approach to the reception of the sacraments. The attacks made on Jesuits by Blaise Pascal (1623-1662) in the eighteen *Lettres Provinciales* were influenced by his friendship with Port-Royal, a convent with strong Jansenistic leanings."

[46] Cf. Fulton J. Sheen, *Old Errors and New Labels* (Alba House, 1931).

[47] Cf. Hitchcock, *History of the Catholic Church*, 190, 207.

1. Rome;

2. Constantinople;

3. Alexandria;

4. Antioch;

5. Jerusalem.

Two Schools of Thought

More importantly, however, we should note that of the five ancient patriarchal sees, two, in particular, Alexandria and Antioch, played a significant role in developing distinct (even rival) schools of theology.

The Alexandrian school[48] produced a "high" Christology,[49] emphasizing the divinity of Christ[50] and an allegorical interpretation of the Bible.[51]

The Antiochean school,[52] on the other hand, adopted a "low" Christology,

---

[48] Cf. O'Collins, Farrugia, *A Concise Dictionary of Theology*, 5: "**Alexandrian Theology.** A theology that began in Alexandria as a catechetical school toward the end of the second century A.D. It interpreted the Scriptures with an allegorical bias and, as the classic Christology from above, focused on the Word becoming flesh and the divine nature of the Incarnate Christ. The many famous exponents of Alexandrian theology include St. Pantaeunus (d. ca. 190), St. Clement of Alexandria (ca. 150-ca. 215), Origen (ca. 185-ca. 254), St. Athanasius of Alexandria (d. 373), Didymus the Blind (ca. 313-398), and St. Cyril of Alexandria (d. 444)."

[49] Cf. Hitchcock, *History of the Catholic Church*, 82, 84.

[50] Cf. O'Collins, Farrugia, *A Concise Dictionary of Theology*, 144f: "**Logos-Sarx Christology.** (Gr. 'Word-flesh'). A Christology from above, characteristic of Origen (ca. 185-ca. 254) and St. Cyril of Alexandria (d. 444) and centered on the eternally preexistent Logos who descends into the world. The Alexandrian school normally did well in maintaining the genuine divinity and true unity of Christ as an acting subject. For some Alexandrians, the most serious challenge came in showing His real humanity and facing the question: How could the eternal Word of God take on a genuinely and fully human way of acting? As for *Logos-Sarx* Christology in its relationship to *Logos-Anthropos*, Alois Grillmeier (1910-1998) has pointed out that they cannot simply be identified with Alexandria and Antioch respectively, since there are important counter-examples."

[51] Cf. Hitchcock, *History of the Catholic Church*, 46, 87.

[52] Cf. O'Collins, Farrugia, *A Concise Dictionary of Theology*, 13: "**Antiochean Theology.** An orientation in theology, connected with the Christian community of Antioch, where it emerged with a very distinct exegetical profile in the fourth century. It stressed the literal and historical interpretation of the Bible but also looked for a *theoria* (Gr. insight) that went beyond the mere letter of the text. While open to the danger of inadequate *dyophysism* (Gr. two natures) by not properly relating the divine and human natures in the one Person of Jesus Christ, its emphasis on His full humanity partly anticipated modern Christology from below. Antiochene theology is generally thought to have been shaped by the martyr St. Lucian of Antioch (d. 312), who had studied at Edessa, and developed by St. Eustathius of Antioch (d. ca. 336) and Diodore of Tarsus (d. ca. 390); it reached its high point with

emphasizing the humanity of Christ,[53] and a literal interpretation of the Scriptures. For either school, the real danger, however, lay in overemphasis, even to the point of downgrading or denying one or the other approach to Christology and biblical exegesis.[54]

According to Acts 11:26, in Antioch the disciples were for the first time called Christians.

Saint Ignatius of Antioch, the successor of Saint Peter in the See of Antioch, was martyred in a Roman arena in A.D. 107, torn apart by lions. He was the first Christian writer to use the expression, *The Catholic Church*.[55]

Protocouncil of Jerusalem[56]

All of the ecumenical councils look to the Council of Jerusalem in A.D. 51 as their "prototype." At the Council of Jerusalem, the Apostles, under the leadership of Peter and James, decided that Gentile converts to Christianity were no longer obliged to observe all the legal prescriptions of the Old Testament.[57]

The main requirements of the Old Testament "Law" (*Torah*),[58] from which the Gentiles were exempted, were circumcision and kosher dietary laws. However, for the sake of not scandalizing their Jewish brethren in the Faith, the Gentile converts were required to abstain from unchastity, from eating the meat of strangled animals

---

St. John Chrysostom (ca. 347-407), Theodore of Mopsuestia (ca. 350-428), and Theodoret of Cyrrhus (ca. 393-ca. 466)."

[53] O'Collins, Farrugia, *A Concise Dictionary of Theology*, 145: "**Logos-Anthropos Christology.** (Gr. Word-man). A Christology from below, characteristic of Theodore of Mopsuestia (ca. 350-428) and the school of Antioch, and concerned to maintain the full humanity of Jesus Christ. Since the Antiochenes began with the duality of natures (the full human nature of Christ and His divine nature), they had to face the question: How are Christ's divinity and humanity united in one acting subject? Their Christology could go astray by abandoning the real unity of Christ and ending up with two subjects: the assuming Word and the man Jesus who is assumed."

[54] Cf. Hitchcock, *History of the Catholic Church*, 82, 84.

[55] Cf. Benedict XVI, *The Fathers*, 13.

[56] Cf. Hitchcock, *History of the Catholic Church*, 61.

[57] Cf. Acts 15.

[58] The primary meaning of the Hebrew word *Torah* is "instruction." It evolved into a term designating the first five books of the Bible, in which the "Law" of God revealed to Moses is contained.

or meat offered in sacrifice to idols. At this "proto-council," the Council Fathers ratified their determinations with the bold exclamation: "For it seemed good to the Holy Spirit and to us too [...]."

The decisions of the Council of Jerusalem are particularly significant because they helped stave off an early group of heretics, known as the Judaizers, who argued that full observance of the Mosaic Law was absolutely necessary for salvation.

Already in the second century, Catholic bishops convened in regional synods or councils, in order to handle together matters of doctrinal and disciplinary concern for their respective local churches. As these local synods or councils increased, the bishops began to see the need for a wider gathering that eventually became the premise for the Ecumenical Council.[59]

Acts 15 is also significant because it provides a Scriptural basis for the Catholic doctrine of infallibility. The Holy Spirit, who is God, can neither deceive nor be deceived (see Act of Faith). If the Holy Spirit could teach infallibly on matters of faith and morality through weak and frail human instruments like Peter, James and the other Apostles gathered at the Council of Jerusalem, why could He not continue to do so through the Successors of the Apostles, the bishops, in communion with the Bishop of Rome? After all, did not Jesus promise the Apostles that He would send them the Holy Spirit as their Second Paraclete (Advocate), who would lead them into the fullness of truth? (cf. John 14:25-26).

Now we stand poised to examine the first seven of the twenty-one councils acknowledged as ecumenical by the Catholic Church and the Orthodox Churches alike, occurring as they did before the schism of 1054.

---

[59] Our English word "ecumenical" is derived from the Greek word *oikoumene or oikomene,* through the Latin word *ecumenicus,* meaning "universal."

PART II

Chapters Three to Nine focus on the contributions of the first seven Ecumenical Councils that established a firm doctrinal and devotional foundation for the united Church of the first Christian millennium.

CHAPTER THREE:
FIRST COUNCIL OF NICAEA[1]
(325 A.D.)

Constantine's Council

The earliest Ecumenical Councils were customarily convoked by the Roman Emperor.[2] The First Council of Nicaea[3] was convoked by the first Christian Emperor, Constantine the Great, during the pontificate of Pope Saint Sylvester I.[4] The Council was attended by approximately three hundred bishops,[5] with sessions held from May 20 until the end of August in A.D. 325.

---

1   Cf. Hitchcock, *History of the Catholic Church*, 13, 83, 90, 188, 477n2, 496.
2   Cf. Pier Franco Beatrice. *Introduction to the Fathers of the Church: The Most Significant Figures of the Fathers of the Church Presented in the Context of the Christian Life of the First Centuries and of Their Own Writings* (Edizioni Istituto San Gaetano, 1987), 194: "The liberty conferred on the Church by Constantine in 313 represented an absolute novelty fraught with consequences for the life and organization of the communities as well as for Christian literature. With regard to the ecclesiastical hierarchy, a series of close ties were established between the hierarchy and the structures of the empire which did not always foster clear and correct reciprocal relations. If on the one hand the bishops obtained grants and favors from the emperors, these latter in their turn felt themselves to be invested with a certain ecclesiastical authority which permitted them even to convoke ecumenical councils and to actively intervene personally in theological questions in order to influence personally the development of the discussions and final decisions."
3   Cf. CCC, 465. Nicaea corresponds to the modern-day seaside resort town of Iznik in Turkey, at one time the Roman province of Asia Minor.
4   Dante comments on the alleged "Donation of Constantine," noting the ill-fated relationship forged between the secular state and the Church during the Emperor Constantine's reign: "O Constantine, what misfortune you caused! Not by becoming Christian, but by the dowry you gave to the first rich pope" [*Inferno*, Canto 19, lines 115-117].
5   Cf. Tony Lane, *The Lion Concise Book of Christian Thought* (Lion Publishing LTC, 1987), 28: "About 220 bishops were present, mostly from the East. Later tradition gave the number as 318, probably derived from Genesis 14:14!"

Arius' Antagonism[6]

The Council's main objective was to correct the heresy of Arius,[7] a priest of Alexandria in Egypt, who did not believe that Jesus possessed the same divine substance as the Father. Arius' principal aim was to safeguard at all costs a strict monotheism,[8] the unity and indivisibility of God's "substance" (Greek: *ousia*). Arius, however, ended up making Jesus into either a subordinate emanation of the Father or the highest of all the Father's creatures, thus forcing the Church into a dogmatic definition.

Mike Aquilina explains the tremendous negative impact of Arius:

> In 313, the new Emperor, Constantine, whose mother was Christian, issued the Edict of Milan, which decreed universal toleration of Christianity. Peace had come, but it would not last. In 318, Arius of Alexandria began to preach his heresy — that Jesus was not truly divine or coeternal — and soon Arianism was sweeping the Church. With an alarming suddenness, Arius won over a great number of bishops, theologians, and imperial officials. As Blessed John Henry Newman wrote, the whole world awoke to find itself Arian. It was this controversy, which involved the core Christian doctrines of the Trinity and the Incarnation that forced the fourth century to be a golden age. There was no alternative. The only way the Church could counter the eloquence and apparent reasonableness of Arius was with more eloquent, and more reasonable, and most importantly, more holy men.[9]

---

[6] Cf. Hitchcock, *History of the Catholic Church*, 82-83, 89, 90, 98, 103, 111, 124, 132, 190, 206. Hitchcock remarks on the "theological context" in the early Church and the so-called *Odium Theologicum* or "Theological Hatred," that it sometimes engendered as in the case of opposition to Arius and his followers. On page 89, Hitchcock writes: "When an Arian bishop entered the public baths of his city, for instance, everyone else withdrew, unwilling to share the water with a heretic." On page 90, our author notes: "Sometimes such partisanship manifested itself in rioting, and Basil and Gregory of Nazianzen lamented that in some ways ecumenical councils brought out the worst in bishops. Cyril actively encouraged mob violence at Alexandria, and the debates at Nicaea and other councils sometimes erupted in strife, as when St. Nicholas of Myra (d. ca. 350) (the original of the Santa Claus legend) reportedly pulled the beard of an Arian bishop in vexation." The reader should note that another version of this story has St. Nicholas of Myra, a bishop in attendance at the Council of Nicaea, slapping Arius himself in the face.

[7] Arius lived from ca. 250 to ca. 336.

[8] Lane, *The Lion Concise Book of Christian Thought*, 28: "Like Origen, [Arius] believed that the Father is greater than the Son, who in turn is greater than the Holy Spirit. But unlike Origen, Arius did not believe that it was possible to have a hierarchy of divine beings. He brought a radical monotheism to Origen's system and concluded that the Father alone is God."

[9] Aquilina, *The Fathers of the Church*, 114-115.

The Fight for Orthodoxy

A key part of defending the Church's orthodox theology, not so much at the Council of Nicaea but after its conclusion, lay in distinguishing the Greek term *homoousios* ("of the *same* substance" with the Father) of the Council Fathers from the term *homoiousios,* whereby the simple addition of the Greek letter *iota* on the part of the so-called "Semi-Arians,"[10] changed the definition of the Greek term to mean "of a *similar* substance" with the Father.

Here, it deserves mentioning that this marked the first time in Church history that non-scriptural terminology (*ousia*) had been introduced into official creedal statements—not always fully appreciated by many so-called "Bible-believing" Christians today, who accept the doctrine of Nicaea without realizing that the doctrine of Christ's divinity could not have been properly explained and taught had the Council Fathers at Nicaea relied solely on scriptural categories.

Lane explains the decisive role that recourse to non-scriptural terminology played in the first ecumenical council:

> Jesus Christ is "of one substance with the Father." The Greek word *homoousios* (of one substance) was the most controversial word in the [Nicene] creed. There were qualms about the use of a non-scriptural term, but it was necessary because the Arians could twist all scriptural phrases. For example, Jesus is "begotten" by God—but so are the dewdrops (Job 38:28)! The word *homoousios* had the added advantage that the Arians had already declared it to be unacceptable. The non-scriptural term was used to safeguard the scriptural truth of the deity of Christ.[11]

Athanasius *Contra Mundum*

The great hero of the first ecumenical council was Saint Athanasius of Alexandria.[12]

---

[10] Cf. O'Collins, Farrugia, *A Concise Dictionary of Theology*, 240: "**Semi-Arianism.** The teaching of Bishop Basil of Ancyra (Ankara) and others after Nicaea I (325). They did not follow the Arian view of Christ being only the first among creatures but did not yet endorse the orthodox doctrine of his being *homoousios* (Gr. of one substance) with the Father. They called the Son *homo-i-ousios* (Gr. of a similar nature) to the Father. Although their term was heretical, the difference of only an "I" created a platform of dialogue that helped many Semi-Arians toward full orthodoxy."

[11] Lane, *The Lion Concise Book of Christian Thought*, 29.

[12] John Henry Newman wrote that Athanasius was "a principal instrument after the Apostles by which the sacred truths of Christianity have been conveyed and secured to the world."

Athanasius[13] was born toward the end of the third century (ca. 296) and died in A.D. 373. He lived under the tutelage of Alexander, the Bishop of Alexandria, and was ordained a deacon by him.

When the Council of Nicaea was convoked in A.D. 325, Athanasius, while still an archdeacon, accompanied Bishop Alexander to the proceedings. Alexander had addressed a circular letter to the Church of Alexandria about the dangers of Arius' theology. When Alexander died in 328, Athanasius succeeded him as Bishop of Alexandria.

During the course of his forty-six years as Bishop of Alexandria, Athanasius suffered exile because he stood firm on the doctrine of Christ's true divinity taught by the Council and opposed by Arius and his followers. Andrew Louth remarks:

> The authority of the Bishop of Alexandria was extensive, covering the whole of Egypt, and Nubia and Libya besides [...]. Athanasius was bishop of Alexandria for nearly fifty years—until his death in 373—though during this time he was deposed, both by church synod and emperor, and was expelled from his see five times, on the first two occasions (A.D. 335-337, 339-346) spending his exile in the West. These periods in the West were important, for they enabled him to establish links with Latin Christians, more generally inclined to support Nicaea.[14]

Athanasius was unpopular not only with his fellow bishops who capitulated to the Arian heresy, but also with political rulers who sided or sympathized with Arius. Athanasius stood his ground.

Fortunately, from 346-356, Athanasius was no longer persecuted or suffering exile and so was able to exercise his episcopal ministry at Alexandria. Hill reflects on Athanasius' prominence in the anti-Arian fight of the fourth century in the East, together with Gregory of Nazianzus, while figures like Hilary of Poitiers[15] and Marius Victorinus led the charge in the West:

> Like most Christian thinkers of this period, Athanasius believed that Jesus saved people through who He was. Irenaeus, nearly two centuries earlier, had taught that in Christ divinity and humanity meet. Through Him, divinity is introduced into humanity, and It spreads, almost like a benign infection, restoring what was lost in Adam.

---

[13]   Cf. Hitchcock, *History of the Catholic Church*, 79, 83-84, 91, 98, 321.

[14]   Hill, *History of Christianity*, 82.

[15]   Cf. Hitchcock, *History of the Catholic Church*, 60, 84-85.

Vestiges of Alexandria, Egypt. Source: Dennis Jarvis, Wikimedia.

> Athanasius' point was therefore simple: how could this happen if Jesus were not really God? [....] Certainly the people of Alexandria seem to have largely opposed Arianism. They supported Athanasuis, and on one occasion his unfortunate successor, George the Cappadocian, was lynched by a mob who murdered him by the curious method of tying him to a camel and burning it.[16]

The main thrust of Athanasius' teaching was to defend the mystery of the Incarnation or enfleshment of God in Christ Jesus against those who, like Arius, denied Jesus' divinity. Athanasius' best known work, which happens to be his longest, is entitled *Orations against the Arians*.

Other key works of Athanasius in the field of apologetics include an apology written in two parts: *Against the Greeks* and *The Incarnation of the Word*. Athanasius is also known for a letter that he addressed to the Christian churches of Egypt in which he listed the books of the New Testament. Athanasius' Canon or list corresponds to that of the twenty-seven books we venerate as the New Testament Scriptures today.[17]

Athanasius was also a fine hagiographer or biographer of saints. He composed an excellent biography, *The Life of Saint Anthony of Egypt*,[18] who is considered the Father of Christian monasticism[19] in the East, while Saint Benedict

---

[16] Hill, *History of Christianity*, 84.

[17] Cf. Hitchcock, *History of the Catholic Church*, 79.

[18] Cf. Hitchcock, *History of the Catholic Church*, 91: "While still a recent convert, [Augustine] felt his heart wrenched by Athanasius' account of Anthony of the Desert, and he returned to Africa to found a monastery."

[19] Cf. O'Collins, Farrugia, *A Concise Dictionary of Theology*, 163f: "**Monasticism.** (Gr. life alone). A movement among baptized believers who respond to Christ's call to perfection (Matthew 5:48; 19:16-26) by giving themselves through poverty, celibacy, and obedience to a life of prayer, common worship, and service. Toward the end of the Roman persecution an ascetic existence in the deserts of Egypt, Palestine, and Syria began to provide a heroic alternative to real martyrdom. In Egypt St. Antony the Abbot (ca. 251-356) and St. Pachomius (ca. 290-346) helped to organize their followers around a rule of life and spiritual guides, thus preparing the way for the two standard forms of monasticism: *anachoretism*, or the life of hermits, and *cenobitism*, or life in common. Deeply influenced by St. Basil the Great (ca. 330-379), Eastern monasticism helped to promote Western monasticism through such writings as the *Life of St. Antony* by St. Athanasius of Alexandria (ca. 296-373) and the *Conferences* of St. John Cassian (ca. 360-435). After St. Martin of Tours (d. 397) and St. Augustine of Hippo (354-430), St. Benedict of Nursia (ca. 480-ca.550) and his rule essentially shaped the future of monasticism in the West. Dominicans, Franciscans, and other active religious orders have offered an alternative to a strictly contemplative monastic life. In the East, however, religious are mainly monks, although Latin influence has encouraged some Western type congregations."

of Nursia[20] is considered the Father of Christian monasticism in the West.[21]

Athanasius defended the divinity of the Holy Spirit against an obscure heretical sect from Egypt known as the *Tropici* by writing letters to their local bishop, Serapion. Serapion sought episcopal advice from Athanasius on how to deal authoritatively with the *Tropici* who, although admitting to the divinity of the Son, denied the co-equal divinity of the Holy Spirit.

Relying on texts like John 15:26, Athanasius effectively argues in favor of the Holy Spirit as one of the three Persons of the Blessed Trinity, distinct from the Father and the Son but in an eternal communion with them both.

Athanasius' Christian anthropology was a fruit of his orthodox Christology. Athanasius believed that the Incarnation made possible man's spiritual divinization, something not possible for either Adam or man after Adam's fall. In a word, Athanasius taught that *God became man so that men might become like gods.*

Historians have attributed to Athanasius a popular epithet; he was called *contra mundum* (against the world) because his strong stance against the Arian

---

[20] Benedict (ca. 480-ca.547) was born in Nursia (Norcia, Italy) and studied rhetoric in Rome. Benedict then decided to live as a hermit at Subiaco (Sacro Speco), but soon gained disciples. Benedict later founded twelve small monasteries, culminating in the establishment of the Abbey of Montecassino where he died and was buried together with his twin sister, Saint Scholastica. His "Rule" for Monks, based on earlier monastic rules of East and West, set the standard for monastic rules in the West. He is thus regarded as the Father of Western Monasticism. Benedictine monks painstakingly preserved classical literature which they copied by hand and faithfully transmitted the orthodox Christian Faith throughout the erroneously termed "Dark Ages" and then again throughout the Middle Ages. The monks accomplished the latter most notably through their teaching in the first Catholic schools (precursors of the first European universities) and illuminated manuscripts. Thus, it is fitting that Pope Paul VI declared Saint Benedict "Patron of Europe." Benedict's most famous biography was penned by Pope Saint Gregory the Great, who was himself a monk. To Pope Gregory is ascribed the systematization of a form of Western monastic chant. Hence, it is called "Gregorian Chant." Saint Benedict's liturgical memorial is observed on July 11.

[21] Cf. Hitchcock, *History of the Catholic Church*, 105-106, 107, 151-152, 329, 352, 465, 467, 484, 524. Hitchcock reflects: "Benedict's first community of monks tried to poison him because of his severity [....]. Benedict's *Rule* was characteristically Western in its practicality. Although there were strict dietary rules—never any meat and long seasonal fasts—he moderated hermetical asceticism, defined monastic organization, regulated the details of daily life, and showed concern for the material needs of the community. The exhortation *ora et labora* ("Pray and Work") became a kind of motto for the monastic life, with monks bound to sing the daily Office in common and to support themselves through manual labor. Benedict and his followers did not extol manual labor for its own sake; they shared the general Christian belief of its necessity solely due to the Fall. But labor was an ascetic practice that had spiritual value, and the fact that it was integral to the lives of the monks gave it a dignity that it did not have in the classical world" [105f].

heresy put him in direct opposition to so many, even among his fellow bishops who favored the Arian heresy. In fact, strangely enough, history tells us that the Arian heresy flourished more after the Council than it did before.

This fact should serve as a reminder to those who naively think that just because the Magisterium pronounces authoritatively on a given matter, whether it concerns faith, morals or liturgical discipline, that the desired obedience and implementation of such teachings will be automatic.

Without belaboring the point, we find that few bishops took seriously the implementation of the Council of Trent save, for example, Saint Charles Borromeo.[22] Today, certain members of the clergy and laity continue to misinterpret and therefore to implement improperly the teachings of the Second Vatican Council, preferring the so-called "spirit of the Council" to its real content.

Regarding the persistent ill effects of the Arian heresy, Blessed John Henry Newman's remark that *Arius groaned and the whole world woke up to find that it had become Arian* meant that the shift from orthodoxy to heterodoxy had been slow and imperceptible to the average believer, hierarchy included, during the Arian controversy.

Even the Emperor Constantine, who first legalized Christianity and who presided over Nicaea I, was ironically baptized on his death bed by an Arian priest and not by an orthodox Catholic priest.

In this regard, Cardinal Newman reflects in his study on the Council of Nicaea and Athanasius' theological treatises that the "sense of the faithful" (*sensus fidelium*)[23] prevailed time and again while the teaching of certain bishops faltered in the ongoing fight against the Arian heresy and subsequent heresies, such as Semi-Arianism (which tended to deny the divinity of the Holy Spirit).

---

[22] Charles Borromeo lived a brief life of forty-six years, 1538-1584. He was the Archbishop of Milan from 1565 to 1584. Saint Philip Neri, his contemporary, so admired Charles' apostolic zeal that he exclaimed, "But this man is a man of steel." The great Italian poet, Alessandro Manzoni, in his celebrated masterpiece, *I Promessi Sposi* ("The Betrothed") praised the hands-on care for the plague victims of Milan demonstrated by Archbishop Borromeo, noting in this regard: "It was called the plague of Saint Charles. So strong is charity!" Saint Charles Borromeo's liturgical memorial is celebrated on November 4.

[23] Cf. O'Collins, Farrugia, *A Concise Dictionary of Theology*, 241: "**Sensus Fidelium.** (Lat. sense of the faithful). The instinctive sensitivity in matters of faith exercised by the whole body of believers, whose appreciation and discernment of revelation are guided by the Holy Spirit (John 16:13; 1 John 2:20, 27). This sense of faith gives rise to and manifests itself in the *consensus fidelium* (Lat. consensus of the faithful), as a cause produces its corresponding effects. Those who have helped to develop this idea include John Henry Newman (1801-1890), Matthias Joseph Scheeben (1835-1888), and Johann Adam Möhler (1796-1838)."

Nevertheless, some of the most formidable opponents of Arianism and Semi-Arianism were bishops and priests, like the fourth-century Cappadocian[24] Fathers—Saints Basil the Great, Gregory of Nazianzen and Gregory of Nyssa.

Arius tended to exaggerate various strains of the thought of the third-century biblical scholar, Origen of Alexandria, thus incurring the judgment of Alexander, Patriarch of Alexandria.

The Friends of Arius

Arius had several supporters. Two in particular stand out: Eusebius of Nicomedia and Eusebius of Caesarea. Eusebius of Caesarea[25] was a Church historian and contemporary of Athanasius of Alexandria and Eusebius of Nicomedia. He was a staunch defender of Constantine as evidenced in his biography of the Emperor.

---

[24] Cappadocia is a rural region of eastern Turkey, west of the Euphrates River. The Hittites ruled Cappadocia until the sixth century B.C., when the Persians took over in 585 B.C. The Seleucids eventually gained control. However, around 255 B.C. Cappadocia had self-rule. Under the Emperor Tiberius in A.D. 17, Cappadocia became a Roman province. One can infer from texts like 1 Maccabees 15:22, and later Acts 2:9, that a Jewish community existed in Cappadocia. 1 Peter 1:1 suggests that Christians in Cappadocia were the recipients of that apostolic letter. Today, at Görem, Turkey, one can visit the ancient underground cave dwellings of Christian monks featuring some of the most precious frescoes in the world.

[25] In Israel there are two ancient cities known as Caesarea: Caesarea Maritima and Caesarea Philippi. Eusebius was from Caesarea Maritima. As the name Maritima implies, it is located along the Mediterranean seacoast. After Augustus won the Battle of Actium against Marc Antony in 30 B.C., he gave the town as a gift to Herod the Great, who named it in Augustus Caesar's honor.

Caesarea Maritima was the capital of the Roman government of Palestine for almost seven centuries. The Roman Procurator Pontius Pilate had his permanent residence at Caesarea Maritima in the first century A.D. From here he would have traveled south to Jerusalem at the time of the Passover to preside at Jesus' trial. Caesarea Maritima boasts outstanding archeological ruins like Roman aqueducts, amphitheater, hippodrome and fortress.

Caesarea Philippi, located in Upper Galilee (Northern Israel), on the southern slope of Mt. Hermon, is near one of the sources of the Jordan River. In ancient times the city was the site of a temple area dedicated to the pagan god, Pan, the protector of shepherds. Hence, the Greek name: *Panias* or, in Arabic, *Banyas*. Caesar Augustus gave the city, known in Latin as *Panion*, to Herod the Great. When Herod's son Philip was named tetrarch (ruler), the city was renamed in honor of Philip and Caesar Augustus. Against the backdrop of this large natural rock formation still visible at Caesarea Philippi, Jesus received Peter's confession of faith, naming him in turn "the rock" (Aramaic: *cephas*; Greek: *petra*) on which He intended to build His Church. Cf. Matthew 16:13-19; Mark 8:27-29.

The First Council of Nicea, wall painting at the church of Stavropoleos, Bucharest, Romania. Source: Kostisl, Wikimedia.

Eusebius was definitely a better historian than theologian as he tended to write in favor of the Arian doctrine, in confused and ambiguous terms. When it became clear that the Council Fathers at Nicaea had decided that Arius' teachings were heterodox, Eusebius changed his position, backing away most reluctantly from his own Arian beliefs. This was also a politically advantageous move on Eusebius' part because he had to curry favor with Constantine who had convoked the Council in the hope that the agreement of the bishops on the essential doctrine of Christ's divinity would serve to restore unity to his empire being torn apart by the Arian controversy.

Lane confirms our profile of Eusebius as a half-hearted supporter of the Council's cause against Arius:

> Eusebius wrote a number of apologetic, biblical and dogmatic works. He was not as acute a theologian as a historian. He supported the heretic Arius and was provisionally excommunicated at the Council of Antioch, early in 325. At the great Council of Nicaea, later that year, he had the opportunity to rehabilitate himself, which he did.

But this was at the price of signing the Creed of Nicaea, which he was able to do only with great anguish and not a little duplicity. His letter to his church at Caesarea survives, in which he hastily explains his actions, lest rumours should precede him. He justifies his signature of the Creed with an interpretation of it which blatantly empties it of its intended meaning. But Eusebius' theological shortcomings should not be allowed to obscure his achievement as a historian. His *History of the Church* was not particularly well written, but it laid a foundation for the history of the early Church on which others built. In the following century Socrates, Sozomen and Theodoret wrote sequels to Eusebius' History.[26]

Eusebius of Nicomedia, on the other hand, openly lent his support to Arius in misappropriating a key biblical text ("For the Father is greater than I")[27] to defend Arius' position that Jesus was not co-equal to the Father.

Language Games

Compounding these facts was Arius' own equivocal use of *homoousios* on the eve of the Council as he convinced certain individuals that his usage was not meant to contradict the meaning afforded the same term by the bishops.

It is believed that Bishop Hosius[28] of Cordoba,[29] at the behest of the Emperor Constantine, made a direct intervention with regard to the Nicene Creed.[30] Bishop Hosius suggested to Constantine that *homoousios to Patri* (of

---

[26] Lane, *The Lion Concise Book of Christian Thought*, 27f.

[27] John 14:28.

[28] *Hosius* is sometimes spelled *Osius*.

[29] Córdoba (English: Cordova) is a city in southern Spain, near Granada and Seville. It is located in the region of Andalusia (Arabic: *al-Andalus*), conquered by the Arab-Berbers in 711 and made into an Islamic Caliphate. Córdoba evolved into a place perhaps unique in all of Christendom where Jews, Christians and Muslims lived together peacefully. Córdoba produced noted scholars like Maimonides (Jew, 1135-1204) and Averroes (Arab, 1126-1198), whose writings, especially their Aristotelian philosophical commentaries greatly influenced medieval Christian thinkers like St. Thomas Aquinas (1225-1274). Cordoba boasts many architectural jewels like its still-extant Great Mosque and Roman Bridge, not to mention statues of local heroes Maimonides and Averroes. The Great Mosque, commonly referred to as *Mezquita-Catedral* ("Cathedral-Mosque") has served alternately as a Catholic cathedral and mosque throughout the centuries. After the "Reconquest" (*Reconquista*) of Spain in 1236 by King Ferdinand III of Castille, the mosque once again became a functioning and flourishing Catholic church (officially: St. Mary of the Assumption) as it remains today in the Diocese of Córdoba.

[30] Hitchcock, *History of the Catholic Church*, 83, 134, 371. Cf. 83: "Some time after Nicaea, a new creed was formulated to summarize orthodox beliefs. As against the Gnostics, the Nicene Creed affirmed that there is one God who is 'Creator of heaven and earth and of all things visible and invisible.' Against the Arians, the Creed stated that Jesus 'was one substance with

one substance with the Father) be added to the Nicene Creed, which Constantine then mandated.

Lane draws out the implications of the collaboration of Hosius and Constantine:

> At Nicaea, Arius was condemned by the use of the word *homoousios* in particular. The Emperor himself advocated the word, probably at the instigation of his western ecclesiastical advisor, the Spaniard Hosius. It was a word which was congenial to the West, which since Tertullian had thought of the Trinity as three Persons in one substance. It was also congenial to the Antiochenes—the minority school in the East who stressed the unity of the Godhead, but were less clear about the distinctness of Father, Son and Holy Spirit. But it was not a congenial word to the Origenists (such as Eusebius of Caesarea), the majority in the East and at the Council. They feared that it would lead to either of two extremes. It could imply a materialist division of God's substance into three. It could open the door to Monarchianism—the blurring together of Father, Son and Holy Spirit. These fears were not without foundation where the Antiochenes were concerned. The Origenists accepted the term and signed the creed, in deference to the emperor, but they were not won over. As a recent writer put it, "theologically the victory of the *homoousios* was a surprise attack, not a solid conquest."[31]

A Council to End All Councils

In the Byzantine Rite, the Sunday before Pentecost[32] is celebrated in honor of the "The Fathers of the First Council."

---

the Father, by whom all things were made,' and against the Docetists (below) that He actually 'suffered, died, and was buried.'" cf. 134: "The Creed was part of the liturgy in the East as early as the fifth century, adopted in the West in the sixth, and mandated for general use by Charlemagne. In the eleventh century, the Church at Rome acceded to the request of the emperor, St. Henry II (1002-1024) to adopt this Frankish custom, thereby making it universal. The Creed was followed by intercessory prayers for the Church, chanted by the deacon. Since by now almost everyone was baptized as an infant, the Liturgy of the Catechumens was no longer considered distinct from the rest of the Mass, and no one was excluded."

[31] Lane, *The Lion Concise Book of Christian Thought*, 29.

[32] According to the Acts 2, the Feast of Pentecost marks the birthday of the Church, when the Holy Spirit descended upon the Apostles "fifty days" after Jesus' Resurrection. The word Pentecost is of Greek origin, meaning "fiftieth." The Jewish Feast of Pentecost mentioned in the Bible was referred to by the Jews as the Feast of *Shavuot* or Feast of "Weeks," occurring between the Feast of Passover and the Feast of Tabernacles, a period of seven weeks or fifty days. *Shavuot* or Pentecost was originally an agricultural festival celebrating the first-fruits, especially of the newly harvested grain. After the destruction of the Temple of Jerusalem by the Romans in A.D. 70, it became a festival in thanksgiving to God for the gift of the *Torah* given to Moses on Mt. Sinai. Cf. Genesis 8: 20-22; 9:8-17; Exodus 19:1; Leviticus 23: 15-16; Numbers 28:26-31; Deuteronomy 16:9; Acts 2:1-42, 20:16; Romans 11:16; 1 Corinthians 16:8.

The *Kontakion*[33] of the Divine Liturgy reads:

> The preaching of the Apostles and the decisions of the Fathers have established the true faith of the Church which she wears as the garment of truth fashioned from the theology from on high; she justly governs and glorifies the great mystery of worship.

We make our own the conclusions of Tony Lane and Jonathan Hill:

> The fourth-century debate about the Person of Jesus Christ can seem remote to us today, especially because of the unfamiliar terms used. At times it can appear like an obscure philosophical argument. But the point at issue is fundamental and central to the Christian Faith. Is Jesus Christ merely a (super-) creature sent by God, or is He the revelation of God Himself? Does "God so loved the world so much that He gave His Only Son" (John 3:16) in fact only mean that He sent one of His creatures? The deity of Jesus Christ is the foundation of all true Christian faith. Without this, there is no true revelation of God in Jesus. Without this, the Christian doctrine of salvation is undermined. Arius raised one of the most important issues in the history of theology and the early Fathers were right to state the full deity of Jesus Christ clearly in opposition to him.[34]

Hill's analysis affords us an opportunity not only to recall the most important contributions of the first ecumenical council but also to debunk many myths or legends that have cropped up time and again regarding the Council of Nicaea and the Emperor Constantine. In notable fashion Dan Brown's *The Da Vinci Code* has embodied and emboldened such conspiracy theories that Hill summarily dismisses here:

> The "symbol" of Nicaea would become one of the most important Christian texts ever to be produced, the basis for the "Nicene

---

[33] Cf. O'Collins, Farrugia, *A Concise Dictionary of Theology*, 132: "**Kondakion.** (from Gr. short). One of the oldest and most important forms of liturgical hymns in the Eastern church, going back to the fifth or sixth century and probably so named because of the short wooden stick around which the text was wrapped. The name, however, may have come from the fact that the composition succinctly sets the tone for the liturgical celebration that follows. A *kondakion* may contain from eighteen to thirty (or more) strophes. The composition has a title, followed by a poignant *proiomion* or introduction that summarizes the spirit of the feast and climaxes in the *ephymion* or refrain. Then follows a series of *oikoi* (houses) or stanzas, the first of which is called *hirmos*, each ending with the refrain. The *oikoi* are often linked acrostically, each strophe beginning with a different letter of the alphabet. St. Romanos the Melodian, who was born in Homs near Edessa toward the end of the fifth century and served as deacon in Constantinople, is the most famous composer of *kondakia*."

[34] Lane, *The Lion Concise Book of Christian Thought*, 29-30.

Creed" which is still recited in churches today. The Creed is similar in form to another text, the "Apostles Creed," which was developing at around the same time [...]. At the same time, the bishops condemned anyone who said that there was a time when the Son did not exist—one of Arius' key doctrines. In modern times, a number of wild claims have been made about the Council of Nicaea, often by conspiracy theorists hoping to show that Christianity was an invention of the Emperor Constantine. We are told, for example, that the bishops were severely divided over the question of Arius, and the pro-Arius faction was silenced only by force on the Emperor's orders; that Arius himself was beaten; and that at this Council, Constantine decreed which books should be considered part of the Bible, effectively rewriting the history of the early Church. In fact, the ancient sources tell us that only seventeen bishops supported Arius at the sessions, and by the end their number had been reduced to two. Arius was questioned at length, but there is no evidence that he was mistreated. The Council did consider a number of other issues, including some of Church organization and the date of Easter, but not the question of the Canon of Scripture, which was settled half a century later. And although Constantine chaired the opening session and the final vote, he seems to have been absent from the intervening discussions and to have made few positive contributions beyond a plea of unity. That might have been the end of it. But Arius continued to make a noise, and he had supporters. The Emperor became convinced that they spoke for the majority of the Church, and at Nicaea he had been hoodwinked by a minority partisan group. In A.D. 336, he ordered the Church to reverse the condemnation of Arius. Suddenly the Church had a new and unprecedented problem. Instead of persecuting the Church, the Emperor was telling it what to do. Constantine was the sole master of the Roman Empire and, as far as he was concerned, this made him the sole master of the Church too; he even called himself a "bishop." The immediate problem was solved by the timely death of Arius, which occurred in a remarkably grotesque fashion at a public toilet in Constantinople, where he suffered an unpleasant hemorrhage. Constantine himself died the following year.[35]

---

[35] Hill, *History of Christianity*, 81.

CHAPTER FOUR:
FIRST COUNCIL OF CONSTANTINOPLE
(A.D. 381)

The New Rome

On the shores of the Bosphorus River is located the modern-day city of Istanbul,[1] the only city in the world that straddles two continents, Europe and Asia. However, in the fourth century this city was known as Byzantium. When the first Christian Emperor, Constantine,[2] moved from Rome to Byzantium he decided to establish his imperial capital city there.

To no one's surprise, the Emperor renamed the city after himself (i.e., Constantinople). Subsequently, Constantinople became known as the "New Rome,"[3] and the eastern half of the Roman Empire as the Byzantine Empire. The Byzantine Empire would last until the Ottoman Turks captured Constantinople in 1453.

Hill documents the conversion of Constantine, the establishment of Constantinople and the rise of Christianity after the city's founding. He cites the original historical documents from the period, most notably, *The Life of Constantine* and *Ecclesiastical History* by Eusebius of Caesarea and *The Edict of Milan* issued by Constantine and his Co-Emperor (arch-rival) Licinius, which legalized Christianity as a religion of the Roman Empire in A.D. 313.

Constantinople as the "New Rome" would never have existed had not Constantine defeated Licinius at the Battle of the Milvian Bridge in 312. As Eusebius relates:

> [Constantine] said that about noon, when the day was already beginning to decline, he saw with his own eyes the trophy of a cross of light in the heavens, above the sun, and bearing the inscription:

---

[1] Istanbul is the Turkish name for Constantinople—still the name of the episcopal see of the Greek Orthodox Patriarch who lives in Istanbul.

[2] Cf. Hitchcock, *History of the Catholic Church*, 54, 56-58, 60, 65, 68, 83, 97, 103.

[3] In certain circles, with the ascendancy of Russia in the eighteenth century, the city of Moscow became known as the "Third Rome."

Arch of Constantine, Rome. Source: Karelj, Wikimedia.

> CONQUER BY THIS.[4] At this sight he himself was so struck with
> amazement and his whole army also, which followed him on the
> expedition and witnessed the miracle.[5]

Hill explains that Constantine later told Eusebius that in preparation for the
Battle at the Milvian Bridge he was hoping for a sign from one of the gods that
would portend his victory, but that he never expected to become a visionary of
the Christian Sign of the Cross.

Having won that crucial victory, Constantine became sole ruler of the
Roman Empire and his soldiers now had emblazoned on their shields the Greek
initials of Christ's name, a symbol we refer to as the Chi-Rho.

---

4   In Greek: *En tauto nike*; in Latin: *In hoc [signo] vinces*.
5   Eusebius' *The Life of Constantine*, as cited in Hill, *History of Christianity*, 72.

As Hill notes, Constantine succeeded in several areas. He reformed the Roman army, boosted the economy, uprooted administrative corruption, established political unity and staved off foreign threats of invasion. Hitchcock summarizes Constantine's "moral revolution" and its apparent contradictions:

> By his decrees, Constantine also sought to bring about a kind of moral revolution: establishing Sunday as a day of rest, in commemoration of Christ's Resurrection; abolishing crucifixion; forbidding the branding of criminals on the face, since the face is the image of the soul; depriving slave-owners of the power of life and death over their slaves. Usury (excessive interest on loans) was condemned, there was a widespread freeing of slaves, and charitable works were extolled. He expressed horror at the bloodiness of pagan sacrifices, in contrast to the unbloody sacrifice of Christ, but the bloody games in the circuses were not suppressed for another century, until a monk ran into the amphitheatre in protest and was torn to pieces by the beasts. Christianity revitalized the Roman family as the basis of all social life by enjoining fidelity on both husband and wife—holding up Paul's ideal relationship between them as like that of Christ and the Church—and including even slaves as part of the family. Because sexual relations were permitted only within marriage, slaves were now allowed to marry. Constantine enacted a series of severe laws concerning sexual conduct, including death by torture of a man who seduced a virgin. The new order curbed patriarchal authority in one important respect—no longer did fathers have power of life and death over their newborn children. Divorce had been easy among the Romans, but in Constantine's decrees, it was allowed to women only if their husbands committed murder or practiced magic and to men only if their wives were unfaithful, sold their bodies, or induced abortions. For the most part, the Church recognized the legitimacy of a second marriage after divorce, if the couple did suitable lengthy penance. The "Pauline privilege" allowed a Christian to separate from a pagan spouse ("Do not be mismated with unbelievers" [2 Corinthians 6:14]), but often a Christian wife was the instrument of her husband's conversion. Though a moral reformer, Constantine was also ruthless and cruel, even to the point of having his wife and his son murdered because of a suspicion that they were plotting against him. The murders so disturbed his mother Helena that, as expiation of her son's sins, she set out on her famous quest for the true Cross, which led eventually to the unearthing of three crosses near Jerusalem that were venerated as the execution instruments of Jesus and the two thieves.[6]

---

[6]   Hitchcock, *History of the Catholic Church*, 57f.

Constantine's attitude toward Christianity, however, was ambivalent since he remained a pagan for all practical purposes until his death-bed conversion, preferring the cult of *sol invictus* (unconquered sun) to worshipping the Son of God. Hill reports:

> Pagan gods remained on the coins until A.D. 320, and the Emperor retained the old pagan title of *pontifex maximus*. Meanwhile, however, his armies continued to march under the Christian Chi-Rho sign. Sunday was made a holiday, and soldiers had to attend church parades. Most strikingly of all, the Emperor founded a new capital in the East. Known as the New Rome, this city was built on the site of an ancient town called Byzantium, on the west coast of the Bosphorus, the channel linking the Black Sea to the Mediterranean. The city was provided with all the amenities of Roman civilization, a forum, a basilica, public baths and the rest, as well as the trappings of the imperial court. But unlike in Old Rome, there were no temples. Indeed, Constantine decreed that no pagan rites would ever be performed in his new capital. Instead, churches were built. New Rome was a potent symbol of the new Empire, an Empire whose centre of gravity was shifting eastwards into the Greek-speaking half of the Mediterranean, and which was built upon the worship of the Christian God, not of pagan deities. New Rome was usually known as Constantinople — "the city of Constantine" — and by the end of the fourth century it was not only the imperial capital but the largest and most culturally vibrant city in the Eastern Empire. It would remain the most important Christian city in the world for over a thousand years.[7]

The First Council of Constantinople[8] was convoked by Emperor Theodosius I during the pontificate of Pope Saint Damasus I[9] and was attended by approximately

---

[7] Hill, *History of Christianity*, 73.

[8] Cf. Lane, *The Lion Concise Book of Christian Thought*, 35: "The Council of Constantinople, in its third canon (law or edict), created a major source of future strife: 'The Bishop of Constantinople is to be honoured next after the Bishop of Rome, because Constantinople is the New Rome.' This canon was unpopular at Rome because it implied that Rome's primacy was based on its position as the secular capital. At this time the Roman bishops were beginning to claim a special position as heirs of Peter. The canon was even more unpopular in Alexandria, which had previously been the number two see or bishopric, after Rome. The bishops of Alexandria, who were ambitiously and immensely powerful, did not miss opportunities to humiliate the bishops of Constantinople, who had little power, despite their theoretical status. This can be seen in the affair of John Chrysostom, Cyril of Alexandria's attack on Nestorius, and the struggle preceding the Council of Chalcedon in 451."

[9] Pope Saint Damasus I (circa 305-374) was probably born in Spain. He fought ardently to promote greater unity between the Churches of East and West. He commissioned St. Jerome to produce the Vulgate, promoted careful study of the Sacred Scriptures and the cult of the martyrs by honoring their relics and helping to compile the stories of their lives. He also was

one hundred and fifty bishops,[10] lasting from May through July in A.D. 381.[11]

Pneumatological and Christological Heresies

The Council sought primarily to defend the divinity of the Holy Spirit against the heretical groups known as the Pneumatochians,[12] Macedonians,[13] and to a lesser degree the Christological heresies of Apollinarius.[14] For instance, Kelly writes:

---

among the first to begin the classification of documents for the archives of the Church at Rome. Saint Damasus' liturgical memorial is December 11.

[10] Cf. Lane, 34f: "This was very much the Cappadocian Fathers' council. The Gregories [Nazianzen and Nyssa] were both present at the council. Gregory of Nazianzus played a leading role, although it ended his career as a bishop. The heresies which the Cappadocians had fought were rejected at the council, in accordance with their teaching."

[11] Cf. O'Collins, Farrugia, *A Concise Dictionary of Theology*, 51f: "**Constantinople, First Council of** (381). Convoked by Emperor Theodosius I to consolidate the unity of faith after the long Arian controversy, this Council was attended, as planned, only by Eastern bishops (according to tradition 150 of them; in reality 146). Neither Pope Damasus I (pope 366-384) nor any other bishops from the West were officially represented. When the first president of the Council, St. Mellitus of Antioch, died, St. Gregory of Nazianzus (ca. 329-ca.389) presided for some time before resigning; the Council then chose St. Nectarius (d. 397) as its president and bishop of Constantinople. The Council confirmed and expanded the Nicene Creed, proclaimed the divinity of the Holy Spirit against the Pneumatomachians, and upheld the full humanity of Christ against the Apollinarians. It gave the see of Constantinople the place of honor in Christendom after Rome. It was recognized later as the Second Ecumenical Council—partly through Chalcedon, which promulgated the Nicene-Constantinopolitan Creed."

[12] Cf. O'Collins, Farrugia, *A Concise Dictionary of Theology*, 205: "**Pneumatochians.** (Gr. 'spirit-fighters'). A late fourth-century sect that denied the full divinity of the Holy Spirit. The sect members are also improperly called Macedonians, possibly because they were joined after his death by followers of Bishop Macedonius of Constantinople (d. ca. 362). They were condemned at the First Council of Constantinople (381), which defined the divinity of the Spirit in vital and biblical terms but without calling the Spirit consubstantial with the Father and the Son."

[13] Cf. Johannes Quasten, *Patrology* [Volume III]: *The Golden Age of Greek Patristic Literature* (Christian Classics, Inc., 1986), 259. Quasten refers to a sermon by Pope St. Gregory the Great entitled: *Sermo de Spiritu Sancto adversus Pnuematomachos Macedonianos* (Sermon on the Holy Spirit against the Pneumatochians and Macedonians). Quasten comments: "This sermon is directed against the *Pneumatomachi* (contenders against the Spirit). Macedonianus, the leader of the sect and the chief representative known to us of the Arian teaching with regard to the Holy Spirit, had been appointed bishop of Constantinople after the deposition of Paul (a Nicene), but was himself in turn deposed by the Synod of Constantinople in 360."

[14] Cf. O'Collins, Farrugia, *A Concise Dictionary of Theology*, 15: "**Apollinarianism.** A christological heresy coming from a bishop of Laodicea, Apollinarius (ca. 310-ca. 390). Intent on defending Christ's full divinity against the Arians, he undercut His full humanity by holding that Christ had no spirit or rational soul, this being replaced by the divine Logos. His overriding concern was thus to establish a strict unity in Christ, as is shown in his formula, 'the one incarnate nature of the Logos.' Note that Apollinarius' name sometimes appears as Apollinaris."

The real heresy of Apollinarius, we know, consisted in his refusal to admit the completeness of the Lord's humanity. The Word, he thought, could not have assumed a free, intelligent human soul without introducing a disastrous duality into the Saviour's being [...]. His doctrine was that Christ had but a single nature and that the flesh was something, as it were, adventitious and added to the divinity.[15]

Nicene-Constantinopolitan Creed[16]

It was therefore necessary to amplify the Nicene Creed to emphasize that Mary's virginal conception of Our Lord came about by the power of the Holy Spirit. It is precisely at this point in the Nicene Creed, more properly known as the Nicene-Constantinopolitan Creed, that we bow at the words: *Et homo factus est* (And became man), except on the Solemnities of the Annunciation (March 25) and Christmas (December 25), when we kneel.[17]

The Constantinopolitan additions to the Nicene Creed clarified belief in the personhood and co-equal divinity of the Holy Spirit. These clarifications should be familiar to us:

> I believe in the Holy Spirit, the Lord, the giver of life, who proceeds from the Father (and the Son) *[Filioque]*,[18] who with the Father and the Son is adored and glorified, who has spoken through the prophets.

---

[15] J.N.D. Kelly, *Early Christian Creeds* [third edition] (Longman Group UK Limited, 1993), 334.

[16] An alternate spelling is Niceno-Constantinopolitan.

[17] In the Extraordinary Form of the Roman Rite, commonly known as the Tridentine Rite, priest and people kneel during the same verse at all times.

[18] Cf. O'Collins, Ferrugia, *A Concise Dictionary of Theology*, 90f: "**Filioque.** (Lat. 'and [from] the Son'). A phrase added to the Nicene-Constantinopolitan Creed at the Fourth Synod of Braga, Spain (675)—its addition at the Third Synod of Toledo (589) seems to be an interpolation—indicating (a) that the Holy Spirit proceeds from the Father and the Son, and (b) that the three Persons of the Trinity are perfectly equal. Emperor Charlemagne (ruled 771-814) promoted the addition; in 1013 St. Henry II (ruled 995-1024) ordered the whole Latin Church to add the 'Filioque' to the Creed. The Greek Orthodox Church objected strongly to this insertion, since it jeopardized the 'monarchy' of the Father (the single, originated principle) by introducing a second principle for the procession of the Spirit—a view expressly rejected by the Catholic Church. After the time of Patriarch Photius of Constantinople (ca. 800-895), the 'Filioque' has often been considered the greatest point of difference separating East and West. The Council of Florence (1438-1445) did not insist that the Greeks accept the 'Filioque' addition, provided they acknowledge the truth behind it, as they did. While many Orthodox continue to reject the 'Filioque' as heretical, some follow Vasilij V. Bolotov (d. 1900), the Russian patristic scholar who understood it to be a free opinion of St. Augustine (354-430), or join with St. Gregory Palamas (1296-1359) in seeking to mediate between East and West on this point."

A Latin or Western apologetic for the addition of the *Filioque* to the Nicene-Constantinopolitan Creed relates in part to the fact that the synod fathers of Toledo made this addition precisely because Semi-Arianism was still spreading like wild-fire in the West, while in the East it was no longer a prevailing heresy.

Furthermore, the West legitimately teaches that the theological term *Filioque* is in accord with the teachings of Sacred Scripture which affirms in various places, but especially in John's Gospel, that the Spirit is the gift of both the Father and the Son.[19]

The Church explains the mode of the Holy Spirit's communication in the Trinitarian life by employing other theological terms such as "procession" and "spiration" (breathing), so that the Holy Spirit is said to "proceed" from both the Father and the Son or to be "spirated" ("breathed forth") by both the Father and the Son from all eternity.

Excursus: *Filioque* Controversy

The *Filioque* controversy (which eventually helped foster disunity and finally formal schism between the majority of the Eastern Churches and the Apostolic See of Rome in 1054) is a complex topic that can only be summarized here.

Lane inaugurates our discussion by underscoring the main theological differences between the Churches of East and West regarding the addition of the *Filioque* to the Creed:

> In the East the belief was and is that the Holy Spirit proceeds from the Father through the Son. In the West, however, the belief grew that the Holy Spirit proceeds from the Father and the Son. (This minor verbal difference reflects an underlying difference in approach to the doctrine of the Trinity). In the West, it became customary to add the words "and the Son" (*Filioque* in Latin) into the Creed. Rome was always cautious and conservative, but finally she followed suit in the eleventh century and also added the word *Filioque*. This helped to precipitate the breach between Rome and Constantinople in 1054.[20]

The expression *Filioque* was added to the ecumenical creed (originally formulated and fought over in the East in the fourth century) by a local synod of bishops held in Toledo (Spain) in the sixth century.

---

[19] Cf. John 15:26.
[20] Lane, *The Lion Concise Book of Christian Thought*, 35.

The Third Council of Toledo held in 589 was convoked by Bishop Leander of Seville[21] in reaction to the nobles and bishops who were Arian Visigoths. At that Council Bishop Leander was only able to convert King Reccared and eight Arian bishops to orthodox Christianity. Ironically and sadly enough, the addition of the *Filioque* to the Nicene-Constantinopolitan Creed at that Council, which was meant to bring about unity between Catholics and Arians, only succeeded in sparking further division between the Churches of East and West until schism began to erupt in 1054.

James Hitchcock explains how the "Photian Schism" of the ninth century served as an ominous harbinger of the so-called Schism of 1054:

> In 858, Emperor Michael III the Drunkard (842-867) deposed Patriarch Ignatius of Constantinople (d. 877) and appointed the layman Photius (d. 897) in his place, an act that Pope Nicholas I denounced after Ignatius appealed to him. Photius soon claimed authority in southern Italy, and Nicholas excommunicated him, whereupon Photius accused the Western church of heresy, because of the doctrine of Purgatory and the word filioque in the Creed. Then a Byzantine council declared Nicholas deposed. However, after an imperial coup, the new emperor, Basil I the Macedonian (867-886), sent Photius to a monastery and restored Ignatius. (Neverthless Photius would be restored and removed yet one more time before his death.) The Fourth Council of Constantinople (869-870) affirmed the authority of the see of Rome, although the Council was later repudiated in the East. The extent of papal authority remained uncertain in the East. In 903, Emperor Leo VI, having been widowed three times, married a fourth wife, for which he was excommunicated by the Eastern bishops. He then obtained a dispensation from Rome, which the Eastern clergy refused to recognize.[22]

---

[21] Leander and his brother, Isidore of Seville, are venerated as patron saints of Spain. Isidore, former Archbishop of Seville and Doctor of the Church, lived from around 560 to 636. His most notable contribution was copious writings that influenced the medieval study of the history of the Church and the Iberian Peninsula (Spain and Portugal). He is sometimes mentioned as "the last scholar of the ancient world," an expression first used by the historian Montalembert. The Mozarabic Rite (proper to Toledo, Spain) is attributed to his genius. In the Ordinary Form of the Roman Rite, the chant for Option A of the Memorial Acclamation is an adaptation of a haunting Mozarabic melody. The liturgical memorial of Isidore of Seville is April 4.
[22] Hitchcock, *History of the Catholic Church*, 190f.

In 1054, a papal legation travelled to Constantinople under the leadership of the French Cardinal Humbert of Silva Candida[23] (former Archbishop of Sicily) to seek clarifications from the Patriarch of Constantinople, Michael Cerularius,[24] about certain grievances he and his followers had against the Pope and the Latin Church in general. Both entourges were warmly received by the Patriarch of Constantinople, Constantine IX (1042-1055).

Greek Orthodox scholar, Timothy (Kallistos) Ware, explains:

> In 1054 there was a great quarrel. The Normans had been forcing the Greeks in Byzantine Italy to conform to Latin usages; the Patriarch of Constantinople, Michael Cerularius, in return demanded that the Latin churches at Constantinople should adopt Greek practices, and in 1052, when they refused he closed them. This was perhaps harsh, but as Patriarch he was fully entitled to act in this manner.[25]

Cerularius also believed that he should be referred to as "Ecumenical Patriarch." Pope Leo IX[26] thought this title inappropriate and one that undermined his own authority as Supreme Pontiff of the Catholic Church. Cerularius and his followers, some more extreme than himself, also railed against, indeed actively persecuted, the Latin Church for other reasons, for so-called abuses like using unleavened bread (Greek: *azymes*)[27] rather than leavened bread in the Eucharistic Liturgy; not singing the "Alleluia" during fast days; eating the meat of strangled animals; enforcing mandatory celibacy for all clergy; encouraging fasting on Saturday. Ware comments further:

---

[23] He was also known as Humbert de Moyenmoutier; he died in 1061.

[24] His Greek name was Kerullarios; he died in 1059.

[25] Timothy Ware, *The Orthodox Church* (Penguin Books, 1997), 58.

[26] Pope Leo IX was born in Egisheim (Upper Alsace-Lorraine) on June 21, 1002 and died on April 19, 1054. Enthroned on February 12, 1049, Leo IX became the most significant, reform-minded German Pope of the Middle Ages.

[27] Cf. O'Collins, Farruggia, A Concise Dictionary of Theology, 23: "**Azymes.** (Gr. 'without yeast'). Thin bread baked without yeast (see Genesis 19:3), eaten during a week-long OT feast commemorating the Exodus from Egypt (Exodus 12:15; 23:15; 34:18). On account of its fermentation, leavened bread came to signify corruption (Matthew 16:6; 1 Corinthians 5:7). Since the Synoptic Gospels report the Last Supper to have taken place on the first day of the feast of Azymes (Matthew 26:7; Mark 14:12; Luke 22:7), unleavened bread is used in the Latin Mass. Most Eastern churches, however, follow St. John, who dates the Last Supper and Crucifixion to just before the feast of Azymes began (John 13:1; 18:28; 19:14, 31). This difference provided one of the immediate pretexts for the schism of 1054 between East and West. Archbishop Leo of Ohrid accused the Latins of being 'azymites' or 'infermentari.' The Council of Florence (1439) taught that both unleavened and leavened bread may be used for the Eucharist. All Easterners, except the Armenians and the Maronites, use leavened bread."

In 1053, however, Cerularius took up a more conciliatory attitude and wrote to Pope Leo IX, offering to restore the Pope's name to the *"Diptychs."*[28] The *"Diptychs"* were tablets that contained the names of all the patriarchs in communion with the Pope. These *"Diptychs"* were placed on the altar and the names of the patriarchs were mentioned in the course of the Divine Liturgy, usually in the context of the litanies.

Ware continues his analysis of the events of 1054:

> In response to this offer, and to settle the disputed questions of Greek and Latin usages, Leo in 1054 sent three legates to Constantinople, the chief of them being Humbert, Bishop of Silva Candida. The choice of Cardinal Humbert was unfortunate, for both he and Cerularius were men of stiff and intransigent temper, whose mutual encounter was not likely to promote good will among Christians. The legates, when they called on Cerularius, did not create a favourable impression. Thrusting a letter from the Pope at him, they retired without giving the usual salutations; the letter itself, although signed by Leo, had in fact been drafted by Humbert, and was distinctively unfriendly in tone. After this the Patriarch refused to have further dealings with the legates.[29]

Consequently, on July 16, 1054, Cardinal Humbert, having lost all patience with Cerularius, placed a Bull of Excommunication of Patriarch Cerularius on the high altar of the Church of *Hagia Sophia* (Church of the "Holy Wisdom") in Constantinople.[30] Kallistos Ware concludes:

> [...] among other ill-founded charges in this document, Humbert accused the Greeks of omitting the *Filioque* from the Creed! Humbert promptly left Constantinople without offering any further explanation of his act, and on returning to Italy he represented the whole incident as a great victory for the see of Rome. Cerularius

---

[28] Ware, *The Orthodox Church*, 58. Cf. O'Collins, Farrugia, *A Concise Dictionary of Theology*, 65: "**Diptychs.** (Gr. 'twofold, doubled, double writing tablets'). The names of people, living and dead, to be read during the Eucharist, originally written on two tablets, joined together by hinges. Naming prominent persons meant communion with them, whereas striking their names off the list signified excommunication. The use of diptychs of the living continues on more solemn occasions in Byzantine liturgies."

[29] Ware, *The Orthodox Church*, 58.

[30] These mutual excommunications were only lifted on December 7, 1965, by Pope Paul VI and Patriarch Athenagoras I.

and his synod retaliated by anathematizing Humbert (but not the Roman Church as such). The attempt at reconciliation left matters worse than before.[31]

Breathing with Both Lungs

It must be noted that, from the Catholic Church's perspective, the addition or omission of the *Filioque* in the Creed does not signify a qualitative change in the Creed's theological orthodoxy.

As a matter of fact, Byzantine Rite Catholics have the option to omit the *Filioque* during the Divine Liturgy, where the Creed is preferably sung as an integral part of the Eucharistic *synaxis* (assembly). In the Roman Rite the Creed is only used on Sundays and Solemnities.

On the occasion of the Solemnity of Saints Peter and Paul[32] in Rome (June 29, 2004), St. John Paul II, together with the Ecumenical Patriarch of Constantinople, Bartholomew I recited the Nicene-Constantinopolitan Creed in Greek without the *Filioque;* that event commemorated the fortieth anniversary of the encounter between Pope Paul VI and the Ecumenical Patriarch of Constantinople, Athenagoras I, in Jerusalem.

Thus, once again, the Bishop of Rome and the Patriarch of Constantinople proved the importance of *breathing with both lungs*,[33] and so took another significant step in the third Christian millennium towards reestablishing the unity of these sister-Churches of East and West whose Christian witness once stood undivided during the first millennium.

This fact has caused some theologians and historians to speculate that if the Churches of East and West had never been formally divided in 1054, the Protestant Reformation would never had occurred in the sixteenth century.

---

[31] Ware, *The Orthodox Church*, 58f.

[32] The Solemnity of Sts. Peter and Paul is believed to be as old as the liturgical celebration of Christmas in the Roman Rite. In the fourth century there were actually three Masses celebrated to commemorate Peter and Paul on this day: 1) At St. Peter's Basilica in the Vatican; 2) At the Basilica of St. Paul Outside the Walls; 3) In the Catacombs of St. Sebastian where the earthly remains of the Apostles were first interred for a time, hidden away from the prying hands of the pagan Roman persecutors.

[33] This was a venerable expression of St. John Paul II.

Ecumenical unity is definitely something to reflect on historically and theologically but, even more so, a reality for which to pray daily following the example of the Lord Jesus who, on the night before He died, asked His Heavenly Father: *Ut unum sint*[34] ("That they might be one)!"[35]

---

[34] See Pope John Paul's Encyclical on Ecumenism, *Ut Unum Sint*, in J. Michael Miller's *The Encyclicals of John Paul II* (Our Sunday Visitor, Inc., 1996), 895-976.

[35] John 17:11.

CHAPTER FIVE:
COUNCIL OF EPHESUS[1]
(A.D. 431)

Ephesus, Pagan and Christian

Ephesus[2] was a thriving port-city during the Roman Empire. In the first and second centuries A.D. Ephesus was the fourth largest city of the Roman Empire.

The ruins of Ephesus, like Hadrian's Temple and Trajan's Fountain and Amphitheater, are among the most extensive, best preserved and breathtaking of the ancient world still extant today. The Amphitheater was excavated by Austrian archeologists in the twentieth century. It was perhaps into this Amphitheater that Saint Paul and his companions, Gaius and Artistarchus, were dragged according to the account of Acts 19:23-24. The famed Library of Celsus alone merits a visit to Ephesus.

The Lion Concise Bible Encyclopedia paints a vivid picture of Ephesus in Roman and early Christian times:

> The most important city in the Roman province of Asia (western Turkey). Ephesus was a bridgehead between East and West. It stood at the end of one of the great caravan trade routes through Asia at the Cayster River. By Paul's day the harbour was beginning to silt up. But the city was magnificent, with streets paved in marble, baths, libraries, a market-place and theatre seating more than twenty-five thousand people.[3] The temple to Diana at Ephesus was one of the seven wonders of the ancient world, four times the size of the Parthenon at Athens. There had been a settlement at Ephesus since the twelfth century B.C. But by New Testament times the population had grown to something like a third of a million, including a great many Jews. Ephesus soon became an important centre for the early Christians, too. Paul made a brief visit

---

[1]   Cf. O'Collins, Farrugia, *A Concise Dictionary of Theology*, 76. Ephesus is the first Ecumenical Council for which we have the "Acts" (*Acta*) of the council.

[2]   In the New Testament, Ephesus and/or the Ephesians are mentioned more than twenty times.

[3]   The actual capacity is closer to twenty-four thousand.

on his second missionary journey, and his friends Aquila and Prisca stayed on there. On his third journey he spent over two years at Ephesus, and the Christian message spread widely throughout the province. Sales of silver images of Diana began to fall off. People's incomes were threatened and there was a riot. Paul wrote his letters to Corinth from Ephesus. And some of his letters from prison (Philippians, etc.) may have been written from Ephesus. Timothy stayed behind to help the church when Paul left. Paul later wrote a letter to the Christians at Ephesus. One of the letters to the seven churches in Revelation was also addressed to them. There is a tradition that Ephesus became the home of the apostle John.[4]

As related in the Acts of the Apostles,[5] Saint Paul successfully evangelized the Ephesians by preaching outdoors for weeks on end in the city's marketplace.[6]

The Ephesians were indeed difficult to evangelize. Fornication with prostitutes was prevalent among the numerous sailors who visited Ephesus daily. Eventually the mouth of the Cayster River silted up completely—stopping the ebb and flow of maritime commerce. The Ephesians were given to much pagan idolatry, especially the cult of the fertility goddess, *Artemis* (Latin: *Diana*).

Recall how the silversmiths of Ephesus, who manufactured popular images of Diana, rioted when Saint Paul dared to preach to them the doctrine of "monotheism" (belief in one God), crying out as they did so: *Great is Artemis of the Ephesians!*[7]

The statue of the "Great" Artemis was known in Greek as the *Artemision*. In and around the *Artemision*, the goddess Artemis was often depicted in statuary as being covered with what appear to be multiple breasts, alluding to her fertility.

Mary's Last Days

It is a privilege to visit the extraordinary ruins of ancient Ephesus and to pray in the holy house[8] of the Blessed Virgin Mary. At Ephesus, according to an ancient tradition, Mary lived out her final years in the company of John the Beloved Disciple to whom Jesus had entrusted her from the Cross.[9]

---

[4] *The Lion Concise Bible Encyclopedia* (Lion Publishing PLC, 1987), 81f.

[5] Cf. Acts 18:19-21, 24-26; 19:1-20:1; 20:16-38; 21:27-22:30; 1 Corinthians 15: 32; 1 Timothy 1:3; 2 Timothy 1:18; 4:12; Revelation 1:11; 2:1-7.

[6] Greek: *agora*; Latin: *forum*.

[7] Acts 19:28.

[8] Cf. Reverend Carl G. Schulte, C.M., *The Life of Sr. Marie de Mandat-Grancey and Mary's House in Ephesus* (Tan Books, 2010).

[9] Cf. John 19:25-27. In the cultural milieu of Jesus' time, it would have been very strange to entrust one's mother to a stranger if, in fact, one had other siblings. This text helps under-

The Dormition of the Virgin *by Theophanes the Greek, 1392.*

Many Christians hold that Mary lived at Ephesus until her glorious and bodily Assumption. Eastern Christians refer to the mystery of Mary's Assumption as the mystery of her "falling asleep" (Greek: *koimesis*).[10]

Another tradition holds that it was at Jerusalem rather than at Ephesus that the Blessed Virgin Mary fell asleep and was assumed into Heaven, having finished her earthly course.

As a matter of fact, there are at least two churches in Jerusalem, the one Greek Orthodox near the Mount of Olives, the other, the Catholic Benedictine

---

score the doctrine of Mary's Perpetual Virginity.

[10] Cf. O'Collins, Farrugia, *A Concise Dictionary of Theology*: "Assumption replaced *dormition* ('falling asleep') when Rome adopted the feast in the seventh century."

church known as "Dormition Abbey" on Mount Zion,[11] both of which claim to be the site of Mary's passing from this world to the next.

Theologians, like Saint John Paul II and Blessed John Henry Newman, have speculated as to whether or not Mary died in imitation of her Divine Son. Nevertheless, Mary's death is neither a part of the dogmatic definition of the Assumption (Venerable Pope Pius XII, 1950) nor a constitutive element of Eastern Orthodox belief.

In visiting Ephesus, one may see what archeologists claim are the remains of the Basilica of Saint Mary in which the Third Ecumenical Council was celebrated.[12] In the vicinity are particularly striking remnants of an ancient altar and baptismal font.

Furthermore, on a hill not far from Ephesus, in the Turkish town of Selçuk, one discovers the Basilica of Saint John the Apostle, which contains what many believe is the empty tomb (sarcophagus) of the Apostle John, the Beloved Disciple, who rested on Our Lord's chest at the Last Supper. According to tradition, John was the youngest of the Apostles, the last to die, and the only Apostle to die of natural causes. His confreres were all martyred.[13] After the death of John the Evangelist (circa A.D. 100), Divine Revelation officially ended.

Nestorianism[14]

The main protagonist of the Christological controversy leading up to the Council of Ephesus was Nestorius who was first a monk at Antioch and later appointed Patriarch of Constantinople (A.D. 428-431). He sought in his theological musings to maintain a clear distinction between the two natures of Christ, human and divine. James Hitchcock underscores a quasi-causal effect between Nestorius' questionable teachings and those of his monastic mentor, Theodore of Mopsuestia, who was posthumously condemned:[15]

---

[11]   Alternate spelling: Sion.

[12]   Cf. Henry Chadwick, *The Early Church* (Volume One) *of the Pelican History of the Church* (Penguin Books, 1967), 198.

[13]   One tradition holds that an attempt was made to kill John by boiling him in a vat of oil. This attempt was miraculously foiled.

[14]   Cf. O'Collins, Farrugia, *A Concise Dictionary of Theology*, 174: "**Nestorianism.** The heresy (condemned in 431 at the Council of Ephesus) that in Christ there are two different persons, one human and the other divine, who are separate subjects linked by a manifest union of love. It was wrongly attributed to Nestorius (d. ca. 451), a monk from Antioch who became the Patriarch of Constantinople (428-431). He opposed a popular Marian title, *Theotokos* (Gr. 'Mother of God'), apparently fearing that it threatened the full and distinct divinity and humanity of Christ, but was willing to accept the title if interpreted correctly."

[15]   Cf. O'Collins, Farrrugia, *A Concise Dictionary of Theology*, 267: "Selected writings from

Theodore of Mopsuestia (d. ca. 428), anxious to counter any suggestion that God suffered or could in any way change, taught that in Jesus there were actually two "persons" united together—the divine dwelling in the human as in a temple—of which only the human was incarnate, suffered, and died. Theodore denied that the prophecies of the Old Testament pertained to Jesus and spoke of a "loving accord" between Christ and His Father rather than of complete equality.[16]

Thus it was that Nestorius favored a mere moral union between the two natures of Christ, rather than a hypostatic[17] union, which means a real and substantial union between the Divine Word and the Sacred Humanity that the Lord Jesus assumed from the Blessed Virgin Mary and which was consubstantially united to His Divine Person.

Mary: Theotokos[18] or Christotokos?

Nestorius rejected the title *Theotokos* (God-bearer) for Our Lady in favor of *Christotokos* (Christ-bearer) in his preaching and teaching, even though the Marian title of *Theotokos* pervaded the devotional and doctrinal language of the time.[19]

---

three authors accused of favoring Nestorianism, whom Justinian I (emperor 527-565), had condemned posthumously as a good-will gesture to the Monophysite opposition to the Council of Chalcedon (451). The condemnation touched the works and person of Theodore of Mopsuestia (ca. 350-428), the writings that Theodoret, Bishop of Cyrrhus (ca. 393-ca.466) directed against St. Cyril of Alexandria (d. 444), and the letter that Ibas of Edessa (bishop 435-449) sent in 433 to Maris, bishop of Hardascir in Persia. Though summoned to Constantinople in 547, Pope Vigilius (pope 537-555) refused at first to subscribe to such posthumous condemnation and opposed any tampering with Chalcedon's teaching. After being forced to come to Constantinople, in his *Iudicium* of 548, he condemned propositions from Theodore, yet only insofar as they might lend themselves to a Nestorian interpretation. When an ecumenical council, Constantinople II (553), was convoked, Vigilius eventually signed the condemnation of the Three Chapters, an act that led to a serious schism in the West, which was healed only around 689. However unfortunate the circumstances, this unusual censuring may be interpreted as a guarantee that there is nothing in church doctrine that would warrant the Nestorian error."

[16] Hitchcock, *History of the Catholic Church*, 85.

[17] "Hypostatic" derives from the Greek words *hypo* (under, beneath) and *stasis* (standing).

[18] Cf. O'Collins, Farrugia, *A Concise Dictionary of Theology*, 266: "**Theotokos**. (Gr. 'God-bearer'). A title given to Our Lady and used at least as early as Origen (ca. 185-ca. 254) to express the fact that she gave birth to the Son of God. In Latin, although the exact equivalent is *Deipara*, the title often appears as *Deigenetrix* (Lat. "Mother of God'). When Nestorius of Constantinople called into question this popular title, the Council of Ephesus (431) condemned him and, in upholding the unity of Christ's person, proclaimed the legitimacy of the title *Theotokos*. It was not just a man (or a humanity) that Mary begot but the Son of God Himself."

[19] Cf. Jaroslav Pelikan, *Mary Through the Centuries: Her Place in the History of Culture* (Yale

This outright rejection of *Theotokos* in favor of *Christotokos* was indicative not only of Nestorius' theological confusion, but likewise of his pastoral insensitivity and disregard for the *sensus fidelium* (sense of the faithful).[20]

However, as recent ecumenical dialogue and signed agreements between the Assyrian Churches[21] and the Church of Rome have underscored, Nestorius and his followers seem to have misunderstood the precise significance of the title *Theotokos* since they believed, for example, that the term *Theotokos* signified that Mary was being considered the Mother of the eternal divine essence, which she is not.

Even our common experience attests that a woman is not the mother of an individual nature but the mother of an entire person. Therefore, by saying that Mary is the God-bearer, the Mother of God, the Church affirms that Mary is the Mother of Jesus Christ, the Incarnate Son of God. Jesus possesses two natures, human and divine, in the unity of His divine Person. Our Lord possesses His divine nature from all eternity, while His human nature was assumed from the Blessed Virgin at the moment of His conception.[22]

University Press, 1996), 59-62. Pelikan explains that St. Athanasius of Alexandria in his writings against the Docetists who denied the full humanity of Jesus mentions Mary's commemoration (*mnēmē*) and office (*chreia*). However, scholarship is inconclusive about the precise meaning of those terms. In all likelihood, Mary's commemoration referred to a liturgical festival (*mnēnē*) held in honor of Mary's Divine Maternity (*chreia*) on the Sunday after Christmas. Thus, in the revised Roman calendar, the first liturgical celebration of the New Year (January 1) is the Solemnity of Mary, Mother of God. According to the Tridentine calendar, January 1 is the Feast of Our Lord's Circumcision.

[20] Pier Franco Beatrice comments on the volatility of Nestorius: "Like Chrysostom, Nestorius also came from Antioch. Unlike his illustrious predecessor in the episcopal see of Constantinople, however, he did not hesitate in the course of his orations to express bold novelties which disturbed the Christian world. According to Nestorius, there are two natures in Christ, the human and divine. Up to this point, there is nothing unusual. However, in Nestorius' view, the two natures are distinct to such an extent that there is no contact at all between the two. Consequently, Mary could not strictly speaking be called 'Mother of God' according to the ancient and affectionate expression of popular faith, but only 'Mother of the man Jesus'" (*Introduction to the Fathers of the Church*, 321). cf. Pelikan, *Mary Through the Centuries*, 1996, 54-65.

[21] The Assyrian Churches remained faithful to Nestorius' teachings even after the Councils of Ephesus and Chalcedon.

[22] Henry Chadwick sheds light on this point: "But believers felt deeply that to question the full legitimacy of saying that the eternal Word died, or that Mary was Mother of God, was distressing to pious ears. Was not the Eucharist a re-enactment of the miracle of Bethlehem, at which the life-giving Body and Blood of Christ were offered to be received by the faithful? Nestorius' distinctions between the humanity of Christ and the eternal Word appeared to prejudice the divine pledge of immortality in the sacrament. Cyril's language, on the other hand, allowed one to say without fear that at Bethlehem the Ancient of Days was an hour or two old. Nothing caused so much scandal as the remark of Nestorius that 'God is not a baby two or three months old'" (*The Early Church*, 198).

Nestorius' Nemesis

The main opponent of Nestorius in this Christological controversy was Saint Cyril of Alexandria, Patriarch of Alexandria. Cyril wrote three letters, in effect three theological treatises, to Nestorius inviting him to recant his heretical notions in light of a careful exposition of the Church's orthodox teaching. Cyril also sent Nestorius a letter written by Pope Celestine to the same effect, to which Cyril then added twelve anathemas against Nestorius.

Council of Ephesus

The Council of Ephesus[23] was convoked by the Emperor Theodosius II[24] during the pontificate of Pope Saint Celestine I. The five sessions of the Council took place between June 22 and July 17 in A.D. 431.

As the Council of Ephesus opened, it did so without the Palestinian-Syrian [Antiochean] delegates, led by John of Antioch, a strong Nestorian sympathizer and, at the time, Patriarch of Antioch.[25]

When Nestorius got word concerning his supporters' conspicuous absence, he refused to attend the Council. After the Council, once he and his theology had been condemned, Nestorius asked for permission to retire to a monastery in Antioch, which, in fact, he received.[26]

---

[23] See CCC, 466.

[24] Theodosius II reigned from A.D. 408 to 450.

[25] Cf. Lane, *The Lion Concise Book of Christian Thought*, 46: "The Antiochene party of bishops, who supported Nestorius, was late in arriving. Cyril, who already had the support of Rome, waited fifteen days and then started the Council. Nestorius was deposed. Four days later the Antiochenes arrived. They refused to acknowledge Cyril's Council and set up their own, which condemned Cyril. There were only about thirty Antiochene bishops, compared with over two hundred at Cyril's Council. Two weeks later the Western [Papal] delegates arrived and confirmed Cyril's Council. It came to be seen as the third of the Ecumenical Councils. The outcome was confusion and division in the East. Alexandria split from Antioch. Eventually, there was a settlement, in 433. Cyril accepted a moderate Antiochene document called the *Formula of Reunion*, while the Antiochenes agreed to accept the deposition of Nestorius. Despite accusations to the contrary, Cyril did not go against his earlier teaching in accepting the *Formula of Reunion*. It did not say all he might have said and its wording was not identical to his, but the primary point for which he had fought against Nestorius, the Incarnation, was clearly stated. Alleged points of contradiction between the *Formula* and Cyril's teaching elsewhere are illusory."

[26] Pier Franco Beatrice notes: "The followers of Nestorius, excluded from ecclesial communion, continued as the autonomous Nestorian church which spread towards the Syriac East. It prospered there and even penetrated the frontiers of distant China. Centuries before Marco Polo, these Nestorians were the first Christians to arrive in China!" (*Introduction to the Fathers of the Church*, 323).

What, then, are the teachings of the Council of Ephesus and their implications for us? The Council clearly teaches that Jesus is not a hybrid or, shall we say, a schizophrenic personality, but one divine Person with two natures, human and divine.

Likewise, the Council affirms that Mary's Divine Maternity affords her a unique union and intimacy with the Son of God Incarnate that justifies her

Byzantine icon in the Basilica of St. Paul Outside the Walls, Rome.

title of *Theotokos*. As Blessed Newman reflected time and again, the title *Theotokos* acts as a safeguard or bulwark of the Church's orthodox Christology and Mariology. Also implied in the Council's decrees is a belief in Mary's Perpetual Virginity.

Jaroslav Pelikan dedicated an entire chapter of his book, *Mary Through the Centuries* to our topic. He explains:

> The name *Theotokos* appears in some manuscripts of the works of Athanasius. Yet the textual evidence leaves ambiguous the question of how often Athanasius did use the title *Theotokos* for Mary. In any event, it receives negative corroboration from its appearance, during the lifetime of Athanasius, in the attacks on the Church by the Emperor Julian "the Apostate," who criticized the superstition of the Christians for invoking the *Theotokos* […]. It was moreover, in honor of the definition by the Council of Ephesus of Mary as Theotokos that right after the Council Pope Sixtus III built the most important shrine to Mary in the West, the Basilica of Santa Maria Maggiore in Rome; its celebrated mosaic of the Annunciation and the Epiphany gave artistic form to that definition. A few centuries later John of Damascus would summarize the orthodox case for this special title: "Hence it is with justice and truth that we call holy Mary Theotokos. For this name embraces the whole mystery of the divine dispensation *[to mystērion tēs oikonomias]* […]." And he argued elsewhere, that is what she was on the icons: *Theotokos* and therefore the orthodox and God-pleasing substitute for the pagan worship of the demons. At the same time, the defenders of the icons insisted that "when we worship her icon, we do not, in pagan fashion *[Hellēnikōs]*, regard her as a goddess *[thean]* but as the *Theotokos.*"[27]

The Robber Synod

As an historical footnote to the Council of Ephesus, we mention the so-called "Robber Synod," also known as the "Robber Council." It got this nickname from the orthodox Catholic bishops who remarked disparagingly that the council was not a *judicium* (judgment) but a *latrocinium* (robbery). Why this assessment?

The "Robber Synod" was deliberately held at Ephesus A.D. 449 to counteract the Ecumenical Council of Ephesus held in A.D. 431. In brief, Dioscorus, Patriarch of Alexandria, convinced Emperor Theodosius II to call an alternate synod at Ephesus in order to vindicate Nestorius, as well as the Monophysite notions of

---

[27] Pelikan, *Mary Through the Centuries*, 55-57 *passim*.

Eutyches and his Alexandrian disciples—who had already been condemned at a synod in A.D. 448. Needless to say, the Catholic Church was never hoodwinked by the "Robber Synod"; she never acknowledged it as having any official weight.

Excursus: The Seven Wonders of the Ancient World

1. The Great Pyramid of Cheops (Khufu) near El Giza'. It was built between 2650 and 2630 B.C. by Cheops, King of Egypt;

2. The Hanging Gardens of Babylon were planted on terraces of the ziggurats, which were pyramidal temples;

3. The Statue of Olympian Zeus, created by the Greek architect Phidias, was situated on a plain of ancient Elis, Greece. Olympia was the site of the first "Olympic Games." The remains of ancient Olympia are still impressive to behold;

4. The Temple of Artemis at Ephesus: After Alexander the Great conquered Ephesus in 334 B.C., the *Artemision* burned in 356 B.C. The *Artemision* that was rebuilt in Hellenistic times was the one that came to be revered as one of the ancient wonders of the world;

5. The Mausoleum of Halicarnasus was a tomb erected around 350 B.C. near the present-day Turkish seaside resort town of Bodrum. It was erected by Artemis, the widow of the prince of Caria, whose name was Mausolus (hence the word mausoleum);

6. The Colossus of Rhodes was a bronze statue of the Greek god Apollo (the god of art and light) that stood at the entrance to the great harbor of Rhodes;

7. The Pharos (Lighthouse) of Alexandria was built by Ptolemy.[28]

Regrettably, of these Seven Wonders of the Ancient World, only the Great Pyramid of Cheops (Khufu) at Giza (near Cairo) remains standing.

---

[28] Cf. Peter D'Epiro and Mary Desmond Pinkowish, *What Are the Seven Wonders of the World?* (First Anchor Books Division, 1998), 179.

CHAPTER SIX:
COUNCIL OF CHALCEDON
(A.D. 451)

Jesus Christ, True God and True Man

Convoked by the Emperor Marcian during the pontificate of Pope Leo, the Council of Chalcedon[1] was attended by approximately six hundred bishops, with seventeen sessions held between October 8 and November 1 in A.D. 451.

O'Collins and Farrugia offer background information for this council:

> [The] Fourth Ecumenical Council, [was] held in 451 at a city now called Kadi-Köy (Turkey) on the other side of the Bosphorus from Constantinople. The Council was convoked to deal with the Mono-physite heresy of Eutyches (ca. 378-454), whose strong opposition to those who divided Christ into two sons seems to have led him into the opposite error. This was to reduce Christ to one of His two natures, the divine, or to a third nature that originated from both and was the only one to remain after the Incarnation. Condemned in 448 at a home [local] synod held in Constantinople, Eutyches was rehabilitated the following year at a synod in Ephesus summoned by Emperor Theodosius II (reigned 408-450). Leo I (pope 440-461) branded the Synod of Ephesus (449) a "latrocinium" (Lat. "brigandage") because its violent and uncanonical procedure robbed him of his right to judge, expressed in the famous *Tome to Flavian,* the Patriarch of Constantinople (d. 449). When Theodosius II fell from his horse and died, Emperor Marcian, who had married the late Emperor's sister St. Pulcheria (399-453), in agreement with the pope, convoked a new Council at Chalcedon. This brought together between 500 and 600 bishops, all of them Easterners, except for three papal legates and two bishops from Africa. The Council Fathers condemned Eutyches, as also did Dioscorus, Patriarch of Alexandria, his former patron. Dioscorus (d. 454), however, was himself deposed for having dared to excommunicate Pope Leo. The council affirmed

---

[1] Cf. CCC, 467.

An illuminated manuscript depicting the meeting of St. Leo the Great with Attila the Hun. Source: Csanády, Wikimedia.

the one person of Christ in His two natures, divine and human. It specified that "the one and the same Christ, Son, Lord, and Only-Begotten" was made known in these two natures, which, without detriment to their full qualities, continue to exist "without confusion or change, and without division or separation," while belonging to only one person and not two. Moreover, the Council enacted twenty-seven canons concerning disciplinary matters. Jerusalem became a patriarchate, the fifth, but Pope Leo refused to recognize the twenty-eighth canon, which assigned Constantinople, "the new Rome," wide jurisdictional powers, second only to old Rome itself.[2]

Aquilina profiles Pope Saint Leo the Great who reigned from A.D. 440-461 and provides context for the events leading up to the Council of Chalcedon:

> Roman-born, Leo served in the Church's diplomatic corps before ascending to the papacy. He was a prolific teacher and preacher, issuing many letters and homilies on doctrinal matters. The rebel who forced the crisis of Leo's pontificate was Eutyches, an archimandrite (or archabbot) in Constantinople, who argued that the two natures of Jesus Christ were so closely connected that they became one — His human nature was absorbed by the divine. Disciplined by Patriarch Flavian of Constantinople, Eutyches appealed to Pope Leo. Meanwhile, in the spring of 449, the emperor Thedosius II, who supported Eutyches, convened a puppet council at Ephesus. The council, which Leo called a "Robber Synod," was a disaster. The dissident bishops refused to hear the Pope's Letter to the Council, and Patriarch Flavian was beaten to death. Leo pressed for a Council that would be legitimate and truly universal in scope. But this was not possible until the accession of a new emperor who was open to the idea. The Council convened in Chalcedon in the fall of 451. At Chalcedon, papal representatives read Leo's Letter to the earlier Council at Ephesus.[3]

Monophysitism

Chalcedon was convoked to combat Eutyches' heresy of Monophysitism — an exaggeration of the Alexandrian position concerning the divinity of Christ — already condemned by Pope Leo the Great. The word Monophysitism is comprised of two Greek words — *monos,* meaning "alone" or "sole" and *physis,* meaning "nature." The Monophysites professed that Christ Jesus possessed only one nature, a divine nature and not a human nature.

Leo's Tome to Flavian

Pope Leo's "Tome" or "Letter" to Flavian, Patriarch of Constantinople, was instrumental in condemning the Monophysitism of Eutyches and his supporters.

---

[2]   O'Collins, Farrugia, *A Concise Dictionary of Theology*, 38f.
[3]   Aquilina, *The Fathers of the Church*, 205f.

Not surprisingly the leaders of the "Robber Council" refused to recognize the validity of Leo's Tome.[4]

Chalcedonian Formula

Leo's Tome is crucial for what has become known as the "Chalcedonian Formula." The essential Christological teaching of the Council can be summarized in the following way: Jesus' natures, human and divine, are to be understood as being separate, without confusion or mixture between them. Therefore, the human and divine natures of Our Lord are consubstantially united in the single reality of His divine Person.

Lane cites the key section of the "Chalcedonian Formula":

> *[The Synod]* opposes those who rend the mystery of the Incarnation into a duality of Sons [of which Nestorius was accused]; it expels from the Priesthood those who dare to say that the Godhead of the Only-Begotten is passible/capable of suffering *[Arius or Eutyches?]*; it resists those who imagine a mixture of Christ *[Eutyches]*; it drives away those who fancy that the "form of a servant" [i.e. humanity] which He took from us was of a heavenly or some other [non-human] substance [of which Apollinarius was falsely accused]; and it anathematises those who imagine that the Lord had two natures before their union, but only one afterwards *[Eutyches]*. Following the holy Fathers, we confess with one voice the one and only Son, Our Lord Jesus Christ, is perfect in Godhead and perfect in manhood, truly God and truly man, that He has a rational soul and a body. He is of one substance *[homoousios]* with the Father as God, He is also of one substance *[homoousios]* with us as man. He is like us in all things except sin. He was begotten of His Father before the ages as God, but in these last days and for our salvation He was born of Mary the Virgin, the *Theotokos*, as man. This one and the same Christ, Son, Lord, Only-begotten is made known in two natures [which exist] without confusion, without change, without division, without separation. The distinction of the natures is in no way taken away by their union, but rather the distinctive properties of each are preserved. [Both natures] unite into one person and one *hypostasis*. They are not separated or divided into two persons but [they form] one and the same Son, Only-Begotten, God, Word, Lord Jesus Christ, just as the Prophets of old [have

---

4   Cf. Hitchcock, *History of the Church*, 86: "Not solely because of Leo's intervention, Chalcedon adopted the formulation; and, although not immediately accepted everywhere, its decrees would serve as the touchstone of all later orthodox belief."

spoken] concerning Him and as the Lord Jesus Christ Himself has
taught us and as the Creed of the Fathers has delivered to us.[5]

Furthermore, the Council taught that Jesus was equally and fully
true God and true Man, consubstantially united to the Father as to
His Divinity, and consubstantially united to man as to His Humanity, like us in all things, save sin.[6]

"Roma Locuta Est: Causa Finita Est!"[7]

The Council Fathers, having heard the letter to Flavian read aloud, cried
out with one voice: *Peter has spoken through Leo.*[8] This is essential testimony to
the unique authority that the Pope exercised in the early Church, bearing in
mind that all the decrees of an Ecumenical Council were not considered valid
until ratified by the Bishop of Rome. Finally, it should be noted that the Bishop
of Rome did not attend these early ecumenical councils in person but sent at
least two or three delegates, usually deacons, to represent him. Chadwick concludes:

> Leo's Tome was received with courteous approval and pronounced to
> be in line with established orthodoxy.[9]

---

[5]   Lane, *The Lion Concise Book of Christian Thought*, 49f.

[6]   Cf. Chadwick, *The Early Church*, 203f.

[7]   A famous expression used by St. Augustine of Hippo. Literally these words are translated
      as "Rome has spoken, the case is finished." In other words, the declarations of the Pope on
      matters of faith and morals, not to mention discipline in the Church, are definitive.

[8]   This saying is also cited as: "Peter has spoken through the mouth of Leo."

[9]   Chadwick, *The Early Church*, 203.

CHAPTER SEVEN:
SECOND COUNCIL OF CONSTANTINOPLE[1]
(A.D. 553)

Chalcedonian Aftermath

As creatures of the twenty-first century, we might be tempted to consider the proceedings of the early church councils as antiquated "hang-ups," amounting to a mere "war of words," a veritable "much ado about nothing." However, as this chapter will endeavor to explain, nothing could be further from the truth.

The Second Council of Constantinople[2] was convoked by the Emperor Justinian I during the pontificate of Pope Vigilius against those who tried to make of Christ's human nature a kind of personal subject. It was attended by approximately one hundred and sixty-five bishops, with eight sessions lasting between May 5 and June 2 in A.D. 553.

Lane explains the Council's complex historical background and ramifications for Christendom. Therefore, it should become eminently clear to the reader why the Second Council of Constantinople was anything but a trivial affair:

> The Council of Chalcedon led to bitter division in the East. The Antio-
> chene School, who were in the minority, supported Chalcedon. A
> large number of Alexandrians opposed Chalcedon and held to Cyril's
> formula: "the one incarnate nature of the Word." They were therefore
> called Monophysites (from the Greek for "sole nature"). They rejected
> Chalcedon with its doctrine of "two natures." In between these two

---

[1] Cf. O'Collins, Farrugia, *A Concise Dictionary of Theology*, 52: "**Constantinople, Second Council of.** (553). The Fifth General Council, [was] convened by Emperor Justinian I (reigned 527-565) to bring peace to the Church in the East. In order to win over the Monophysites, Justinian encouraged the one hundred and sixty-five bishops present (practically all Easterners) to condemn Theodore of Mopsuestia (ca. 350-428), Theodoret of Cyrrhus (ca. 393-ca. 458) and Ibas of Edessa (435-457) for Nestorianism. After considerable harassment, Pope Vigilius (pope 537-555) dropped his opposition to the proceedings and accepted the Council."

[2] Cf. CCC, 468.

groups was another, sometimes called the "neo-Alexandrians." These were enthusiastic Alexandrian supporters of Cyril's teaching who were happy to accept Chalcedon. They saw it as a protection against possible misinterpretation of Cyril. They argued that Chalcedon should be accepted in the same way that Cyril himself accepted the *Formula of Reunion.* They held to Chalcedon, but interpreted it in a strongly Cyrilline way. The Monophysites controlled Egypt and other areas of the East. They were too powerful to be ignored or suppressed. Their objections to Chalcedon fell into two classes. *First,* they complained that certain Alexandrian/Cyrilline teaching was missing from Chalcedon: the "one incarnate nature" formula, the term "hypostatic union" and the idea that Christ was *"one out of two natures."* All of these terms were found in Cyril. *Secondly,* they objected to passages in Chalcedon which, they believed, divided Jesus Christ into two: the phrase "in two natures" and several passages in Leo's *Tome.* The Eastern Emperors struggled to resolve the controversy. At first Chalcedon was upheld. Then in 482 the Emperor Zeno issued a *Henotikon,* which proclaimed the only criteria for orthodoxy to be the Nicene Creed and Cyril's *Anathemas [of Nestorius].* Those who taught otherwise, "whether at Chalcedon or in any other synod whatever," were anathematized. This united the East—but at the price of schism from the West. Zeno's successor, Anastasius, went further and openly rejected Chalcedon. But when he died, his successors, Justin and Justinian, opted for Chalcedon and peace with Rome. In 553 Justinian called the Council of Constantinople, the fifth of the Ecumenical Councils. It sought to appease the Monophysites by presenting a Cyrilline interpretation of Chalcedon [...].[3]

Lane concludes his analysis of the Council of Constantinople as follows:

Most importantly, the Council showed that Chalcedon was to be understood in an Alexandrian way. The bishops confess "that we receive the four holy synods, that is, the Nicene, the Constantinopolitan, the first of Ephesus and that of Chalcedon, and we have taught and do teach all that they defined respecting the one faith." The aim was to placate Monophysite fears that Chalcedon had opened the doors to Nestorianism. The anathemas also show that the Cyrilline terms missing from Chalcedon (such as "hypostatic union") were acceptable as long as they were not understood to imply a mixture or confusion of the two natures. Finally, an Alexandrian formula popular with the Monophysites was approved: one of the Trinity was crucified in the flesh.[4]

---

[3]   Lane, *The Lion Concise Book of Christian Thought,* 57.
[4]   Ibid.

The Trinity *by G.A. de Sacchis, c. 1535.*

Communication of Properties[5]

The theological notion of *communicatio idiomatum* (communication of properties) is best understood in relation to the Christology clarified at this Council. Everything in Christ's human nature is to be attributed to the divine

---

[5]   Cf. O'Collins, Farrugia, *A Concise Dictionary of Theology*, 47: "**Communicatio Idiomatum.** (Lat. /Gr. 'interchange of properties'). Exchange of attributes because of the union of divinity and humanity in the one person of the incarnate Son of God. This means that attributes of one of His natures may be predicated of Him even when He is named with reference to the other nature, for example, 'the Son of God died on the Cross,' and 'the Son of Mary created the world.' This method of attribution calls for certain distinctions, so as not to confuse the two natures. The Son of God precisely as divine did not die on the Cross, nor did the Son of Mary precisely as human create the universe."

Person, as its proper subject, not only His miracles, but also His sufferings and even His death on the Cross.

It is theologically correct to state that God in Christ suffered and died. However, it is unacceptable to believe that the divine essence which is "impassible" (i.e., incapable of suffering) underwent suffering and death during Our Lord's Passion and Death.

Liturgy as *Locus Theologicus*[6]

In the Divine Liturgy of Saint John Chrysostom, there is a *troparion* or hymn entitled in Greek, *O Monogenes* (O Only-Begotten Son). Its principal aim is to teach orthodox Trinitarian, Christological and Mariological doctrines against Nestorianism and Monophysitism.

This liturgical hymn of the Byzantine Liturgy inculcates the truth of the Incarnation affirmed at Constantinople II in a sublime and poetic fashion:

> O Only-Begotten Son and Word of God, immortal being, you who deigned for our salvation to become incarnate of the Holy Mother of God and Ever-Virgin Mary, you who without change became man and were crucified, O Christ our God, you who by your death have crushed death, you who are one of the Holy Trinity, glorified with the Father and the Holy Spirit, save us!

Furthermore, as Henry Chadwick notes, a controversy arose between the adherents of the Chalcedonian Council of 451 and the Monophysites who rejected that Council's decrees. This controversy was not merely theological or speculative in nature, but one that came to be expressed: "in the popularly comprehensible form of a liturgical difference"[7] Chadwick explicates this point:

> Before 451 both the churches of Syria and Constantinople had come to use as a liturgical acclamation the "Trisagion," viz. "Holy God,

---

[6] Cf. O'Collins, Farrugia, *A Concise Dictionary of Theology*, 144: "**Locus Theologicus.** (Lat. 'place of theology'). The main themes of Christian faith (*loci communes* or common topics), or else fundamental principles and sources for medieval, baroque, and Neo-Scholastic theology (and Renaissance humanism) in systematically presenting doctrines. In a posthumous work *De locis theologicis* (1563) Melchior Cano (1509-1560) displayed the impact of the new humanism. He enumerated seven *loci* that depend, directly or indirectly, on divine authority and revelation: (1) God's Word in Scripture; (2) The Tradition of the Apostles; (3) The Universal Church; (4) Councils; (5) Papal Teaching; (6) The Fathers of the Church; and (7) Theologians and Canonists. As additional helps Cano named natural reason; philosophers and jurists; and history and tradition. Cano's method has exercised a great influence but needs to allow more for mystery and to incorporate the themes of salvation history and liturgy."

[7] Chadwick, *The Early Church*, 208.

Holy Mighty, Holy Immortal, have mercy upon us." As early as 431 Apollinarian sympathizers were adding "crucified for us" after "Immortal." At Antioch under a Monophysite patriarch about 460 this strengthened version of the Trisagion passed into use. The Chalcedonians rejected the addition, as implying that God was crucified, and re-interpreted the Trisagion to refer not to Christ but to the Trinity.[8]

The Catechism and Chalcedon

Consequently, the Catechism of the Catholic Church instructs us that the humanity of Jesus is assumed, not absorbed. Jesus has full human faculties of intellect and will:

> Everything that Christ is and does in this nature [i.e., His human nature] derives from "one of the Trinity." The Son of God therefore communicates to His humanity His own personal mode of existence in the Trinity. In His soul as in His body, Christ thus expresses humanly the divine ways of the Trinity: "The Son of God [...] worked with human hands; He thought with a human mind. He acted with a human will, and with a human heart He loved. Born of the Virgin Mary, He has truly been made one of us, like to us in all things except sin."[9]

Excursus: Patripassianism[10]

The heresy of *Patripassianism*[11] holds that God the Father suffered with His crucified Son in a co-equal manner. Why is *Patripassianism* a heresy? To answer this question we need to define the limits of our God-centered language.

---

[8] Chadwick, *The Early Church*, 208.
[9] CCC, 470; cf. *Gaudium et Spes* 22:2.
[10] Cf. O'Collins, Farrugia, *A Concise Dictionary of Theology*, 194: "**Patripassianism.** (Lat. 'suffering of the Father'). A term coined by Tertullian (ca. 160- ca. 220) for that form of Monarchianism that we call modalism, in his campaign against Praxeas (lived ca. 200), whom he mocked as having driven out the Spirit and crucified the Father. Another modalist, Noetus (lived ca. 200), asserted that it was the Father who had been born and had suffered on the Cross."
[11] Cf. Hitchcock, *History of the Catholic Church*, 86: "Modalism, also called Sabellianism after one of its leaders, was an early third-century attempt to understand the Trinity as 'modes' of a single Person—the same Being manifesting itself in three different ways. It was sometimes called Patripassianism—'the Father suffered'—leading Tertullian to jibe that the modalists had crucified the Father."

To speak of God, as Thomas Aquinas taught, we fallible human beings must make recourse to analogies.[12] We know that our human language is incapable of grasping fully the divine mystery.[13]

The Church, in the Catechism, also speaks of the *analogia fidei*, or "analogy of faith."[14] In fact, it is much easier, theologically speaking, to make apophatic[15] statements about God than cataphatic[16] statements. This means that it is easier for us to say who or what God is *not* rather than to say who or what He actually *is*.

In theological parlance this manner is referred to as the *via negativa*.[17] For the most part, through the centuries Christian mystics and aescetics belonging to the Eastern tradition have been more adept at using such apophatic language with regard to God than Western theologians, a most notable exception being Thomas Aquinas.[18]

---

[12] Cf. O'Collins, Farrugia, *A Concise Dictionary of Theology*, 284: "**Via Affirmationis, Negationis, Eminentiae** (Lat. 'way of affirmation, way of negation, exalted way'). Three rules of speaking analogously about God that were classically formulated by St. Thomas Aquinas (ca. 1225-1274). Our experience of human goodness, for example, allows us to predicate goodness of God. At the same time, God is not good in the limited way that human beings may be said to be good. Finally, being Goodness itself, God is good in an excellent way that transcends our understanding and language."

[13] Cf. CCC, 39-43.

[14] CCC, 114.

[15] Cf. O'Collins, Farrugia, *A Concise Dictionary of Theology*, 16: "**Apophatic Theology.** (Gr. 'prohibiting,' 'negative'). Central concept in Eastern theology, often translated as negative theology. It points out the inadequacy of all attempts to describe the absolute mystery of God. Any affirmation about God has to be qualified by a corresponding negation and the recognition that God surpasses in an infinite way our categories. Knowledge of God is never purely intellectual but calls for an ascent to God through moral and religious purification, classically described in *The Life of Moses* by St. Gregory of Nyssa (ca. 330-ca. 395)."

[16] Cf. O'Collins, Farrugia, *A Concise Dictionary of Theology*, 35: "**Cataphatic Theology.** (Gr. 'affirmative'). Sometimes called positive theology, it is a complementary concept to apophatic theology. Despite the radical inadequacy of our categories, we may nonetheless assert much that is true of God as revealed unsurpassably in Jesus Christ and known to us through the Holy Spirit. However, apophatic theology insists that even after the divine self-revelation and self-gift in grace, God remains the primordial mystery."

[17] The Latin phrase *via negativa* translates literally as: "the negative way." However, the use of the word "negative" in this phrase does not correspond to its modern connotation. Rather, the word "negative" is meant to express a "privation" on man's part; his inability to speak of God in definitive terms.

[18] Thomas Aquinas, Priest and Doctor of the Church, lived from around 1225 to 1274. He was an illustrious philosopher, who "baptized," to the best of his ability, the philosophy of Aristotle. His philosophy is so highly regarded by the Catholic Church that it is termed *philosophia perennis* (perrenial philosophy). Thomas' theological prowess, best exemplified by his *Summa Theologiae*, *Summa Contra Gentiles* and numerous Commentaries on Sacred Scripture, earned him the honorific title of *Doctor Angelicus* (Angelic Doctor). As a young

Insofar as all analogies "limp," we must be content with certain limitations in our theological discourse. Consequently, to speak of divine compassion, from the perspective of our own human emotions, is perfectly understandable.

Occasionally, the sacred authors of the Bible describe God as relenting and changing His mind. For example, the peoples of Sodom were spared destruction for a time in response to the repeated supplications of Abraham. Or, for example, the Bible speaks of God as having sympathized with His chosen people, Israel, as they endured slavery in Egypt.[19] Such anthropomorphic descriptions of God are meant to be understood figuratively, not literally.

To do otherwise would be paramount to saying that God experienced suffering in the exact same way as we humans do. Such a statement would be incorrect because all suffering entails change. Change is an essential characteristic of creatures, not their Creator, for "immutability" is one of the essential attributes of God as we learn in Aquinas' *Summa Theologica*.[20]

Moreover, one can speak figuratively of God the Father as having felt anguish as He beheld His Only-Begotten Son's Passion and Death without falling into the heresy of *Patripassianism*.

Thus, we read in the Catechism of the Catholic Church:

> He is truly the Son of God who, without ceasing to be God and
> Lord, became man and our brother.[21]

---

man he was very taciturn in the classroom, earning him the nickname, "The Dumb Ox," from his classmates. One of the oldest Pontifical universities in Rome (1580) is named in his honor, "The University of Saint Thomas in the City [of Rome]." This University, under the auspices of the Dominicans, Thomas' own religious order, is more colloquially referred to as "The Angelicum." The liturgical memorial of Saint Thomas Aquinas is January 28.

[19] The Hebrew text of Exodus says that God "knew" (*yada*) His people's suffering. Cf. Exodus 3:7. This usage of *yada* denotes God's omniscience.

[20] This text is also referred as the *Summa Theologiae*.

[21] CCC, 469.

Chapter Eight:
Third Council of Constantinople
(A.D. 680 - 681)

Fighting for the Human Soul of Jesus

The debate raging at the time centered on whether or not Jesus possessed one or two wills.

If, as the Council Fathers of Chalcedon taught, Jesus has two natures, human and divine, then would it not follow logically that He also possessed two wills? Not everyone, especially the Monophysites, agreed with this assumption. A conciliatory effort was needed to end the dispute.

The Sixth Ecumenical Council[1] was convoked by the Emperor Constantine IV[2] during the pontificates of Pope Saint Agatho and Pope Saint Leo II. It was attended by approximately one hundred and seventy bishops, with sixteen sessions being held at Constantinople between November 7, 680, and September 6, 681.

The Council of Constantinople III took place because there was major fallout (as we have already examined in our treatment of the Second Council of Constantinople) from the Council of Chalcedon in 451.

Ironically, as Lane explains, the theological discussions that ensued only led to further confusion and division over the Chalcedonian Formula:

> Sergius, Patriarch of Constantinople, proposed the formula, taken from the moderate Monophysite Severus of Antioch, that Christ had one "theandric" (divine/human) energy, by which he performed both divine and human acts. On the basis of this formula, Constantinople agreed with [Alexandria] Egypt, but objections came from the Patriarch of Jerusalem. Sergius then proposed another formula: that Jesus Christ had only one will. Pope Honorius of Rome agreed

---

[1] Cf. CCC, 475.
[2] He was also known as Pogonatos, reigning from 668 to 685.

Icon of Christ Pantocrator *("Ruler of All") by Metropolitan Jovan Zograf, 1384.*

and in 683 he and Sergius published an *Exposition of the Faith*. This outlawed debate about one energy or two. Instead it proclaimed "the one will of Our Lord Jesus Christ," and maintained that not even Nestorius would have dared to say that Jesus Christ had two wills. But within a few years another pope, John IV, was to condemn the view that Jesus Christ had only one will (called Monothelitism, from the Greek for "sole will"). It was also opposed by Maximus the Confessor. In 649 Pope Martin called a synod at Rome which proclaimed that Jesus Christ had two wills, but he was exiled for his pains. Thereafter Roman opposition to Monothelitism was more muted, until the time of Pope Agatho (678-81). He managed to persuade the Eastern Emperor to call another Council at Constantinople, the Sixth Ecumenical Council.[3]

Pope Agatho's letter to the Fathers of the Third Council of Constantinople makes many arguments in favor of the doctrine of two wills in Christ. Lane helps us digest the Pope's most convincing argument:

> It was argued that without a human will Jesus would have had an incomplete human nature and would not have been truly man. Without a human will there would be no human obedience or virtue. Jesus would then cease to be our pattern and example. If He had no human will, we could not say that He "has been tempted in every way, just as we are" (Hebrews 4:15). This argument, which echoes the argument used by the Cappadocian Fathers against Apollinaris' denial of Jesus' human soul, is the most powerful.[4]

Clarifications of the Catechism

The Catechism of the Catholic Church notes that the Church refuted those who:

> asserted that in Christ the divine Word had replaced the soul or spirit. Against this error the Church confessed that the eternal Son also assumed a rational, human soul.[5]

Further clarification is offered by the Catechism in several places:

> The human soul that the Son of God assumed is endowed with a true human knowledge [...]. This is why the Son of God could,

[3] Lane, *The Lion Concise Book of Christian Thought*, 59.
[4] Ibid., 60.
[5] CCC, 471.

when He became man, "increase in wisdom and in stature, and in favor with God and man."[6]

Likewise, we should consider this teaching:

> But at the same time, this truly human knowledge of God's Son expressed the divine life of His person [...]. Such is first of all the case with the intimate and immediate knowledge that the Son of God made man has of His Father. The Son in His human knowledge also showed the divine penetration He had into the secret thoughts of human hearts.[7]

The Catechism continues:

> By its union to the divine wisdom in the person of the Word Incarnate, Christ enjoyed in His human knowledge the fullness of understanding of the eternal plans He had come to reveal. What He admitted to not knowing in this area, He elsewhere declared Himself not sent to reveal.[8]

Monothelitism

Against the heresy of Monothelitism[9] that posited only a single will, a divine will in Jesus, the Catechism summarizes the response of the Sixth Ecumenical Council:

> [...] at Constantinople III in 681, the Church confessed that Christ possesses two wills and two natural operations, divine and human. They are not opposed to each other, but cooperate in such a way that the Word made flesh willed humanly in obedience to His Father all that He had decided divinely with the Father and the Holy Spirit for our salvation. Christ's human will "does not resist or oppose but rather submits to His divine and almighty will."[10]

Chadwick elucidates our discussion of the heresy of Monothelitism:

> The principal architect of the theological destruction of Monothelitism was Maximus the Confessor (c. 580-662),[11] who was moved

---

6   Ibid., 472; cf. Luke 2:40, 52.

7   Ibid,, 474.

8   Ibid.

9   The word *Monothelitism* is derived from the Greek words *monos* (one) and *thelēma* (will).

10 CCC, 475.

11 Cf. Hitchcock, *History of the Catholic Church*, 192: "St. Maximus the Confessor (d. 662),

to give the Chalcedonian Christology the profoundest study that it received in antiquity. He saw that the Monophysite doctrine implied a pessimistic estimate of human nature. Chalcedon, he urged with arguments of the most subtle refinement, safeguarded the autonomy of manhood and granted an independent status and positive value to the order of creation. The Christ who is known in two natures is able to be the model for our freedom and individuality, and for a mystical union in which man's separateness as a creature is respected.[12]

---

the last of the great Greek Fathers, had been secretary to Emperor Heraclius (610-641). He became a monk and was savagely mutilated for his oppostion to the Monothelitism of Emperor Constans II Pogonatus (641-668). Maximus was also instrumental in the final condemnation of Monophysitism, proposing that the mystical union of two natures in Christ affirmed the goodness of creation and the inherent dignity of human nature. Maximus was the most prestigious of the various Easterners who acknowledged the primacy of Rome."

[12] Chadwick, *The Early Church*, 211.

CHAPTER NINE:
SECOND COUNCIL OF NICAEA
(A.D. 787)

Iconography versus Iconoclasm

An expression goes that behind every good man there is a good woman. Analogously, as we have already seen in the chapters on Nicaea I and Ephesus, we can say behind every ecumenical council there is a good man, namely, for the former, Saint Athanaisus of Alexandria, and, for the latter, Saint Cyril of Alexandria.

The Second Council of Nicaea, the Seventh Ecumenical Council, was no exception to this rule. Although, unlike Athanasius and Cyril, the Father of the Church we will now examine did not live to attend the Council he so greatly inspired.

Saint John Damascene[1] was probably born of Arab Christian parents. Like his father, John was a lawyer. He later became a monk of the famous Monastery of San Saba, located outside Jerusalem. His writings, especially homilies and treatises, were effective in combatting the heresy of Iconoclasm and in promoting devotion to the Blessed Virgin Mary. In particular, Saint John Damascene defended Mary's Dormition, her bodily and glorious Assumption into Heaven.

In the second of his three sermons on the Dormition, Saint John directly addresses the Holy Virgin Mary:

> Your sacred and happy soul, as nature will have it, was separated in death from your most blessed and immaculate body; and although the body was duly interred, it did not remain in the state of death, neither was it dissolved by decay [...]. Your most pure and sinless body was not left on earth but you were transferred to your heavenly throne, O Lady, Queen, Mother of God in truth.

---

[1]   Hitchcock, *History of the Catholic Church*, 90.

An anonymous author added a passage to one of Saint John's sermons on the Dormition in which he tells the story, now legendary, of how the Eastern Emperor Marcian (d. 457) made a direct request from the Bishop of Jerusalem present at the Council of Chalcedon in A.D. 451, for the relics of the Virgin Mary to be brought to Constantinople. The bishop is said to have replied that

The Marriage of the Virgin, *Raphael, 1504.*

Mary died in the presence of the Apostles; but her tomb, when opened later at the request of Saint Thomas, was found empty, and thus the Apostles concluded that the body was taken up to Heaven.

Other legends, contained in a book known as *Legenda Aurea* (Golden Legends) about Mary's Assumption abound and were incorporated into artistic depictions of that Fifth Glorious Mystery of the Holy Rosary through the centuries.

There are several other examples as well: the Apostles were miraculously whisked away from the various sites of their apostolic preaching to be present together at Mary's tomb; when they arrived they did not find Mary's body in the tomb but flowers instead. Finally, Mary is said to have lowered her girdle to Saint Thomas the Apostle as a sign of her heavenly presence and intercessory power.

According to a popular tradition, Saint John Damascene, an iconographer by avocation, had his right hand chopped off by Muslims, so that he would not paint any more so-called "graven images." The Virgin Mary interceded for him, and his right hand was miraculously restored.

Saint John Damascene is also known as John of Damascus because he came from Damascus,[2] which is the ancient and present capital of Syria.

Jaroslav Pelikan cites a beautiful passage from Saint John of Damascus that he characterizes as "a catalogue raisonné of Byzantine" icons. The Father of the Church, in his treatise *On the Images* (3:2) writes:

> Because the one who by excellency of nature transcends all quantity and size and magnitude, who has His being in the form of God, has now, by taking upon Himself the form of a slave, contracted Himself into a quantity and size and has acquired a physical identity, do not hesitate any longer to draw pictures and to set forth, for all to see, Him who has chosen to let Himself be seen: His ineffable Descent from Heaven to earth; His Birth from the Virgin; His Baptism in the Jordan; His Transfiguration on Mount Tabor; the Sufferings that have achieved for us freedom from suffering; the Miracles that symbolized His divine nature and activity when they were performed through the activity of His [human] flesh; the Burial, Resurrection, and Ascension into Heaven by which the Savior has accomplished our salvation—describe all of these events, both in word and in colors, both in books and in pictures.[3]

---

[2] See Excursus at the end of this Chapter.
[3] Pelikan, *Jesus Through the Centuries*, 92.

Second Council of Nicaea

Convoked by the Empress Irene during the pontificate of Pope Adrian I, the Second Council of Nicaea[4] was attended by approximately three hundred bishops. Eight sessions were held between September 24 and October 23 in A.D. 787.

Smashing Icons

The Council aimed primarily to combat the heresy of *Iconoclasm* (meaning literally, "smashing icons") that thrived under the influence of Islam's strict prohibition of images. Fathers of the Church, like Saints John Damascene, Germanus of Constantinople and Andrew of Crete,[5] living in the seventh and eighth centuries, were great advocates of the Church's position concerning the valid use of icons based on Sacred Scripture and Sacred Tradition.

Incarnational Principle

These intrepid Fathers argued that the First Commandment[6] was a condemnation of idolatry and therefore not applicable to the Christian veneration of icons in light of the mystery of the Incarnation.

The Old Testament itself contains internal evidence that the use of certain man-made images was not considered idolatrous, especially since their construction was commanded by God Himself and destined to adorn His sanctuary alone.[7] Hitchcock notes:

> Saint John of Damascus (or Damascene, d. 749), the most important theologian of the age, was an iconophile who pointed out that the Jews in fact had images, notably the Ark of the Covenant, and that icons represented the history of Christ in the same way as the Gospels did.[8]

---

[4] Cf. CCC, 476-478.

[5] Crete is the fifth largest Mediterranean island. It was the capital of the ancient Minoan civilization, the remains of which, excavated by Sir Arthur Evans in 1900, can be seen at the archeological site of *Knossos* as well as in the archeological museum of Crete's capital city, *Heraclion*, which is named after the Greek mythological hero, Heracles or Hercules, known for his twelve labors. The palace at *Knossos* is associated in Greek mythology with the Labyrinth, which was the dwelling place of the mythological creature, the Minotaur, killed by Theseus. According to Acts 27:8, Crete's best port of anchorage was located in the southern half of the island. Sailors gave it the Greek nickname *Kali Limenes* or "Fair Havens," literally "Beautiful or Good Port."

[6] Cf. Exodus 20:4-5. This text concerns the divine injunction not to make any graven images.

[7] Cf. Exodus 25:16-19; Numbers 21:8-9; 1 Kings 6:23-29, 7:25-45.

[8] Hitchcock, *History of the Catholic Church*, 194.

Famous 15th-century icon of the Trinity by Andrei Rublev.

Lane gets to the heart of the matters at stake leading up to the Second Council of Nicaea:

> The icondules claimed that the Incarnation is the warrant for visible representations of God—in Jesus Christ the invisible God became visible man. They accused the iconoclasts of Docetism—of not taking seriously the humanity of Jesus Christ. They also accused them of Manichaeism (the denial of the goodness of physical creation),

since they would not allow material representations of Jesus Christ. The debate was polarized in that neither side allowed the possibility that there could be representations of Jesus Christ without being worshipped (as with a modern visual aid).[9]

Nicaea II's essential definition of the legitimate use of icons as opposed to Iconoclasm reads:

> Following the royal pathway and the divinely inspired authority of our Holy Fathers and the traditions of the Catholic Church, we define with all certitude and accuracy that, just like the figure of the precious and life-giving Cross, the venerable and holy images (in painting, mosaic and of other fit materials) are to be set up in the holy churches of God, on the walls and in pictures, in houses and by the roadside. This means images of our Lord, God and Saviour, Jesus Christ, of our undefiled Lady, the *Theotokos*, of the honourable angels and of all saints and holy men. For the more men see them in artistic representation, the more readily they will be aroused to remember the originals and to long after them. Images should receive due salutation and honourable reverence, but not the true worship of faith which is due to the divine nature alone. In accordance with ancient pious custom, incense and lights may be offered to images, as they are to the figure of the precious and life-giving Cross, to the Book of the Gospels and to other holy objects. For the honour paid to the image passes on to its original and he who reveres the image reveres in it the person represented.[10]

Distinctions with a Difference

Given this theological framework, three linguistic distinctions developed that still serve us in offering an apologetic for iconography as opposed to iconoclasm as James Hitchcock points out:

> [John Damascene] formulated what became the standard teaching concerning the venerations of saints even in the West, distinguishing among different Greek terms: *latreia* ("worship") for God alone, *hyperduleia* ("high honor") for Mary, and *duleia* ("honor") for the saints.[11]

---

[9]   Lane, *The Lion Concise Book of Christian Thought*, 62.

[10] Lane, *The Lion Concise Book of Christian Thought*, 63.

[11] Hitchcock, *History of the Catholic Church*, 194. Alternate spellings for these terms: *latria, hyperdoulia, doulia*.

Common Sense Apologetic

In common sense terms, we can argue that if venerating an icon or statue is tantamount to idolatry, then so too is the respect we pay to flags, statues (e.g., Statue of Liberty, Lincoln Memorial in Washington D.C.) and the photos of family members we carry around in our wallets and so proudly show off to friends and strangers alike.

Magisterial Response

The Catechism, following the teachings of Nicaea II, puts forth the Church's defense of the reality of Jesus' Sacred Humanity as worthy of artistic depiction:

> Since the Word became flesh in assuming a true humanity, Christ's body was finite. Therefore, the human face of Jesus can be portrayed; at the Seventh Ecumenical Council (Nicaea II in 787) the Church recognized its representation in holy images to be legitimate.[12]

In addition, the Catechism relates:

> At the same time the Church has always acknowledged that in the body of Jesus "we see our God made visible and so are caught up in the love of the God we cannot see." The individual characteristics of Christ's body express the divine person of God's Son. He has made the features of His human body His own, to the point that they can be venerated when portrayed in a holy image, for the believer "who venerates the icon is venerating in it the person of the one depicted."[13]

The Triumph of Orthodoxy

Christ's lay faithful, led by their pastors, the bishops and priests, rejoiced in the final deliberations of the Council Fathers, so much so that a liturgical feast was established to commemorate the victory of Nicaea II. This feast known as the Feast of the Holy Images or "The Triumph of Orthodoxy" is observed by Greek Orthodox Christians and Byzantine Catholics on the First Sunday of Lent.

Another celebration commemorating the felicitous outcome of the Second Council of Nicaea is celebrated on the Sunday following October 10 according to the Byzantine liturgical calendar.

---

[12]   CCC, 476; See also, CCC, 478, "on the heart of the Incarnate Word."
[13]   CCC, 477.

History records how the laity and clergy celebrated the Council's decisions by carrying lighted torches and icons during an all-night vigil procession.

The Troparion for the Feast of the Holy Images reads:

> We bow before your sacred image, O gracious Lord, and beg forgiveness for our offenses, O Christ our God: for you, of your own will, deigned to ascend the Cross in your human nature to deliver from bondage under the enemy those whom you created. Therefore we gratefully cry out to you: "Through your coming to save the world, O Savior, you have filled all with joy."

The Kontakion for that same Liturgy links the mystery of Mary's Divine Maternity and the mystery of the Incarnation:

> O Mother of God, through you in the Incarnation, the indescribable Word of God became describable, for through the divine goodness the Word spoken from eternity became an Image. May we who believe in salvation clothe ourselves with the same Image both in word and deed.

Theological Beauty

Finally, Henry Chadwick provides valuable insight in terms of the significance, historical, theological and spiritual, of Christian art and the Iconoclast controversy that the Fathers of the Second Council of Nicaea so adamantly fought to stamp out. He writes:

> A considerable body of Christian art of the fifth, sixth and seventh centuries has survived, and illustrates the very high quality of artistic achievement that characterized the age. The splendid mosaics of the churches at Ravenna or Rome, the Rossano Codex of the Gospels, the Syriac Gospel Book written in 586 by the Mesopotamian monk Rabula (now in Florence), the doors of Santa Sabina in Rome, and many other examples, witness to an artistic renaissance of the first distinction, devoted to the expression of Christian themes and unrestrained by any inhibitions about portraying Christ and the saints. Yet these representations of Christ caused pain to those who remembered an older austerity and reserve. The icons were the object of an undercurrent of mistrust which emerged in the eighth century as the bitter iconic controversy, when the Emperor Leo the Isaurian in 726 initiated by edict a full-scale programme of destroying all such pictures. The icons had become an accepted and loved part of church

decoration, and were deeply valued by devout souls. The controversy grew into a major conflict between church and state in the Byzantine Empire lasting over a century, and (since the emperors were icono-clast and the papacy was not) contributed to a still further widen-ing of the estrangement between Rome and Byzantium [...]. The decision to restore icons was taken by the Empress Irene (780-790). In face of growing hostility in both the Church and army her firm hand led the Second Council of Nicaea (787) formally to condemn the iconoclasts. The failure of Irene and her successors to achieve prosperity for the empire brought a reaction in favour of Iconoclasm again from 814 until 843, the iconophile cause being maintained meanwhile by the monks of Studios at Constantinople under their Abbot Theodore. But on the First Sunday in Lent 843 the Empress Theodora restored the icons for the last time with a procession that in the eyes of posterity marked "the Triumph of Orthodoxy," and made possible the gradual redecoration of the churches under the Patriarch Photius from 858 onwards.[14]

Excursus: Damascus

Damascus, like Jericho, is considered one of the world's oldest continually inhabited cities. *The Lion Concise Bible Encyclopedia* notes its historic signifi-cance in the context of the Bible:

> Damascus was already known in Abraham's day, and is often men-tioned in the Old Testament. King David captured the city, but it soon gained its independence. Damascus is the home of Naaman, who came to the prophet Elisha for healing. The prophet later went to Damascus to advise on the king's health. Isaiah predicted the destruction of Damascus. And after a series of attacks the Assyr-ians captured the city in 732 B.C., carried away its treasures and many of its peoples, and reduced its power. From 64 B.C. to A.D. 33 Damascus was a Roman city. Paul was on his way to Damascus to persecute the Christians when he met with Jesus Himself, and the whole direction of his life was changed. He had to escape from the city later, when the Jews persecuted him.[15]

In visiting Damascus one can walk in the "footsteps of Saint Paul." It was on the road leading from Jerusalem to Damascus that Saul, later Saint Paul, was

---

[14] Chadwick, *The Early Church*, 282-284 *passim*.
[15] *The Lion Concise Bible Encyclopedia*, 62-63. Cf. Genesis 14:15, 15:2; 2 Samuel 8:5; 1 Kings 20:34; 2 Kings 5; 8:7-15; Isaiah 17; Acts 19.

blinded by a heavenly light and heard the Savior's voice from Heaven: "Saul, Saul, why do you persecute me?"

To appreciate from an artistic perspective Paul's conversion experience, one should first read its account in Acts 9:1-19 and then perhaps study its artistic rendition by the Italian painter Caravaggio (born: Michelangelo Merisi), a treasure found in Rome's Church of Santa Maria del Popolo.

At Damascus there is also the site where Paul was healed of his blindness by a Christian from Damascus named Ananias. Having had Ananias' hands laid on him, the future Apostle was filled with the Holy Spirit (cf. Acts 9: 10-19).

Another important spot in Damascus is the place where Ananias helped lower Paul in a basket over a wall in order to escape from the city when sought by the Jews (cf. Acts 9: 23-25). Acts 9: 19-22 recounts how Saint Paul preached in Damascus for several days, "confounding" the Jews "by proving that Jesus was the Christ." Simply put, Paul's effective preaching is what incited the Jews of Damascus to persecute him.

Certain Muslims believe that at the end of time *Allah* (God) will send *Issa* (Jesus) to judge the world, appearing on the parapet of the great Ummayad Mosque of Damascus.

PART III

Chapters Ten to Twenty-One seek to unpack the thought of select Fathers, situating each Father in chronological order, with particular attention paid to his cultural and historical background.

CHAPTER TEN:
THE APOSTOLIC FATHERS[1]

The *Apostolic Fathers* lived during the era of the Apostles or in a generation proximate to the death of one or more of the Apostles. Many of these Fathers were in fact disciples or at least close personal acquaintances of the Apostles who, in turn, handed on in their teaching the Deposit of Faith to a growing number of ecclesial communities in the Mediterranean world.[2]

Lane introduces us to the Apostolic Fathers:

> The Apostolic Fathers are the earliest Christian writers outside the New Testament, belonging to what is called "the sub-apostolic age." Their writing forms a bridge between the New Testament and the Apologists who wrote later in the second century, the most noteworthy being Justin Martyr. They help us to understand the transition from the apostolic church of the first century to the Catholic Church of the end of the second century as described by Irenaeus.[3]

These budding churches took great pride in claiming a sort of pedigree, a link to a particular Apostle, his teaching and practices. Unfortunately, in the minds of many believers at that time, the distinction between tradition (with a lower

---

[1] Cf. O'Collins, Farrugia, *A Concise Dictionary of Theology*, 17: "**Apostolic Fathers.** The name for the oldest nonbiblical and orthodox Christian writers, commonly adopted after Jean Baptiste Coteiler published in 1672 the so-called *Epistle of Barnabas* (first century), St. Clement of Rome (d. ca. 96), St. Ignatius of Antioch (ca. 35-ca. 107), the *Shepherd of Hermas* (second century), and St. Polycarp of Smyrna (ca. 69-ca. 155), as well as the acts of the martyrdom of Clement, Ignatius and Polycarp. In 1765 Andrea Gallandi added the *Epistle to Diognetus*, a defense of Christianity, and Papias of Hierapolis (ca. 60-130). Philotheos Bryennios published in 1883 what may be the oldest work in this whole group, the anonymous *Didache* (Gr. 'teaching'). These writings shed invaluable light on the passage from the NT church to post-apostolic Christianity. Some modern scholars wish to exclude those authors who probably were not directly connected with the Apostles, or whose mentality is not so close to the NT. This suggests listing as Apostolic Fathers only St. Clement, St. Ignatius of Antioch, St. Polycarp, and Papias, as well as St. Quadratus (second century), who around 124 addressed to Emperor Hadrian the oldest apology for Christian faith."

[2] The Romans referred to the Mediterranean as *Mare Nostrum* or "Our Sea."

[3] Lane, *The Lion Concise Book of Christian Thought*, 13.

case t) and Tradition (with a capital T) was not always so clear, thus giving rise
to heated disputes over such disciplinary matters as the proper date for the celebration of Easter, even to the extent of helping to foment schism.

St. John the Evangelist writing his Gospel

CHAPTER ELEVEN:
CLEMENT OF ROME

(D. A.D. 101)

Corinth and the Corinthians

Corinth was a major city in the ancient world, strategically located on the isthmus between the Greek mainland and the Peloponnesus. The Gulf of Corinth boasted two commercial ports: one on the Aegean Sea and the other on the Adriatic Sea. In 146 B.C., the Romans occupied Corinth and utterly destroyed it, killing the men and selling the women and children into slavery.

In 44 B.C., Julius Caesar sought to rebuild Corinth. Strabo's *Geography* refers to a thousand temple prostitutes at Corinth. Based on Strabo's description of Corinth, it gained a reputation as the ancient world's version of "sin city."

Saint Paul first arrived in Corinth in A.D. 50. According to Acts 18:1-3, among the first locals he met were two Christians: Prisca and Aquila. Due to the ethnic diversity of Corinth, about half of the Corinthians mentioned in the New Testament had Greek names, while the other half had Latin names.

Thanks to the excavations of the American School of Classical Studies at Athens we can see how many archeological ruins at Corinth attest to the historicity of the New Testament. For example:

> One inscription mentions the name of Erastus the aedile, an official in charge of public works (possibly the "city treasurer" of Romans 16:23; cf. 2 Timothy 4:20). In the center of the forum was found a platform *(Gk: bēma)* constructed in ca. A.D. 44, probably Gallio's "tribunal" at Paul's trial (Acts 18:12, 17). In the Lerna Asclepium and in other temples of the city can be seen the ruins of sacred dining halls that illuminate 1 Corinthians 8 and 10. An early first-century Latin inscription refers to the *macellum*,[1] as Paul uses the Greek *makellon* in speaking of the "meat market" (1 Corinthians 10:25). And a crude,

---

[1]   In Italian, to describe a happening like a scholastic exam as *un macello* means that it was a "killer event." Thus, *un macello* refers to any difficult situation or undertaking.

undatable Greek inscription on a broken lintel stone seems to announce the "Synagogue of the Hebrews." Again, in the forum have been excavated rows of shops of the type Paul would have shared with his fellow tentmaker Aquila. A contemporary villa gives a good understanding of the limitations on the size of the "house-churches," perhaps explaining why factions arose in Corinth (several house-churches) and why there was discrimination in the communal meals of the general assembly (the dining room could only accommodate a select few, according to a Roman custom of ranking guests).[2]

Clement of Rome

Pope Clement I[3] reigned from A.D. 92 to A.D.101. According to the Martyrology known as the *Martyrium Sancti Clementis* (The Martyrdom of Saint Clement), he died in exile near the Black Sea.[4]

Clement's *Letter to the Corinthians* was written circa A.D. 96-98. Pope Benedict relates:

Clement's intervention—we are still in the first century—was prompted

St. Clement of Rome, detail of an 11th-century mosaic depicting various Church Fathers, found in the Church of St. Sophia of Kyiv. Source: Wikimedia.

---

2   *Harper's Bible Dictionary* (The Society of Biblical Literature, 1985), 183-184.
3   Cf. Benedict XVI, *The Fathers*, 7-12.
4   The liturgical memorial of Pope St. Clement is November 23. Clement's name appears in the Roman Canon or First Eucharistic Prayer in the first list of saints that precedes the words of consecration.

by the serious problems besetting the Church in Corinth: the elders of the community, in fact, had been deposed by some young contestants. The sorrowful event was recalled once again by Saint Irenaeus who wrote: "In the time of this Clement, no small dissension having occurred among the brethren in Corinth, the Church in Rome dispatched a most powerful letter to the Corinthians exhorting them to peace, renewing their faith, and declaring the tradition which it had lately received from the Apostles."[5]

According to Saint Irenaeus' list, tracing Apostolic Succession in the See of Rome from his time back to the time of the Apostle Peter, we discover that Pope Clement was the fourth Bishop of Rome, the third Successor of Saint Peter. Irenaeus lauds Clement of Rome as having seen:

> the blessed Apostles and conversed with them and had yet ringing in his ears the preaching of the Apostles, and had their tradition before his eyes, and not he only, for many were then surviving who had been taught by the Apostles.[6]

Tertullian believed that Saint Peter himself had consecrated Clement a bishop. Eusebius of Caesarea, a Church historian living in the fourth century, documents the order of the first popes after Peter, leading up to Clement, namely, Linus (A.D. 80) and Anicletus (80-92).[7]

Clement's House-Church

In Latin, "house-church" is rendered *domus ecclesia* or *ecclesia domus*.

Already in New Testament times,[8] the early Christians worshipped in their homes, where they were relatively safe. Using one's home as a place of worship first became necessary when the Christians were officially expelled from the synagogues and lacked buildings of their own.

---

[5]   Benedict XVI, *The Fathers*, 8; cf. Irenaeus of Lyons, *Adversus Haereses*, 3: 3, 3.

[6]   Irenaeus of Lyons, *Adversus Haereses*, 3: 3, 3. Cf. Benedict XVI, *The Fathers*, 7.

[7]   Cf. Benedict XVI, *The Fathers*, 7f: "Eusebius of Caesarea, the great 'archivist' of Christian beginnings, presents it in these terms, 'there is extant an epistle of this Clement which is acknowledged to be genuine and is of remarkable merit. He wrote it in the name of the Church of Rome to the Church of Corinth, when a sedition had arisen in the latter Church. We know that this epistle also has been publicly used in a great many churches both in former times and in our own." See also, Eusebius of Caesarea, *Historia Ecclesiastica* (*Ecclesiastical History*), 3:16.

[8]   Cf. Acts 1:12-14, 2:42, 46, 28:30; Romans 16:3-5.

Sometimes Christian homes were expanded to take the form of a church. This tradition continued in the centuries leading up to the legalization of Christianity that took place during the reign of the Emperor Constantine in the fourth century.

The oldest extant "house-church" (A.D. 231) is Dura-Europos in Syria. It is located along the Euphrates River near the Iraqi border. In that house-church there is room for about 100 people.

The visitor notices a little platform from which the presiding bishop would have celebrated the Sunday Eucharist and preached. In a separate corner of the room there is also a Baptistery covered by a baldachin and decorated with paintings. On the walls are depicted scenes of the Old Testament and of the Gospels such as Adam and Eve, David and Goliath, Christ the Good Shepherd, Christ walking on water, a woman processing with a candle.

Other notable examples of house-churches have been excavated in other parts of the world. For example, archeologists have unearthed the house of the Apostle Peter at Capharnaum[9] and about twenty or so structures in Rome.

In Rome, one should visit the Church of San Clemente (Saint Clement) located in the general area between the Colosseum[10] and the Basilica of Saint John Lateran.[11] There we discover not only the tomb of Saint Clement under the high altar, but also, at the lowest level of this four-tiered church, the remains of a pagan banquet table (*triclinium*) dedicated to the Persian god Mithras.

---

[9]   Alternate spelling: Capernaum. From the Hebrew words: *Kfar* and *Nahum,* meaning "Nahum's village."

[10] The Colosseum (A.D. 80) was named after a colossal statue of Nero that once stood nearby. The Colosseum is more accurately referred to as the "Flavian Amphitheatre," named after the Flavian imperial dynasty that had it built. This was the most famous amphitheater in Roman times, seating about forty-five thousand spectators. Inside the Colosseum gladiatorial fights were held as well as simulated naval war games. Occasionally, Christians were martyred in the arena and were thrown as food to lions, tigers and bears.

[11] Contrary to a popular assumption, the Basilica of St. John Lateran and not St. Peter's Basilica is the cathedral church of the Bishop of Rome. The term "Lateran" refers to the noble Roman family that originally owned the land that the Emperor Constantine then gave to his wife, Fausta, and later bequeathed to Pope Melchiades I (Meltiades). For several centuries, especially during the Middle Ages, the Popes resided at the Lateran palaces before moving definitively to the Vatican. The return to Rome occurred at the conclusion of the Great Western Schism of the fourteenth century that saw legitimate popes exiled in Avignon, France. During this period of exile, it was not uncommon for one or more "anti-popes" (illegitimate contenders) to claim the right to the papacy. The Dedication of the Basilica of St. John Lateran is celebrated on November 9.

The cult to Mithras was very popular among the Roman soldiers living in the first century A.D., who learned about Mithraism as they ventured further and further into the Eastern half of the Roman Empire. There are theologians who hold that this mystery cult is a type of *praeparatio evangelica* (preparation for the Gospel) with Baptismal and Eucharistic overtones. That Mithraism helped prepare a way for the Gospel is understandable when one considers that its devotees believed in the resurrection of the mythological god Mithras and practiced killing bulls in whose "sacred blood" members were immersed as a type of ritual initiation.[12] It is also speculated that the neophytes[13] drank the blood of the slaughtered bull as a way of spiritually consummating the sacrifice, helping to forge their new fraternal bonds as members of the Mithraic cult.

A Case of Mistaken Identity

Certain scholars have tried to identify Pope Clement with Titus Flavius Clemens, who was a cousin of the Emperor Domitian and who served at the imperial court. Pagan historical documents claim that Titus Flavius Clemens was martyred in the late first century for "impiety" toward the pagan gods and for "atheism." These charges were commonly made against Christians because of their monotheistic beliefs and subsequent refusal to participate in any pagan worship.

Not to participate in pagan worship was considered a serious breach of one's duties as a citizen of the Empire, just as the ancient Greeks would have considered it a serious breach of one's duties as a citizen of the *polis* or "city-state."

Plato, recounting the trial of his mentor Socrates[14] in his *Apologia*, notes that Socrates (who was dubbed the "Athenian Gadfly") had been accused by the Athenian governing body of having corrupted the youth with his philosophy and of being an atheist, since he posited the notion of a single supreme deity and did not appear to render homage to the Greek Pantheon, as did other ordinary citizens.

---

[12] As the Mithraic catechumens stood in a pit, perhaps underneath a type of grate, the bull's throat would be sliced open, so that its blood came streaming down upon them.

[13] From the Greek, meaning those who were most recently initiated into discipleship of Jesus Christ through Baptism.

[14] The Socratic Method in philosophy makes use of deductive reasoning. The philosopher asks questions of his students hoping to elicit correct answers based on their own knowledge and reasoning abilities. This method is also known as the "meutic" method, so called because it is likened to a "mid-wife" helping a pregnant woman give birth.

As we know, Socrates refused to plead guilty to these trumped-up charges and decided to take his life by drinking poison (perhaps hemlock). In the Middle Ages Socrates was revered by Christians as a type of Christ, insofar as he was a just and wise man innocently condemned.

In any case, there does not seem to be convincing historical evidence to identify Saint Clement with Titus Flavius Clemens.

Clement's Letter to the Corinthians

Clement's *Letter to the Corinthians* highlights some key facts about its author: That he prayed for the well-being of civil authority, as Saint Paul urges us to do in 1 Timothy 2:1-2; had little or no knowledge of Roman military life; was heavily influenced by Stoic philosophy and Egyptian folklore; had an excellent familiarity with the Old Testament texts which he often quoted or alluded to in his Letter.[15]

For instance, Clement insists that a connection needs to be maintained between faith and good works, the hallmarks of Christian holiness:

> Let us come before the Lord, then, in sanctity of soul, lifting pure and undefiled hands to Him, loving our gentle and merciful Father who has made us His chosen portion. For it is written: "When the Most High divided the nations, when He scattered the sons of Adam, He set up the boundaries of nations according to the number of the angels of God. His people, Jacob, became the portion of the Lord; Israel was the allotment of His inheritance."[16] And in another place He says: "Behold, the Lord takes to Himself a nation from the midst of the nations, as a man takes the first-fruits of his threshing floor, and from that nation shall come forth the Holy of Holies."[17] Since we are a portion of the Holy One, let us do all that belongs to holiness, fleeing from evil speech, and abominable and impure

---

[15] See the Second Reading of the Office of Readings for Tuesday of the First Week in Ordinary Time: Clement of Rome, *Letter to the Corinthians* (31-33). He writes: "Finally, with His own holy and undefiled hands, [God] made man, the highest of His creatures, the copy of His own image. *Let us make man,* God said, *in our image and likeness. And God made man, male and female He made them.* Then, when He had finished making all His creatures, God gave them His approval and blessing: *Increase and multiply,* He charged them. We must recognize, therefore, that all upright men have been graced by good works, and that even the Lord Himself took delight in the glory His works gave them. This should inspire us with a resolute determination to do His will and make us put our whole strength into the work of living a Christian life."

[16] Deuteronomy 32:8-9.

[17] Deuteronomy 4:34. Cf. Deuteronomy 14:2; Numbers 18:27; Ezechiel 48:12.

embraces, from drunkenness and from rioting, and detestable lusts, foul adultery, and detestable pride. For God, He says, "resists the proud but gives grace to the humble."[18]

In his *Letter to the Corinthians*, Saint Clement gives preeminence to the Church of Rome. His tone is gentle but authoritative. The Pope's intervention in the affairs of the local church at Corinth is to be received with a spirit of docility and obedience. Pope Benedict comments:

> Thus, we could say that this letter was a first exercise of the Roman primacy after Saint Peter's death. Clement's letter touches on topics that were dear to Saint Paul, who had written two important letters to the Corinthians, in particular the theological dialectic, perennially current, between the *indicative* of salvation and the *imperative* of moral commitments.[19]

Almost Made It into the Bible

The significance of this letter is also revealed in the fact that by A.D. 170, it was being read during the Sacred Liturgy,[20] almost on a par with the readings from Sacred Scripture. Clement's Epistle can best be understood against the background of Saint Paul's Epistles to the Corinthians since both men found the Corinthians to be a contentious people, prone to creating rivalries and factions that wounded the unity of Christ's Mystical Body, the Church.

Mike Aquilina appraises the value of Pope Clement's *Letter to the Corinthians*:

> Saint Clement's *Letter to the Corinthians* received due reverence in Corinth, where, In 170 A.D., it was still read during liturgies along with a letter from then-current pope, Soter.

> Eusebius related that other churches also revered Saint Clement's letter, and we know that some even numbered it among the books of the New Testament. Saint Polycarp quoted from this text in his own Letter to the Philippians. Clement of Alexandria was one of several

---

18 Clement of Rome, *Letter to the Corinthians*, 30-34; cf. 1 Peter 5:5; Proverbs 3: 34; James 4:6.

19 Benedict XVI, *The Fathers*, 8.

20 In the Office of Readings, the writings of Clement appear thirteen times.

Fathers who advocated the inclusion of Clement of Rome's Letter in the Canon of Scriptures. One should also note that a so-called Second Letter to the Corinthians has been attributed at times to Clement. However, his authorship is believed by most scholars to be quite dubious. One of the most striking passages in the Letter is an effusion of praise for the natural order in the created world. A pope, a mystic, and a poet at heart, Saint Clement saw a world charged with God's grandeur[21]: Creation reflects the unity and harmony of the Persons of the Trinity, and creation provides a model for unity and harmony in the Church.[22]

In his letter, Pope Clement also praises the Lord for the beauty and order of the created universe — a theme that is related to the beauty and good order he was seeking to re-establish in the Church at Corinth falling apart at the seams in many ways.

Confusion at Corinth

The principal aim of Clement's Letter was to stave off schism in the local church. In so doing, he laid down certain parameters, rules and regulations that he expected the Corinthians to follow for the sake of the common good.

Pier Franco Beatrice grasps the conciliatory aims of Pope Clement's *Letter to the Corinthians*:

> With his summons to amendment and penance, to bending "the knees of the heart," Clement aims at restoring the damaged authority of the local hierarchy. This hierarchy constitutes the foundation and the guarantee of the peace and harmony of the members who make up the Church, the true Body of Christ. The intensive use of the Sacred Scriptures is intended to show how much hatred has injured humanity and, to the contrary, what benefits the concord willed by the Creator produces.[23]

In reference to the Sacrament of Penance, Clement writes:

---

[21] The Jesuit poet, Gerard Manley Hopkins, wrote a poem in which he praises creation as charged with the grandeur of God.

[22] Aquilina, *The Fathers of the Church*, 54.

23 Beatrice, *Introduction to the Fathers of the Church*, 20.

> Let us fix our eyes on Christ's Blood and understand how precious it is to His Father, for, poured out for our salvation, it has brought to the whole world the grace of repentance.[24]

Pope Clement, in that same letter,[25] attests to the Lord's will that only men be ordained to the sacred priesthood and episcopacy,[26] having borne witness to the doctrine of Apostolic Succession as established directly by Our Lord.[27]

A Pope's Prayer for Public Officials

Finally, Pope Clement[28] provides, according to the Catechism "the Church's most ancient prayer" for political authorities. Pope Benedict comments:

> The prayer for rulers and governors acquires special importance. Subsequent to the New Testament, it is the oldest prayer extant for political institutions. Thus, in the period following their persecution, Christians, well aware that the persecutions would continue, never ceased to pray for the very authorities who had unjustly condemned them. The reason is primarily Christological: it is necessary to pray for one's persecutors as Jesus did on the cross. But this prayer also contains a teaching that guides the attitude of Christians toward politics and the state down the centuries. In praying for authorities, Clement recognized the legitimacy of political institutions in the order established by God; at the same time, he expressed his concern that the authorities would be docile to God, "devoutly in peace and meekness exercising power given them by [God]." Caesar is not everything. Another sovereignty emerges whose origins and essence are not of this world but of "the heavens above": it is that of Truth, which also claims a right to be heard by the state.[29]

Clement's prayer reads thus:

> Grant to them, Lord, health, peace, concord, and stability, so that they may exercise without offense the sovereignty that you have given them. Master, heavenly King of the ages, you give glory, honor, and power over the things of earth to the sons of men. Direct, Lord, their

---

24 Clement of Rome, *Letter to the Corinthians*, 7:4; cf. CCC, 1432.
25 Clement of Rome. *Letter to the Corinthians*, 42:4.
26 Cf. CCC, 1577.
27 Cf. Clement of Rome, *Letter to the Corinthians*, 42:44; cf. CCC, 861.
28 Clement of Rome, *Letter to the Corinthians*, 61.
29 Benedict XVI, *The Fathers*, 11. Cf. CCC, 1900.

counsel, following what is pleasing and acceptable in your sight, so that by exercising with devotion and in peace and gentleness the power that you have given to them, they may find favor in you.[30]

---

30 Benedict XVI, *The Fathers*, 11. See Monday of the First Week of Ordinary Time, the Second Reading of the Office of Readings: Clement of Rome, *Letter to the Corinthians* (59: 2-60:4; 61:3). In this reading we find a timeless prayer of intercession: "Lord, we entreat you to help us. Come to the aid of the afflicted, pity the lowly, raise up the fallen, show your face to the needy, heal the sick, convert the wayward, feed the hungry, deliver the captives, support the weak, encourage the fainthearted. Let all nations know that you alone are God; Jesus Christ is your Son; and *we* are your people and the sheep of your flock."

CHAPTER TWELVE:
IGNATIUS OF ANTIOCH
(D. A.D. 107)

Catholic to the Core

In the Bible there are two places named Antioch: Antioch in Syria and Pissidian Antioch. We are concerned here with Antioch in Syria. Before we consider who Saint Ignatius was and the significance of his teachings let us recall the importance of the city with which he was so closely affiliated.

Harper's Bible Dictionary explains:

> Antioch [...] (Syrian), (modern Antakya in Turkey) founded by
> Seleucus Nicator in 300 B.C. and conquered by Rome in 64 B.C.
> Located on the Orontes River in the northwestern corner of the
> Roman province of Syria, it was the province's capital, the third larg-
> est city of the empire, a center of Greek culture, and a commercial
> hub. Jews inhabited Antioch from its foundation and enjoyed the
> rights to observe their own customs. The various synagogues of the
> city sent representatives to a council of elders presided over by a
> 'ruler.' Large numbers of Antiochene Gentiles were attracted to Jew-
> ish worship. Nicolaus of Antioch, one of the seven Hellenist lead-
> ers in Jerusalem (Acts 6:5), was among those Gentiles who became
> Jewish proselytes. The first Jewish war (A.D. 66-73) occasioned
> anti-Jewish riots in Antioch, but on the whole Judaism enjoyed a
> peaceful life at Antioch and thus provided early Christians a stable
> matrix. Public order, a prosperous urban culture, a Judaism used to
> contact with Gentiles, an intellectual and religious milieu open to
> many currents, interest in mystery cults, fine roads and lines of com-
> munication—all these factors favored Antioch as an energetic center
> for Christian missionary outreach.[1]

---

[1]   Cf. Harper's Bible Dictionary, 33: See also, Raymond Brown and J. Meier, *Antioch and Rome* (Paulist Press, 1983); G. Downey, *A History of Antioch in Syria from Seleucus to the Arab Conquest* (Princeton University Press, 1961); W. Meeks and R. Wilken, *Jews and Christians in Antioch* (Scholars Press, 1978).

Ignatius'[2] epithet was *Theophorus*, meaning from the Greek "God-bearer." Early biographies attest that he was a disciple of Saint John the Evangelist. Fourth-century biographies attest that he was bishop at Antioch for forty years, having been installed there personally by the Apostles Peter and Paul. We can recall thus that Peter is believed to have been the first bishop of Antioch where, according to the Book of Acts, the disciples of Jesus were first called Christians.[3]

Saint Ignatius is the first Christian author to refer to the Catholic Church, doing so in his *Letter to the Smyrnnaeans*:

> Where there is Christ Jesus, there is the Catholic Church.[4]

Strangely enough, despite such a long pontificate in the key apostolic See of Antioch, we know very little about his episcopal career. However, Benedict XVI notes:

> Eusebius of Caesarea, a fourth-century historian, dedicated an entire chapter of his *Church History* to the life and literary works of Ignatius. Eusebius writes: "The Report says that [Ignatius] was sent from Syria to Rome, and became food for wild beasts on account of his testimony to Christ. And as he made his journey through Asia under the strictest military surveillance (he called the guards "ten leopards" in his *Letter to the Romans*, 5:1), "he fortified cities where he stopped by homilies and exhortations and warned them to be especially on their guard against the heresies that were then beginning to prevail, and exhorted them to hold fast to the tradition of the Apostles."[5]

The Letters of Saint Ignatius

Ignatius' Letters to the Churches of Asia Minor were written as he was being brought by ship to Rome to await martyrdom. These writings are the essential source of our knowledge about Saint Ignatius' thought. It can be plainly noted, for example, in his *Letter to the Smyrnnaeens*, that he opposed the Docetist heresy. Ignatius argued that Jesus did not merely *seem* to have a body, to die on the cross, and to rise again. Rather, He truly did all this according to the reality of His sacred humanity for the sake of our salvation.

Along these lines, Ignatius describes the Gnostic heresies as *biting insidiously*, so much so that he deems them *difficult to heal*, even through his efforts

---

2   Cf. Benedict XVI, *The Fathers*, 11-18.
3   Cf. Acts 11:26.
4   Ignatius of Antioch, *Letter to the Smyrnaeans*, 8:2. Cf. CCC, 830.
5   Benedict XVI, *The Fathers*, 13f.

of dialogue, apologetics and evangelization. Ignatius proceeds, in his *Letter to the Ephesians*:

> One only is the physician bodily and spiritual; generated and not generated; made flesh and God; in death and true life; born of Mary as likewise born of God, at first, passible, afterwards, impassible, Jesus Christ, Our Lord.[6]

We can compare what Saint Ignatius writes here to what the Fathers of the Council of Chalcedon stated in A.D. 451 against the heretical notions of Eutyches:

> Following the holy Fathers, we unanimously teach and confess one and the same Son, Our Lord Jesus Christ, the same perfect in divinity and perfect in humanity, the same truly God and truly man, composed of rational soul and body; consubstantial with the Father as to His Divinity and consubstantial with us as to His Humanity, "like unto us in all things, but sin" [cf. Hebrews 4:15]. He was begotten from the Father before all ages as to His Divinity and in these last days, for us and for our salvation, was born as to His Humanity of the Virgin Mary, the Mother of God.[7]

Furthermore, Ignatius courageously told the Roman Christians not to intercede on his behalf with the Roman Emperor, lest his death sentence be commuted:

> I beg you not to show an unseasonable goodwill toward me. Let me become food for the wild beasts, through whose favor it will be granted me to attain to God.[8]

As Saint Ignatius made his way from Antioch to Rome for martyrdom in the Colosseum, his already well-established fame spread, causing many fellow Christians and bishops to greet him along the way, encouraging him to "keep the faith."

---

[6] Ignatius of Antioch, *Letter to the Ephesians*, 7:2.

[7] Denzinger-Schönmetzer, *Enchiridion Symbolorum, definitionum et declarationum de rebus fidei et morum* (1965), 301. Cf. CCC 467.

[8] Cf. Benedict XVI, *The Fathers*, 14: "Thus, Ignatius implores the Christians of Rome not to prevent his martyrdom since he is impatient 'to attain to Jesus Christ.' And he explains, 'It is better for me to die on behalf of Jesus Christ than to reign over all the ends of the earth [...]. Him, I seek who died for us: Him I desire, who rose again for our sake [...]. Permit me to be an imitator of the Passion of my God!" cf. Ignatius of Antioch, *Letter to the Romans*, 5-6.

It was during two of his layovers in Asia Minor, at Smyrna and Troas, that he composed six epistles to the Churches of Ephesus,[9] Magnesia,[10] Smyrna,[11] Tralli,[12] Philadelphia[13] and Rome.[14] Saint Ignatius also wrote a seventh letter to his personal friend, Saint Polycarp[15] of Smyrna.

Ignatius wrote against the Judaizers to defend Christianity against the accusation of being just another heretical sect of Judaism. Ignatius defended the Church's belief in the divinity of Christ as consonant with the Jewish doctrine of monotheism.

He upheld the doctrine of the Real Presence of Our Lord in the Eucharist in his *Letter to the Smyrnaeans* against the Gnostics and strictly linked the valid celebration of the Eucharistic Sacrifice and Banquet to the authoritative ministry of the bishops, priests, and deacons.

Pope Benedict cites Ignatius' *Letter to Polycarp* on the spiritual communion Christians are called to maintain with their local bishop and clergy:

---

9   See the Second Reading for the Office of Readings for the Sunday of the Second Week in Ordinary Time: Ignatius of Antioch, *Letter to the Ephesians* (2: 2-5, 2): "For Jesus Christ, our life, without whom we cannot live, is the mind of the Father, just as the bishops, appointed over the whole earth, are in conformity with the mind of Jesus Christ."

10 See the Second Reading for the Office of Readings for the Sixteenth Sunday in Ordinary Time: Ignatius of Antioch, *Letter to the Magnesians* (1: 1-5, 2): "We should really live as Christians and not merely have the name."

11 See the Second Reading of the Office of Readings for the Fourth Sunday in Ordinary Time: Ignatius of Antioch, *Letter to the Smyrnaeans* (1-4, 1): "[Jesus] was of the *race of David* according to his flesh, but God's Son by the will and power of God; truly born of the Virgin and baptized by John, [...]. truly nailed to a cross in the flesh for our sake under Pontius Pilate [...]. and just as truly rose from the dead."

12 See the Second Reading of the Office of Readings for Tuesday of the Twenty-Seventh Week in Ordinary Time: Ignatius of Antioch, *Letter to the Trallians* (1:1-3, 2; 4: 1-2; 6: 1; 7: 1-8, 1): "[...] All should respect the deacons as Jesus Christ, just as all should regard the bishops as the image of the Father, and the clergy as God's senate and the College of the Apostles."

13 See the Second Reading of the Office of Readings for Thursday of the Twenty-Seventh Week in Ordinary Time: Ignatius of Antioch, *Letter to the Philadelphians* (1: 1-2, 1; 3: 2-5): "Be careful, therefore, to take part in only the one Eucharist; for there is only the one flesh of our Lord Jesus Christ and one cup to unite us with His blood, one altar and one bishop with the presbyters and deacons, who are his fellow-servants. Then, whatever you do, you will do according to God."

14 See the Second Reading of the Office of Readings for the Tenth Sunday in Ordinary Time: Ignatius of Antioch, *Letter to the Romans* (1: 1-2, 2): "To the Church which rules over the Romans, a church worthy of God, worthy of honor and praise, worthy to be called blessed, worthy to receive the answer to its prayer, pure, and preeminent in love among Christian communities, observing the law of Christ and bearing the Father's Name."

15 See the Second Reading of the Office of Readings for Friday of the Seventeenth Week in Ordinary Time: Ignatius of Antioch, *Letter to Polycarp* (1: 1-4, 3): "[...] Remaining firm like the anvil under the hammer. The good athlete must take punishment in order to win. And above all we must bear with everything for God, so that he in turn may bear with us."

My soul be for theirs who are submissive to the bishop, to the presbyters and the deacons, and may my portion be along with them in
God! Labor together with one another; strive in company together;
run together; suffer together; sleep together; and awake together as
the stewards and associates and servants of God. Please Him under
whom you fight, and from whom you receive your wages. Let none
of you be found a deserter. Let your Baptism endure as your arms;
your faith as your helmet; your love as your spear; your patience as
a complete panoply.[16]

In reference to the Gnostics, Ignatius writes:

They abstain from the Eucharist and from prayer because they confess not the Eucharist to be the flesh of Our Savior Jesus Christ,
which suffered for our sins, and which the Father, of His goodness,
raised up again. Those, therefore, who speak against this gift of God,
incur death in the midst of their disputes.[17]

Regarding the validity of the Eucharist and the apostolic ministry, Ignatius
exhorts the Smyrnaeans:

See that you follow the bishop, even as Christ Jesus does the Father,
and the priests as you would the Apostles. Reverence the deacons
as those who carry out the appointment of God. Let no man do
anything connected with the Church without the bishop. Let only
the Eucharist be regarded as legitimate, which is celebrated under
[the presidency of] the bishop or him to whom he has entrusted it.[18]

Saint Ignatius speaks authoritatively on the question of the authority of
bishops with regard to the Sacrament of Baptism and the practice of the "love-
feast" (Greek: *agape*) that usually preceded or followed the Eucharist, and sometimes unfortunately received more attention than the actual celebration of the
Eucharist.

---

[16] Ignatius of Antioch, *Letter to Polycarp* 6: 1-2, as found in Benedict XVI's *The Fathers*, 16.

[17] Ignatius of Antioch, *Letter to the Smyrnaeans*, 6, 2.

[18] Polycarp of Smyrna, *Letter to the Smyrnaeans* 8:1. Cf. CCC 1369. Pope Benedict XVI cites
Ignatius' *Letter to the Ephesians* (4:1-2) in his book, *The Fathers*, 15: "It is fitting that you
should concur with the will of your bishop, which you also do. For your justly renowned
presbytery, worthy of God, is fitted as exactly to the bishop as the strings to the harp. Therefore, in your concord and harmonious love, Jesus Christ is sung. And man by man, you
become a choir, that being harmonious in love and taking up the song of God in unison you
may with one voice sing to the Father [...]."

In Saint Paul's time, the neophytes among the Corinthians were notorious for this latter abuse.[19] Once again, reference must be made to Saint Ignatius' *Letter to the Smyrnaeans*:

> It is not lawful without the bishop either to baptize or to celebrate a love-feast; but whatsoever he shall approve of, that is also pleasing to God, so that everything done may be secure and valid.

The Catechism of the Catholic Church[20] cites Saint Ignatius' *Letter to the Ephesians* as teaching:

> Mary's virginity and giving birth, and even the Lord's death escaped the notice of the prince of this world: these three mysteries worthy of proclamation were accomplished in God's silence.[21]

A Father Fed to the Lions

Ignatius' martyrdom (A.D. 107) was anything but silent. It took place in the Roman arena. Saint Ignatius arrived in Rome on the last day of the gruesome public games. He was led into the Flavian Amphitheatre (Colosseum) where his flesh was torn apart by ravenous lions according to the customary blood sport of the pagan Romans. Jaroslav Pelikan relates:

> A story in *The Martyrdom of Ignatius* has Ignatius telling the emperor Trajan[22] to his face, "I have the Christ the King [within me], may I now enjoy His Kingdom."[23]

The memorial of Saint Ignatius of Antioch is celebrated on October 17.[24]

---

[19] Cf. 1 Corinthians 11:17-22; 12:27-34.

[20] CCC, 498.

[21] Ignatius of Antioch, *Letter to the Ephesians* 19:1.

[22] In A.D. 112, Pliny the Younger, Governor of Bythinia, wrote a letter to the Emperor Trajan in which he described Christian practices as he had observed them. Pliny described how the Christians were accustomed to gathering on the same day (most likely, Sunday) before dawn to sing to Christ "as to a god." They also celebrated what is known in Latin as a *sacramentum*. In Roman military terms a *sacramentum* was the solemn oath of a soldier. In the context of Pliny's letter, it refers to the Christians pledging not to commit evil acts like fraud, theft, adultery and lying. Pliny notes that, besides this gathering, the Christians would gather on a separate day, not to celebrate what was the Eucharistic Sacrifice and Banquet that included eating the Body and Blood of Christ, but for what he termed an "ordinary and innocent meal." Trajan wrote to Pliny instructing him not to persecute the Christians proactively but simply to interrogate them when he encountered them. If they refused pagan worship, then Pliny should have them prosecuted.

[23] Pelikan, *Jesus Through the Centuries*, 49.

[24] In the Office of Readings, the writings of St. Ignatius of Antioch are cited fifteen times.

The Martyrdom of St. Ignatius of Antioch. *Source: Wikimedia.*

His name is mentioned in the Roman Canon or First Eucharistic Prayer in the second list of saints that follows the words of consecration.

Thomas Weinandy, in his article, "Ignatius of Antioch," concludes our section with these insights:

> In the early years of the second century, Ignatius, bishop of Antioch, was arrested and taken to Rome to suffer martyrdom in the Colosseum. In the course of his travels, this lively and energetic man met and wrote to other Christian communities. In his seven letters to the communities at Ephesus, Magnesia, Tralles, Rome, Philadelphia and Smyrna and to Polycarp of Smyrna he was primarily concerned with three issues: the unity of the church as lived in communion with the bishop and fostered in the Eucharist, the danger of heresy, and the glory of martyrdom. For Ignatius (d. ca. AD 107) the unity of the church was of supreme importance because this unity consisted of Christ (the Head) and His body. This unity was first of all founded upon a unity of faith—all believed in the one true Gospel (thus his concern for heresy which destroys the unity of faith). It was the bishop, as the earthly presence of Christ and successor to the Apostles, who is the foundation of this present unity; for he is the authentic

teacher and defender of the Gospel and the pastor who oversees the proper care and harmony of all the faithful. The fullest expression and fostering of this unity, "a symphony of minds in concert," is found in the Eucharist, for there the local faithful, in union with the bishop, gather to hear the Gospel and to come into communion with Christ by receiving His risen Body and Blood, which is "the medicine of immortality." The greatest heresy that faced Ignatius was Docetism (from the Greek word *dokesis* meaning "to seem"), which held that the Son/Word of God only "seemed" or "appeared" to take on human flesh, but actually did not. Thus all that pertained to Jesus' humanity—birth, eating, suffering, dying and so on—was only apparent and not real. The Docetists argued that, if the Son/Word was truly God, He could not truly assume human flesh; for to do so would jeopardize and destroy His divine nature. God could not actually suffer and die. In response to this, first Ignatius argued that Jesus, being the true Word of the Father, was the full revealer of the Father. He speaks from the Father's "silence" and the Word as the Father's "mouthpiece." As such Jesus is truly God. Ignatius calls Jesus God on fourteen occasions and on eight of these actually refers to Him as *ho Theos,* "the God"—in Greek, names are preceded by the definite article. This is very surprising at such an early date, since the New Testament seems very hesitant to call Jesus simply "God." Second, what is also surprising, Ignatius is one of the first, if not the first, to use "the communication of idioms," that is, the predicating of divine and human attributes of one and the same person. He can speak of "divine blood" or "the passion of my God." This is a very strange use of language. God does not have blood. God cannot suffer. However, if God becomes man, then God does have blood, and He can suffer, not as God but as man. This is why Ignatius used such language. It allowed him to express boldly and even scandalously, contrary to the Docetists, the truth of the Incarnation. To the Ephesians Ignatius could write about Jesus in a marvellous, poetic fashion: "Very flesh, yet Spirit too; Uncreated, and yet born; God-and-Man in One agreed, Very-Life-in-Death indeed, Fruit of God and Mary's seed At once impassible and torn By pain and suffering here below: Jesus Christ, whom as Our Lord we know." Ignatius' main argument for upholding the truth of the Incarnation is based on the doctrine of salvation. If the Son of God only pretended to be a man, if His "human" life were a mere charade and thus His birth, baptism, suffering and death were simply pantomime, then our salvation is mere pretense and counterfeit. It has no reality either. This leads to Ignatius' third concern, the glory of martyrdom. Ignatius pointedly told the church at Tralles that, when he arrives in Rome, he will be eaten by real lions with real teeth. He will shed real blood. He will actually suffer and truly die. If Jesus only pretended to shed blood and only feigned suffering and death, then [Ignatius] is the most to be pitied. He is but a fool. Moreover, it is in becoming a martyr that one fully proclaims the Gospel by imitating Jesus Himself. Equally, martyrdom fulfills what takes place in Baptism in that one dies and rises with Christ and so fully becomes an authentic Christian. Lastly, martyrdom is the living out of the Eucharist, for there, in receiving the Body and Blood of Christ, we are conformed into His likeness and thus in laying down one's life for Christ is fully conformed into the true likeness of Christ.[25]

---

[25] Hill, *History of Christianity*, 51.

CHAPTER THIRTEEN:
POLYCARP OF SMYRNA
(C. A.D. 89 - 155)

Episcopal Pedigree

Polycarp[1] of Smyrna[2] was born around A.D. 69. He became a young disciple of Saint John the Evangelist. As a middle-aged man, he became the episcopal colleague of Saint Ignatius of Antioch. As an elderly man, he became the master teacher of the future Saint Irenaeus of Lyons. By the time of his death at the age of eighty-six, he had left a singular legacy of faith to future generations of Christian disciples and martyrs.[3]

Only one of his supposed two letters has come down to us. Many scholars believe that two letters have come down to us as one letter. In his letter, like Saint John, his mentor, Polycarp shows much concern about the persecution of Christians at Smyrna.[4]

Polycarp Was No Pushover

Furthermore, he fought on other significant battle fronts, engaging in dis-

---

[1] Polycarp is a Greek name, comprised of two words, that literally means: "much fruit."

[2] Cf. *Harper's Bible Dictionary*, 960f: "Smyrna, an ancient city (modern Izmir, Turkey) on the west coast of Asia Minor. It is one of the seven cities mentioned in the Book of Revelation (1:11). It lay at the end of a major east-west road, possessed an excellent harbor, and was surrounded by rich farmland. The city's leadership was consistently loyal to Rome. A temple dedicated to the worship of Rome (*dea Roma*; Lat., 'the goddess Rome') was built there in 195 B.C. The message addressed to Smyrna reflects conflict between Christians and Jews (Revelation 2: 9-10). It may be that local Jewish leaders were appearing before the city authorities or the Roman governor (cf. Acts 17:5-8) and accusing their Christian neighbors of crimes. Polycarp, Bishop of Smyrna, was martyred in A.D. 156. The account of his martyrdom makes clear that there was great hostility between the local Jewish and Christian communities at that time. Information about the Christians in Smyrna between the time of the composition of the Book of Revelation and the Martyrdom of Polycarp is available in the Letters of Ignatius, Bishop of Antioch, written early in the second century."

[3] Cf. Lane, *The Lion Concise Book of Christian Thought*, 14: "A stirring account of [Polycarp's] martyrdom survives in *The Letter of the Smyrnaeans on the Martyrdom of Polycarp*."

[4] Cf. Revelation 2:8-11.

putes with the heretics Marcion and Valentinus. Irenaeus recounts a meeting between Polycarp and the hubris-filled Marcion. Being quite enamored of his own celebrity, Marcion asked Polycarp if he recognized him. Polycarp answered him, without batting an eyelash:

> Of course, I can always recognize the offspring of Satan!

In his *Letter to the Philippians*, Polycarp strenuously urged his flock to practice Christian virtue, exhorting them to put off the old man of unrighteousness so as to be clothed anew with the righteousness of Christ which they first received at Baptism.

Following Our Lord's teaching in the Gospel, Polycarp stressed that even though the Philippians were still living in a pagan society, they should not be afraid to be counter-cultural in order to persevere in the integrity of their heavenly citizenship. In that same letter, Polycarp makes reference to how Ignatius' letters were being widely circulated throughout the Church, lending further weight to the importance of the Apostolic Tradition.

Regarding the practice of Christian virtue, Polycarp writes:

> Teach your wives to walk in the faith given to them, and in love and purity, tenderly loving their own husbands in all truth, and loving all others equally in all chastity; and to train up their children in the knowledge and fear of God. Teach the widows to be discreet as respects the faith of the Lord, praying continually for all, being far from all slandering, evil-speaking, false-witnessing, love of money, and every kind of evil; knowing that they are the altars of God [...]. Let the young men also be blameless in all things, being especially careful to preserve purity, and keeping themselves in, as with a bridle, from every kind of evil. For it is well that they should be cut off from the lusts that are in the world.[5]

Quartodecimans Controversy

At the age of 80, Pope Anicletus called Polycarp to Rome to help him resolve the Easter Date Controversy[6] that had arisen between the churches of Asia Minor and Rome.

---

5   Polycarp of Smyrna, *Letter to the Philippians*, 5.
6   This controversy is known as the "Quartodecimans" controversy because of the insistence that Easter be celebrated on the "fourteenth" (*quartodecimus* in Latin) day of the month of Nisan.

The Asian Churches, claiming to follow the tradition of the Apostle John, celebrated Easter on the fourteenth day of the month of Nisan (March or April) in conjunction with the Jewish feast of Passover (Hebrew: *Pesach*). This meant that the celebration of Easter could fall on any day of the week.

The Pope, on the other hand, desired that Easter would be always celebrated on the Sunday following the fourteenth day of the month of Nisan, Sunday being the "first day of the week," and, more importantly, the Day of the Lord's Resurrection according to the Gospel accounts.[7] Although the meetings between Polycarp and Pope Anicletus were positive, the reaction to the Pope's decision on the part of the local churches of Asia Minor was not.

Bearing Fruit Even Unto Death

Having borne the brunt of the local clergy and lay faithful in this regard, Polycarp's imminent martyrdom now began to appear on the horizon. Saint Polycarp was martyred because he refused to worship the Emperor Marcus Aurelius upon his return to Smyrna from Rome.

Within a few months of Saint Polycarp's death, the Church of Smyrna published an account of his martyrdom as a circular letter to the entire Catholic world—a prototype of a bishop's pastoral letter and a papal encyclical. This pastoral letter became in short order the forerunner of an important literary genre in the early Church known as "Acts of the Martyrs" (*Acta Martyrum*), which provide vivid and detailed accounts of how the early martyrs died, so as to receive the unfading crown of glory.

This style of letter was truly innovative and its popularity caught on like wildfire, so much so that multiple copies of the anonymous letter were made and then read for centuries to come as a means of fortifying Christians, most especially those enduring persecution for the sake of the Gospel.

Finally, we turn our attention to the awe-inspiring prayer that Polycarp prayed in preparation for his martyrdom in A.D. 155. It is a masterpiece of early Christian theology and spirituality. Polycarp, lifting his gaze heavenward, prayed thus:

---

[7]   Today, our custom in the West, following the Gregorian calendar, is to celebrate Easter on the Sunday following the first full moon of the vernal (spring) equinox. The date of Easter in the East differs because the Christians of the East continue to follow the Julian calendar, which the Gregorian calendar replaced in the West.

O Lord God Almighty, the Father of your beloved and blessed Son Jesus Christ, by whom we have received the knowledge of you, the God of angels and powers, and of every creature, and of the whole race of the righteous who live before you, I give you thanks that you have counted me worthy of this day and this hour, that I should be counted in the number of your martyrs, in the chalice of your Christ, to the resurrection of eternal life, both of soul and body, through the incorruption given by the Holy Spirit. Among them may I be accepted this day before you as a rich and acceptable sacrifice, as you, the ever-truthful God, have preordained, have revealed beforehand to me, and now have fulfilled. I praise you for all things, I bless you, I glorify you, along with the everlasting and heavenly Jesus Christ, your Beloved Son; with Him, to you and the Holy Spirit, be glory now and forever. Amen.[8]

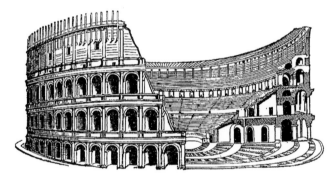

The second-century account of his martyrdom is the oldest such account that has come down to us from apostolic times. As he faced death, the angry mob shouted out at him, accusing him of having disrupted the unity and harmony of their pagan lives because of his fidelity to Christ and the Church: "This is the father of the Christians, the destroyer of our gods, who teaches many not to sacrifice or worship."

In response, the Roman magistrate in charge of his death urged Polycarp to reconsider his actions: "Have respect for your age. Revile Christ and I will release you."

---

[8] *Martyrium Polycarpi*, 1, 6-11, 13-16, as found in Claire Russell's *Glimpses of the Church Fathers*, 21.

Polycarp remonstrated:

> For eighty-six years I have been His servant, and He has done me no
> wrong. How can I blaspheme my King who saved me?

At that, the Roman magistrate had Polycarp burned alive at the stake.

The liturgical memorial of Saint Polycarp of Smyrna is February 23.[9]

---

9 In the Office of Readings the Epistles or Letters of St. Polycarp are cited five times. See the
   Second Reading for the Twenty-Sixth Sunday in Ordinary Time: *Letter to the Philippians*
   (1: 1-2, 3): "[…] Put aside empty talk and popular errors […]. All who refuse to believe in
   [Jesus] must answer to God for the blood of His Son"; See the Second Reading for Tuesday
   of the Twenty-Sixth Week in Ordinary Time: *Letter to the Philippians* (6: 1- 8, 2): "Presbyters should be sympathetic and merciful to everyone, bringing back those who have wan-
   dered, visiting the sick; they must not neglect widows and orphans, or the poor […]. They
   should refrain from anger, human respect and prejudice; avarice should be wholly alien to
   them. Nor should they be rash in judging others, since they know that we are all debtors
   through sin"; See the Second Reading for Thursday of the Twenty-Sixth Week in Ordinary
   Time: *Letter to the Philippians* (12: 1-14): "[…] Keep all the saints in your prayers. Pray too,
   for our rulers, for our leaders, and for all those who are enemies of the cross. In this way,
   your good works will be seen by all men, and you will be perfected in him." On February
   23, the Memorial of St. Polycarp of Smyrna, we read in the Divine Office from a letter on
   the martyrdom of St. Polycarp written by the Church of Smyrna (13: 2-15, 2): "[…] Like
   a ship's sail swelling in the wind, the flame became as it were a dove encircling the martyr's
   body. Surrounded by the fire, [Polycarp's] body was like bread that is baked, or gold and silver white-hot in a furnace, not like the flesh that has been burnt. So sweet a fragrance came
   to us that it was like that of burning incense or some other costly and sweet-smelling grain."

CHAPTER FOURTEEN:
THE PRE-NICENE FATHERS

Those known as the Pre-Nicene Fathers[1] are so called because they lived in the period preceding the First Ecumenical Council held at Nicaea in A.D. 325. Some of these Fathers are also known collectively as the Church's first "apologists," and it is interesting to note that for the most part these writers were laymen and not priests. We hear a great deal about "apologetics" in the Church today. Often people think of the word "apology," and immediately associate it with its present connotation of asking pardon for one's errors or offenses.

Apologetics doesn't mean having to say you're sorry

The original definition of the Greek word *apologia* (hence, our English words: "apology" and "apologetics") did not refer to a confession of one's errors or offenses but, on the contrary, to the oral or written "defense" that one made of firmly held beliefs in the face of opposition.

The Fathers we will examine upheld the Apostolic Tradition, the orthodox teachings of the Church on faith and morals, by forging Catholicism's apologetic against the attacks of heretics who were the forerunners of the early Church's most formidable enemy, the fourth-century heretical priest Arius of Alexandria who provoked the Emperor Constantine to convoke Nicaea I.

Newman on the Pre-Nicene Fathers

Blessed John Henry Newman, whose conversion to Catholicism in 1845 was undoubtedly due in large part to his discovery of patristic writings as an Anglican in the 1820s, and more specifically to his in-depth study of the Arian controversy and the writings of Saint Athanasius of Alexandria, wrote his own *Apologia pro Vita Sua*,[2] comparable in many respects to Saint Augustine's autobiography,[3] *The Confessions*.

---

[1] The Pre-Nicene Fathers are also known as the Ante-Nicene Fathers. The prefix "ante," meaning "before," to be distinguished from the prefix "anti," meaning "against."

[2] Newman's *Apologia pro vita sua*, or "A Defense for his life," chronicles Newman's theological, philosophical, spiritual and psychological development, the development of his ideas, from his childhood to his conversion to Catholicism in 1845 until 1864 when the book was first published.

[3] In hindsight, *The Confessions* of St. Augustine is considered the first psychological autobiography ever written.

In his 1865 apologetical Letter to the Anglican Reverend Doctor Edward B. Pusey (Regius Professor of Hebrew at Oxford University and former member of the Oxford Movement), Newman referred to the Pre-Nicene Fathers, such as Saint Justin Martyr, Saint Irenaeus of Lyons, and Tertullian as a "three-fold cord," that powerfully combined to bear witness to the antiquity of the Church's doctrine of Mary as the New Eve.

Newman reasoned that these Fathers (and many others after them) inferred the doctrine of Mary as the New Eve mainly from their study of the antithetical parallelism between Christ and Adam highlighted in the writings of Saint Paul;[4] the *Protoevangelium*, or "First Gospel," found in Genesis 3:15; and the apocalyptic vision of the woman in Revelation 12:1-6.

Therefore, in an indirect fashion, Newman posited the notion that these Pre-Nicene Fathers gave us in rudimentary form a Marian apologetic as regards the doctrines of Our Lady's sinlessness, perpetual virginity, divine maternity and intercessory power—in a word, her singular cooperation in the economy or plan of our eternal salvation.

One discovers, by the way, that the Church rarely formulates her teaching into dogmatic definitions except when she finds her teachings being attacked or when the development of a particular doctrine is deemed by the Magisterium to have matured enough so as to merit a dogmatic encapsulation. Noteworthy examples of dogmatic definitions are the Immaculate Conception (1854) by Blessed Pope Pius IX and the Assumption (1950) by Pope Pius XII.

Gospel Inculturation

During the Pre-Nicene period, the Church Fathers labored to find adequate means for inculturating the Gospel message in a society whose Jewish roots were now being forced to intertwine with Greco-Roman branches. The Hellenistic culture of the Church's earliest centuries, saturated with the pagan philosophies of Socrates, Plato and Aristotle[5] was a major influence on how the Fathers transmitted the Hebraic thought of the Sacred Scriptures into a predominantly Greek mindset.

Although certain Fathers resisted the process of "hellenization" (for example, Tertullian quipped: "What does Athens have to do with Jerusalem?"), others, like Justin Martyr, Irenaeus of Lyons and Clement of Alexandria, deemed it indispensable.

---

[4]   Cf. Romans 5:12-20; 1 Corinthians 15:22, 45-50.
[5]   "SPA" is a useful mnemonic device. It helps one remember the names of the Greek philosophers, Socrates, Plato and Aristotle in chronological order.

At the same time, they demonstrated their firm willingness to correct the process of hellenization when necessary, as we find in the case of the Gnostic heretics who exploited Platonic philosophy to advance a so-called "secret knowledge," or *gnosis* that corrupted the *kerygma*—a Greek theological term that denotes "the original proclamation of the Gospel message."

For the most part, however, the ancient Greek philosophers did a tremendous service to the early Church by providing technical terminology, a whole new extra-biblical vocabulary (for example, the Greek word *hypostasis* meaning "substance"), which the Fathers then employed to stake out clearer lines in their all-important discussions concerning Trinitarian and Christological doctrines.

This fortuitous development is all the more detectable to us today when we study, for example, the highly philosophical language constitutive of the Nicene-Constantinopolitan Creed, commonly known as the Nicene Creed, which we profess every Sunday at Mass.

Nowhere in Sacred Scripture will one find such creedal expressions that explain Jesus' divinity in the philosophical terms employed in the Nicene Creed: Jesus Christ is *consubstantial with the Father*, (*homoousios to Patri*).

Nevertheless, it is precisely this sort of language that was officially adopted by councils and incorporated into decrees that allowed the early Church to form her own apologetic meant to preserve the orthodoxy of her scripturally based teachings while, at the same time, allowing those teachings to interface with cultures and languages that had already evolved from their biblical moorings, or never had any.

The Pressures of Persecution and Backsliding

The Pre-Nicene Fathers also grappled with other key issues that added different contours to their apologetic. Living in centuries of Christian persecution, these Fathers were faced with the pastoral challenge of how to deal with those being persecuted.

Some of them desired martyrdom at all costs. Others sought to preserve their lives by fleeing from martyrdom at all costs. Still others were tempted to give into the demands of their persecutors to avoid execution.

Many Christians did fall into this final category and belonged to a group known collectively as the *lapsi* since they "lapsed" from the practice of the Faith under the threat of persecution.

Certain *lapsi* succumbed to the practice of burning incense before the statue of a pagan god or one of the emperors, living or deceased.[6] Other *lapsi*, for example, apostasized, that is, renounced Christianity, even for a temporary period, because they succumbed to the pressure to hand over the Church's sacred books (*libelli*) to the Roman authorities.[7]
There were also *lapsi* who purchased certificates from Roman officials that stated falsely that they had adhered to the requirements of pagan worship.

The Fathers of the Church held heated debates as to whether or not repentant *lapsi* should be allowed to return to the one true fold. And if so, under what conditions would they be allowed to return? Would they have to do severe public penances for a prolonged period? Or, could they simply be welcomed back privately by their local bishop before whom they would make a renewal of their profession of faith?

Christians, who had been gravely affected by the defections of the *lapsi*, desired that they incur the strict punishment of being denied access to the sacraments until they were *in extremis*, that is to say, until they were on their deathbeds.

Many Christians voiced their strong opinion that the *lapsi* should never be readmitted into communion with the Church because they interpreted their acts as treasonous, clearly indicative of having committed the sin of blasphemy against the Holy Spirit, a sin of ultimate despair of God's mercy, which, according to Our Lord's teaching in Matthew 12:32, was unpardonable:

> And whoever says a word against the Son of Man will be forgiven;
> but whoever speaks against the Holy Spirit will not be forgiven,
> either in this age or in the age to come.

At a different level, the early Christian apologists strove to defend the Church against the absurd claims of pagan persecutors that they consented to infanticide; that they were cannibals because they ate and drank the Body and Blood of Christ their God; that they were atheists because they refused to worship the gods of the established Pantheon; that they were seditious because they hailed Christ as their King, indeed the King of kings and Lord of lords.

---

[6] These *lapsi* were known as the *thuriferari* (incense-bearers). One should recall that some of
     the emperors demanded divine titles while they were still alive, and expected furthermore
     that a cult be established for them on a par with the other gods and goddesses of the pagan
     Pantheon, hence the erection of statuary in their honor.

[7] These *lapsi* were known as the *libellatici*.

Chapter Fifteen:
Justin Martyr[1]
(C. A.D. 100 - 165)

The Church's First Apologist

Justin[2] was born in the early half of the second century (circa A.D. 100) in the Palestinian town of Flavia Neapolis,[3] located in Israel's central region of Samaria.[4]

Although Justin was a Samaritan by birth, both his parents were pagans. Because Justin's father Priscus was a veteran soldier of the Roman Empire, Justin was considered a Roman citizen. He was fortunate to receive an excellent classical education, being trained in rhetoric, history, and poetry at philosophical schools run by the Pythagoreans,[5] Peripatetics,[6] Stoics[7] and Platonists.[8]

---

[1] *Martyr* is not Justin's proper last name but an epithet.

[2] Cf. Benedict XVI, *The Fathers*, 19-23.

[3] Flavia Neapolis ("the new city of Flavius") was founded in A.D. 72 on the site of the ancient biblical city of Shechem in Samaria. Today, this city corresponds to Nablus in the Palestinian territories. In the time of Augustus Caesar, the province of Samaria was renamed Sebaste, the Greek equivalent of the Latin title *Augustus*, chosen to honor Rome's first emperor.

[4] Samaritans were considered heretics by the Jews because they intermarried with pagans, accepted only the first five books of the Bible, and insisted on worshipping Yahweh (YHWH) not in the Temple of Jerusalem but at Mount Gerizim in Samaria. Recall Our Lord's dialogue with the Samaritan woman at Jacob's well recounted in chapter four of John's Gospel.

[5] The Pythagoreans were followers of the Greek philosopher and mathematician Pythagoras, who lived in the sixth century B.C. The main beliefs of the Pythagoreans were centered on the transmigration of souls and the idea that numbers were the ultimate elements in the universe.

[6] The Greek-based word "peripatetic" literally means "to walk about/around." The Peripatetics were followers of Aristotle who followed him around or walked about the Lyceum as he taught them.

[7] The Stoics derived their name from the *stoa* or "porch" in Athens where they used to gather around their founder Zeno to discuss their philosophical notions. Zeno's school, founded circa 303 B.C., proposed the belief that all things, properties, relations are governed by unvarying natural laws, and that the truly wise man was the one who pursued virtue for its own sake through the exercise of reason and indifference to the outside world, all human emotions and passions.

[8] The followers of the Greek philosopher Plato (B.C. 427- 347) who taught, among other things, that the objects we perceive on earth with our senses are real only insofar as they imitate or participate in an invisible, independent world of immutable ideas, logical forms or essences

For a time, as a Platonist, Justin believed himself to have been on the verge of achieving the goal of all philosophy, namely, the vision of God.[9] Like the later Augustine of Hippo, Justin made his way to conversion through an ongoing experimentation with various philosophies until at last he was baptized at Ephesus and could be found wearing the philosopher's "shawl" (*pallium*), preaching the Gospel.[10]

Apologetics for Free, not Fees

Justin was not content to be a wandering philosopher, so he headed to Rome where, during the reign of the stoic philosopher Emperor Marcus Aurelius (A.D. 138-161),[11] he opened the first school of Christian philosophy — free of charge. In this way, Justin may be viewed as having "baptized" the idea of the pagan Greek philosophers Plato (founder of the Academy), and Aristotle (founder of the Lyceum and private tutor of Alexander the Great).

According to Tatian, one of Justin's pupils and a Christian apologist in his own right, Justin's noble efforts to found a Christian school of philosophy were ultimately frustrated by the active persecution of Crescens, a cynic philosopher, and by the harsh interrogations of Junius Rusticus, pagan prefect of Rome at the time. Eventually, this persecution led to Justin's being condemned to die a martyr's death in A.D. 165, along with six of his companions.[12] Unfortunately, we have only three extant works of Justin's much larger corpus.

---

which in effect constituted for the Platonists the world of essence and reality.

9   Cf. John Paul II, *Fides et Ratio* (38) as cited in Benedict XVI's *The Fathers*, 21. Saint John Paul II describes St. Justin as a "pioneer of positive engagement with philosophical thinking—albeit with cautious discernment [...]. Although he continued to hold Greek philosophy in high esteem after his conversion, Justin claimed with power and clarity that he had found in Christianity 'the only sure and profitable philosophy' (*Dialogue with Trypho*, 8:1)."

10   Cf. Lane, *The Lion Concise Book of Christian Thought*, 15: "In this way, Justin anchored his Christian faith in his Greek heritage. When he became a Christian he did not renounce philosophy, he became a true philosopher. He said that the relationship between the philosophers and Christ is that between the incomplete and the complete, between the imperfect and the perfect. So while Justin was positive toward his Greek past, he was not bound by it."

11   A copy of an ancient equestrian statue of the Emperor Marcus Aurelius adorns the "Capitol Hill" (Italian: *Campidoglio*) of Rome. Marcus Aurelius wrote an important work documenting his stoic philosophical musings, entitled *Meditations*.

12   The *Acta Sancti Justini* (The Acts of Saint Justin) has left us a stunning and detailed account of his gruesome martyrdom. Justin and his companions were accused of impiety, that is, not worshipping the pagan gods. Subsequently, they were scourged and then beheaded. The liturgical memorial of St. Justin Martyr's "birthday into Heaven" (death) is celebrated on June 1.

Justin Corrects an Emperor

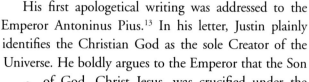

His first apologetical writing was addressed to the Emperor Antoninus Pius.[13] In his letter, Justin plainly identifies the Christian God as the sole Creator of the Universe. He boldly argues to the Emperor that the Son of God, Christ Jesus, was crucified under the Roman Procurator of Syria, Pontius Pilate.

Referring to the Holy Spirit, he attaches the adjective "prophetic" and attributes to Him the inspiration of the prophetic texts that point to the Death and Resurrection of Jesus, the everlasting Christ.

In this same apology, Justin describes the Sacrament of Baptism as being administered with the Trinitarian formula in accord with Christ's mandate to the Apostles in Matthew 28:16-20.

Justin criticizes the Emperor for his unfair treatment of Christians. He argues that the Emperor's persecution of Christians as so-called "atheists" is ludicrous, given their objective beliefs. Furthermore, Justin says that there are pagan philosophers in Rome who claim to be atheists and who incite men to immorality yet they go unscathed. Why? Should not the Emperor Antoninus Pius hold himself to higher standards of justice, to the noble Roman *pietas*[14] in dealing with pagans and Christians alike?

Justin's Letter to the Roman Senate

Justin's second apologetical letter is addressed to the Roman Senate. He tells the imperial senators that Christian doctrines are on a much higher plane than man-made doctrines because they have as their primary premise the mystery of the Incarnation of God's definitive "Word" (*Logos*).

Pagan philosophers, so Justin reasons, even the noblest among them like Socrates, were but a partial preparation for the coming of the fullness of the truth. Justin asserts that the pagan philosophers, but to a lesser degree than the Old Testament patriarchs and prophets, carried within themselves the *Logos* or

---

[13]   Antoninus Pius lived from A.D. 86-181, reigning from A.D. 131-181.

[14]   *Pietas* was a catch-all term used in pagan Rome to express the virtues that all good citizens were expected to exemplify in relation to family, religion and the state. The epic poet Virgil, writing in the first century A.D., describes in his masterpiece, *The Aeneid,* how his main character Aeneas was indeed a "pious" (Latin: *pius*) Roman.

Word of God. The Greek expression that Justin uses to describe this belief is *Logos Spermatikos* (Seed of the Word).

Finally, Justin strengthens his apologetic when he claims that Christian doctrine is far superior to pagan doctrine, because the former has a universal appeal while the latter caters mainly to the higher, intellectual classes. Chadwick explains:

> Justin was convinced that in the high-minded Stoic ethics of human brotherhood, there was much for a Christian to welcome. With varying results the divine Sower had sown the seed of truth, admittedly not always in wholly fertile ground [...]. In the universal reason of the divine Word all rational beings have, and both Abraham and Socrates are "Christians before Christ." Christ's ethical teaching proclaimed the way to true happiness, for he was not only man but God, acknowledged in the manger by the Magi, vindicated by His wonderful acts, by the fulfillment of prophecy in the Gospel story, and by the astounding diffusion of the Gospel in the world. So the truths only partially apprehended in the aspirations of the greatest classical philosophers of Greece find their fulfillment, and correction, in the framework of the Christian faith.[15]

Justin's Order of the Mass

Concerning the celebration of the Eucharistic Sacrifice and Banquet, Justin offers us the following description that lays down in broad outline the parts of the Mass as we can still recognize them in all of *the great liturgical families*.[16]

Justin writes to the Emperor around A.D. 155, wherein we find this remarkable description in Justin's third apologetical work, the one for which he is most famous, the *Dialogue with Trypho the Jew*:

> On the day we call the day of the sun, all who dwell in the city or country gather in the same place. The memoirs of the apostles and the writings of the prophets are read, as much as time permits. When the reader has finished, he who presides over those gathered admonishes and challenges them to imitate these beautiful things. Then we all rise together and offer prayers for ourselves [...] and for the others, wherever they may be, so that we may be found righteous by our life and actions, and faithful to the commandments, so as to obtain

---

[15] Chadwick, "The Early Christian Community," in *The Oxford History of Christianity*, 52-53 *passim*.

[16] CCC, 1345.

eternal salvation. When the prayers are concluded, we exchange the kiss. Then someone brings bread and a cup of water and wine mixed together to him who presides over the brethren. He takes them and offers praise and glory to the Father of the universe, through the Name of the Son and of the Holy Spirit and for a considerable time he gives thanks (Greek: *Eucharistein*) that we have been judged worthy of these gifts. When he has concluded the prayers and thanksgivings, all present give voice to an acclamation by saying: "Amen."

When he who presides has given thanks and the people have responded, those whom we call deacons give to those present the "eucharisted" bread, wine and water and take them to those who are absent. This food we call the Eucharist, which no one is allowed to share except the one who believes that our teaching is true, and who has been washed with the washing that is the remission of sins, and unto regeneration, and so lives as Christ has handed down. For we do not receive these as common bread and common drink: but just as Jesus Christ Our Savior, having been made flesh by the Word of God, had both flesh and blood for our salvation, so likewise have we learned that the food over which thanks has been given by the prayer of the Word which comes from Him, and by which our blood and flesh are nourished through a change, is the Flesh and Blood of the same Incarnate Jesus. For the Apostles in the memoirs composed by them and that are called Gospels have thus handed on what was commanded them; namely, that Jesus took bread, and when He had given thanks, said, "Do this in remembrance of Me; This is My Body"; and that, in like manner, having taken the cup and given thanks, He said, "This is My Blood," and gave it to them.[17]

Justin and Interreligious Dialogue

In terms of Christian apologetics, Saint Justin Martyr was masterful. His *Dialogue with Trypho* is without a doubt the best example of his apologetical prowess.[18] In his *Dialogue,* Justin strives to make a coherent defense of Catholic Christianity to the objections of Judaism, all the while explaining his own process of intellectual and spiritual conversion to Catholicism. For example, as regards the nature of the Eucharist as a sacrifice fulfilling all others, he cites in his *Dialogue with Trypho* the

---

[17] Justin Martyr, *Dialogue with Trypho*, 1: 65-67.

[18] Cf. Chadwick, "The Early Christian Community," in *The Oxford History of Christianity*, 52: "In a style modeled on the Platonic dialogues, Justin here interpreted Old Testament prophecies which he saw fulfilled in Jesus and in the present life of the Church, already spreading throughout the known world."

prophecy of Malachi 1:10-12, that a pure sacrifice will be offered to the glory of God's Name from the rising of the sun to its setting. Justin comments:

> Already, then, did He prophesy about those sacrifices that are offered to Him in every place by us Gentiles, speaking, that is, about the Bread and Cup of the Eucharist.[19]

Great Minds of Great Fathers Think Alike

Justin's apologetic concerning the Church's Eucharistic theology and discipline confirms much of what Ignatius of Antioch wrote in this regard during the Post-Apostolic period. For example, Saint Ignatius instructs the early Christians at Smyrna in Asia Minor, who were deliberately refusing to receive Holy Communion:

> They abstain from the Eucharist and from prayer because they do not confess that the Eucharist is the Flesh of Our Savior Jesus Christ, which suffered for our sins and which, in His goodness, the Father raised [...]. It would be better for them to show love in order that they also might rise.[20]

Regarding the sacrificial nature of the Mass, Ignatius, reminiscent of Paul's teaching in 1 Corinthians 10:16-17, writes to the Christians at Philadelphia in Asia Minor:

> Be careful to observe only one celebration of the Eucharist; for there is only one Flesh of Our Lord Jesus Christ and one cup of union with His Blood, one altar of sacrifice, as there is one bishop with the presbyters and my fellow-servants, the deacons.[21]

Finally, as for the unity of the Mass, Ignatius insists in his *Letter to the Ephesians* that only one Eucharistic assembly, led by a single bishop, is permissible with:

> breaking one bread that is the medicine of immortality and the antidote against dying that offers life for all in Jesus Christ.[22]

Old Man by the Sea

Strangely, or better yet, providentially enough, Justin's conversion was aided in part by a mysterious old man whom he encountered along the seashore, who

---

[19] As cited in *The Hidden Manna: A Theology of the Eucharist* by James O'Connor (Ignatius Press, 1988), 22.

[20] As cited in *The History, Theology and Psychology of Eucharistic Devotion* by Father Benedict Groeschel, C.F.R., and James Monti (Our Sunday Visitor, 1996), 37.

[21] Ibid.

[22] Ignatius of Antioch, *Letter to the Ephesians*, 20, 2. See CCC, 1331.

engaged Justin in a discussion about the purpose of philosophy. In the course of their colloquium, as Justin recounts it in the *Dialogue with Trypho* 1-8, he replied that the primary end of the study of philosophy was to lead man to happiness.

The old man concluded his own apologetic to Justin by exhorting him to seek the wisdom of God, not in speculative philosophical knowledge but rather in prayer and in the inspired writings of the prophets. Justin enthusiastically took up this gauntlet and never put it down until his death in A.D. 165.

His reading of the prophets of the Old Testament led him to recognize Jesus of Nazareth as the promised "Lord" (*Kyrios*) and "Messiah" (*Christos*), the "Word" (*Logos*) and "Wisdom" (*Sophia*) of God.

We can conclude with some thoughts of Benedict XVI:

> In taking his leave, the old man urged [Justin] to pray that the gates of light would be opened to him.[23] The story foretells the crucial episode in Justin's life: at the end of a long philosophical journey, a quest for the truth, he arrived at the Christian faith.[24]

The relics of St. Justin Martyr, found in Stift Lilienfeld, Lower Austria. Source: Karl Gruber, Wikimedia.

---

[23] Cf. Wilken, *The Spirit of Early Christian Thought*, 6: "As Justin finished his conversation, the old man, to Justin's surprise, did not try to convince him of the teachings he had presented but ended the colloquy with a prayer that the 'gates of light' would be opened and Justin would be receptive to what he heard. After his prayer the old man left, but his words had fallen like hot coals on dry kindling. 'A flame was kindled in my soul,' writes Justin, 'and I was seized by love of the prophets and of the friends of Christ. While I was pondering his words in my mind, I came to see that this way of life alone is sure and fulfilling.'"

[24] Benedict XVI, *The Fathers*, 20.

CHAPTER SIXTEEN:
IRENAEUS OF LYONS

(C. A.D. 115 - 202)

Father of Theology

Irenaeus of Lyons,[1] a great apologist, nicknamed by some the "Father of Theology," was born in Smyrna between A.D. 115 and A.D. 125. No details concerning his death (circa A.D. 202) are known for certain. According to Saint Gregory of Tours, he died as a martyr during the persecutions of the Roman Emperor Septimius Severus.

It is interesting to note that the first person to publish Irenaeus' landmark work, *Adversus Haereses* (Against the Heresies), was the Renaissance humanist, Erasmus of Rotterdam, in 1526.[2]

Classical Curriculum

Saint Irenaeus owed much of his early intellectual formation to his avid study of Homer's classical works, the *Iliad* and the *Odyssey*, as well as to the works of Plato. His later theological and spiritual formation occurred under the tutelage of Saint Polycarp, Bishop of Smyrna, whose own mentor had been Saint John the Evangelist, also credited with having written the Book of Revelation (Apocalypse).

Along these lines, Eusebius of Caesarea, the "Father of Church History" living in the fourth century, reports these words of Irenaeus acknowledging his indebtedness to the pedagogy of Saint Polycarp of Smyrna:

> Polycarp learned everything from eyewitnesses of the Word of Life, and he proclaimed Him (Christ) in full harmony with what is taught in the Sacred Scriptures. These things [...] that I heard attentively

---

[1] Cf. Benedict XVI, *The Fathers*, 24-29.
[2] A certain expression commenting on Erasmus' theological method says that "Erasmus laid the egg that Luther hatched."

at that time I then conserved in my memory not just on the written page but in my innermost heart.[3]

Ecclesiastical Diplomat

A particular tradition holds that Polycarp sent Irenaeus to be a young missionary priest in the Roman province of Gaul (now France).[4] There Irenaeus, epitomizing the significance of his Greek name meaning "peace" (hence the proper name: Irene), eventually succeeded Photinus as bishop of Lyons. Both as a missionary priest and bishop, Irenaeus was adept at exercising prudent, diplomatic, peacemaking skills by interceding with the Bishop of Rome in order to reconcile the schismatic sect known as the Montanists,[5] which Tertullian joined toward the end of his life in A.D. 230.

Irenaeus' apology (i.e., a defense) on behalf of the Montanists was centered on his conviction that although they admittedly espoused certain extreme beliefs[6] and practices[7] they nonetheless adhered, for the most part, to the deposit of the apostolic faith.[8]

Irenaeus also offered an apologetic to the Pope on behalf of the Christians of Asia Minor who celebrated Easter according to a different tradition than the Roman tradition. According to previous decrees given by the Bishop of Rome to the churches of Asia Minor, Easter was to be celebrated each year on a Sunday and never on a weekday. It was about this same delicate matter that Saint Polycarp of Smyrna negotiated unsuccessfully with the Pope in his own time.

Ultimately, however, Irenaeus firmly expounded his conviction that the beliefs and practices of the Church of Rome, founded by the glorious Apostles

---

[3] Eusebius of Caesarea, *Ecclesiastical History*, IV, 14, 3.

[4] Cf. Benedict XVI, *The Fathers*, 24: "We do not know when [Irenaeus] moved from Asia Minor to Gaul, but his move must have coincided with the first development of the Christian community in Lyons: here, in 177, we find Irenaeus listed in the college of presbyters. In that very year, he was sent to Rome bearing a letter from the community in Lyons to Pope Eleutherius. His mission in Rome saved Irenaeus from the persecution of Marcus Aurelius that took a toll of at least forty-eight martyrs, including the ninety-year-old Bishop Pontinus of Lyons, who died from ill treatment in prison. Thus, on his return, Irenaeus was appointed bishop of the city. The new pastor devoted himself without reserve to his episcopal ministry that ended in about 202-203, perhaps with martyrdom."

[5] Recall that the Montanists derive their name from Montanus of Phrygia whose beliefs were eventually condemned by Pope Zephyrinus in the third century A.D.

[6] For example, the Montanists failed to appreciate the Church as a divine institution possessing the authority to forgive sins.

[7] For example, the Montanists practiced a rigorous asceticism and ecstatic spirituality because they believed in the imminent return or second coming of Christ.

[8] Cf. Aquilina, *The Fathers of the Church*, 83.

Peter and Paul, should be the standard for those of all the other churches. The Bishop of Lyons explains:

> Because of its supremacy, it is necessary that with the Church of Rome all of the churches should be joined, that is to say all the faithful from every place in which the ancient tradition of the apostles has been preserved by those living in whatever part of the world.[9]

Irenaeus also offers us invaluable testimony to the unbroken line of apostolic succession in the See of Saint Peter, listing all the Popes from the time of Peter to the twelfth pontiff, Eleutherius, reigning in his own day.[10]

Irenaeus and Anti-Gnosticism

Irenaeus, however, did not dally with the various heretical sects known collectively as the Gnostics. Lane explains Irenaeus' visceral aversion to Gnosticism:

> [Irenaeus] challenged the Gnostic claims to secret apostolic traditions. He argues that if the Apostles had had special teaching to pass on, they would have entrusted it to the churches they had founded. He points to the different churches founded by the Apostles and shows how there has been a continuous succession of open public teaching in these churches since that time. In support of this, he lists the leaders of these churches, beginning with those appointed by the apostles themselves. Furthermore, these churches, scattered throughout the empire, all teach the same doctrine.[11]

As a matter of fact, Irenaeus could not tolerate the notion that so-called Christians arrogantly claimed to possess secret knowledge about the mysteries of faith that Christ neither revealed to His Church through the teaching of the Apostles nor intended to be handed down as the Deposit of Faith by the successors of the Apostles to all the faithful but only to a select number of especially illuminated initiates.[12]

---

9   Irenaeus of Lyons, *Adversus Haereses* 3: 3, 2-3.

10   Cf. Irenaeus of Lyons, *Adversus Haereses* 3:3, 2-3. Pope St. Eleutherius reigned from approximately A.D. 175-189.

11   Lane, *The Lion Concise Book of Christian Thought*, 16. Cf. Irenaeus of Lyons, *Against the Heresies* 3: 3, 1.

12   Lane, *The Lion Concise Book of Christian Thought*, 16f: "Irenaeus' argument is quite powerful. This writer discovered that for himself once when debating with two self-confessed 'Gnostics' who had given him a lift. He first tried to answer them from the New Testament, but this did not work. They, like their second-century forebears, did not accept what

A statue of St. Irenaeus of Lyons, found in Copenhagen, Denmark. Source: Wikimedia.

Tracing the Roots of Apostolic Tradition

The Gnostic claims plainly undermined Irenaeus' own episcopal authority and pedigree.[13] Benedict XVI highlights three distinguishing characteristics of Irenaeus' *genuine concept of the Apostolic Tradition:*[14]

they called '*your* Scriptures.' As Irenaeus himself put it, 'when they are refuted from the Scriptures, they turn round and accuse these same Scriptures, as if they were not correct or authoritative.' Orthodox Christianity and Gnosticism are two religions, with two different sets of Scriptures. The question is: which religion and which set of Scriptures goes back to the Apostles? It is this question, which is answered by Irenaeus' argument—and it is hard to see how it could be answered otherwise."

13 This term is used in ecclesiastical parlance as a reference to the manner by which an individual bishop, duly consecrated, is able to trace his episcopal lineage to one or more of the Apostles.

14 Benedict XVI, *The Fathers*, 27.

Apostolic is "public," not private or secret [...], the succession of bishops, the personal principle, and Apostolic Tradition, the doctrinal principle, coincide. b) Apostolic Tradition is "one." [...] whereas Gnosticism was divided into multiple sects [...] c) Lastly, the Apostolic Tradition as he says in the Greek language in which he wrote his book, is "pneumatic," in other words, spiritual, guided by the Holy Spirit: in Greek, the word for "spirit" is *pneuma*. Indeed, it is not a question of a transmission entrusted to the ability of more or less learned people, but to God's Spirit who guarantees fidelity to the transmission of the faith.[15]

Fragmentary Apologetics

Before we proceed to highlight aspects of Saint Irenaeus' apologetical writings against the Gnostic heretics, it would be worthwhile to mention the other fragmentary writings[16] that make up his patrimony to the Church.

First, we recall Irenaeus' *Letter to Pope Victor I* [17] to which we have already alluded and, in which, Irenaeus explained the position of the Eastern bishops regarding the proper date for the celebration of Easter.

Second, there is his work, *Demonstratio Praedicationis Apostolicae* (Demonstration of the Apostolic Preaching), of which we have only an Armenian translation of the original Greek. Thirdly, Irenaeus wrote two letters to a Roman priest by the name of Florian, who had fallen under the Gnostic spell and whom he sought to bring back to the one true fold of Christ's Church. Irenaeus responded to the Gnostics by writing a celebrated apologetical treatise in five volumes entitled *Adversus Haereses* (Against the Heresies).[18] This work is also referred to as *Against Those Falsely Called Gnostics*—a title aimed at debunking the sect's elitist claims to an occult archive of Divine Revelation.[19]

---

[15] Benedict XVI, *The Fathers*, 27-28 *passim*.

[16] Chadwick, *The Early Church*, 80: "Apart from fragments, two complete works from his pen have been preserved, though neither survives in his original Greek."

[17] Pope Victor I reigned from A.D. 189 to A.D. 199.

[18] Unfortunately, only an ancient third-century Latin version of Irenaeus' original Greek text has survived.

[19] Cf. Benedict XVI, *The Fathers*, 25: "As a writer, [Irenaeus] pursued a two-fold aim: to defend true doctrine from the attacks of heretics, and to explain the truth of the faith clearly. His two extant works—the five books of *The Detection and Overthrow of the False Gnostics and Demonstration of the Apostolic Preaching* (which can also be called the oldest 'catechism of Christian doctrine')—exactly corresponded with these aims."

Irenaeus' Theology

Irenaeus' theology demolishes the tenets of Gnostic revelation according to which material creation was to be despised and the Son of Man considered a mere demi-urge, a divine emanation or emissary inferior to the Father.

Irenaeus also refused to accept the Gnostics' view of revelation as secret knowledge. He was not in the least convinced that the Gnostics had obtained knowledge that provided them with a perfect means of achieving an immediate, mystical, and esoteric experience of God, to which only their intelligentsia could be privy.

Concerning the doctrine of the Holy Trinity, Saint Irenaeus writes:

> There is only one God the Father who is over all [...] and who is the head of Christ, the Word who is in every thing and is Himself the Head of the Church; the Holy Spirit who then is in all of us and who is the living water that the Lord offers to those who have right (orthodox) faith in Him.[20]

Regarding pneumatology[21] Irenaeus writes:

> Where there is the Church, there is also the Spirit of God; and where the Spirit of God is, there is the Church, and every kind of grace; but the Spirit is the truth.[22]

In terms of his Christian anthropology, a favorite citation of Irenaeus is: *Gloria Dei homo vivens; visio Dei, vita hominis* (The glory of God is man fully alive; the vision of God is the life of man). Man, so the Bishop of Lyons argues, is:

> the compendium of the works of God, of all His wisdom, and of all His truth.[23]

Irenaeus' Christocentric soteriology comes to light in this excerpt from *Adversus Haereses:*[24]

---

[20]   Irenaeus of Lyons, *Adversus Haereses* 5: 18, 2.
[21]   *Pneuma* is the Greek work for "spirit." Pneumatology is the technical term given to that branch of theology in which the Third Person of the Blessed Trinity, the Holy Spirit, is studied.
[22]   Irenaeus of Lyons, *Adversus Haereses*, 3: 25, 7.
[23]   Ibid., 3:20, 2.
[24]   Ibid.

Christ assumed a flesh similar to ours in order to condemn sin and, as the One condemned, to cast it out from human flesh. The goal of Christ had been likewise to propel man to be like unto Himself, making man to be an imitator of God and inserting him into the law of His Father, so that he might see God. The Word of God, who dwelt in man, in order to permit man to comprehend the Father, became the Son of Man to render man capable of understanding God and of becoming familiar with the God dwelling in him, according to the good will of the Father.

Leonardo da Vinci's famous depiction of the Last Supper.

We profit by reflecting on the Eucharistic faith of Saint Irenaeus:

> Vain in every respect are they who reject the entire dispensation of God, and deny the salvation of the flesh, and spurn its regeneration, saying that it is not capable of incorruption. But if this flesh is not saved, then neither did the Lord redeem us by His Blood, nor is the cup of the Eucharist the Communion of His Blood, or the bread that we break the Communion of His Body [...]. When, therefore, the cup that has been mixed and the bread that has been made receive the Word of God and become the Eucharist and the Body of Christ, from which the substance of our flesh is increased and supported, how can they affirm that the flesh is incapable of receiving the gift of God, which is life eternal, which flesh is nourished from the Body and Blood of the Lord and is a member of Him? [...]. And just as the vine planted in the ground fructifies in its season, and as a grain of wheat falling into the earth and decomposing rises with manifold

increase by the Spirit of God Who continues all things and then, through the wisdom of God, serves for the use of men, and having received the Word of God become the Eucharist, which is the Body and Blood of Christ: so also our bodies, having been nourished by this Eucharist and then placed in the earth and suffering decomposition there, shall rise at their time, the Word of God granting them resurrection unto the glory of God the Father.[25]

The Four Marks of the Church

Irenaeus' two most important works, *Demonstration of the Apostolic Preaching* and *Against the Heretics*, provide us with ample material concerning his understanding of the four marks of the Church. The unity of the Bible, comprised of the Old and New Testaments, is fundamental to his understanding of the unity of the Church against the various Gnostic sects that abounded in his time, the Gnostics being the principal proponents of the heresies he sought to confute.

Also, in response to the Gnostic heretics, Irenaeus defends the unity of the two natures (human and divine) in the one Person of Christ Jesus, for if Our Lord is divided then how can the Church claim that her unity flows from Him as Head of the Mystical Body?

The Bishop of Lyons affirms without hesitation that the unity of the Catholic Faith and the unity of the Church are interdependent. God, in His plan of salvation that includes all men, has purposely willed that this interdependency exist until at last all things will be "recapitulated" in Christ at the end of time.

In the meantime, the Church's structure is a visible reminder of the unity God the Father has willed for men in His Divine Son. Irenaeus believes that the Church of Rome is the lynchpin for the unity of all the other local churches in the Catholic Church. He sets out to prove apostolic succession in the See of Peter as a way of manifesting the superior catholicity of the Diocese of Rome. Union with Rome is a *sine qua non* for the Church to be manifestly her whole self, that is to say, one, holy, catholic, and apostolic.

A Papal Appraisal

Benedict XVI summarizes the theological contributions of Saint Irenaeus of Lyons:

---

[25] Irenaeus of Lyons, *Adversus Haereses*, 5: 2, 2-3.

Firmly rooted in the biblical doctrine of creation, Irenaeus refuted the Gnostic dualism and pessimism which debased corporeal realities. He decisively claimed the original holiness of matter, of the body, of the flesh no less than that of the spirit. But his work went far beyond the confutation of heresy: in fact, he emerges as the first great Church theologian who created systematic theology; he himself speaks of the system of theology—that is, of the internal coherence of all the faith. At the heart of his doctrine is the question of the "rule of faith" and its transmission. For Irenaeus the "rule of faith" coincided in practice with the *Apostles' Creed,* which gives us the key for interpreting the Gospel, for interpreting the Creed in the light of the Gospel. The Creed, which is a sort of Gospel synthesis, helps us understand what it means and how we should read the Gospel itself.[26]

Excursus: Irenaeus in the Liturgy of the Hours

The liturgical memorial of Saint Irenaeus of Lyons is celebrated on June 28. In the Liturgy of the Hours, the works of Irenaeus are cited fourteen times.

Here are examples of Irenaeus' work. This comparison of Eve and Mary is the topic of the Second Reading for Friday of the Second Week of Advent. In the Second Reading for the Wednesday of the Third Week of Advent, we read from Irenaeus' treatise, *Adversus Haereses* (4: 20, 4-5):

> There is one God, who by His word and wisdom created all things and set them in order. His Word is our Lord Jesus Christ, who in this last age became man among men to unite end and beginning, that is, man and God.

On December 19, during the Advent season, the Church has us read once again from Irenaeus' *Adversus Haereses* (3: 20, 2-3):

> God is man's glory. Man is the vessel which receives God's action and all his wisdom and power. Just as a doctor is judged in his care for the sick, so God is revealed in His conduct with men [...]. For this reason the Lord Himself gave as a sign of our salvation, the one who was born of the Virgin, Emmanuel.

In the Second Reading for Thursday of the First Week in Ordinary Time, Irenaeus teaches us:

---

[26] Benedict XVI, *The Fathers,* 26.

From the beginning the Son is present in creation, reveals the Father to all, to those the Father chooses, when the Father chooses, and as the Father chooses. So, there is in all and through all one God the Father, one Word and Son, and one Spirit, and one salvation for all who believe in Him.[27]

A most memorable line of Irenaeus is found in the Second Reading for Wednesday of the Fourth Week in Ordinary Time:

The Word of God became man, the Son of God became the Son of Man, in order to unite man with himself and make him, by adoption, a son of God.[28]

[27] Ibid., *Adversus Haereses*, 4:6, 3.5.6.7.
[28] Ibid., 3:19, 1-3, 20:1.

CHAPTER SEVENTEEN:
TERTULLIAN OF CARTHAGE
(A.D. C. 155 - 225)

Father of the Church Turned Schismatic

Quintus Septimus Florens Tertullianus, more commonly referred to as Tertullian,[1] was born in Carthage[2] in North Africa circa A.D. 155. His father was a centurion employed in proconsular service of the Roman Empire.

As a young man, Tertullian moved to the Eternal City to practice law. While in Rome, Tertullian's reputation as a skilled lawyer grew by leaps and bounds, soon making him one of the most sought-after attorneys in the whole Mediterranean world. In his late thirties, around A.D. 193, Tertullian converted from paganism to Catholic Christianity.

He soon decided to return to his native Carthage to render wholehearted service to Christ and the Church. A fiery personality and a highly intellectual convert, Tertullian exhibited, in his skillful writing and rhetoric, a great deal of intolerance not only toward pagans but also toward his fellow Christians who proved themselves unfaithful to the Gospel message, or even lukewarm; he judged that they lacked the type of Christian grit that Christ had demanded of all His disciples.[3]

---

[1] Cf. Benedict XVI, *The Fathers*, 46-50.

[2] Modern-day Tunis.

[3] Cf. Pelikan, *Jesus Through the Centuries*, 25: "The North African thinker Tertullian, the first important Christian writer to use Latin, may serve as an illustration of such a combination at the end of the second century. Warning his fellow believers against attending shows and spectacles of Roman society, Tertullian urged them to wait for the great day coming, when the victorious Christ would return in triumphal procession like a Roman conqueror and would lead in his train, as prisoners, the monarchs and governors who had persecuted His people, the philosophers and poets who had mocked His message, the actors and other 'ministers of sin' who had ridiculed 'His commandments.' 'And so,' he wrote elsewhere, 'we never march unarmed [...]. With prayer let us expect the angel's trumpet.' Yet this same Tertullian could declare, in response to the charge of treason against the Roman Empire: 'We also pray for the emperors, for their ministers and for all in authority, for the welfare of the world, for the prevalence of peace, for the *delay* of the final *consummation*.'"

Too Hard on Himself

Tertullian had a particularly hard time accepting the realities of apostasy and sexual immorality among his North African co-religionists. Eventually, Tertullian's pursuit of truth and integrity would lead him to condemn those who dared to call themselves Christians despite the fact that they had fallen into mortal sin after Baptism. Tertullian made a mass appeal for catharsis in the Church. His appeal, however, became a bit too radical when his vision of a "purer Church" translated into his joining a schismatic sect known as the Montanists.

The sect was founded by a man named Montanus, who claimed to have secret knowledge revealed to him directly by the Holy Spirit. This sect, which took root in North Africa, created a false dichotomy between the so-called "spiritual" or "charismatic" Church and the institutional Church represented by the hierarchy. The sect took particular aim at the bishops, the successors of the Apostles. Unfortunately, although Tertullian was often disillusioned by Montanism, he never reconciled with the Church, dying in schism around A.D. 220.[4]

The Epitome of Pithy Theology

Tertullian, unlike the other Pre-Nicene Fathers we have already examined, was not so keen on engaging pagan philosophy and culture in his apologetics. Tertullian vehemently expressed his opposition to such an inculturation of the Gospel with biting sarcasm and wit to dispel the very notion.[5]

Nonetheless, Tertullian often employed his sarcasm and wit to convey profound, albiet debatable, theological insights.[6] For example, in his work, *Concerning the Flesh of Christ*, Tertullian exults in the paradox of the Incarnation denied by the Gnostic heretics. Tertullian coins some classic theological expressions like:

---

[4] Cf. Benedict XVI, *The Fathers*, 49: "Rigid in his positions [Tertullian] did not withhold blunt criticism and he inevitably ended by finding himself isolated [...]. One sees that in the end he lacked the simplicity, the humility, to integrate himself with the Church, to accept weakness, to be forbearing with others and with himself."

[5] Tertullian once quipped as a way of setting the Christians apart from the pagans: "We share everything in common except our wives."

[6] Cf. Benedict XVI, *The Fathers*, 47: "The originality of [Tertullian's] thought, however, together with an incisive efficacy of language, assured him a high position in ancient Christian literature. His apologetical writings are above all the most famous. They manifest two key intentions: to refute the grave accusations that the pagans directed against the new religion; and, more propositional and missionary, to proclaim the Gospel message in dialogue with the culture of the time."

credo quia absurdum est (I believe because it is absurd) and *credo quia impossibile est* (I believe because it is impossible).

We discover other pithy expressions in Tertullian that help encapsulate his theology and spirituality. For instance, Tertullian says: *Sanguis Christi et Christianorum, medulla Scripturarum* (the blood of Christ and of Christians is the bone marrow of the Scriptures).

Regarding the apparent absurdity of Christian martyrdom at the hands of pagans, whom Tertullian directly derided as barbaric, inhuman, and godless, he boldly dares the pagans to kill the Christians, taunting them with his famous remark: *Semen est sanguis Christianorum* (The blood of Christians is [effective] seed).[7]

It was from the very early martyrs of Christian North Africa that Tertullian derived much of his own strength in bearing witness to Christ as a theologian and teacher.

A Great Rhetorician

Indeed, Tertullian may be considered the first great theologian of the Latin Church, being the first Christian writer to use Latin to compose theological treatises. Although he also wrote some treatises in Greek, the *lingua franca* of the Mediterranean basin, most of his writings were in Latin.

Jonathan Hill characterizes Tertullian as a lawyer who:

> expertly picked holes in the official [Roman] policy. If Christians really committed these crimes and deserved death, he sneered, why did the authorities adopt the "don't ask, don't tell" policy of Trajan?[8]

Patrick Hamel weighs the evidence for the literary claim that Tertullian was the finest of Latin theologians in his era. Some patristic scholars would argue that Tertullian was to the Latin Church what Origen was to the Eastern Church during the Pre-Nicene period. Other scholars claim that the bragging rights to best Latin theologian of the entire patristic period would have to go to either Tertullian or Augustine, even if simply based on literary genius.

Hamel makes strong arguments from all sides in Tertullian's favor:

---

7   Cf. Benedict XVI, *The Fathers*, 47. See also, Irenaeus of Lyons, *Apologeticus*, 50:13. Occasionally, this original expression of Tertullian is misquoted as: *sanguis Martyrum, semen Christianorum*, that is, "the blood of Martyrs is the seed of Christians."

8   Hill, *History of Christianity*, 55.

He is the most prolific of all the Latin writers, most original and personal. In no one else is Buffon's phrase, "the style is the man," more justified (Ebert)—he always spoke from the heart. His writings are (1) apologetic; (2) dogmatico-polemic; (3) practico-ascetical. The personal note is always present, whether he writes carried away with holy zeal that is harshly rigorous, or as a Montanist raging against the alleged laxity of the Catholic Church. A born controversialist, powerful adversary, eloquent and fiery, a man of biting satire and compact logic, he often overshoots the mark, writes without moderation, sweeps away opposition rather than convinces. His expression is bold, concise, rugged, involved; he does not bother with beauty of form—he is "daringly creative and suddenly enriches the Latin tongue." With Saint Augustine he is the greatest Western theologian. Western theology is in his debt for many technical terms. Indeed, in a certain sense, he created the clear language of Western theology.[9]

Tertullian: A Theological Giant

Although Tertullian expressed some extremist[10] and schismatic views, his theological prowess was demonstrated in a particular way in his ability to defend the Church's teaching against several Trinitarian and Christological heresies[11] stemming from the Gnostic views of Hermogenes,[12] Valentinus,[13] Marcion,[14]

---

[9] Patrick Hamell, *Handbook of Patrology* 70f.

[10] For instance, Tertullian did not accept the Church's doctrine of Mary's perpetual virginity, arguing that the brothers and sisters of Jesus mentioned in the Bible were born from the union of Mary and Joseph. Furthermore, Tertullian did not believe that Mary remained a virgin *in partu*, that is, "while giving birth" to the Christ-Child.

[11] For the Feast of the Apostles Philip and James (May 3), we read in the Liturgy of the Hours from Tertullian's *Prescription of Heretics* (20: 1-9, 21: 3; 22). Tertullian writes on the apostolicity of the local churches in communion with one another: "Every family has to be traced back to its origins. That is why we can say that all these great churches constitute that one original Church of the Apostles; for it is from them that they all come. They are all primitive, all apostolic, because they are all one. They bear witness to this unity by the peace in which they all live, the brotherhood which is their name, the fellowship to which they are pledged. The principle on which these associations are based is common tradition by which they share the same sacramental bond."

[12] Hermogenes was a Gnostic who held a dualist theory, contrary to the biblical doctrine of creation.

[13] Tertullian maintained, as Kelly explains, that "[Christ] entered into the Virgin, as the angel of the Annunciation foretold, and received His flesh from her (*Adversus Praxeam*, 26). The birth was a real one; He was born from her and not, as the Gnostic Valentinus alleged, simply through her, as if she were a mere channel through which He passed (cf. *De carne Christi*, 20: *Patrologia Latina* 2: 830-831)" (J.N.D. Kelly, *Early Christian Doctrines*, (Harper-Collins, 1991),150.

[14] Hubert Cunliffe-Jones gives Tertullian credit as a champion of orthodoxy: "Against Marcion

Adoration of the Name of God, *Goya 1772*.

Praxeas,[15] among others. Furthermore, his contribution to Trinitarian theology should not go unappreciated since he practically coined the terms by which the concept of Trinity as *una substantia, tres Personae* (one substance, three Persons) is understood in the West.

In considering Tertullian's Mariology, for example, one begins to appreciate even more his avid defense of an orthodox Christology, especially those truths concerning the reality of the Incarnation.[16]

Jones highlights Tertullian's efforts defending the goodness of creation, the reality of the Incarnation, and the efficacy of the sacramental system against Gnostic dualism. Furthermore, Jones illustrates how Tertullian's controversies with Praxeas and Marcion led him to formulate precise soteriological conclusions:

> Against Praxeas, it is the Son, distinct from the Father, Who became Man; against Marcion, the Son became fully Man, and did not assume a human disguise. Tertullian therefore asserts the scandalous paradox of the Incarnation with the utmost possible vigour. The subject of the human experience of Christ, the subject, indeed, of the Incarna-

and Valentinus he asserts the reality of Christ's birth. He did not simply appear as man without deriving actual humanity from Mary" [*A History of Christian Doctrine*, 60].

[15] Cf. Kelly, *Early Christian Doctrines*, 121, for some historical background concerning the identity of Praxeas and his theology.

[16] Cf. Benedict XVI, *The Fathers*, 48: "[Tertullian's] writings are important as they also show the practical trends in the Christian community regarding Mary Most Holy, the Sacrament of the Eucharist, matrimony and reconciliation, Petrine primacy, prayer [...]."

tion, is none other than the Son. "The Son of God was born; one is not ashamed to confess it, just because it is shameful. And the Son of God died; one can believe it, just because it is absurd. And he was buried and rose; it is certain, just because it was impossible" (cf. *De Carne Christi*, 17, 5). That is, God the Son Who lived and died is the essential truth on which Tertullian's soteriology depends; for like Irenaeus, he interprets the work of Christ for salvation as an interchange of places with mankind [*admirabile commercium*]: "God lived with man, so that man might be able to live with God; God became small so that man might become great" (cf. Mark 2:27).[17]

Jesuit Father Bertrand de Margerie lists and explains Tertullian's hermeneutical principles, among which are included the *regula fidei* (the rule of faith) and the principle of totality, by which was excluded any heretical attempt to interpret the whole Bible in the light of a few isolated sentences.[18]

These criteria of biblical interpretation helped Tertullian in his apologetical work against the Gnostics who relied on an exaggerated form of literary and/or allegorical interpretation to oppose orthodox beliefs.

Tertullian: Man of Head and Heart

The reader may benefit from a quick overview of some of Tertullian's other contributions to patristic theology and spirituality. In his treatise on prayer, the first of its kind in Christian literature (written between A.D. 198 and A.D. 200), Tertullian attests that the New Testament is a source of prayer surpassing anything in the Old Testament precisely because of God's singular nearness to man in Christ Jesus.

Let this brief excerpt serve as an example:

> Prayer is the offering in spirit that has done away with the sacrifices of old [...]. We are true worshippers and true priests. We pray in spirit and we offer in spirit the sacrifice of prayer. Prayer is an offering that belongs to God and is acceptable to Him: it is the offering He has asked for, the offering He planned as His own. We must dedicate this offering with our whole heart, we must fatten it on faith, tend it by truth, and keep it unblemished through innocence

---

[17] Jones, *A History of Christian Doctrine*, 58f.

[18] Bertrand de Margerie, S.J., *An Introduction to the History of Exegesis* [Volume 2: The Latin Fathers] (Saint Bede's Publications, 1991), 14.

and chastity, and crown it with love. We must escort it to the altar
of God in a procession of good works to the sounds of psalms and
hymns. Then it will gain for us all that we ask of God.[19]

Tertullian obviously valued the importance of the necessary ingredients that go
into making proper recourse to the Sacrament of Penance,[20] namely, a thorough
examination of conscience, sincere contrition (sorrow) for one's sins, confession, a firm purpose of amendment, absolution,[21] and the performance of a
suitable penance. It should be noted that the Sacrament of Penance has sometimes been sadly dubbed by contemporary theologians of East and West as "the
Lost (Forgotten) Sacrament" since an eroded sense of sin and of the sacred has
conspired to accelerate a decline in its use over the past several decades.

In his work *On Penance*, Tertullian offers the following observations concerning the attitude toward sin and confession in his own day as well as sound
advice, based on Gospel principles, on how to turn the tide in favor of God and
the salvation of souls:

Yet most men either shun confession, as being a public exposure of
themselves, or else defer it from day to day. I presume they do so
as being more mindful of modesty than of salvation; just like men
who, having contracted some malady in the more private parts of

---

[19]   Tertullian of Carthage, *De Oratione* (On Prayer), 28-29. The Church presents this text of
Tertullian "On Prayer," as the Second Reading of the Divine Office for Thursday of the
Third Week of Lent. Cf. Benedict XVI, *The Fathers*, 48.

[20]   The reader should recall that in the earliest centuries of the Church the Sacrament of
Penance was performed in public. Individual private confession, also known as auricular
confession, was only gradually introduced in the West due to the practice of the Irish monks
living in the ninth century. The sinner would be marked out as such by sackcloth and ashes,
following Old Testament custom. The penances incurred could be quite severe and last for
long periods before the sinner was officially reconciled with the Church. All sin was believed
to offend at one and the same time God Himself and the Church, the Mystical Body and
Spotless Bride of Christ.

[21]   Jaroslav Pelikan underscores the theology of the Cross and the forgiveness of sins: "But the
Gospel of the Cross pervades the New Testament and early Christian literature. Christ was
the 'Lamb of God who takes away the sins of the world' (John 1:29). The prophecy of the
fifty-third chapter of the Book of Isaiah about the suffering servant who was 'wounded for
our transgressions, bruised for our iniquities' was taken to refer to Jesus on the Cross. The
use of the Sign of the Cross, as a mark of identification and as a means of warding off the
power of demons, is not mentioned as such in the New Testament; but it appears very early
in Christian history, and when it is mentioned it is already being taken for granted. Tertullian declares that 'at every forward step and movement, at every going in and out [...] in all
the ordinary actions of daily life, we mark upon our foreheads the Sign,' and the Sign of the
Cross became the prime evidence for the existence of an unwritten tradition that everyone
observed even though it was not commended in the Bible" (*Jesus Through the Centuries*, 96).

the body, avoid the privity of physicians, and so perish with their own bashfulness. Truly you are honourable in your own modesty: bearing an open forehead for sinning, but an abashed one for deprecating! I give no place to bashfulness when I am a gainer by its loss; when itself in some sort exhorts the man, saying, *Respect not me; it is better that I perish through you than you through me* [...]. Grand indeed is the reward of modesty, which the concealment of our fault promises us! If we do hide something from the knowledge of man, shall we equally conceal it from God? Are the judgments of men and the knowledge of God so put on a par? Is it better to be damned in secret than absolved in public? *It is a hard thing thus to come to admit sins and confess them.* Hard, I grant; for evil does bring to misery; but where repentance is to be made, the misery ceases, because it is turned into something salutary. Miserable it is to be cut, and cauterized, and racked with the pungency of some medicinal powder. Still, the things which heal by unpleasant means do, by the benefit of the cure, excuse their own offensiveness, and make present injury bearable for the sake of the greater good we can enjoy in the future.[22]

In his apologetical letter addressed to Roman governors who in their provinces were presiding over mass and cruel persecutions of Christians, Tertullian offers one of the most memorable lines describing the essence of Christianity as contrasted to paganism, namely: "See those Christians, how they love one another."

In the context of this same apology, Tertullian, using admirable rhetorical devices, describes how the cruelty with which the pagan Romans treat Christians (whether doing so under the direction of hateful governors or subject to frenzied mob rule) clearly contrasts with the seemingly absurd charity, forgiveness and self-control exhibited by Christians in obedience to the example and teachings of Christ.

Tertullian had these scathing words for the merciless, evil powers during his time of upheaval, when morality and law in effect had very little to do with each other:

> Think about your own experiences. How often do you inflict gross cruelties on Christians, partly because it is your own inclination,

---

[22] *Tertullian of Carthage*, De Poenitentia (On Penance), 7: 4-10.

and partly in obedience to the laws! How often, too, the hostile mob, paying no regard to you, takes the law into its own hand, and assails us with stones and flames! With the frenzy of Bacchanalia,[23] they do not even spare the Christian dead, but tear them, now sadly changed, no longer entire, from the rest of the tomb, from the asylum we might say of death, cutting them to pieces, rendering them asunder. Yet banded together as we are—ever so ready to sacrifice our lives—what single case of revenge for injury are you able to point to, though, if we believed it right to repay evil with evil, a single night with a torch or two could achieve an ample vengeance? But away with the idea of a divine sect avenging itself by human fires, or shrieking from the sufferings in which it is tried [...].[24]

"What does Athens have to do with Jerusalem?"

While Tertullian does not reflect the Church's understanding of the proper relationship between theology and philosophy, between faith and reason, his remarks are fascinating since they are characteristically polemical:

> What indeed has Athens to do with Jerusalem? What concord is there between the Academy and the Church? What between heretics and Christians? Our instruction comes from the Portico of Solomon (cf. Acts 3:11), who had himself taught that the Lord should be sought in simplicity of heart (cf. Wisdom 1:1). Away with all attempts to produce a mottled Christianity of Stoic, Platonic, and dialectic composition! We want no curious disputation after possessing Christ Jesus, no inquisition after enjoying the Gospel! With our faith, we desire no further belief.[25]

The Rule of Faith

In conclusion, we rely on Tertullian's own recourse to the *rule of faith* (*regula fidei*) in defending Christian doctrine against the heretics:

> It is clear that all doctrine which agrees with the apostolic churches—those moulds and original sources of the faith—must be considered true, as undoubtedly containing what those churches received from the Apostles, the Apostles from Christ, Christ from God. And all

---

23 *Bacchanalia* is a term that refers to the celebrations held in ancient Rome in honor of the god Bacchus, considered the god of wine and revelry. This festival was usually held in the winter.

24 As cited in Aquilina, *The Fathers of the Church*, 90f.

25 Ibid.

doctrine must be considered false which contradicts the truth of the churches and Apostles of Christ and God.[26]

[26] Tertullian of Carthage's *Prescription [Against] the Heretics,* as cited in Hill's *History of Christianity,* 67.

CHAPTER EIGHTEEN:
CLEMENT OF ALEXANDRIA
(A.D. 150 - 215)

Knowledge of Christ is True Power

Although later called "the Alexandrian," Titus Flavius Clemens was born in Athens and died in Jerusalem. Since his parents were pagan, Clement of Alexandria's[1] early education was in pagan philosophy.

Once converted to Catholic Christianity, Clement, like Tertullian, believed that the claims of Gnostics to a secret knowledge were manifestly heretical. Unlike Tertullian, Clement did not consider the refutation of the Gnostic heresy to be a premise for mounting a full frontal assault against all pagan schools of thought and philosophy.[2]

Preparing for the Gospel

Clement believed that grains of truth could be found in certain pagan philosophies which serve as a *praeparatio evangelica* or "preparation for the Gospel."[3] For Clement, however, the true *"gnosis"* or "knowledge" was to be

---

[1] Cf. Benedict XVI, *The Fathers*, 30-34.

[2] A son of the Alexandrian school of theology whose underpinnings were more Platonic than those of the school at Antioch, Clement of Alexandria, like Origen and other early Fathers of the Church, manifested dualistic, Platonic tendencies (not to be confused with Gnostic dualism/docetism) in some areas of his thought. For instance, Clement applied a strict Greek notion of asceticism (e.g., Stoicism) to the mystery of the Incarnation which tended to deny that the God-Man possessed and exercised real human passions.

[3] Cf. Pelikan, *Jesus Through the Centuries*, 42f: "It was Clement of Alexandria who made the most effective and profound use of the image of Odysseus at the mast as a foreshadowing of Jesus. Circe's instructions to Odysseus and his band were two-fold: to avoid the allurements of the Sirens by stopping their ears and to tie Odysseus to the mast so that he alone would hear the call of the Sirens but would triumph over it. Both parts applied to Christian believers. They were to avoid sin and error 'as we would a dangerous headland, or the threatening Charybdis. Or the mythic Sirens' as Odysseus ordered his helmsman: 'You must keep her clear from where the smoke and the breakers are, and make hard for the sea rock lest, without you knowing, she might drift that way, and you bring all of us into disaster.' But they could do this because of Jesus, the Logos and Word of God, the Christian Odysseus:

fully identified only with the Gospel preached by the one, holy, catholic and apostolic Church.

Clement argued for a complementary relationship between *fides et ratio*, faith and reason. One does not need to make a grand leap of faith to conclude that Clement would have agreed with those later medieval scholastics, like Thomas Aquinas, who referred to theology as "The Queen of the Sciences" (*Regina Scientiarum*) and termed philosophy "The Handmaiden of Theology" (*Ancilla Theologiae*).

As head of the Catechetical School at Alexandria in Egypt, Clement taught that the only true and lasting knowledge was derived from a loving relationship with Christ, God's eternal "Wisdom" (*Sophia*) and "Word" (*Logos*) Incarnate.

Clement's Search for Divine Wisdom

Clement should also be acknowledged for his commitment to the defense of Christian tradition. He traveled far and wide to make sure that his teaching was rooted in the sources of the Apostolic Tradition. No superficial thinker, Clement's profound passion for the truth and authentic love of Christian wisdom[4] kept him in constant contact with the great Christian thinkers of his day who were handing on the teachings of the Apostles. Clement epitomized the meaning of the Latin adage: *discimus docendo* (we learn by teaching).[5]

'Sail past their music and leave it behind you, for it will bring about your death. But if you will, you can be the victor over the powers of destruction. Tied to the wood [of the Cross], you shall be freed from destruction. The Logos of God will be your pilot, and the Holy Spirit will bring you to anchor in the harbor of Heaven.' During the Byzantine period various Christian commentaries on both the *Iliad* and the *Odyessy* carried out this image and in the process helped to protect the ancient classics against the misplaced zeal of religious bigotry. And a fourth-century Christian sarcophagus, made of marble and now preserved in the Museo delle Terme in Rome shows Odysseus at the mast, which rises to the yardarm to form a cross. As a later Byzantine sermon was to put it, 'O man, do not fear the loudly roaring waves in the sea of this life. For the cross is the pattern of a strength that cannot be broken, so that you may nail your flesh to that unlimited reverence for the Crucified One and so with great pain arrive at the haven of rest.' The story of Odysseus at the mast became a permanent component of the Gentile 'types of Christ.'"

4 Our English word *philosophy* derives from the Greek word *philosophia*, meaning "love of wisdom."

5 Cf. Benedict XVI, *The Fathers*, 30: "From Athens [Clement] inherited that marked interest in philosophy that was to make him one of the pioneers of the dialogue between faith and reason in the Christian tradition. While he was still young, he arrived at Alexandria, the 'city-symbol' of that fertile junction between the different cultures that was a feature of the Hellenistic age. He was a disciple of Pantaenus until he succeeded him as head of the Catechetical School. Many sources testify he was ordained a priest."

Clement the Catechist

Origen of Alexandria, Clement's successor as head of the Catechetical School of Alexandria, found out as a young boy that Clement was a most admirable teacher, who displayed his broad intellectual abilities in his theological, spiritual, catechetical, philosophical and poetical writings.

With his students Clement shared his immense knowledge of philosophy and theology, and, in particular, his knowledge of Sacred Scripture, until he was forced to flee Alexandria during the severe persecutions of the Roman Emperor Septimius Severus.

Clement fled to Cappadocia in Asia Minor (modern-day Turkey) where he vigorously preached the Gospel. In the year 211, Clement stayed with his former disciple Alexander at Jerusalem. According to Eusebius' *Ecclesiastical History,* a letter of Alexander, Bishop of Jerusalem, to the churches at Antioch was sent through Clement.

In this letter Alexander commends Clement to the Antiochean Christians, recalling that Clement had successfully strengthened and given increase to his local church of Jerusalem. In this regard the bishops of the Catholic Church, as well as her priests, can learn how to express their solicitude for all the churches;[6] to contribute to the general edification of the Church as true churchmen who shun being identified as mere functionaries, CEOs, or members of an exclusive club; and to foster genuine fraternity among their ranks, a fraternity rooted in a single-minded love of Christ the High Priest and Head of the Mystical Body, the Church.

A Christian Trilogy

Clement can be credited with having written the first treatise of Christian theology, or one could say that he wrote a treatise that served as the first *Introduction to Christianity.*[7] He produced three important works that can be considered a sort of trilogy: the *Protreptikos,* the *Paidagogos,* and the *Stromata.*

---

[6]   The Latin expression is *sollicitudo omnium ecclesiarum,* first used by St. Paul and promoted by the Second Vatican Council, the Magisterium of Pope John Paul II, and that of Benedict XVI.

[7]   Joseph Ratzinger, later Benedict XVI, wrote a work of the same title in 1963.

Part One

The *Protreptikos* (which means a book designed to exhort and to convert) is, in effect, Clement's appeal to pagans to accept his proofs of the false teachings of pagan philosophies and religions that they might accept the invitation to follow Christ, the surest way to true contemplation of God. Clement's appeal to pagans is one of urgency with respect to the Gospel.

Perhaps here we would do well to recall the stirring words of Pope Benedict XVI's homily delivered on the occasion of his inauguration as Supreme Pontiff on April 24, 2005:

> How often we wish that God would show Himself stronger, that He would strike decisively, defeating evil and creating a better world. All ideologies of power justify themselves in exactly this way; they justify the destruction of whatever would stand in the way of progress and the liberation of humanity. We suffer on account of God's patience. And yet, we need His patience. God, who became a lamb, tells us that the world is saved by the Crucified One, not by those who crucified Him. The world is redeemed by the patience of God. It is destroyed by the impatience of man.

Part Two

The *Paidagogos*, which is essentially a treatise on moral theology, underscores Our Lord's role as the supreme teacher of truth. In this work,[8] Clement addresses catechumens and all Christians on how to comport themselves in a distinctly Christian manner, while still living in a predominantly pagan society oftentimes hostile to the Christian message and mores. For example, Clement instructs his audience on how to cultivate the virtues of modesty, prudence and temperance in using the public baths, in attending banquets, in conversation, and in dress.

He also reflects on the nature of Christian conjugal love with regard to chastity, a virtue which many people in our contemporary society are tempted to identify solely as a virtue of celibates. Against the Gnostics, who claimed that human nature had become utterly corrupt, Clement strongly affirms the goodness of human sexuality even after the Fall of Adam and Eve.

---

[8]   In some respect, Clement's *Paidagogos* can be considered a forerunner of St. Augustine of Hippo's masterly work *De Magistro* ("On the Teacher"). In this work, Augustine engages in a dialogue with his illegitimate son Adeodatus (Latin: "given by God") about the central role that the Lord Jesus plays in the instruction of the Christian mind and soul as to the nature of divine wisdom that both fulfills and yet surpasses the wisdom of the Hebrew prophets and pagan philosophers.

The Alexandrian did concede, however, that after the Fall Adam's and Eve's wills and rationality were so weakened and their passions so severely debilitated that they were all the more prone, as are we, to give in to lustful temptations. Hence, the necessity of safeguarding one's chastity at all times.

Part Three

The *Stromata*, a Greek word which means "tapestries," is a treatise that is woven out of the seamless garment of Christian doctrines that Clement compares and contrasts to pagan beliefs in such a way that the relation between faith and reason is more clearly delineated and likewise the profile of an ideal Christian in which there can be no hypocrisy, duplicity or dichotomy between what one believes and how one applies those same beliefs to the various sectors of one's life, public and private.

Clement's teaching in the *Stromata* finds an echo in the *Protreptikos*, where he states:

> The condition for following Christ is this: whatever our proposals be
> so too our discourses, whatever our discourses be so too our actions,
> and whatever our works be so too our life.[9]

Wealth and Christians

In a treatise known by the Latin title *Quis dives salvetur?* (What rich man can be saved?), Clement remarks about the right and wrong uses of riches from a Christian perspective. Of course, we know that money, like eating, drinking and sleeping, has neutral moral value in and of itself.[10] However, if one is spending beyond his means, if one is a glutton, a drunkard or slothful, then these actions acquire a negative moral value. Clement would argue, much in line with the thought of Aristotle and of Saint Thomas Aquinas later, that *virtue stands in the middle*,[11] that vice is the extreme to be avoided at all costs.[12]

Clement's Doctrine

What are some other examples of Saint Clement's teachings?

He insists that the Catholic Church safeguards Sacred Tradition, what Tertullian had referred to as the *Regula Fidei* (The Rule of Faith). In other words,

---

[9]   Clement of Alexandria, *Protreptikos*, 12.
[10]   Cf. Clement of Alexandria, *Quis dives salvetur?*, 15.
[11]   Latin: *In medio stat virtus*.
[12]   Cf. *Protreptikos*, 4.

The Annunciation, *a mosaic by Pietro Cavallini, dated 1291. Source: Wikimedia.*

the Church teaches not a mere human science or knowledge, but the very science and knowledge of God entrusted in a particular way to the care of Saint Peter, whom Clement describes as:

> the chosen one, the excellent one, the first of the disciples, for whom alone, except for Himself, Our Lord paid the tribute.[13]

In the *Paidagogos,* Clement identifies his belief in the Most Holy Trinity, God: *one in nature and three in Persons.*[14]

Hippolytus broke from communion with Pope Callistus on disciplinary matters even though they agreed firmly on doctrinal matters, such as the condemnation of Sabellius and the heresy he helped spearhead, namely, Monarchianism, which held that the Son and the Spirit were inferior or subordinate to the monarchy of the Father.

The Triune Godhead has certain attributes or perfections, such as eternity, goodness and the desire to save all mankind.[15] To this effect, the Catechism of the Catholic Church cites Clement of Alexandria:

---

[13]   *Quis dives salvetur?*, 21.
[14]   *Paidagogos*, 1: 2.
[15]   Ibid., 1: 9.

Just as God's will is creation and is called "the world," so his intention is the salvation of men, and it is called "the Church."[16]

As regards the Second Person of the Trinity, Saint Clement writes that the Son of God is: The Word, who became Incarnate in order to free us from our sins.[17] Furthermore, Clement reflects on the Incarnation in relation to Christ as our teacher, our pedagogue *par excellence*.[18]

Both of these reasons for the Incarnation are explained in the Catechism:

> The Word became flesh for us in order to save us by reconciling us with God, who "loved us and sent His Son to be the expiation of our sins"[19] [...]. The Word became flesh so that thus we might know God's love: "In this the love of God was made manifest among us, that God sent His only Son into the world, so that we might live through Him."[20]

For Clement of Alexandria, the Church's belief in the Holy Spirit, the Third Person of the Blessed Trinity, assures us of three key doctrines, namely, that we have free will,[21] that we need grace,[22] and that we should hope in the resurrection of the body on the Last Day.[23]

In emphasizing unity as one of the four distinguishing marks of the Church, Clement writes with much enthusiasm:

> What an astonishing mystery! There is one Father of the universe, one Logos of the universe, and also one Holy Spirit, everywhere one and the same; there is also one virgin become mother, and I should like to call her "Church."[24]

Clement explains that this virgin mother feeds her children with the holy milk of the one Logos.[25] In the *Paidagogos*[26] Clement speaks of Baptism[27] as:

---

16 Ibid., 1: 6, 2. See CCC, 760.

17 *Protreptikos*, 11.

18 *Paidagogos*, 1, 6.

19 CCC, 457.

20 Ibid., 458.

21 *Protreptikos*, 11.

22 Clement of Alexandria, *Stromata*, 2:4.

23 *Paidagogos*, 1: 4.

24 Ibid., 1: 6, 42 as cited in CCC, 813.

25 Cf. Kelly, *Early Christian Doctrines*, 201.

26 Clement of Alexandria, *Paidagogos*, 16, 26.

27 Cf. Benedict XVI, *The Fathers*, 31: "[...] Clement's catecheses accompanied the catechumens and the baptized step by step on their way, so that with the two 'wings' of faith and reason they

imparting regeneration, enlightenment, divine sonship, immortality, remission of sins; the sonship, he explains, is the result of the regeneration worked by the Spirit.[28]

Regarding the Sacrament of the Holy Eucharist, Clement teaches that:

to drink of Jesus' blood [. . .] is to participate in Jesus' incorruptibility.[29]

Clement and Cosmetics

An adage asserts that beauty is in the eye of the beholder. Clement had a more objective view of beauty rooted not merely in his Platonic idealism but in the concrete love he bore Our Incarnate Savior, who is the most beautiful among the sons of Adam. Concerning the topic of true beauty, Clement helped to encapsulate the teaching of the Wisdom literature of the Bible (e.g., Proverbs, Sirach) in the phrase:

Man looks at the eyes but God looks at the heart.[30]

Furthermore, Clement writes:

It is not so much the exterior aspect of man that needs to be beautified but rather the soul[31] that needs to be made beautiful with the ornamentation of goodness. One could also add that the body must be embellished with the virtue of temperance.[32]

Do Not Be Afraid

Clement offers us the following encouragement as we seek God during our pilgrimage of faith:

No impediment opposes him who tends toward the knowledge of God, not the lack of instruction, not poverty, not the obscurity of one's name, not misery [. . .]. A splendid hymn to God is immortal man, built upon justice, in whom the words of truth have been inscribed.[33]

---

might reach intimate knowledge of the Truth which is Jesus Christ, the Word of God."

[28]   *Paidagogos*, 207.

[29]   Ibid., 213.

[30]   Ibid., 3: 2.

[31]   Cf. Pelikan, *Jesus Through the Centuries*, 44: "[. . .] quoting the Book of Psalms and Plato's *Republic* on the Final Judgment, Clement could conclude, 'It follows this that the soul is immortal,' a doctrine on which Scripture and philosophy were agreed."

[32]   *Protreptikos*, 10.

[33]   Ibid.

Using striking common-sense analogies, Clement succeeds in upholding the virtue of fraternal correction when he explains:

> Just as the mirror is not evil with the man who is ugly, since it shows him what he is, and as the physician is not evil with the sick person when he tells him that he has a fever, so no one who admonishes, desires evil for the person who is sick in the soul. In fact he who admonishes does not put extra sins onto that person, but rather he shows him the sins he already has, so that he might distance himself from that bad behavior.[34]

The reader familiar with Saint Augustine's masterpiece, *De Civitate Dei* (The City of God), in which he contrasts the eternal values of the City of God and the temporal values of the City of Man, may find a prophetic voice in Clement's discussion of the "two persecutions" that he sees at work in the City of Man.

In *Quis dives salvetur?* Clement, relying on excellent theological, spiritual, and psychological insights, offers the following advice or spiritual direction:

> Persecution befalls us from outside forces when men persecute the faithful whether because they are considered enemies, or because they are envious, or because their goal is one of personal gain, or because they have received a diabolical suggestion; but another and much worse persecution is born from within the soul of someone who has been corrupted by impious and lustful desires, by evil hopes and vain fantasies. This last persecution is quite grave and ruinous, because it erupts from within and gives no respite; he who suffers from it cannot free himself from it since he carries the enemy within himself wherever he goes. The test that comes from outside can help to tone a person, but the one that rises up from within is a bearer of death and can lead one to despair of salvation and to despise God. If you suffer from this persecution, turn to the Gospel and to the Lord, patron and comfort of your soul, who will give you a life that will have no end. If you have sinful belongings or ties, free yourself from them and procure peace for yourself. The things that you see are temporal; eternal instead are those that are not seen; the first are destined to perish, nor do those things give any support to you if they are sustained; instead in the future eternal life is stored up for you.

---

[34] *Paidagogos*, 1, 9.

Wrestling with God

Clement, then, makes us wise to the true nature of the eternal life that is the ultimate goal of the Christian life, which should be comprised of prayerful vigilance and a type of ongoing spiritual struggle with Almighty God reminiscent of Jacob's wrestling with an angel that proves one's ardor and fervor, one's "desire for God" (*desiderium Dei*). Man is not only "capable of union with God" by nature (*capax Dei*), but also through his arduous "work" (*homo faber*) in fighting the good fight of the faith, in "running out the course" of his eternal salvation to the finish line (*homo viator*). He can, with the help of God's grace, make a bold claim to his heavenly inheritance. Clement comments thus:

> The Kingdom of Heaven does not belong to the one who sleeps nor to the one who lives sluggishly, but it belongs to violent men who are successful in taking possession of it. This is the only violence that can be considered good: to force God to decide and to steal from God eternal life. God enjoys being conquered in this contest; He indeed helps souls with such valor.[35]

---

[35] *Quis dives salvetur?*, 21.

CHAPTER NINETEEN:
ORIGEN OF ALEXANDRIA

(A.D. 185 - 254)

"Man of Steel," "Biblical Maestro"

Origen of Alexandria had a tendency to go to extremes his whole life long. Having interpreted literally Jesus' teaching in Matthew 19:12, *There are eunuchs who have made themselves eunuchs for the sake of the kingdom of heaven*,[1] Origen is believed to have castrated himself.[2]

When Origen was just seventeen he enthusiastically sought out martyrdom, in imitation of his father, Leonides,[3] who had been martyred during the persecutions of the Emperor Septimius Severus. Much later, during the reign of the Emperor Decius, Origen underwent the cruelest of tortures and eventually died

---

[1] The discipline of priestly celibacy is based on Matthew 19:12 and several other texts like Matthew 19:27-29; Luke 18:29-30; 1 Corinthians 7:7-9, 27, 29, 32-35, 38.

[2] See. John McGuckin's article "A Christian Philosophy: Origen," in Hill, *History of Christianity*, 67: "It was a story reported a century after his death by Eusebius, bishop of Caesarea, but it is highly unlikely, as Origen himself speaks of those who interpret the Gospel text on castration (Matthew 19:12) in a literal way as little better than fools[...]. A text, therefore, had several layers of meaning. For Origen, those who stayed only with the literal meaning of the biblical text were unenlightened souls who had not realized that Jesus gave some of His teaching in the valleys and some on mountain tops. Only to the latter disciples, those who could ascend the mountains, did Jesus reveal Himself transfigured (see Mark 9)." It was also rumored that the priests of Origen's time questioned the validity of his priestly ordination because of his castration. According to a long-standing tradition castration is an impediment to valid priestly ordination. In the Middle Ages, a man, upon being elected pope, had to be examined to make sure that he had all the proper male sexual organs. Otherwise, he could not be legitimately confirmed as pope, so much, therefore, for the medieval legend of the female Pope Joan.

[3] Cf. Benedict XVI, *The Fathers*, 35f: "[Origen's] whole life was pervaded by a ceaseless longing for martyrdom. He was seventeen years old when, in the tenth year of the reign of the Emperor Septimius Severus, the persecution against Christians was unleashed in Alexandria. Clement, his teacher, fled the city, and Origen's father, Leonides, was thrown into prison. His son longed ardently for martyrdom but was unable to realize his dream. So he wrote to his father, urging him not to shrink from the supreme witness of faith. And when Leonides was beheaded, the young Origen felt bound to welcome the example of his father's life."

from his wounds, a death akin to that of a martyr[4] in fulfillment of his life-long wish.[5] Origen died at the age of sixty-nine, in the ancient Phoenician city of Tyre, located on the Mediterranean Coast near the border between modern-day Israel and Lebanon.

Origen's fame as a learned and holy man had spread so far and wide that his grave became an automatic pilgrimage site among the early Christians for centuries following his death.

Man of Steel

As a result of Origen's tenacity, even in the face of the worst tortures, Eusebius of Caesarea nicknamed Origen *Adamantius* or "man of steel" in his *Ecclesiastical History*. The story is told that when the Roman soldiers were arresting Origen's father and confiscating the family property, his mother deliberately hid Origen's clothes so that he would not run outside in order to join his father in martyrdom.[6]

Other examples of his extremism could be pinpointed in his having accepted priestly ordination from two wandering bishops without his bishop's consent, and in his having speculated on some heretical beliefs. Certainly, one could argue quite reasonably that since Origen believed himself to be a loyal son of the Church, feeling with the Church[7] on matters of faith and morals, that his skewed speculative notions only constituted material and not formal heresy (since these matters were not yet formally defined).

The difference between a material and formal heretic can be explained thus: A material heretic is one who teaches heresy perhaps unwittingly, that is to say,

---

[4]   The English word "martyr" derives from the Greek word for "witness." The martyrs bear supreme witness to Christ *usque ad effusionem sanguinis*, ("to the point of shedding their blood.") Cardinals wear scarlet red because they make a promise to shed their blood for the Pope, if required.

[5]   While Origen was imprisoned, he wrote letters (no longer extant), in which he spells out his ardor for the Christian Faith and his willingness to bear witness to Christ with the courage of a martyr. Cardinal Newman once wrote: "Many a man will live and die upon a dogma: no man will be a martyr for a conclusion" (Section 6 of the "Tamworth Reading Room," *Discussions and Arguments*).

[6]   A more mature Origen reflects on martyrdom in his Commentary on the Gospel of John (28:18): "For our persecutors who have not yet shed our blood, we do not want to be occasions of sin so that they might become even more impious. For this reason we avoid them, as much as we can. If we were to do the opposite they would bear an even greater fault and a harsher punishment whenever we, in our egoism, would have thought only about our own advantage and we would have let ourselves be killed even when it would not have been strictly necessary."

[7]   This expression derives from the Latin saying *sentire cum ecclesia*.

without the intention of being a heretic. A formal heretic, on the other hand, is one who not only teaches heresy but also deliberately chooses to be identified as such in clear opposition to the legitimate authority and disciplinary action of the Church.

Among Origen's heretical notions were his acceptance of Plato's theory that the soul preexists the body, allowing for man to be born with innate knowledge from the world of ideas, and that on the Last Day hell will be completely emptied because the infinite love of God would not permit a single creature, not even Satan and his fallen angels, to be eternally damned or definitively excluded from the recapitulation of all things in Christ enunciated in the teachings of Saint Paul.

Biblical Maestro

So, what did Origen get right? Given what we have already mentioned about Origen, we can say firstly that Origen's desire for martyrdom, while a bit extreme, was nonetheless most admirable. Secondly, we cannot but relish the tremendous contributions Origen made to the fields of systematic theology and to the study of Sacred Scripture. Indeed, some scholars refer to Origen as the father of both of these branches of sacred theology.

Pope Benedict offers several valid reasons why Origen was a brilliant scripturist:

> Theology to [Origen] was essentially explaining, understanding Scripture; or we might say that his theology was a perfect symbiosis between theology and exegesis [...]. The central nucleus of Origen's immense literary output consists in his "threefold interpretation" of the Bible [...]. First of all, he read the Bible, determined to do his utmost to ascertain the biblical text and offer the most reliable version of it [...]. Secondly, Origen read the Bible systematically in his famous Commentaries. They reproduced faithfully the explanations that the teacher offered during his lessons at Alexandria and Caesarea. Origen proceeded verse by verse with a detailed, broad, and analytical approach, with philosophical and doctrinal notes. He worked with great precision in order to know completely what the sacred authors meant. Lastly, even before his ordination to the priesthood, Origen was deeply dedicated to preaching the Bible and adapted himself to a varied public. In any case, the teacher can also be perceived in his Homilies, wholly dedicated as he was to the systematic interpretation of the passage under examination, which he analyzed step by step in

the sequence of the verses. Also in his Homilies Origen took every opportunity to recall the different dimensions of the sense of Sacred Scripture that encourage or express a process of growth in the faith: there is the "literal" sense, but this conceals depths that are not immediately apparent. The second dimension is the "moral" sense: what we must do in living the Word; and finally, the "spiritual" sense, the unity of Scripture which throughout its development speaks of Christ. It is the Holy Spirit who enables us to understand the Christological content; hence, the unity in the diversity of Scripture.[8]

Origen the Teacher

Origen had an outstanding reputation as a teacher, so much so that the Roman Emperor's mother took him as a tutor, as did the Roman governor of Arabia and the bishops of Palestine.[9]

According to the historical recollections of Saint Epiphanius of Salamis, Origen was a most prolific writer, with a corpus of more than six thousand writings, including at least one hundred letters (regrettably, we have only a small portion of his entire literary output extant).[10] He was able to accomplish this amazing feat due in part to the generous benefaction of one of his former students, a wealthy man who had been persuaded by Origen to recant a particular heresy. As a result, the wealthy "revert" to Catholic Christianity supplied Origen with seven full-time stenographer-secretaries.[11]

With his own father off to receive the crown of red or bloody martyrdom, Origen took it upon himself to support his mother and several younger brothers and sisters by teaching. Already by the age of eighteen, only a year after his father's arrest, Origen was a renowned teacher, attracting numerous students from all over the Egyptian capital of Alexandria.

---

[8]   Benedict XVI, *The Fathers*, 36-39 *passim*.

[9]   See John McGuckin's article, "A Christian Philosophy: Origen," in Hill, *The History of Christianity*, 67: "In AD 212 Origen travelled to Rome and heard the theologian Hippolytus lecture. It was the first of many tours and book-buying expeditions. He began to receive government invitations to present philosophical discourses, and his fame as a thinker extended far beyond Christian circles, making him the first truly international philosopher the Christian movement could boast of."

[10] Cf. Benedict XVI, *The Fathers*, 37: "St. Jerome, in his Epistle 33, lists the titles of 320 books and 310 homilies by Origen. Unfortunately, most of these works have been lost, but even the few that remain make him the most prolific author of Christianity's first three centuries. His field of interest extended from exegesis to dogma, to philosophy, apologetics and ascetical theology. It was a fundamental and global vision of Christian life."

[11] Cf. Aquilina, *The Fathers of the Church*, 105-106 *passim*.

When Clement of Alexandria fled from Roman persecution, Origen, still in his teens, was appointed by Demetrius Bishop of Alexandria, director of the catechetical school at Alexandria, which was considered to be the most prestigious Christian educational institution in the world at the time.

One of Origen's most famous pupils was the Father of the Church, Saint Gregory of Pontus, also called "the Wonder-Worker." During the early part of his life, Origen traveled around the whole basin of the Mediterranean Sea from his natal city of Alexandria to the Eternal City of Rome, from Greece to Palestine, then on to the Arabian Desert—evangelizing and uprooting heresy.

Origen in Love with the Church

Thus, Origen proved his predilection for the Church as the "Body of Christ" while exhorting us, for example, in his *Commentary on Psalm* 31, obviously read in light of Matthew 25:31-46: "Christ assumes all of us into Himself: and He Himself says, that in us He suffers hunger, that He has thirst in us, that in us He is nude and sick, a guest and one who is imprisoned; and He says that whatsoever would have been done to one of His disciples would have been done to Him."

Along these same lines, Origen's ecclesiology, focused on the real unity of Christ as Head with the members of His Mystical Body, the Church, affords us this bit of common-sense observation:

If one part of our body hurts us [...], no one says: "I'm well but my stomach hurts me," rather [he says] "I'm not well, because my stomach hurts me."

A Traveling Evangelist

In 231, Origen settled for twenty years in the city of Caesarea in Palestine. The Bishop of Caesarea asked Origen to found a school of theology, but this did not inhibit Origen from continuing his journeys of evangelization to Antioch (Syria) and Arabia. One example of Origen's successful efforts at evangelization is related to his having brought back to the Catholic fold a bishop by the name of Beryllus of Bostia, who had espoused the heresy known as Patripassionism, which holds that the Father underwent suffering, and therefore change, as His Son died on the cross.[12]

---

[12] Cf. Russell, *Glimpses of the Church Fathers*, 77f.

Allegorical Musings

The school of theology at Alexandria, as has already been mentioned, tended to lend its support to allegorical interpretations of Holy Writ, with a focus on the divinity of Christ.[13] This tendency to overemphasize the allegorical sense of Sacred Scripture can be attributed in part to the influence that Philo of Alexandria had on Christian biblical studies. Philo was a Platonist and a Greek-speaking Jew of the Alexandrian Diaspora living in the first century A.D., who favored the allegorical sense in his interpretation of the Old Testament.

This is not to say that the Alexandrian school, to which Clement and Origen belonged, did not accept the literal sense. Rather, the Alexandrians accepted the allegorical sense of the Bible as a subdivision of the spiritual sense that was often barely distinguishable in their interpretation from the literal sense of the Bible.

Thus, the Alexandrians had a knack for interpreting a single pericope or passage of the Bible as encompassing both the literal sense and the spiritual sense with all its subdivisions, namely, the allegorical sense, the moral sense and the anagogical sense (from the Greek word *anagogein,* meaning "leading toward" Heaven).[14]

Here we must add that the allegorical sense usually included texts that are deemed Christological or Messianic prophecies, as well as other texts that have to do with typology.[15] J.N.D. Kelly explains and illustrates Origen's exegetical methodology:

---

[13] In reference to the Eucharistic Sacrifice as the new Passover of the Lord, Origen writes allegorically: "The Passover still takes place today, [...] and those who sacrifice Christ come out of Egypt, cross the Red Sea, and see Pharaoh engulfed." cf. Wilken, *The Spirit of Early Christian Thought*, 34.

[14] Cf. Benedict XVI, *The Fathers*, 39: "[...] In the ninth *Homily on Numbers* [Origen] likens Scripture to [fresh] walnuts: 'The doctrine of the Law and the Prophets at the school of Christ is like this,' the homilist says; 'the letter is bitter, like the [green-covered] skin; secondly, you will come to the shell, which is the moral doctrine; thirdly, you will discover the meaning of the mysteries, with which the souls of the saints are nourished in the present life and the future."

[15] Cf. Benedict XVI, *The Fathers*, 44-45 *passim*: "[...] in [Origen's] ninth *Homily on Leviticus*, he alludes to the 'fire for the holocaust,' that is, to faith and knowledge of the Scriptures which must never be extinguished on the altar of the person who exercises the priesthood. He then adds: 'But each one of us has within him' not only the fire; he 'also has the holocaust and from this holocaust lights the altar so that it may burn for ever.' If I renounce all my possessions, take up my cross and follow Christ, I offer my holocaust on the altar of God; and if I give up my body to be burned with love and achieve the glory of martyrdom, I offer my holocaust on the altar of God."

An admirer of Philo, he regarded Scripture as a vast ocean, or (using a different image) forest, of mysteries; it was impossible to fathom, or even perceive, them all, but one could be sure that every line, even every word, the sacred authors wrote was replete with meaning. Formally he distinguished three levels of signification in Scripture, corresponding to the three parts of which human nature is composed: the bodily, the psychic and the spiritual. The first was the straightforward historical sense, and was useful for simple people; the second was the moral sense, or the lesson of the text for the will; the third was the mystical sense with relation to Christ, the Church or the great truths of the faith. In practice Origen seems to have employed a slightly different triple classification, comprising (a) the plain historical sense, (b) the typological sense, and (c) the spiritual sense in which the text may be applied to the devout soul. Thus when the Psalmist cries (3, 4), "Thou, O Lord, art my support, my glory, and the lifter up of my head," he explains that it is in the first place David who speaks; but, secondly, it is Christ, who knows in His Passion that God will vindicate Him; and thirdly, it is every just soul who, by union with Christ, finds His glory in God.[16]

Origen the Exegete

Some consider Origen the Church's first true exegete or interpreter of the Bible insofar as he applied himself rigorously to the study of the original languages (e.g., Hebrew and Greek) long before Saint Jerome produced the Latin Vulgate in the fifth century; Origen utilized his in-depth knowledge of linguistic morphology and etymology in a painstaking word-for-word study of the individual books; he compiled the first critical edition of the Bible known as the *Hexapla* (because it consisted of "six" parallel columns) in which Origen wrote respectively the original Hebrew text without vowels, the Hebrew text transliterated into Greek letters to fix and facilitate pronunciation, followed by

---

[16] Kelly, *Early Christian Doctrines*, 73. Cf. Benedict XVI, *The Fathers*, 41-42 *passim*: "[Origen] was convinced that the best way to become acquainted with God is through love, and there is no authentic *scientia Christi* ("knowledge of Christ") without falling in love with Him [...]. In his Letter to Gregory, Origen recommends, 'while you attend to this *lectio divina*, seek aright and with unwavering faith in God the hidden sense which is present in most passages of the divine Scriptures. And do not be content with knocking and seeking, for what is absolutely necessary for understanding divine things is *oratio* ("prayer"), and in urging us to this the Savior says not only 'knock and it will be opened to you,' and 'seek and you will find,' but also 'ask and it will be given you [...].' Just as the man [Adam] and the woman [Eve] are 'two in one flesh,' so God and the believer become 'two in one spirit.' The prayer of the Alexandrian thus attained the loftiest level of mysticism, as is attested to by his Homilies on the Song of Songs.'"

four popular translations (namely, those of Aquila,[17] Symmachos, the Septuagint and Theodotion). He is also credited with having discovered two translations of the Psalms by anonymous scholars.

The historian Hans Lietzmann in his two-volume work, *A History of the Early Church*, offers the following estimation of Origen as a biblical scholar:

> Anyone who seeks to understand Origen's heart must watch him as a Bible student. It was in the Bible and here alone, that the way to knowledge opened out for a Christian; here spoke the Lord through His Holy Spirit to the spirit which had taken up a dwelling in man: and, without the revelation of the Logos, it was simply impossible to enter into God's presence. Origen used to lift his hands in prayer when he was struggling to find a right meaning, and he felt the kiss of the lips of the Logos when a divine secret was revealed to him apart from worldly learning; but he always worked on the basis of academic principles and, as is shown by the case of the *Hexapla,* he carried out serious philological work in a most extensive measure, and developed a method of allegorical exegesis carefully thought out, and based on the Alexandrian tradition. His commentary on the Gospel of John proves how his methods of work could maintain their place in the face of the Gnostic methods of Herakleon the Valentinian. His work became the model for Biblical exegesis as practiced in the entire Greek Church. Copied out and imitated, it held good from century to century, long after his theology had been condemned. His Bible commentaries still reveal, therefore, many aspects of his religious life and theological thought, aspects re-appearing in his principal, systematic works [. . .].[18]

---

[17] Cf. Chadwick, *The Early Church*, 102: "[. . .] Aquila, a Gentile who, after becoming a Christian for a time, became a proselyte to Judaism about 140 produced a version [translation of the Bible] which took literalism to fanatical ends."

[18] Lietzmann, *A History of the Early Church* [Volume 1], 581-582 *passim*.

Excursus: Origen of Alexandria in the Liturgy of the Hours

Origen's writings are found in the Office of Readings on eight occasions.

For Tuesday of the Fifth Week in Ordinary Time we read from Origen's eighth homily on Genesis: "[...] *And Abraham, looking about him, saw a ram caught by the horns in a bush.* We said before that Isaac is a type of Christ. Yet this also seems true of the ram [...]. Christ is the Word of God, but *the Word became flesh.* Christ therefore suffered and died, but in the flesh. In this respect, the ram is the type, just as John said: *Behold the Lamb of God, behold Him who takes away the sins of the world.*"

On Monday of the Fourth Week of Lent the Second Reading of the Liturgy of the Hours is from Origen's ninth homily on Leviticus: "[...] There is a deeper meaning in the fact that the high priest sprinkles the blood toward the east. Atonement comes to you from the east. From the east comes the one whose name is Dayspring, He who is mediator between God and men. You are invited then to look always to the east: it is there that the sun of righteousness rises for you, it is there that the light is always being born for you. You never walk in darkness. Do not let the night and mist of ignorance steal upon you. So that you may always enjoy the light of knowledge, keep always in the daylight of faith, hold fast always to the light of love and peace."

The Office of Readings for Wednesday of the Tenth Week in Ordinary Time is from Origen's fourth homily on the Book of Joshua in which he addresses the newly baptized: "[...] You have recently abandoned the darkness of idolatry, and you now desire to come and hear the divine law. This is your departure from Egypt. When you became a catechumen and began to obey the laws of the Church, you passed through the Red Sea; now at the various stops in the desert, you give time each day to hear the law of God and to see the face of Moses unveiled by the glory of God. But once you come to the baptismal font and, in the presence of the priests and deacons, are initiated into those sacred and august mysteries which only those know who should, then, through the ministry of the priests, you will cross the Jordan and enter the Promised Land. There Moses will hand you over to Jesus, and He Himself will be your guide on your new journey."

See also, Origen's writings in the Divine Office for Thursday of the Tenth Week in Ordinary Time; Thursday of the Twenty-Second Week in Ordinary Time; The Solemnity of Christ the King; June 2: Optional Memorial of Sts. Marcellinus and Peter, Martyrs; Second Reading for the Common of the Dedication of a Church in Ordinary Time.[19]

---

[19] Cf. Benedict XVI, *The Fathers*, 35-45. See also Henry Chadwick, *The Early Church*, 110-113.

Father of Systematic Theology

Origen is considered the "Father of Systematic Theology" mainly because he produced early on in his career a *magnum opus* consisting of four books, entitled in Greek, *Peri Archon* (On First Principles).[20] We are fortunate that this work has been handed down practically in its entirety, receiving much acclaim, criticism and correction in later periods by such learned men as Rufinus of Aquileia and Saint Jerome, thus allowing us to decipher more of his original intent.[21]

Origen's Reflections on the Trinity

In this work, one discovers Origen's explanations of the dogma of the Trinity. Admittedly, Origen tends toward subordinationism by placing the Father above the Son as the monarch of the Trinity. On the other hand, Origen does not conceive this subordination of the Son to the Father as expressive of the Son's being any less eternal than the Father.

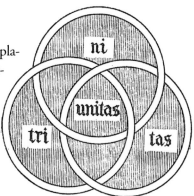

For Origen, the Son is eternally generated, not becoming the Son merely at the moment of His Incarnation. Moreover, Origen explains that eternity pertains also to the Holy Spirit, the only One who, together with the Son, knows the Father.[22] Despite his subordinationist tendencies, Origen clearly distinguishes between the spiritual, eternal Persons of the Trinity and all created reality. He writes:

---

[20] Cf. Chadwick, *The Early Church*, 104: "The defense of orthodoxy against heresy occupied much of Origen's attention. He saw that an answer to Gnosticism could not be made piecemeal by taking particular points in isolation, but only by providing a coherent and all-embracing view of the nature of Christian doctrine, within which the central Gnostic questions (the problem of evil, the place of matter in the divine purpose, free will, divine justice) could find an answer by being seen in a wider and deeper perspective. It was to provide this broad interpretation of Christian theology that Origen wrote his controversial work *On First Principles*."

[21] Chadwick, *The Early Church*, 104: "It was translated into Latin at the end of the fourth century by Rufinus of Aquileia, who frankly explained that he had altered some passages to bring them into conformity with more orthodox opinions expressed in Origen's other writings. Jerome, however, published an exact version of the principal passages which Rufinus had thus mitigated and qualified, so that it is still possible to discover the original meaning of the work."

[22] See Origen's *Commentary on the Gospel of John*, 2:10, 75.

In fact, in the Trinity alone, who is the Creator of all, the good exists in a substantial way: the other beings possess the good only in an accidental manner and as such it can decrease.[23]

Once again, we turn to Hanz Lietzmann for a general assessment of this essential writing of Origen:

> This work was the first Christian system of theology, the first bold attempt to combine Christian pronouncements about God, the world, and man, in a closely-knit, and strictly logical, system of doctrine, and it stands in majestic isolation in the history of the early Church. No theologian of the East, and none of the West, dared to attempt again this immense task. Their own scholarship was devoted to single issues, and their compositions were not more learned than was necessary for instruction appropriate to catechumens.[24]

Origen the Apologist

In terms of Origen's apologetical writings, we recall his principal work, *Contra Celsum* (Against Celsus).[25] Celsus had the audacity to claim that the infancy narratives of the Gospel according to Saints Matthew and Luke were mythological accounts. In turn, Celsus proposed his own crude anti-Marian mythology that Origen adamantly refuted. Celsus asserted that Mary was an adulterous woman (repudiated by Joseph for this very reason), who had become pregnant with Jesus by means of an illicit relationship with a certain pagan Roman soldier by the name of Pantera.

Consequently, in his treatise Origen defends, among other truths, the virginity of Mary, together with the doctrine of Jesus' virginal conception. He does this not only in reaction to Celsus' bizarre claims but more significantly as a way of reprimanding the Gnostics and the Ebionites, Jewish converts to Christianity who insisted on still living according to the strict precepts of the Torah. These

---

23 Origen of Alexandria, *Concerning First Principles*, 1: 6, 2.
24 Lietzman, *A History of the Early Church*, 567.
25 Cf. Wilken, *The Spirit of Early Christian Thought*, 10-11 *passim*: "Celsus wrote his book against Christianity about A.D. 170, and for several generations it received no response. But in the middle of the next century Origen of Alexandria, one of the boldest and most original minds in the Church's history, wrote a detailed refutation of Celsus' *True Doctrine*. Entitled *Against Celsus*, Origen's treatise adroitly fields Celsus' criticisms, patiently explains where he misunderstands things, and on the points that count meets him argument for argument. It is a learned, subtle book, and among early Christian writings written in defense of the faith only Augustine's *City of God* rivals it in profundity [...]. Thomas Jefferson had two copies of *Against Celsus* in his library, the Greek text and a French translation."

The Nativity, *mosaic in the Basilica of St. Mary Major, Rome.*

Ebionites, to whom Celsus had made reference as a way of defending his own denial of the divinity of Christ, could not reconcile the "unicity" (oneness) of God with the doctrine of the Incarnation.

Furthermore, Origin defends the unity of the Divinity and Sacred Humanity of Christ the Logos Incarnate against the pagan assaults of Celsus. Origen also teaches Celsus about the divine activity of the Holy Spirit when he writes:

> Even today we find traces of that Holy Spirit who was seen in the
> form of a dove: Christians cast out demons, heal different maladies,
> and some of them see future events through the will of the Word.[26]

Unlike the Christian apologists who preceded him, Origen was not so much concerned with discussing Jesus' role as the intermediary power through whom the Father created the universe. Rather, Origen focused on the relation between immanence and transcendence, divinity and humanity, in the one Person of Christ.

Origen tended to emphasize the soul as the principle of unity in Our Lord's Person. He rejected any notion of a merely moral union between the humanity

---

[26] Origen of Alexandria, *Contra Celsum*, 1: 46.

and divinity in the Person of Christ, as was held by the heretic Paul of Samosata and later would be expounded on by Nestorius.

Origen's Christology, however, falls short since its Platonic philosophical underpinnings led him nonetheless to consider the humanity of Christ, His soul and body, as absorbed into the divinity of Christ.

The Mystical Body

Origen defended the orthodoxy of the Church against inaccurate and vile remarks about the early Christians, such as:

> There is a new race of men born yesterday, with neither homeland nor traditions, allied against all religious and civil institutions, pursued by justice, universally notorious for their infamy, but glorying in common execration: These are the Christians.

Origen, who was fiercely proud of his Catholic Christian identity, retorts in his *Contra Celsum* ("Against Celsus") that the Christians have a deep-seated, noble—indeed sacred—tradition that is derived from the unified teaching of the Apostles and their successors, the bishops:

> The teaching of the Church has been handed down through an order of succession from the Apostles, and remains in the churches even until the present day. That alone is to be believed which is not at variance with the ecclesiastical and apostolic tradition.

More directly, Origen defends Christians against the attacks of Celsus when he asserts that Christians are not bound together by material reasons only (e.g., civic duty); rather, their unity is derived from constant prayer and an eschatological hope that their priestly service to God and neighbor on earth will bring them to enjoy eternal fellowship and citizenship in the Heavenly homeland. Origen writes:

> If Celsus desires that we serve as officers in the army for the sake of our homeland, let him know that we do that also, but not for the sake of being seen by men or obtaining empty glory from them. In secret, in the very core of our being prayers are sent up as though from priests on behalf of fellow citizens. Christians are more beneficial to their homeland than other people. They instruct their fellow citizens, teach piety towards the God who guards the city and lift up to some divine and heavenly city those who have lived well in the smallest cities. It might be said to them, "You have been faithful in a small city, come into a great one."[27]

---

[27] Origen of Alexandria, *Against Celsus*, 8:74.

Origen has a profound sense of the Church as the Mystical Body of Christ. Christ the Head, crucified and risen, reigns gloriously in Heaven at the right hand of the Father. However, according to Origen, Our Lord's joy is incomplete until at last all the members of His Body are reunited with Him in Heaven. Thus, the doctrine of the communion of saints is a sure consolation not only to us but even to Jesus.

Origen extends this notion to describe the bonds of affection that link the saints in Heaven to us here below. He says that the saints miss us, that our present absence from Heaven leaves a void in the perfect lot of the saints. Therefore, Origen writes this splendid passage about the unity of the Church in relation to the communion of saints:

> Neither the Apostles have obtained their full share of joy. Not even the saints, having left earth, receive the complete reward of their merits, but await also us: even if we are hesitant, even if we are lazy. There cannot be perfect happiness for them until they express sorrow for our errors and weep for our sins.... See, therefore, that Abraham waits yet to obtain his perfect state. Also Isaac and Jacob and all the prophets await us in order to receive together with us perfect beatitude.... In fact one only is the body that waits to be glorified; one only is the body [...]. that will rise on the day of judgment [...]. Therefore, you will have joy leaving this life if you will have been a saint. But then there will be full joy, when no member of your body [i.e., the Church] will be missing. Since also you will have waited for others, so too for you will others have awaited.[28]

Origen's Spirituality

We turn our attention now to some of Origen's less dogmatic treatises, namely, his *Treatise on Prayer* and his *Commentary on the Gospel of St. Luke*.

Origen's *Treatise on Prayer*, in which he reflects on the petitions of the Lord's Prayer, was written during a later stage of his life. This work is considered the first treatise of its kind in early Christian literature. Here are two sample passages:

> When speaking about praying, it is very useful to keep oneself in the presence of God and to speak with Him as one converses with a friend who is physically present. Just as images which are stored in the memory give rise to thoughts whose figures are thought about

---

[28] Origen of Alexandria, *Homily 8 on Leviticus,* 2.

in the mind, so too we believe that it is useful to recall God present in the soul. He controls all our movements, even the slightest ones, when we are willing to show gratitude to the One we know to be present within us, to this God Who examines the heart and scrutinizes the thoughts [...]. The person, who in fulfillment of his duties unites them to his prayer, and in prayer to his deeds, prays without ceasing; for virtuous actions and the fulfillment of the precepts become part of prayer. We then come to realize that the precept *pray without ceasing* can only be fulfilled if we are able to say that the life of a person is a great continuous prayer.[29]

On March 25 the Church celebrates the great mystery of God's condescension in the Incarnation. With that as our focus, we can meditate on a passage from Origen's beautiful commentary on the Gospel of Saint Luke, in which he proffers a reflection on Our Lady's canticle of praise, the *Magnificat*.[30] In the Roman Rite the *Magnificat* is prayed at Vespers (Evening Prayer) each day, while in the Liturgy of the Hours of the Byzantine Rite the *Magnificat* is the morning canticle of praise. Origen writes:

Let us examine the Virgin Mary's prophecy: *My soul magnifies the Lord, and my spirit rejoices in God my Savior* (Luke 1:46). We will ask ourselves in what way the soul can magnify the Lord, since God can neither be increased nor decreased: He Who is. Why then did Mary say: *My soul magnifies the Lord?* If I consider that the Lord and Savior *is the image of the invisible God* (Colossians 1:15), and if I recognize that my soul has been made as an image of the Creator (cf. Genesis 1:27) to be an image of the image (for in reality my soul is not properly speaking an image of God, but has been created as a likeness to the first image), I can then understand the words of the Virgin Mary [...]. Those who paint images first choose what they want to paint, for example, a portrait of a king. Then, with all their artistic ability, they make the effort to reproduce that one model. Similarly, each one of us, transforming our soul to the image of Christ, forms an image of Him that is more or less large, sometimes dark and dirty, other times bright and clear, which corresponds to the original. Consequently, when the image of the image — that is to say, my soul — has been painted large, and it has been magnified by deeds, with thoughts,

---

[29] Origen's *Treatise on Prayer*, as found in Russell, *Glimpses of the Fathers*, 79: *Patrologia Graeca* 11: 415-530.

[30] The text found in Luke 1:46-55 is pronounced by Mary on the occasion of her visitation to her cousin Elizabeth, pregnant with John the Baptist (the second joyful mystery of the Rosary). *Magnificat* is the first word in Latin of Mary's canticle of praise.

with the word, then the image of God is magnified, and the Lord Himself, of whom my soul is an image, will be glorified in my own soul. But if we are sinners, the Lord, Who previously grew in my image, now decreases and diminishes.[31]

Origin's Last Days and Works

John McGuckin helps us envision Origen's quasi-martyrdom during the systematic persecution of Christians on the part of the Emperor Decius. We can only be moved by Origen's selfless love of Christ and his fellow Christians even to his dying breath. McGuckin writes:

In c. A.D. 249 the accession of the Emperor Decius unleashed a new storm of hostility against the Christians of Palestine. Origen was sought out, and the Roman governor ordered him to be tortured carefully (so that he would not die before denying the faith). He was set in the iron collar and stretched over "four spaces" (ratchet marks in the rack) which would more or less have permanently crippled him. His courage and fidelity, however, outlasted his persecutors' efforts, and in the subsequent peace, in A.D. 253, he was taken into convalescence by the Church, and spent a year dying. Eusebius tells us that the old man's primary anxiety was that he would have time to finish a series of encouraging letters, so that those who had suffered losses in the persecution would not be left "uncomforted." Sadly these last works have not survived. He died aged sixty-nine with a martyr's honour, if not a martyr's crown. If he had possessed that status formally his works might not have suffered the depletions that have reduced them over the centuries. His writings were ordered to be burned in the sixth century, but even so a massive amount has survived, and his influence can be felt in almost all aspects of Christian dogma, spirituality, exegesis, and not least in the desire to connect faith and philosophy in day-to-day Christian living.[32]

---

[31] See Origen's *Homilies on the Gospel of Luke* (8, 1-7), as found in Russell, *Glimpses of the Church Fathers*, 83.

[32] John McGuckin's "A Christian Philosophy: Origen," in Hill, *The History of Christianity*, 67.

CHAPTER TWENTY:
CYPRIAN OF CARTHAGE
(C. A.D. 205 - 258)

Visiting Ancient Carthage

In Francis Ford Coppola's 1970 Academy Award-Winning film *Patton*, the fiery four-star general, brilliantly played by George C. Scott, is portrayed as admiring the ruins of ancient Carthage, located in modern-day Tunisia, over-looking the calm azure waters of the Mediterranean. As "old blood and guts" "Georgie," known for his passionate love of ancient history and especially the history of ancient battles and their famous generals, gazes upon the archeo-logical remains, he turns to one of his companions and says: "I was here." This meant that he actually pictured himself as having been present in Carthage when the Romans finally defeated the Carthaginians and eventually silted up the land with salt[33] in A.D. 146.

In visiting those same ruins of ancient Carthage, a person can relive in his or her mind the three Punic Wars fought between the ancient Carthaginians and Romans. During these wars, when addressing the Roman Senate, Cato ended his speeches with a clever rhetorical device: *Carthago delenda est* (Carthage must be destroyed), until, at last, the Romans did just that.

Carthage was a city where many important early councils were held. In Cyprian's time Carthage was a thriving Christian city until barbarians invaded it while Saint Augustine of Hippo was dying. In later centuries, bands of warrior Muslims destroyed the Christian churches at Carthage.

Imagining and Remembering Cyprian

As we prepare to study Cyprian's thought, with our mind's eye we may want to catch a glimpse of a sixth-century fresco found in the Catacombs of Saint Callistus depicting Pope Cornelius and Cyprian of Carthage dressed in

---

[33] The purpose of sowing salt into the land was to destroy its fertility. This action helps explain the expression "to put salt on someone's wounds."

pontifical[34] vestments, each man holding a jeweled Book of the Gospels in his left hand. In like manner, we can reflect on the fifteenth-century miniature (1475-1482) of an anonymous master who followed the style of Sandro Botticelli, showing Cyprian writing in his cell. That artist had a marvelous knack for painting with precision and detail, for "God is in the details." The liturgical memorial of Pope Saint Cornelius and Saint Cyprian of Carthage falls on September 16.[35] They are mentioned together in the Roman Canon or First Eucharistic Prayer in the first list of saints commemorated before the words of consecration.[36]

Cyprian's Life

Cyprian of Carthage was born Thascius Caecilius[37] Cyprianus in the early third century, probably in A.D. 205. He was born into an upper-class pagan family who saw to it that he received the best classical education available. Cyprian studied rhetoric in his hometown of Carthage. He became a renowned

---

[34] This adjective describes things, actions, vestments, etc. proper to bishops.

[35] See the Office of Readings for the Memorial of Sts. Cornelius, pope and martyr, Cyprian, bishop and martyr: "Cyprian sends greetings to his brother Cornelius. My very dear brother, we have heard of the glorious witness given by your courageous faith. On learning of the honor you had won by your witness, we were filled with such joy that we felt ourselves sharers and companions in your praiseworthy achievements. After all, we have the same Church, the same mind, the same unbroken harmony. Why then should a priest not take pride in the praise given to a fellow priest as though it were given to him? What brotherhood fails to rejoice in the happiness of its brothers wherever they are?

[36] See the Second Reading of the Office of Readings for Saturday of the First Week of Advent. Cyprian writes in his treatise *On the Value of Patience*: "Paul warns us not to grow weary in good works through impatience, not to be distracted or overcome by temptations and so give up in the midst of our pilgrimage of praise and glory, and allow our good past deeds to count for nothing because what has begun falls short of completion."

[37] The reader should not confuse this Caecilius with a later Caecilian, Bishop of Carthage, who in A.D. 311 was condemned by a group of eighty North African bishops for having been ordained by a bishop who had handed over the sacred books of the Church to Roman officials rather than suffer martyrdom. The eighty North African bishops decided to ordain a new bishop of their own choosing to take the place of Caecilian. Thus was spawned an intense, permanent schism in the Church in North Africa that was still boiling over after the Muslim invasions of North Africa in the seventh century. It is a logical inference to conclude that such division among the early Christians was no incentive for the Muslims to convert to Catholic Christianity. However, long before the Muslims arrived, the first Christian Emperor, Constantine, sided with Caecilian against a North African heretic known as Donatus, who claimed that his sect was the only true Church because they denied the validity of the sacraments administered by heretics and schismatics. St. Augustine adamantly disagreed and eventually helped settle this controversy dividing the Church. For example, with regard to the Donatists, he remarks: "The clouds roll with thunder that the House of the Lord shall be built throughout the earth; and these frogs sit in their marshes and croak, 'We are the only Christians!'"

teacher of rhetoric, so much so that his family had even higher hopes for his success. Perhaps they believed that if Cyprian excelled in his studies he would eventually obtain a prominent position, such as governor of Proconsular Africa whose seat was in Carthage.

Cyprian's Baptism

To their dismay and surprise, the forty-year-old Cyprian took the road less traveled when he decided to convert to Christianity circa A.D. 246, a conversion due in no small part to the excellent instruction in the Faith he had received at the hands of an elderly priest named Caecilius or Caecilianus, whose name he took as his own. Cyprian was probably baptized at the Easter Vigil on April 18, 246. About his baptism, Cyprian writes to a certain Donatus that it was like a *second birth* that *restored* him:

> so as to make him a new man [...] what before had seemed difficult was now easy.

Here is Cyprian's description of the effects of his baptism, most especially the effusion of the Holy Spirit, as related in his *Letter to Donatus*, which takes the form of a monologue addressed to a friend while lying under a vine-clad pergola:

> I was bound to the many vices of my past life and I would never have believed it possible to be freed from them [...]. However, the help of the water that regenerates overcame me. The corruption of my preceding life was cancelled and from on high a light was effused into my soul making it pure and clean. I received from Heaven the Holy Spirit and by means of a second birth I became a new man. After this event that which was struck by doubt in my life became suddenly a certitude in a way that I would not know how to describe [...]. I understood that that which the Holy Spirit had already animated began to pertain to God [...]. In using the gifts of God there is no measure or limit, as instead occurs with earthly benefits. The Spirit expands Himself abundantly and is not limited by any confine, nor is He refrained by the borders that surround Him and that refrain within secure confined space. The Spirit gushes forth continually, flows abundantly: It is only necessary that our heart would have thirst and that it would be open. The Spirit that we have received acts with His power, since we participate in a new life.[38]

Cyprian: Priest and Bishop

---

[38]   Cyprian of Carthage, *Letter to Donatus*, 4-5, 1.

Cyprian was ordained a priest around the year 248/249. While still a recent convert to Catholicism, he was appointed Bishop of Carthage and thus the Metropolitan of Africa. Cyprian's career as a bishop lasted only ten years, ending with his martyrdom around A.D. 258/259.

Despite his classical learning, Cyprian proved himself to be a man of action more than a man bent on intellectual pursuits. He is to be admired and emulated for the way in which he courageously faced the concrete challenges posed him in carrying out his priestly and episcopal duties. Many of the challenges he faced hinged on the question of the Church's unity, one of the four distinguishing characteristics of the true Church of Christ.

Bringing Back the Lost Sheep

Regarding the unity of the Church, Cyprian was personally involved in two important controversies in the early Church. The first had to do with the so-called *lapsi*, those who had "lapsed" or apostasized from Christianity and therefore had given up allegiance to the Catholic Church during times of persecution. The question was whether or how the *lapsi* should be re-admitted to full communion with the Church. The second controversy dealt with the re-baptism of heretics.

Cyprian relied heavily on the writings of Tertullian, a third-century Christian writer from North Africa who had joined a rigorist moralistic schismatic sect known as the Montanists. Cyprian is said to have read Tertullian's writings daily. He referred to Tertullian as his "master." Fortunately, Cyprian modified some of Tertullian's harsh moral positions in order to foster Church unity.[39] He wanted ecclesiastical discipline to be reasonable and realistic, a servant to Christian unity, not a deterrent to it. The

---

[39] See the Liturgy of the Hours for Friday of the Thirty-Fourth Week in Ordinary Time: "The world hates Christians, so why give your love to it instead of following Christ, who loved you and has redeemed you? [...]. We ought never to forget, beloved, that we have renounced the world. We are living here now as aliens and only for a time. When the day of our homecoming puts an end to our exile, frees us from the bonds of the world, and restores us to paradise and to kingdom, we should welcome it [...]. There, is the glorious band of apostles, there the exultant assembly of prophets, there the innumerable host of martyrs, crowned for their glorious victory in combat and in death. There in triumph are the virgins who subdued their passions by the strength of continence. There the merciful are rewarded, those who fulfill the demands of justice by providing for the poor. In obedience to the Lord's command, they turned their earthly pilgrimage into heavenly treasure."

unity of the local Church was Cyprian's uppermost concern. When the Novatian controversy sprang up, Cyprian became concerned with the unity of the
universal or Catholic Church, causing Cyprian to side with Pope Cornelius
against the anti-pope Novatian.

Christian Disunity and Persecution

Certain priests were envious of Cyprian's precipitous rise to the episcopal
office, and this too became a source of tension and disunity that Cyprian had
to combat. Disunity heightened when the Emperor Decius began the first systematic persecution of the Church by the Roman Empire, lasting for two years,
A.D. 250-252.[40] Decius had a two-pronged focus to his effort.

First and foremost, he sought to kill the bishops, especially those who held
major sees such as Rome,[41] Alexandria, Antioch, Jerusalem, and Caesarea. In
Cyprian's case, the Emperor initially failed because Cyprian fled his diocese after
having been warned in advance of the imminent onslaught. Cyprian thought it
more prudent to stay alive in self-imposed exile.

While in exile, Cyprian addressed numerous pastoral letters to the clergy
and lay faithful, exhorting them to remain faithful to Christ and the Church
and to imitate the courage of the martyrs.[42] Many of Cyprian's fellow bishops

---

[40] Recall in the Acts of the Apostles that a systematic persecution of the Christians occurred
      under the Pharisee Saul (later St. Paul), which culminated in the stoning of the Church's
      first martyr, the deacon, St. Stephen, whose feastday is December 26.

[41] On January 20, 250, Pope Fabian was killed by decree of the Emperor Decius. See the Second
      Reading of the Liturgy of the Hours for the Optional Memorial of Fabian, pope and martyr.
      The reading is from a *Letter About the Death of Saint Fabian*, Pope, by Saint Cyprian and the
      Roman Church: "Informed of the death of Pope Fabian, Saint Cyprian sent this letter to the
      priests and deacons of Rome: My dear brothers, [...] I was quite happy that his [Fabian's]
      virtuous demise corresponded with the integrity of his administration. Hence I too offer you
      congratulations that you honor his memory with so striking and praiseworthy a testimony.
      Through you we can see quite clearly what an honor for you is the glorious heritage of one
      who was your superior, and what an example of faith and courage it offers us."

[42] St. Perpetua, an early third-century martyr from Carthage, left us a diary recounting the
      events that led up to her martyrdom along with that of several of her companions, most
      notably St. Felicity, with whom she shares an optional memorial on March 7, and whose
      names appear together in the Roman Canon. Perpetua was a young woman who, despite
      the decrees of the Emperor Septimius Severus, decided to convert to Christianity from
      paganism. When Roman officials arrested and imprisoned her, Perpetua was pregnant. As
      she awaited her execution, she received permission from the Romans to keep her baby with
      her while in prison, where she had given birth. About this felicitous piece of news, Perpetua
      writes in her diary: "My prison had suddenly become a palace, so that I wanted to be there
      rather than anywhere else." Her father was distraught over Perpetua's unwillingness to give
      in to the demands of pagan worship in order to be freed from jail. He pleaded with her, as
      she recounts, saying, "Daughter, have pity on my grey head [...]. If I have favored you above

and priests, especially the clergy of Rome, criticized him harshly, deeming him a coward for having fled the gruesome scene of persecution, abandoning his flock. Later on, Cyprian was asked by Rome to explain the meaning of his actions, which he did in his twentieth *Letter*. Cyprian enhanced his self-defense by sending Rome thirteen copies of the pastoral letters he had written while in self-imposed exile.[43]

Secondly, the Emperor Decius tried to force Christians to offer sacrifice to the pagan gods and to burn incense before the statue of the Emperor, and to hand over the sacred books used in Christian worship. Those who cooperated were given a certificate (Latin: *libellus*) that authenticated their apostasy. Those who held these certificates were called *libellatici*.

Reconciling the Lapsed

The questions now arose: Should the *lapsi* be readmitted immediately upon

---

all your brothers [...] do not abandon me! Give up your pride!" Perpetua replied to her father's desperate plea with trust in God's mercy: "It will happen as God wills." Her father, defeated by Perpetua's undying faith, left the prison. The Roman Governor Hilarianus then sought to persuade her to apostatize: "Have pity on your father's grey head; have pity on your infant son. Offer the sacrifice for the welfare of the emperors." Perpetua refused and so recounted in her diary, "We were condemned to the beasts and returned to prison in high spirits." A fellow Christian recorded the events that transpired on the day of Perpetua's martyrdom: "The day of their victory dawned, and they marched from prison to the amphitheatre joyfully as though they were going to Heaven, with calm faces, trembling, if at all, with calm rather than fear."

[43] See the Liturgy of the Hours for the Optional Memorial of St. Stanislaus, bishop and martyr, celebrated on April 11. In Lent this is a Commemoration. Cyprian writes an exhortation based on St. Paul's own exhortation in Ephesians 6: 13-20: "Dear brethren, let us arm ourselves with all our might, let us prepare for the struggle by innocence of heart, integrity of faith, dedication to virtue [...]. Let us take this armor and defend ourselves with these spiritual defenses from heaven, so that we may be able to fight back on the evil day. Let us put on the breastplate of righteousness so that our hearts may be safeguarded, proof against the arrows of the enemy. Let our feet be protected by the shoes of the teaching of the Gospel so that when we begin to trample on the serpent and crush it, we may not be bitten and tripped up by it. Let us with fortitude bear the shield of faith to protect us by extinguishing all the burning arrows that the enemy may launch against us. Let us wear on our head the helmet of spirit to defend our ears against the proclamation of death, our eyes against the sight of accursed idols, and our forehead so that God's sign may be kept intact, our lips so that our tongue may proclaim victoriously its faith in Christ its Lord. Let us arm our right hand with the sword of the Spirit so that it may courageously refuse the daily [pagan] sacrifices, and like the hand—mindful of the Eucharist—that receives the Body of the Lord, stretch out to embrace Him, and so gain from the Lord the future prize of a heavenly crown."

verbal repentance, or only after having completed a long period of severe public penance? Should the confessors, those who had remained steadfast in the Faith and survived despite the persecution, decide on these matters concerning the reconciliation of the *lapsi*? Or should the local bishops make such decisions? Tension between the bishops and the confessors grew when some confessors accused certain bishops of re-admitting the *lapsi* with too much leniency.

For his part, Cyprian as Bishop of Carthage insisted that the authority to decide such issues lay with the local ordinaries (diocesan bishops) and not with the confessors. Nevertheless, Cyprian agreed that the bishops should accept the counsel of the confessors as an advisory board, even if not a deliberative one.

To address these key issues, Cyprian wrote two important treatises, one on the *lapsi*[44] and the other on the unity of the Church.[45] At the Council of Carthage in A.D. 251, the Council Fathers, under the leadership of Cyprian, who had recently returned from a year of hiding, decided that the *lapsi* could be reconciled but only after undergoing a period of penance; those in danger of death, Cyprian held, should be immediately reconciled by a priest, or, in the absence of a priest, by a deacon.[46]

However, in no case, Cyprian argued, should the *lapsi* be treated in the same manner as those who had withstood the persecutions without backsliding. In meting out penances to the *lapsi*, Cyprian also distinguished between those Christians who had truly sacrificed to pagan gods and those who, lacking the courage of their convictions, obtained *libelli* (certificates) perhaps by bribing Roman officials, without, however, really offering pagan sacrifice. In the former case, Cyprian decreed that the *lapsi* should be readmitted to full communion with the Catholic Church only after completion of lifelong penance and when they were on the threshold of death.

In A.D. 252, another council or synod held at Carthage decided that the *lapsi* could be reconciled immediately as if they had already submitted themselves to appropriate penances because the Church was then facing another fierce persecution.

---

[44] See Cyprian of Carthage, *De Lapsis* (On the Lapsed).

[45] See Cyprian of Carthage, *De Ecclesiae Catholicae Unitate* (On the Unity of the Catholic Church).

[46] One should note that the delegation to deacons of the power to reconcile lapsi "on their deathbeds" (*in extremis*) was later reserved only to priests and bishops because a development of doctrine led the Church to see such reconciliatory ministry as integral to the Sacrament of Penance.

Unity, Not Schism

Cyprian's defense of the unity of the Church is also intrinsically related to the Novatian Schism. Novatian, perhaps embittered that he never was consecrated a bishop, declared himself "pope," setting up a rival throne to the legitimate throne of Pope Cornelius, with whom Cyprian maintained a long-term and congenial correspondence. Novatian believed that his church (sect), unlike the Church of Rome and the local churches affiliated with it (e.g., Carthage under Cyprian) would not allow for the re-admission of the *lapsi*.

Cyprian addressed these issues in his writings, especially in his treatise, *De Ecclesiae Catholicae Unitate* (On the Unity of the Catholic Church) by opposing any and all factions within the Church. This treatise was read aloud at the Council of Carthage in A.D. 251. In this treatise, we find many significant passages concerning the four marks of the Church. In particular, Cyprian focuses on the Church's indefectible holiness in relation to Christ, her heavenly Bridegroom. Cyprian also stresses that the Church's unity is intrinsically linked to the communion her members are called to maintain with the Trinity. Lastly, the Church's unity is unfathomable apart from the fidelity of her members to the sacramental and moral life. Cyprian writes:

> The spouse of Christ cannot be defiled; she is uncorrupted and chaste. She knows one home. With chaste modesty she guards the sanctity of one couch. She keeps us for God; she assigns the children whom she has created to the Kingdom. Whoever is separated from the Church will not reap the rewards of Christ. He is a stranger; he is profane; he is an enemy. He cannot have God as a father who does not have the Church as a mother. If whoever was outside the ark of Noah was able to escape, he too who is outside the Church escapes. But the Lord warns, saying: "He who is not with me is against me, and he who does not gather with me, scatters" (Matthew 12:30). He who breaks the peace and concord of Christ acts against Christ; he who gathers somewhere outside of the Church, scatters the Church of Christ. The Lord says, "I and the Father are one" (John 10:30). And again, it is written of the Father and Son and the Holy Spirit: "And these three are one" (1 John 5:7). Does anyone believe that this unity which comes from divine power, which is closely connected with the divine sacraments, can be broken asunder in the Church and be separated by the divisions of colliding wills? He who does not hold this unity, does not hold the law of God, does not hold the faith of the Father and the Son, does not hold life and salvation.[47]

---

[47] Cyprian of Carthage, *On the Unity of the Catholic Church*, 4.

Defending Holy Mother Church

Denominationalism was not an option as far as Cyprian was concerned. Those who divide the Church should have the intellectual and spiritual honesty to leave her fold. According to Cyprian, schismatics like Novatian commit a type of spiritual suicide because they are like branches cut off from the vine; there is no life in those branches.[48]

In Cyprian's *On the Unity of the Catholic Church*, he insists on the reality of one Baptism. He offers us the following similes from nature to conjure up orthodox notions of Catholic unity:

> This unity we ought to hold firmly and defend, especially we bishops who watch over the Church, that we may prove that the episcopate itself is also one and undivided. Let no one deceive the brotherhood by lying. Let no one corrupt the faith by a perfidious prevarication of the truth. The episcopate is one, the parts of which are held together by the individual bishops. The Church is one. With increasing fecundity she extends far and wide into the multitude. Just as the rays of the sun are many but the light is one, and the branches of the tree are many but the strength is one founded in its tenacious root, and, when many streams flow from one source, although a multiplicity of waters seems to have been diffused from the abundance of the overflowing supply, nevertheless unity is preserved in their origin. Take away a ray of light from the body of the sun, and its unity does not allow for any division of its light. Break a branch from a tree, and the branch thus broken will not be able to bud. Cut off a stream from its source, and the stream dries up. The Church, too, bathed in the light of the Lord, projects her rays over the whole world, yet there is one light which is diffused everywhere, and the unity of the body is separated. She extends her branches over the whole earth in fruitful abundance. She extends her richly flowing streams far and wide; yet her head is one, and her source is one, and she is the one mother copious in fruit. By her womb, we are born; by her milk, we are nourished; by her spirit, we are animated.[49]

Cyprian's "Tough Love"

Cyprian took a rather severe attitude toward schismatics, certainly not one ever officially condoned by the Church's Magisterium. He states that even the schismatics who die a martyr's death are not forgiven by God because there

---

[48]   Cf. John 15.
[49]   *On the Unity of the Catholic Church*, 4.

Christ Giving the Keys to St. Peter, *Lorenzo Veneziano, 1370.*

can be no martyrdom outside the Church. As regards the unity of the Church, Cyprian stresses the significance of maintaining communion with the local bishop, who in his turn must be in communion with the Bishop of Rome. Thus Cyprian teaches:

> You ought to know that the bishop is in the Church and the Church is in the bishop. If anyone is not with the bishop, he is not in the Church.

Moreover, Cyprian explains how Saint Peter was established by Christ to be the visible source of the Church's unity:

> The Lord says to Peter: "I say to you that you are Peter, and upon this rock I will build my Church, and the gates of Hell shall not prevail against it; to you I will give the keys of the Kingdom of Heaven, and whatever you will have bound on earth shall be bound in Heaven, and whatever you will have loosed on earth shall be loosed in Heaven." Upon one He builds His Church, and to the same He says after His Resurrection, "Feed my sheep." And though to all His Apostles He gave an equal power, yet did He set up one chair, and disposed the origin and manner of unity by His authority. The other Apostles were indeed what Peter was, but the primacy is given to Peter, and the Church and the chair are shown to be one. And all are pastors, but the flock is shown to be one, which is fed by all the Apostles with one mind and heart. He that holds not this unity of the Church, does he think that he holds the faith? He who deserts the chair of Peter, upon whom the Church is founded, is he confident that he is in the Church?[50]

Dealing with Popes and Bishops

Cyprian's ecclesiology is most admirable. He values the bishop as having supreme authority in his local church, but he also emphasizes the need for bishops to be in union with each other, most especially with the Bishop of Rome, the see which Cyprian termed the *Ecclesia Principalis* (The Principal Church). Cyprian referred to the papacy as *the womb and root of the Catholic Church*.[51] It is out of this frame of mind that Cyprian expressed his belief that Novatian and any of his followers who sought reconciliation with the Catholic Church should be re-baptized. Pope Cornelius thought otherwise.

However, in June of 253, Pope Cornelius was exiled to *Centumcellae*, today

---

[50] Ibid.
[51] Ibid., 48: 3.

known as "Civitavecchia," Rome's port city along the Tyrrhenian Sea. Pope Cornelius died in Civitavecchia and was considered a martyr by Cyprian and the Catholic faithful. He was succeeded by Pope Lucius who shortly after his election was likewise exiled to Civitavecchia, where he died on March 5, 254. He was succeeded by Pope Saint Stephen I on May 12, 254; he immediately took to facing the question of the *lapsi* head-on.

Pope Stephen decided to impose his policy that the *lapsi* and Novatian schismatics not be re-baptized in all the churches, including of course Cyprian's local church at Carthage. This attempt on the part of Pope Stephen was resented by many bishops who wondered if the Pope could legitimately take such an action. A number of Eastern bishops sided with Cyprian on this disciplinary issue and began to put pressure on Pope Stephen to change his policy.

A council was held at Carthage in September of 256 at which Cyprian and his brother-bishops expressed their unanimous decision in favor of the re-baptism of heretics and schismatics. The messengers who brought to Rome the document chronicling the opinions of the bishops at the Carthaginian Council were refused an audience by Pope Stephen. Pope Stephen was so distressed with Cyprian that he actually threatened to excommunicate him if he and his brother-bishops in Africa did not enact the original policy.

However, another widespread persecution intervened under the Emperor Valerian[52] to quell the flame of dissent in the Church. On August 27, 257, Pope Stephen was martyred, and the re-baptism controversy died down. Consequently, the Church in Africa, including the Church at Carthage, and the Church of Rome temporarily adopted two different disciplinary approaches to this doctrinal question, so that re-baptism continued in North Africa until the Holy See finally ruled that this was doctrinally incorrect under the strong influence of Saint Augustine of Hippo who dealt with this same matter in his controversy with the Donatists.

---

[52] See the Liturgy of the Hours for the Optional Memorial of Sixtus II, Pope and Martyr, and Companions, Martyrs, celebrated on August 7. In Cyprian's Epistle 80 we read: "The true state of affairs is this. Valerian has issued an edict to the Senate to the effect that bishops, presbyters and deacons shall suffer the death penalty without delay [...]. I must also inform you that Sixtus was put to death in a catacomb on the sixth of August, and four deacons with him. Moreover, the prefects in Rome are pressing this persecution zealously and without intermission, to such a point that anyone brought before them is punished and his property is claimed by the treasury. I ask you to make these facts known to the rest of our fellow bishops, in order that by the exhortation of their pastors the brethren everywhere may be strengthened and prepared for spiritual combat."

Father of Christian Unity

Cyprian's love of ecclesial unity was woven into his thought and action until he was beheaded near Carthage during the persecution of the Emperor Valerian circa A.D. 258/259. Writing to Donatus, Cyprian explains how his own baptism brought unity to his life. Cyprian remarks that before his conversion he had been a *stranger to truth and to the light*, but that afterwards he attained a knowledge that surpassed the knowledge that he achieved through the superb education he had received as a pagan. And as much as he prized his baptism as an adult, Cyprian, in his forty-fourth letter, for example, defended the apostolic practice of infant baptism, as can be inferred from the baptism of the jailer and his whole household in the Acts of the Apostles.[53]

Cyprian's Sanctity

As a catechumen and then later as a bishop, Cyprian understood that he needed to strive for inner spiritual unity by espousing the evangelical counsels of celibacy and poverty, giving away most of his belongings to the poor.[54] On the occasion of a plague in Carthage, Cyprian wrote a short treatise, *On Mortality*. His exhortations were matched by his willingness to organize a staff of workers and raise a large amount of money so that the sick could be cared for and the dead afforded a decent Christian burial.

In several of his letters,[55] Cyprian alludes to his having had ecstatic visions under what he perceived to be the power of the Holy Spirit.

The Greek word *diabolos*, from which we get our English "diabolical," comes from the verb which means: "to throw into confusion." Satan's[56] primary work is to create chaos and confusion amidst God's creation and in His one, holy, catholic and apostolic Church. Cyprian knew this well.

Holy Patience

Thus in a work which he penned in A.D. 256 entitled, *De Bono Patientiae* ("On the Value of Patience"), Cyprian encourages his flock to resist the confu-

---

[53] Cf. Acts 16: 27-33. See also, Matthew 19: 13-15; Luke 18: 15-17; John 3:3-5; Acts 2: 37-41; 1 Corinthians 1:16; 15:21-22; Colossians 2:11-12.

[54] Already as a catechumen, Cyprian had sold much of his property. His disciples, however, bought back his property and returned it to Cyprian, whereupon he re-sold it.

[55] The corpus of Cyprian's epistolary includes eighty-one letters. Three of these letters are composed in the name of the local councils held at Carthage. Seven letters deal with Cyprian's thoughts on martyrdom sent to the church at Carthage while he was in self-imposed exile. The remaining letters deal with his interventions on the question of the rebaptism of the *lapsi*, his correspondence with Pope St. Cornelius, and miscellaneous topics.

[56] *Satan* is a Hebrew word meaning *adversary*.

sion of the Evil One, so as to be more united in the struggle to keep themselves and their faith free of all anxiety and discouragement. Cyprian describes the unity of life that results from the practice of the virtue of patience when he writes:

> The virtue of patience extends widely and its wealth and abundance proceed from a source that has indeed a single name, but with its full-flowing streams it is diffused through many glorious courses, and nothing in our actions can avail toward the full realization of merit which does not take the power for its accomplishment from that source. It is patience that both commends us to God and saves us for God. It is this same patience which tempers anger, bridles the tongue, governs the mind, guards peace, rules discipline, breaks the onslaught of lust, suppresses the violence of pride, extinguishes the fire of dissension, restrains the power of the wealthy, renews the endurance of the poor in bearing their lot, guards the blessed integrity of virgins, the difficult chastity of widows, and the indivisible love of husbands and wives. It makes men humble in prosperity, brave in adversity, meek in the face of injuries and insults. It teaches us to pardon our offenders quickly; if you yourself should offend, it teaches you to ask pardon often and with perseverance. It vanquishes temptations, sustains persecutions, endures sufferings and martyrdom to the end. It is this patience which strongly fortifies the foundations of our faith. It is this patience which sublimely promotes the growth of hope. It directs our action, so that we can keep to the way of Christ while we make progress because of His forbearance. It ensures our perseverance as sons of God while we imitate the patience of the Father.[57]

The Lord's Prayer

Cyprian's treatise on the Our Father[58] is one of the most precious documents we have from the early Church Fathers. His commentary, *De Dominica Oratione* (On the Lord's Prayer),[59] is a mainstay for the Catechism of the Catholic Church's

---

[57] Cyprian of Carthage, *On the Value of Patience*, 19-20.

[58] See the Office of Readings for the Eleventh Week in Ordinary Time: "The prayer continues: *Your kingdom come.* We pray that God's kingdom will become present for us in the same way as we ask for His Name to be hallowed among us [...]. After this we add: *Your will be done on earth as it is in heaven*; we pray not that God should do His will, but that we may carry out His will. How could anyone prevent the Lord from doing His will? But in our prayer we ask that God's will be done in us, because the devil throws obstacles to prevent our mind and our conduct from obeying God in all things."

[59] See the Liturgy of the Hours for Thursday of the Eleventh Week in Ordinary Time: "As the Lord's Prayer continues, we ask: *Give us this day our daily bread.* We can understand this petition in a spiritual and in a literal sense [...]. Now, we who live in Christ and receive

section on prayer as well as in the Liturgy of the Hours.[60] Here, we offer only one quote that underscores Cyprian's appreciation of the Lord's Prayer[61] as the perfect prayer[62] aimed at Christian unity, for which we all must work and pray at all times. In reflecting on the words, *and forgive us our trespasses as we forgive those who trespass against us* and Jesus' teaching in Matthew 5:24, Cyprian writes:

> God bids us to be peace-loving, harmonious *and of one mind in His house;* He wants us to live with the new life He gave us at our second birth. As sons of God, we are to abide in peace; as we have one Spirit, we should be one in mind and heart. Thus God does not receive the sacrifice of one who lives in conflict; and He orders us to turn back from the altar and be first reconciled with our brother, that God too

the Eucharist, the food of salvation, ask for this bread to be given us every day. Otherwise we may be forced to abstain from this communion because of some serious sin [...]. After this we ask pardon for our sins, in the words: *And forgive us our trespasses.* The gift of God is followed by a prayer for forgiveness, our hearts are aware of our state! This command to pray daily for our sins reminds us that we commit sin every day. No one should complacently think himself innocent, lest his pride lead to further sin."

[60] Cf. CCC, 2782; 2784; 2813; 2816; 2830; 2845. See the Office of Readings for Tuesday of the First Week of Lent: "So, my brothers, let us pray as God our master has taught us. To ask the Father in the words the Son has given us, to let Him hear the prayer of Christ ringing in His ears, is to make our prayer one of friendship, a family of prayer." See too the Sunday for the Eleventh Week in Ordinary Time: "When we pray our words should be calm, modest and disciplined. Let us reflect that we are standing before God. We should please him by our bodily posture and the manner of our speech. It is the characteristic of the vulgar to shout and make a noise, not those who are modest. On the contrary, they should employ a quiet tone of prayer. Moreover, in the course of His teaching, the Lord instructed us to pray in secret. Hidden and secluded places, even our own rooms, give witness to our belief that God is present everywhere; that He sees and hears all; that in the fullness of His majesty, He penetrates hidden and secret places." Again, we read from Cyprian's treatise *On the Lord's Prayer* for Monday of the Eleventh Week in Ordinary Time: "God is then the teacher of harmony, peace and unity, and desires each one of us to pray for all men, even as He bore all men in Himself alone. The three young men in the furnace of fire observed this rule of prayer [...]. Even though Christ had not yet taught them to pray, nevertheless, they spoke as with one voice." See the Second Reading for Tuesday of the Eleventh Week in Ordinary Time: "None of us would ever have dared to utter this [God's] Name unless He Himself had allowed us to pray in this way. And, therefore, dear friends, we should bear in mind and realize that when we call God our Father we ought to act like sons. If we are pleased to call Him Father, let Him in turn be pleased to call us sons [...]. We go on to say: May your name be hallowed. It is not that we think to make God holy by our prayers; rather we are asking God that His Name may be made holy in us."

[61] See the Liturgy of the Hours for Friday of the Eleventh Week in Ordinary Time: "Christ clearly laid down an additional rule to bind us by a certain contractual condition: we ask that our debts be forgiven insofar as we forgive our debtors [...]. This is why He says elsewhere: *The measure you give will be the measure you get.*"

[62] See the Liturgy of the Hours for Saturday of the Eleventh Week in Ordinary Time: "God taught us to pray not only by His words, but also by His actions."

may be appeased by the prayers of one who is at peace. The greatest offering we can make to God is our peace, harmony among fellow Christians, a people united with the unity of the Father, the Son and the Holy Spirit.[63]

Cyprian of Carthage teaches us that our peace and unity are the greatest sacrifice that we can offer to Almighty God. He contrasts the sacrifices of Cain and Abel and reminds us that God looks first and foremost to create inner unity by examining the authenticity of our hearts and their intentions and not so much the sacrifices themselves.[64]

Cyprian's Martyrdom[65]

When it came time for his own sacrifice, we are told a moving account that solidified Cyprian as a champion of Christian unity even till his dying day and created for himself such a legacy that already in the fifth century Saint Jerome could recommend his writings to his spiritual sons and daughters as works replete with faith and devotion.

The *Acts of the Martyrs* are those documents of early Christianity that relate the stories of the martyrdoms of Christians like Cyprian of Carthage. In Cyprian's case, we have a document composed of four fragments, entitled, *The Proconsular Acts of the Martyrdom of the Bishop Cyprian.*

The first fragment deals with the interrogation of Cyprian before the proconsul Aspasius Paternus, which took place on August 30, 257.

The second fragment consists of the narration of Cyprian's exile to Curubis, *Colonia Iulia Curubis*, which was an ancient Roman penal colony located off the coast of Carthage. It also contains an account of Cyprian's return from exile.

---

[63] Cyprian of Carthage, *On the Lord's Prayer*, 23: *Patrologia Latina* 4: 535-536; cf. CCC, 2845.

[64] Cf. Cyprian of Carthage, *On the Lord's Prayer*, 23-24.

[65] In A.D. 406, St. Jerome, basing his arguments on Sacred Scripture, writes eloquently, using clever logical and rhetorical devices, to defend the doctrine of the intercession of saints and the use of relics in his work: *Against Vigilantius* here cited in Hill's *The History of Christianity*, 57: "If apostles and martyrs while still in the body can pray for others, when they ought to be thinking about themselves, how much more must they do so after they have won their crowns, overcome, and triumphed? One lone man, Moses, wins pardon for six hundred thousand armed men [Exodus 32:30], and Stephen, the follower of his Lord and the first Christian martyr, begs forgiveness for his persecutors [Acts 7: 59-60]. So when they have entered life with Christ, will they have less power than before? The apostle Paul says that two hundred and seventy-six souls were given to him in the ship [Acts 27:37]. So when, after his death, he has begun to be with Christ, must he shut his mouth, and be unable to say a word for those who throughout the world have believed in the Gospel ?[...]. In fact the saints are not called dead—they are said to be sleeping."

The third fragment of the *Acts* deals with the interrogation of Cyprian before the proconsul Galerius Maximus that took place on September 14, 258.[66]

The fourth fragment is the actual account of his martyrdom. In this last fragment the following dramatic dialogue is recorded between Cyprian and the proconsul Galerius Maximus leading up to the pronouncement of Saint Cyprian's sentence of execution:

> **Galerius Maximus:** Are you Thascius, known also as Cyprian?
>
> **Cyprian:** I am.
>
> **Galerius Maximus:** Have you presented yourself to people as the head of a sacrilegious movement?
>
> **Cyprian:** I have.
>
> **Galerius Maximus:** The most sacred Emperor has ordered you to offer worship.
>
> **Cyprian:** I will not.
>
> **Galerius Maximus:** Have you a care for your own interests?
>
> **Cyprian:** In such a matter there need be no reflection.
>
> **Galerius Maximus:** You have lived for a long time in a sacrilegious frame of mind, have gathered very many other members of this impious conspiracy around you and have set yourself up as an enemy of the Roman gods and their rites. Our pious and most sacred princes, the august Valerian and Gallienus and our most noble Caesar, Valerian, have not been able to call you back to the observance of their worship. Therefore, since you are the author and admitted leader of the most worthless crimes, you will yourself be a warning for these people whom you have gathered around you in your crime. Respect

---

[66] In the beginning of August of 258, Pope Sixtus II, the successor to Pope St. Stephen I, was martyred together with various deacons, including St. Lawrence (who was roasted to death on a grill) because they refused to hand over the Church's riches to the Roman Empire. Instead, led by St. Lawrence, the poor were presented as the true riches of the Church. While St. Lawrence was being roasted on the grill, he is said to have quipped to his executioners: "Turn me over: I'm done on this side." As an aside, it is worth mentioning that the church in Rome that houses St. Lawrence's grill is known as San Lorenzo in Lucina, "St. Lawrence in Lucina," but is jokingly referred to by the Romans as San Lorenzo in Cucina, "St. Lawrence in the Kitchen," a tongue-in-cheek reference to his mode of martyrdom.

for the law will be confirmed by your blood [. . .]. It has been decided that Thascius Cyprian is to be executed by the sword.

Cyprian: Thanks be to God.

We rely on the *Proconsular Acts of the Martyrdom of Saint Cyprian.* They narrate for us his final dramatic moments in this world and the reaction of the faithful, bearing in mind what Cyprian once wrote in a letter about the intrinsic value of Christian martyrdom:

He who once conquered death, can conquer it in each one of us.[67]

The *Proconsular Acts* recount:

After the sentence was passed, a crowd of [Cyprian's] fellow Christians said: "We should also be killed with him." There arose an uproar among the Christians, and a great mob followed after him. Cyprian was then brought out to the grounds of the Villa Sexti, where, taking off his outer cloak and kneeling on the ground, he fell before the Lord in prayer.[68] He removed his dalmatic and gave it to the deacons, and then stood erect while waiting for the executioner. When the executioner arrived, Cyprian told his friends to give the man twenty-five gold pieces. Cloths and napkins were being spread out in front of him by the brethren.[69] Then the blessed Cyprian covered his eyes with his own hands, but when he was unable to tie the ends of the

---

[67] Cyprian of Carthage, *Letter,* 10: 3.

[68] Russell, *Glimpses of the Church Fathers,* 91f.

[69] In this fashion the early Christians used to collect the blood of the martyrs out of respect and for veneration. The Bible teaches that the life of a man is in his blood. Therefore, blood is sacred. To shed someone's innocent blood is the worst physical crime, so much so that the blood of the innocent (e.g., Abel) cries out to God for vengeance. In the movie *The Passion of the Christ,* the Blessed Virgin Mary and St. Mary Magdalene appear at the scene of Our Lord's scourging. With towels provided them by Claudia, the wife of Pontius Pilate, together they wipe up the Most Precious Blood of Jesus, whose blood, as the Letter to the Hebrews describes, "speaks more graciously than the blood of Abel" (Hebrews 12:24). See also, CCC, 2258-2262. See Hill, *The History of Christianity,* 57: "Another account told of the death of Cyprian, bishop of Carthage who was beheaded in A.D. 258 during the Valerian persecution. It described how the very last thing that the martyr saw was a pile of cloths under the block on which he was to die, placed there by other Christians to catch his blood when he was decapitated. Those bloodstained cloths would become precious relics, for the Christians believed that God was with the martyrs, and their remains were holy. The remains of those who died were generally bought from the executioners at great cost. Many were laid in the catacombs, and these graves would be especially holy places. By the fourth century many of the martyrs' graves in the catacombs had become crypts, that is, small chapels or churches built around the tomb, where the faithful could come and pray in the presence of the martyr."

linen himself, the priest Julian and the sub-deacon Julian fastened
them for him. In this way, the blessed Cyprian suffered, and his
body was laid out at a nearby place to satisfy the curiosity of the
pagans. During the night Cyprian's body was triumphantly borne
away in a procession of Christians who, praying and bearing tapers
and torches, carried the body to the cemetery of the governor Mac-
robius Candidanus which lies on the Mappalian Way near the fish
ponds. Not many days later the governor Galerinus Maximus died.
The most blessed martyr Cyprian suffered on the fourteenth day of
September under the Emperors Valerian and Gallienus, in the reign
of the true Lord Jesus Christ, to whom belong honor and glory for
ever. Amen.[70]

---

[70] As found in the Liturgy of the Hours for the Memorial of Sts Cornelius and Cyprian. Cf.
Claire Russell, *Glimpses of the Church Fathers*, 91f. See the Second Reading of the Common of Martyrs for Several Martyrs: "How blessed is the prison honored by your presence,
how blessed the prison that sends men of God to heaven! Darkness brighter than the sun
itself, more resplendent than this light of the world, for it is here that God's temples are now
established, and your limbs made holy by your praise of God. Let nothing else be now in
your hearts and minds except God's commandments and the precepts of heaven: by their
means the Holy Spirit has always inspired you to bear your sufferings. Let no one think of
death, but only of immortality; let no one think of suffering for a time, but only of glory
that is for eternity. It is written: *Precious in the sight of God is the death of His holy ones.* And
again: *A sacrifice to God is an afflicted spirit; a broken and humble heart God does not despise.*"
Finally, see Cyprian's sermon on the so-called "white martyrdom" of consecrated virginity.
His sermon *On the Dress of Virgins* is the first option for the Common of Virgins in the
Liturgy of the Hours: "Now I wish to address the Order of Virgins. Because their way of
life is more exalted, our concern for them must be greater. If we compare the Church to a
tree, then they are its blossom. Virgins show forth the beauty of God's grace; they are the
image of God that reflects the holiness of the Lord; they are the more illustrious members of
Christ's flock. They are the glory of mother Church and maintain her fruitfulness. The more
numerous her virgins, the greater is her joy."

CHAPTER TWENTY-ONE
AUGUSTINE OF HIPPO
(A.D. 354 - 430)

"Doctor of Grace"

Saint Augustine of Hippo is generally considered the greatest convert and theologian since Saint Paul, as well as the most influential Father of the Church in the West. His statue is one of four Doctors of the Church that grace the "Altar of the Chair" in Saint Peter's Basilica in Rome.[1]

Augustine's Import

His writings dominated theological reflection in the Middle Ages, influencing Christianity's greatest thinkers from Thomas Aquinas to the Protestant Reformer Martin Luther, who interpreted Augustine in contrasting ways.

"From Misery to Mercy"[2]

Our main source of knowledge about Augustine is his autobiography, *The Confessions.*

Augustine was born in Tagaste in modern-day Algeria. His father, Patricius, was a pagan and his mother, Monica, a devout Christian. Augustine received a classical education in Carthage, excelling in philosophy and Latin,[3] but faring poorly in Greek, which language Augustine admittedly loathed.

As a young man, Augustine stole a pear from a neighbor's yard. He would later castigate himself for this action, stating that he did this simply because he wanted to get away with doing something bad. Augustine realized that this

---

[1] The statues, sculpted in bronze by Gian Lorenzo Bernini, depict the Eastern Fathers, Athanasius of Alexandria and John Chrysostom, flanked by the Western Fathers, Ambrose and Augustine.

[2] St. Augustine described the history of salvation as a movement, *a miseria ad misericordiam* ("from misery to mercy"). These words can also be used to describe Augustine's own pilgrimage of faith.

[3] Augustine recounts in *The Confessions* that he enjoyed reading Cicero's work, *Hortensius.* It was this work that piqued Augustine's interest in the serious study of philosophy at age 19 in 373.

action was indicative of an important fact, namely, that he and indeed all men inherited original sin through propagation, together with all its evil consequences like concupiscence.

Augustine searched for God his whole life long. He sought for God in the beauty and goodness of creation and sought truth through philosophical reasoning and discourse. For several years, Augustine dabbled in a variety of philosophies, especially Platonism, even joining the Manichean sect.

He had a child outside of wedlock whom he named *Adeodatus* ("gift from God"). As Augustine experienced a gradual conversion, he struggled, among other things, with celibacy although, at the same time, he admired the early Christian martyrs and felt challenged to imitate the ascetical life of Saint Anthony of Egypt. Thus, a conflicted Augustine famously prayed:

> Grant me chastity and continence, but not yet.[4]

When Augustine began reading the Old Testament instead of classical Greek and Roman philosophy, he found the former "boring" by comparison. The grace of conversion to the Christian Faith would obviously change his estimation of the first half of the Bible. So liberating was the grace of conversion that the Bishop of Hippo would later exhort Christians with these simple words:

> Love, and do whatever you want.[5]

A Mother's Tears for a Prodigal Son

His mother, Monica, shed many a tear and prayed for nearly thirty years that Augustine would become a "Catholic Christian," before she would die. Her prayers were eventually answered due in no small part to the fact that she introduced her son to the saintly bishop of Milan, Ambrose. Ambrose became Augustine's mentor and eventually baptized him in Milan at the Easter Vigil in A.D. 387. The remains of the baptistry, a huge complex, are still visible today.

Augustine's Baptism

A year earlier, in August of 386, still tottering on the fence of pagan vice and Christian virtue, Augustine rushed into a garden in Milan. There he heard the mysterious voice of a child tell him, "*Tolle, lege*" ("Take and read"). Opening his

---

[4]   Augustine of Hippo, *The Confessions*, VIII, 7.
[5]   Augustine of Hippo, *Commentary on the Epistles of John*, Tractate VII, 8.

copy of Saint Paul's Epistles, he turned to Romans 13:13-14,

> Let us conduct ourselves properly as in the day, not in orgies and drunkenness, not in promiscuity and licentiousness, not in rivalry and jealousy. But put on the Lord Jesus Christ, and make no provision for the desires of the flesh.

Contemplation in Action

After his conversion, Augustine and several of his disciples lived a semi-monastic life in North Africa. In 391, Augustine was ordained a priest. In 396, quite reluctantly, he accepted episcopal consecration as a coadjutor, becoming the Bishop of Hippo in 396 and remaining so until his death in 430.

Augustine's "Rule" for community living was eventually adopted as a rule by many religious orders and congregations (e.g., the Dominicans and Servites), most notably by the order that still bears his name the "Augustinians."

The Augustinians are considered neither monks nor mendicants but rather "canons" because they were secular or diocesan clergy, who lived a life of common prayer (chanting daily the Liturgy of the Hours in the cathedral church), penance and study. Often they did this while enjoying the company and leadership of their diocesan bishop.

Augustine was an exemplary priest and diocesan bishop, especially adept at living in peace and harmony with his own priests.

A Theologian's Theologian

Augustine was a most prolific and brilliant writer. He commanded an eloquent Latin prose with a propsensity for puns and other turns of phrase. His corpus consists of numerous sermons; homilies; commentaries on Sacred Scripture (most notably the Psalms and the Gospel of John); fiesty letters to his friend Saint Jerome with whom he often disagreed;[6] major theological treatises on topics like the Trinity, grace and free will; and controversial apologetical

---

[6] A major disagreement between Augustine and Jerome centered on which text to use as the basis of Jerome's translation of the Old Testament into Latin. Augustine believed that Jerome should translate from the Greek Septuagint, which contained the Deuterocanonical books that belonged to the so-called Alexandrian Canon popular with Jews in the Diaspora. Jerome, on the other hand, decided to follow the shorter so-called Palestinian Canon that omitted the Deuterocanonical books. Jerome distinguished the canonical books of Scripture from the so-called ecclesiastical books. He deemed the latter worthy of study, but not of inclusion in the Bible.

works aimed at correcting the errors of heretical and schismatic groups like the Manicheeans, Pelagians and Donatists—all are of incomparable literary, theological and spiritual value.

Augustine's view of history is best ascertained by reading his *magnum opus, City of God*, often compared to Plato's *Republic* in terms of its scholarly profundity and lasting influence. By far, *The Confessions* ranks among the best-known classic works of Christian literature outside the Bible and Thomas à Kempis' *The Imitation of Christ*. The most quoted line of the Confessions is a prayer taken from its First Book:

> [Lord], you have made us for yourself, and our heart is restless until it rests in you.[7]

Attributed to Saint Augustine is the phrase, *cor ad cor loquitur* (heart speaks to heart) that would centuries later be adapted as the mottos of Saint Francis de Sales and Blessed John Henry Newman.

A Saintly Mother-and-Son Combination

The Church honors Augustine as Bishop and Doctor of the Church with a liturgical memorial on August 28, fittingly celebrated a day after the memorial of his mother, Monica.

Saint Monica is buried in the Church of Saint Augustine in Rome, having died of a sudden fever at Rome's ancient port city of Ostia; her intention before becoming ill was to sail back to North Africa.

At Ostia one can still read an inscription with a quote from Augustine's final dialogue with Monica as he himself recounted it in *The Confessions*.

In that famous and touching dialogue at the lido of Ostia, Monica tells Augustine that she had prayed for one principal reason: to see Augustine become a "Catholic Christian" before she died. The stalwart Monica also added a final request that Augustine should not be concerned with a precise burial place for her old body but simply remember to pray for her at the altar of the Lord, that is, at the Eucharistic Sacrifice.

Saint Augustine is buried in the northern Italian city of Pavia. As Augustine was dying, barbarian hordes descended upon North Africa. This trend of barbarian attacks would continue for centuries to come. Barbarian tribes like the Vandals, Huns, Visigoths, Ostrogoths, and numerous others not only successfully breached the once impenetrable frontiers of the Roman Empire and wreaked

---

[7] Augustine of Hippo, *The Confessions*, 1:1.

havoc on Roman cities and villages through rape and pillage but moreover contributed in the long term to the decline and fall of the Roman Empire, unwittingly aiding and abetting Rome's own internal corruption and the rise of Christianity into which many barbarian peoples would gradually inculturate. In a real sense, Augustine's death marked the end of an era in the history of ancient Roman and classical civilization.

Doctor Gratiae

With this background in place, we can focus on Augustine as "Doctor of Grace."

Unlike Cyprian of Carthage, Augustine posited the notion that schismatics and heretics could validly administer the sacraments of salvation because the validity of the sacraments did not depend on the personal holiness of the minister but on the inherent holiness of the sacrament being performed.

This key theological distinction is encapsulated in two Latin phrases, *ex opere operato* and *ex opere operantis.*

The former phrase literally means, "from the work having been worked," that is to say, that a sacrament celebrated by a validly ordained minister according to the mind or theology of the Church is valid in and of itself; this stresses the objective dimension of every sacrament and the divine initiative.

The latter phrase literally means, "from the work of the one doing the work," that is to say, that a sacrament's efficacy but not its validity depends to a certain extent on the minister himself as well as on the recipient of the sacrament, thus holding up the subjective dimension.

These phrases became integral to medieval scholastic and neo-scholastic sacramental theology and helped form the backbone of the Church's defense of the sacraments at the Council of Trent in the sixteenth century against the heretical teachings of the Protestant Reformers. The Church teaches, in line with Augustine and Thomas Aquinas that, while it would be ideal to have the holiness of the sacrament matched by the holiness of the minister, this cannot be a prerequisite for a sacrament's validity lest every person's faith and salvation become matters of precariousness.

This is why Augustine reminds us that Christ is the principal minister of every sacrament. In his *Commentary on John*, Augustine writes:

Whoever the man is who administers the sacrament, even if he is a Judas, it is always Christ who baptizes.[8]

At the same time, Augustine also held that unbelievers, even those who had not heard the Gospel preached to them, could not be saved.

Augustine's Grace-Filled Ecclesiology

In his *Sermon 251* on the "Miraculous Catch" recounted in John 21:1-14, narrating according to the Evangelist the third apparition of the Lord after His Resurrection, Augustine rehearses several key elements of his theology of the Church as one, holy, catholic and apostolic.[9]

Augustine compares the miraculous catch related in Luke 5:1-11 to John 21:1-14. In Luke's story, the fishing expedition of Jesus from Simon's boat, together with Simon's partners James and John, moves the fishermen to leave everything to become Jesus' disciples. In turn, the Lord tells Simon Peter (and thus by extension, James and John) that they were being called instead to become "fishers of men" or His chosen Apostles. In making this comparison, Augustine notes that in Luke's version Jesus has the Apostles cast their net spontaneously, that is, in no particular direction.

For Augustine, this spontaneity symbolized that the Church, represented by the boat of Simon Peter, was casting its net of evangelization in order to haul in all types of fish, all types of men, sinners and saints alike. Thus, the Lucan catch that precedes the Resurrection tells us about the actual state of the Catholic Church in our time. This, too, is a point that Jesus makes clear in the Parable of the Weeds and the Wheat,[10] in which the Lord says that the weeds (wicked) and the wheat (good) are allowed to grow up together until the remaining weeds (those wicked men still unconverted) will be burned or thrown into the fires of Gehenna (Hell).

On the other hand, Saint Augustine notes that, in the passage of John's Gospel, Our Lord specifically commands the Apostles to throw the net over the right side of the ship. This indicates, according to Saint Augustine's allegorical interpretation of the text, that the Catholic Church in the end of times will be constituted only of saints, orthodox believers who like the sheep and not the goats mentioned in Matthew 25 ("The Judgment of the Nations") will be

---

8   Augustine of Hippo, *Commentary on John*, 6:7.
9   Our Lord's promise to Peter that the gates of hell will never prevail against the Church is the scriptural foundation for the doctrine of the Church's indefectibility. Cf. Matthew 16:18.
10   Cf. Matthew 13:24-30.

St. Augustine in His Study, *Botticelli, 1480.*

placed to the right and not to the left of Jesus in the Heavenly Kingdom.

In reference to the symbolism of the boats being on the verge of sinking and yet spared from doing so, Augustine writes that this signifies that the great quantity and diversity of the Church's members might endanger but never succeed in destroying the Church's unity. In speaking about the symbolism of torn nets, Saint Augustine explains that the Church would be threatened by schism (a word derived from the Greek, meaning "to tear away from").

Regarding the fact that the net of the Church's evangelization of all peoples is not torn, Augustine posits the notion of the Church's indefectibility, which means that the Church will never entirely cease to be what she is by reason of her divine institution, namely, one, holy, catholic and apostolic.

Finally, in offering an interpretation of the one hundred and fifty-three large fish caught in John's version of the miraculous catch, Augustine notes the following: a) the fact that the number of these fish is "great" but does not tear apart the barque of Peter means that they represent the true believers, not the heretics who seek to destroy (or sink) the Catholic Church; b) Augustine explains the symbolic significance of the number one hundred and fifty-three in relation to the Church as the New Israel:

> A gradually increasing number derives from ten and seven. Begin with one, go on to seventeen in such a way that you add all the intervening numbers, that is, add three, and it becomes six; add four, and it becomes ten. In this way, add all the numbers up to seventeen and the total is one hundred and fifty-three. Hence, our whole attention ought to be directed to nothing else except the significance of ten and seven, for therein lies the foundation of the one hundred and fifty-three. Now, what is the significance of the ten and the seven? Understand the ten as in the Law. Ten precepts were given first; the Decalogue was inscribed by the finger of God on tablets. In the ten, understand the Law; in the seven, understand the Holy Spirit, for the Holy Spirit is presented in sevenfold form [...]. But why does the Apostle say: "The letter kills, but the spirit gives life"? (2 Corinthians 3:6). How does the Spirit give life? Because He causes the letter to be fulfilled so that it may not kill. The sanctified are those who fulfill the law of God according to the gift of God. The Law can command; it cannot help. The Spirit is added as a helper, and the commandment of God is fulfilled with joy and delight.[11]

Jerome explains that the number one hundred and fifty-three mentioned in John's pericope symbolizes the number of species of fish known in the world at the time. Other explanations given by the early Church Fathers include the following: If you consider the number of nations mentioned in Acts 2 (Saint Luke's account of Pentecost), namely, seventeen, and you multiply that number by nine, the number that symbolizes a novena (as in the nine-day period of prayer addressed to the Holy Spirit before Pentecost)—the result is one hundred and fifty-three.

---

[11] Augustine of Hippo, *Sermon*, 251.

Another explanation goes as follows: Consider the numerical value of the Greek word for fish (*ichthus*)—a symbol of Christ among the early Christians—which is seventy-seven and add that number to the numerical value of the Greek word for Simon (which is seventy-six), that yields one hundred and fifty-three. In other words, Jesus and Peter go together!

PART IV

Chapter Twenty-Two deals with the formation of the Catholic Canon of the Bible, highlighting too its relation to the Jewish, Eastern Orthodox and Protestant Canons.

Chapter Twenty-Two:
The Canon of the Bible

The Formation of the Old Testament

Our studies of the Faith of the Early Church have taken us far enough that we need to consider the origins of the Bible as we know it.

We have all heard of the perennial dilemma, "What came first—the chicken or the egg?" In asking, "What came first—the Catholic Church or the Bible?"[1]—the Catholic response (which is the historically correct one) is not only that the Catholic Church indeed came first, but that the Bible would not exist as we know it if it were not for the Catholic Church and her Magisterium[2] that decided from the earliest centuries of Christianity, under the guidance of the Holy Spirit, which books were truly inspired by God and which were not. In the Catechism, we find the following bold statement of Augustine:

> But I would not believe in the Gospel, had not the authority of the Catholic Church already moved me.[3]

Augustine's statement is an excellent starting point for our discussion of the historical development of the Canon of the Bible.[4] But we can also recall the axiom of Saint Jerome, Father and Doctor of the Church in the fifth century, who dedicated his whole life as a hermit to translating and commenting on the texts of Sacred Scripture: *Ignorance of Scripture is ignorance of Christ.*

---

[1]   Our English word Bible comes from the Greek word *ton biblion*, meaning "book." The plural of the Greek word *ton biblion* is *ta biblia* or "the books." Hence, we speak of the Sacred Scripture in the singular or of the Sacred Scriptures in the plural. The Bible is not so much a single book but a collection of books written over the course of thousands of years by different authors using various literary genres to address the needs of particular audiences.

[2]   *Magisterium* derives from the Latin *magister*, meaning "teacher." In our context, the word Magisterium designates the living teaching office of the Catholic Church comprised of the bishops teaching in communion with the Pope, the Bishop of Rome.

[3]   CCC, 119.

[4]   Cf. Pelikan, *Whose Bible Is It?* (Penguin Books, 2005).

The Old Testament Canon

Canon means "rule" or "list." In the ancient world, a reed was often used as a measuring stick. In this context, "canon" designates the official list of the books of the Bible recognized by the Church as inspired by God. A simple observation reveals that there are differences among Bibles. The Catholic Bible contains forty-six Old Testament books and twenty-seven New Testament books (for a total of seventy-three books), while the Protestant Bible has thirty-nine Old Testament and twenty-seven New Testament books, equaling sixty-six books.

A Second List of Books

What accounts for the difference? The difference lies in the fact that the Catholic canon contains seven additional books: Tobit, Judith, Wisdom, Sirach, Baruch and 1-2 Maccabees. Catholic Bibles also contain an additional six chapters of the Book of Esther (103 verses) and three more chapters of the Book of Daniel (174 verses) found in the Greek manuscripts of the Old Testament and not in the Hebrew manuscripts. In the Catholic and Orthodox Bibles, but not in the Protestant Bible, the additional material from the Book of Daniel consists of the following: The Prayer of Azariah and the Song of the Three Youths (3:23-24); the story of Susanna (chapter 13); the story of Bel and the Dragon (chapter 14).

Catholics refer to these seven Old Testament books as "Deuterocanonical," that is to say, belonging to a "second canon" or "second list" of the Bible; Jews and Protestants refer to them as Apocryphal,[5] thus denying them the official status or canonicity that they attribute to the other books of the Old Testament (Hebrew or Jewish Scriptures) that we hold in common.

Various Christian Orthodox Churches include other Deutero-Canonical books, namely, Psalm 151, 1 Esdras, Odes (with the Prayer of Manasseh), Psalms of Solomon, 3 Maccabees, and more rarely 4 Maccabees (since it has strong pagan overtones). Among Ethiopian Orthodox Christians, the Book of Enoch is afforded quasi-canonical status.

It is interesting that in Jude 1:14-15 the sacred author mentions Enoch and one of his prophecies, even though the Book of Enoch was ultimately deemed apocryphal by the Catholic Church and likewise excluded from the Hebrew Canon. Of course, this merely demonstrates that in Judaism, as in

---

[5]   Sometimes Protestant and ecumenical editions of the Bible, especially study editions, will include the Deuterocanonical books in an appendix under the heading Apocrypha, which is the plural of the Greek word *apocryphon*, meaning "things that are hidden away."

Catholicism, not every truth must be explicitly taught in Scripture. Sebastian R. Fama comments:

> Bible Christians use the shorter canon because it matches the present-day Jewish Canon. They will often quote Romans 3:2, which says: "The Jews are entrusted with the oracles of God." They reason that since God entrusted the Old Testament to the Jews, they should be the ones who determine which books belong in it. This reasoning presents a couple of problems. Firstly, both Old Testament Canons were received from the Jews. Thus neither canon is eliminated by this verse. Secondly, the Jews didn't settle on the Palestinian Canon until at least 90 A.D. at the Council of Jamnia. This was well after authority had passed from the Jews to the Church (Acts 4:19). Ironically it was at the Council of Jamnia that the Jews also rejected the New Testament. Logically speaking, anyone who would consider Jamnia as being authoritative would also have to reject the New Testament.[6]

Catholics revere these seven Old Testament books as belonging to a "second canon" or "second list" because they seem to have been a reference point for the sacred authors of the New Testament, who relied on the Septuagint.

For example, compare Revelation 1:4; 8:3-4 with Tobit 12:15; these texts refer to seven spirits (angels) who stand before the throne of God and offer Him the prayers of the saints. Or compare Hebrews 11:35 and 2 Maccabees 7:29 that speak of the certain hope in the resurrection of the dead on the part of women who were mourning their dead sons, some of whom they had exhorted to be martyred for the Faith.

Perhaps also with a little more difficulty one can see how Saint Paul in writing 1 Corinthians 15:29 may have been influenced by 2 Maccabees 12:44. Saint Paul speaks of being baptized for the dead, a practice that sounds eerie at first and which in the literal sense is in fact forbidden by the Catholic Church. However, the context in which Paul speaks of this practice (cf. 1 Corinthians 15:30-32) suggests to some scholars that this baptism was not so much by means of water, but by means of prayer, fasting and penances offered up on behalf of the faithful departed, a baptism of suffering, as it were, such as is recommended in the Deuterocanonical book of 2 Maccabees.

---

[6] This text can be found at the following web site: http://www.staycatholic.com/the_canon_of_scripture.htm

The Alexandrian Canon

The "second canon" is commonly identified with the so-called Alexandrian Canon because it circulated among the Greek-speaking (no longer Hebrew- or Aramaic-speaking) Jews living outside of Palestine in the "Diaspora" (Dispersion); around one million of these Jews lived in the Egyptian capital of Alexandria from the third century B.C. to the first century A.D.

In the Greco-Roman world, Alexandria (founded by and named after Alexander the Great) was the main cosmopolitan rival of Rome and Athens. Because of its enviable position at the crossroads of the eastern and western parts of the Mediterranean, Alexandria became a commercial, philosophical and religious center of much prestige. It was famous, among other things, for having the largest "library complex" in the world (*mouseion*) and for a massive "lighthouse" (*faros*) in its harbor. These two wonders of the ancient world were most unfortunately destroyed centuries ago, but, at least, the library complex has been innovatively rebuilt according to modern architectural capabilities.

The Alexandrian Canon of the Bible formed the basis for the Septuagint or Greek translation of the Old Testament, upon which the sacred authors of the New Testament relied. The Old Testament is quoted in the New Testament three hundred and fifty times, of which three hundred are from the Septuagint.

In *Whose Bible Is It?* Pelikan explains the legend behind the composition of the Septuagint:

> According to a legend that was originally published under the pseudonym "Aristeas" and is certainly fictitious but that nevertheless achieved wide circulation as well as considerable embellishment over time, King Ptolemy Philadelphius of Egypt in the third century B.C.E.[7] received from Demetrius of Phalerum, director of the celebrated library at Alexandria, the proposal that the Jewish Law, the Torah, should be translated into Greek to fill a serious gap in the holdings of the library's collection; librarians then as now, cannot

---

[7]   B.C.E. is an abbreviation meaning "Before the Common Era," in some quarters now used to replace B.C. (Before Christ). Many secularists tend to favor this abbreviation and its counterpart C.E. (Common Era, to replace A.D., Anno Domini, In the Year of Our Lord) because it seemingly takes Christ out of the picture of mankind's history. But what really constitutes the so-called the "Common Era," anyway? Western calendars, and certainly the global business calendar, have not changed. Whether one uses the B.C.E. and C.E. abbreviations or B.C. and A.D., one still counts the years as occurring before and after Christ. Christ is the Lord of history and His entrance into time at the moment of the Incarnation was anything but a commonplace event; it marked the apex of history. While the word "common" may feign neutrality, it unwittingly still points to Christ as the focal point of history.

stand to see a blank space on their shelves. Ptolemy was proud of his library, and he was also interested in the world religions, having once received an embassy of Buddhist scholars from India. He therefore sent a delegation of which "Aristeas" claims to have been a member, to Eleazar, the high priest at Jerusalem, with the request that six scholars from each of the twelve tribes of Israel be dispatched to Alexandria to carry out this assignment of translating the Torah. According to one version of the Letter of Aristeas, the Greek translations of the entire Jewish Scriptures from the Hebrew, produced individually by each of these seventy-two scholars, turned out to be identical, which was irrefutable evidence that they were divinely inspired. From the legendary number of the translators, this version acquired the name Septuagint (the Latin word for seventy), which is customarily abbreviated as LXX.[8]

The Palestinian Canon and the Masoretic Text

Those Jews who lived in the Greek-speaking Diaspora most likely followed the Alexandrian Canon, and continued to do so if and when they returned to the Holy Land.[9] The Jews living within Palestine followed a shorter canon—lacking the Deuterocanonical books—commonly referred to as the Palestinian Canon. It is based on the so-called Palestinian Canon that the Masoretic text (named after the Jewish scholars the Masoretes) [10]was formed by which the Hebrew text of the Bible received for the first time written marks determining the vowel sounds in between the consonants (since the Hebrew alphabet lacks vowels).

The Divisions of the Bible

For the Jews there is obviously no such reality as the Old Testament. They refer to the Bible as the Hebrew or Jewish Scriptures and sometimes by the term *Tanakh* (TNK).

---

[8] Pelikan, *Whose Bible is It?*, 56-57 passim.

[9] Under the heading "Deuterocanonical Books," Wikipedia states: "Most Septuagint manuscripts include the Deuterocanonical books and passages. Like the New Testament, the Deuterocanonical books were mostly written in Greek. Several appear to have been written originally in Hebrew, but the original text has been lost. Archeological finds in the last century, however, have provided a text of almost two-thirds of the book of Sirach, and fragments of other books have been found as well. One of these books, 2 Esdras, survives only in an ancient Latin translation dated to the second century A.D. but was probably composed in Greek. This particular book is not widely accepted by the Orthodox and is rejected by Catholics. The Septuagint was widely accepted and used by Jews in the first century, even in the Roman Judaea Province, and therefore naturally became the text most widely used by early Christians." http://en.wikipedia.org/wiki/Deuterocanonical_books.

[10] The Hebrew word *Masorah* means "tradition."

The letter T stands for *Torah,* meaning the "Law" that God revealed to Moses on Mount Sinai (Horeb). Although the word *Torah* is occasionally used by Jews to refer to the whole of Sacred Scripture it more precisely designates the first five books of the Bible, also called the Pentateuch (comprised of two Greek words meaning, "a book composed of five scrolls").

Jewish tradition holds that Moses was the principal author, that is, the sacred scribe, who wrote the first five books that include: Genesis, Exodus, Leviticus, Numbers and Deuteronomy. Thus, they are commnoly called "The Law of Moses" or "The Books of Moses."

The Samaritans and Sadducees were groups that, for different reasons, only revered as Sacred Scripture the first five books of the Bible. Indeed, for all Jews, the *Torah* has the same pride of place in their Bibles as do the four Gospels in the New Testament.

The reader should recall that the order in which the books of the Hebrew Scriptures appear as well as the various names or titles attributed to those books do not correspond necessarily to how those books are called and placed within the contexts of the Catholic and Protestant canons of the Old Testament. For example, we refer to the first book of the Bible as the Book of Genesis. However, Genesis is a Greek word, not a Hebrew one. Genesis means: "origin." This same book in the Hebrew Bible simply begins with the Hebrew word: *beresit* meaning: "In the beginning."

The letter N stand for the Hebrew word *Neviim,* meaning: "Prophets." For the Jews, this section of the Bible is divided into two parts: the "Former Prophets" and the "Latter Prophets."

The "Former Prophets," contain the following books: Joshua, Judges, 1-2 Samuel, 1 and 2 Kings.[11] The "Latter Prophets" are furthermore, divided into two sub-sections of the "Major Prophets" and the "Minor Prophets." The "Major Prophets" include the books of Isaiah, Jeremiah and Ezechiel. The "Minor Prophets" include twelve books: Hosea, Joel, Amos, Obadiah, Jonah, Micah, Nahum, Habakkuk, Zephaniah, Haggai, Zechariah and Malachy.

The letter K stands for the Hebrew word, *Ketuvim* or "Writings." These books are: Psalms, Proverbs, Job, Song of Songs (also known as the Canticle of

---

[11]   In some Catholic versions of the Bible, such as the Douay-Rheims, the Books of 1-2 Samuel are listed as 1-2 Kings, while the Books of 1-2 Kings are listed as 3-4 Kings.

Canticles or Song of Solomon), Ruth, Lamentations (of Jeremiah), Ecclesiastes (Qoheleth), Esther, Daniel, Ezra, Nehemiah, 1 and 2 Chronicles.[12]

Often, as evidenced by Jesus' own way of speaking in the New Testament, the Book of Psalms might be mentioned so as to designate all the "writings."

When the Jews returned from exile in Babylon, they rebuilt the walls of Jerusalem and reconstructed the Temple that had been destroyed by the Babylonians. This historic era is known as the Second Temple Period. During this time a large number of other books surfaced that were written by Jews in Hebrew, Aramaic and Greek. These books were eventually excluded from the Hebrew Canon of the Bible, although they were accepted by the Catholic and Orthodox Churches.

Other writings from the Second Temple Period are called Pseudoepigrapha, meaning "false writings." These books include books like: The Testament of the Twelve Patriarchs, 1 and 2 Enoch and Jubilees. These books were rejected as non-canonical by Jews, Catholics and Protestants alike.

According to Talmudic tradition, the official Canon of the Hebrew Bible was not decided until the Council of Jamnia[13] was held circa A.D. 90-100.

The Bible is a Church Document

For the development of the Canon of the Bible, the Catholic Church relied on the assistance of various councils like those at Hippo in A.D. 393 and at Carthage in A.D. 397 and again in A.D. 419. At those early councils, the Fathers of the Church also confirmed the normative use of the Septuagint version of the Old Testament Scriptures.

The majority of the Fathers of the Church, both from the East (e.g., Saints Athanasius of Alexandria, Cyril of Jerusalem, Gregory Nazianzus) and from the West (e.g., Saints Irenaeus of Lyons, Augustine of Hippo, Cyprian of Carthage), with the notable exception of Saint Jerome, accepted the Septuagint, and therefore the seven Deuterocanonical books, as truly inspired by God, faithful to the Apostolic Tradition.

---

[12] According to the Greek Septuagint, 1-2 Chronicles were referred to as 1-2 Paraleipomenon because they were mistakingly thought to have filled in what had been "omitted" (Greek word: *paraleipo* means "to omit") from the books of Kings and Samuel. The present title derives from St. Jerome who, in his Latin Vulgate translation of the Hebrew and Greek texts of the Bible, characterized these books as "The Chronicle of the Whole of Divine History."

[13] Jamnia, formerly Jabneel, was a town four miles away from the Mediterranean Sea. It was destroyed by Judas Maccabeus, who set it on fire. Today Jamnia corresponds to the town of Yibna, twelve miles south of Joppa.

The oldest Greek manuscripts of the Old Testament contain the Deutero-canonical books, not placing them in a separate section but rather including them among the other canonical books. These Greek manuscripts are known as the *Codex Sinaiticus* (Codex of Sinai) and the *Codex Alexandrinus* (Codex of Alexandria).

The *Codex Sinaiticus* is the earliest surviving complete manuscript of the New Testament containing also parts of the Old Testament. It dates to the fourth century A.D. and was written in Greek on parchment. In the nineteenth century, the *Codex Sinaiticus* was discovered at the Monastery of Saint Catherine at the foot of Mount Sinai. The Monastery of Saint Catherine is the world's oldest monastery in continual use and belongs to the Greek Orthodox Church.

The *Codex Alexandrinus* dates from circa A.D. 400-450. It is one of the oldest copies of the Bible. It was hand-written in Greek and probably originated in Alexandria, Egypt, whence the Patriarch of Constantinople obtained it. He later gave the Codex as a present to King Charles II of England in 1627.

The practice of putting the Deuterocanonical books into a class by themselves within the Bible is a Protestant one that goes back to around 1520. Following the teachings of Martin Luther and other Protestant reformers, Protestant Bibles omitted these books because they contained doctrines that they found unacceptable.

For example, prayer for the dead is found in Tobit 12:12 and 2 Maccabees 12:39-45. However, this doctrine has roots in other books that the Protestants do accept such as 1 Corinthians 15:29. Likewise, Protestants objected to the doctrine of the intercession of dead saints, such as we find in 2 Maccabees 15:14, failing to see how this doctrine is also contained in Revelation 6:9-10.[14]

They also rejected the doctrine of the intermediary and intercessory role of angels, as mentioned in Tobit 12:12, 15, and which is yet completely in keeping with what we are taught about the angels in Revelation 5:8; 8:3-4.

The Formation of the New Testament

In the last section, we considered the development of the Old Testament. It is now opportune to consider the development of the New Testament Canon.

The twenty-seven books of the New Testament Canon were written in a form of Greek known as *koiné* or "common" Greek that was a simplified version of the Classical or Attic Greek used in the philosophical writings of Plato and Aristotle,

---

[14] Interestingly, Luther was in favor of removing the Book of Revelation from the New Testament, as well as the Epistle of James and the Epistle to the Hebrews—on his own authority—all because they taught doctrines held by the Catholic Church and rejected by him.

the epic poems of Homer's *Iliad* and *Odyssey*, the tragedies of Sophocles, and the comedies of Aristophanes.

The New Testament books can be roughly dated from A.D. 50 to A.D.100. Many scholars believe that Saint Paul's First Epistle to the Thessalonians was the earliest New Testament writing.

It is amazing to realize that more manuscripts of the New Testament (nearly five thousand) have survived from antiquity than manuscripts of the most important pagan works of antiquity. The oldest fragment of the New Testament is dated to the first half of the second century A.D.—a copy of the Gospel of John. The most ancient manuscripts containing the entire New Testament date to the fourth century A.D.

In 1740 Lorenzo A. Muratori found a precious document that now bears his name: "Muratorium Fragment," sometimes referred to as the *Muratorianum* or "Muratorian Document." The Muratorium Fragment consists of a catalogue of books dating to the second half of the second century A.D. This catalogue indicates the books of the Bible that the Christians of Rome considered to be truly inspired by God. The list of books corresponds to the Canon of the Bible approved by the Council of Trent, except for the Letter to the Hebrews, the Letter of James and 2 Peter. The Muratorium Fragment also refers to the apocryphal text known as the Shepherd of Hermas, whose author is named as the brother of Pope Pius who reigned from A.D. 140 to A.D. 155. The dates for the pontificate of Pope Pius have helped scholars date the Muratorium Fragment to circa A.D. 180.

How are the New Testament writings dated? The two main criteria are the writing material used and the style of writing employed. The oldest manuscripts tended to be written on papyrus parchments with majuscule letters, rather than miniscule letters.

Regarding the origins of the Gospels, the Catechism of the Catholic Church delineates three stages of formation: 1) The life and teaching of Jesus; 2) The oral tradition of the Apostles being led into the fullness of truth under the guidance of the Holy Spirit; 3) The four written historical Gospels that are not meant so much to be biographies of Jesus as different portraits of Him, whose varying perspectives are complementary and not contradictory.[15]

Justin Martyr, who lived from circa A.D. 100 to circa A.D. 160, is the earliest Father of the Church to state clearly that there are more books in the Old Testament Scriptures revered by the Christians than in the Hebrew Scriptures

---

[15] Cf. CCC, 126.

revered by the Jews. He also is the first Church Father to assert quite boldly that the Catholic Church possessed the sole legitimate authority to decide on which books should be considered divinely inspired and entered into the canon.

The second-century Gnostic heretic Marcion misinterpreted Saint Paul as having been anti-Jewish when he teaches that Christians are no longer slaves to the Old Law because they have been freed by the Gospel of grace. Based on this misinterpretation of Paul and also on his typical Gnostic dualism that pitted the material world against the spiritual world, Marcion rejected the Old Testament. He equated the God of Creation with the God of the Old Covenant, to whom he attributed the unflattering characteristics of anger and retribution, enslaving man by means of the Mosaic Law.

On the other hand, Marcion accepted only parts of the New Testament, for example, the Gospel of Luke known as the "Gospel of Mercy" and what he deemed the anti-Jewish portions of the Epistles of Saint Paul that agreed with his understanding of the God of the New Covenant as the God of love and freedom.

On this basis, Marcion proposed his own Canon of the Bible, for which he was roundly condemned by Fathers of the Church like Irenaeus of Lyons. Another, although a less formidable threat to the Christian Canon of the Bible than Marcion's, came from a second-century heretic by the name of Montanus (hence Montanism), who came from Phrygia in Asia Minor.

Montanus attracted followers, especially in northern Africa, among whom were many women, most notably Priscilla and Maximilla, and the early Christian theologian Tertullian, who ironically wrote works in which he condemned the Gnostic heresy of Marcion. The Montanists claimed to be ecstatic prophets, having secret knowledge of apocalyptic visions through the writings of Montanus. They were moral rigorists and so

> preached absolute chastity and the rejection of the world in view of its imminent end which was to accompany the advent of the Holy Spirit, the Paraclete.[16]

Their strict asceticism led them to practice long fasts and to deny that the Catholic Church had the power to forgive mortal sins like adultery. They believed that mortal sin could only be forgiven by a special act of God's grace or if the sinner gave up his life as a martyr; viewed even legitimate "second marriages" as adultery; urged their followers to avoid contact with those whom they con-

---

[16] Beatrice, *Introduction to the Fathers of the Church*, 141.

sidered impure like idolaters and adulterers; rejected the doctrine of apostolic succession and therefore the apostolic authority of the college of bishops in communion with the Pope; and insisted on admitting women to priestly ordination.

For all these reasons, the Montanists too posed a direct threat not only to the legitimate formation of the biblical Canon but indeed to the Church's unity, holiness, catholicity and apostolicity.

Returning to the positive story of the development of the Canon, we find that already from A.D. 150 Papias, Bishop of Gerapolis, attests that the author of the Gospel of Mark was the interpreter or stenographer of Saint Peter while living in Rome. According to Irenaeus of Lyons in his anti-Marcion prologue, written in the second century A.D., the Gospel of Mark was written shortly after the death of Saint Peter in Rome, circa A.D. 65.

Clement of Alexandria, on the other hand, suggests that the Gospel of Mark was actually written during Saint Peter's lifetime. Some biblical scholars assert that Mark, whose audience consisted of pagans living outside of Palestine, was the first Gospel to be written. Others argue for the greater antiquity of Matthew's Gospel because they claim that the Greek text is not the original but that there was an original Aramaic and/or Hebrew text that was lost.

The actual Greek text of Matthew's Gospel, written for an audience of Jewish converts to Christianity, was probably written outside of Palestine, perhaps from Syria (Antioch) between A.D. 80 and A.D. 90. Apart from the dating of the Gospel of Matthew, most of the early Fathers of the Church and Christian writers like Origen of Alexandria, Jerome and Epiphanius of Salamis, following the earliest testimony of Papias, Bishop of Gerapolis in the first half of the second century, agreed that the Apostle Levi or Matthew was indeed its author.

Saint Luke seems to have been aware of the destruction of the Temple of Jerusalem in A.D. 70. Therefore, dating the composition before then seems unlikely. Rather, it is more often dated to the period between A.D. 80 and A.D. 90. The Gospel's intended audience was most likely

Christians of Hellenistic origin, that is to say, Greek-speaking converts unfamiliar with Hebrew/Aramaic terms, customs, and Palestinian geography, much of which is frequently explained by the sacred author. Irenaeus of Lyons was convinced that the author of this Gospel was the disciple Luke whom Paul identified as a physician and mentioned in Colossians 4:14; Philemon 24; and 2 Timothy 4:11.

The Gospel of John stands on its own among the four Gospels. There is nothing inherent in the Gospel to suggest a precise date of the composition or author. According to Irenaeus of Lyons (who was a disciple of Polycarp of Smyrna who, in turn, was a disciple of John the Apostle), authorship of the Fourth Gospel should be attributed to John the Beloved Disciple who rested his head on the Lord's bosom at the Last Supper and who composed his text at Ephesus.

In this regard, Fathers of the Church and early Christian writers like Origen, Clement of Alexandria and Tertullian are of one accord with Irenaeus of Lyons. The fourth evangelist composed his text in reference to a series of Jewish feasts that, unlike the Synoptic Gospels, extends Jesus' public ministry from one to three years. It seems that the Fourth Gospel was composed near the end of the first century A.D.

Origen of Alexandria, like most of the early Fathers of the Church, considered Matthew to be the first Gospel written, precisely because his Jewish audience seemed to be the most logical starting point. It is thanks to these Fathers of the Church who first deliberated on the Canon of the New Testament, that we owe the tradition according to which the four Gospels appear in the Bible in the chronological order in which they were believed to have been composed.

Irenaeus, in his late second-century work, *Adversus Haereses* (Against the Heresies), stated emphatically that only the four Gospels of Matthew, Mark, Luke and John should be considered as divinely inspired Gospels and read by true Christians. Thus, we have an early testimony of a Father of the Church against the divine inerrancy and inspiration of the Gnostic Gospels and other Gnostic literature that tried to pass itself off as authentic, indeed, more authentic than the canonical writings of the Old and New Testaments.

Another indirect contribution of the Fathers of the Church to the development of the Catholic Canon of the Bible came from Eusebius of Caesarea, the author of a history of the Church (*Ecclesiastical History*) and official biographer of the Emperor Constantine in the fourth century.

Five years after the Council of Nicaea (325), Constantine asked Eusebius to produce fifty copies of the Catholic Bible to be distributed among the churches in Constantinople. Eusebius put into his *Ecclesiastical History* and included in the fifty Bibles he distributed to the churches a list of eighteen New Testament books, including some books that were disputed by Christians at the time.

The Council of Laodicea (circa A.D. 360) listed most of the books of the present Catholic Canon, including Baruch (that is considered an attachment to the Book of the Prophet Jeremiah), but not Tobit, Judith, Wisdom, Sirach, 1 and 2 Maccabees, and the Book of Revelation.

The deliberations of several other councils (synods) were helpful in the formation of the New Testament Canon: the First Council of Carthage (393); the Third Council of Carthage (397); the Fourth Council of Carthage (419). In the East, the Trullan Synod of 692 played an important role in this regard as well. The question of the New Testament Canon was likewise an issue that came up during the Council of Florence in 1441 as the Council Fathers sought to reconcile the Jacobites.

Typically, the Epistle to the Hebrews was considered the most problematic book from the perspective of Western Christians because its precise author was unknown. For centuries the book was attributed to Saint Paul, but modern biblical scholarship questions that theory, so much so that almost all Bible translations nowadays refer to it as the Epistle to the Hebrews and no longer as the Epistle of Saint Paul to the Hebrews. From the perspective of Eastern Christians, the canonicity of the Book of Revelation was frequently called into question due to its apocalyptic nature that made it the most difficult book of the New Testament, perhaps of the entire Bible, to interpret.

Perhaps the most significant development in the early Church with regard to the formation of the New Testament Canon may have occurred in A.D. 367, when Saint Athanasius, Patriarch of Alexandria, wrote a circular letter for Easter to the bishops of Egypt in which all twenty-seven of the New Testament books as we know them appeared together for the first time.

The Catholic Canon of the Bible was definitively and solemnly defined only in the sixteenth century at the Council of Trent; the precise date was April 8, 1546. Subsequently, the Fathers of the First Vatican Council confirmed the decision of the Council of Trent on April 24, 1870.

PART V

Chapters Twenty-Three to Twenty-Six are focused on early key Christian writings and they portrayal of the four marks of the Church (one, holy, catholic and apostolic) and her unique role in human history as the universal sacrament of salvation.

CHAPTER TWENTY-THREE:
THE *DIDACHE*

The First Christian Catechism

The Christian document known as *The Teaching of the Twelve Apostles*, more commonly referred to by the Greek word *Didache* ("teaching"), was written around A.D. 93. The author of this anonymous document, which is one of the oldest and most venerated of Christian catechisms, was probably a Jewish convert who wrote in Greek, while based in either Palestine or Syria.

Rome, Crypt of the Popes in the Catacombs of St. Callistus.
Source: Dnalor 01, Wikimedia.

The significance of the *Didache* in the Early Church is evident from the fact that it was cited in many other important writings such as the *Letter of Pseudo-Barnabas* (A.D. 120) and *The Shepherd of Hermas* (A.D. 140). The *Didache* was also a source of catechetical inspiration for early Christian writers like Clement of Alexandria (A.D. 150-215) and Origen of Alexandria (A.D. 185-254).

Although this catechetical document was much revered by the Fathers of the

Early Church, it somehow got lost in the shuffle of history until a Greek copy (dating to 1056) was rediscovered by the Metropolitan Philotheos Byrennios in Constantinople in 1873. Later, large papyrus fragments of the *Didache* dating to the fourth century A.D. were found. Finally, in 430 the *Didache* was found in the Georgian language, which was a translation of the Greek text, attributed to a Bishop Jeremiah.

A central theme of the *Didache* is ecclesial unity. The *Didache* teaches that the common good of all Christ's faithful needs to be secured by fidelity to the norms that regulate Christian doctrine, comportment, the right exercise of charismatic and hierarchical charisms (gifts), and the faithful administration and stewardship of the sacraments like Baptism, the Holy Eucharist and Penance.

Baptism derives from the Greek *baptizein*, meaning "to immerse." Already the *Didache* explains to us the "matter" and the "form" of Baptism. The "matter," of course, is water. The "form" of the sacrament is the Trinitarian formula recited while the person to be baptized is either immersed into the water, or has the water poured over his head (the most common practice of Baptism nowadays, known as *infusion*), or is carefully sprinkled with the holy water.

Certain Christians argue that Baptism can be validly performed in the Name of Jesus only, while yet others claim that immersion is the only valid form of baptism. On the contrary, the Church's immemorial baptismal doctrine and practice is based on the use of the Trinitarian formula handed down by Our Lord to the disciples in the Great Commission recounted in Matthew 28:16-20.

Furthermore, the Catholic Church's teachings about Baptism are firmly rooted in sacred and apostolic Tradition attested to in the *Didache* where it stipulates:

> You should baptize in this way. Having recited all these things, baptize in the Name of the Father and of the Son and of the Holy Spirit in running water. But if you have no running water, use other water and if you cannot use cold water, use warm. If you have neither, then pour water on the head three times in the Name of the Father and of the Son and of the Holy Spirit. [1]

The *Didache* relates that the early Christians gathered together on the first day of the week, that is, Sunday, the Day of the Lord's Resurrection, in order to celebrate the "Eucharist," meaning "thanksgiving." They also referred to the

[1] *Didache*, 7:1-4.

Mass as the *Fractio Panis* or "The Breaking of the Bread." Holy Communion was given only to the baptized; thus the Sacrament of the Holy Eucharist is referred to in the *Didache* as "*the Holy Things given to the holy ones.*"[2]

In the Byzantine Liturgy before the distribution of Holy Communion, the priest raises the chalice and *diskos*[3] while singing or saying: *Holy Things to the holy.*[4]

This expression is intrinsically related to another theological expression, namely, *Communicatio in Sacris* ("Communion in Sacred Realities"), that is, sharing in the sacraments, especially the Holy Eucharist. In this context the *Didache* says that we ought not to give what we regard as holy to the dogs, meaning to the non-baptized; elsewhere, Our Lord exhorts us in the Gospel not to throw our pearls before swine — both admittedly strong expressions.

This language of the early Christians is appropriately harsh or strict because Eucharistic Communion is a serious matter. If the Eucharistic Species were considered mere bread and wine, then such injunctions would carry no weight. But as Saint Paul taught the Christians at Corinth,

> The cup of blessing which we bless, is it not a participation in the blood of Christ? The bread which we break, is it not a participation in the body of Christ? Because there is one bread, we who are many are one body; for we all partake of the one bread.[5]

Again, Saint Paul instructs us:

> Whoever, therefore, eats this bread or drinks the cup of the Lord in an unworthy manner will be guilty of profaning the Body and Blood of the Lord. Let a man examine himself, and so eat of the bread and drink of the cup. For anyone who eats and drinks without discerning the body eats and drinks judgment upon himself.[6]

It is probably with such Pauline injunctions in mind that the *Didache*[7] refers to communal confession of sin, especially sins against fraternal charity, as a rite used in the context of the Mass, so that "our sacrifice might be acceptable."

---

[2]   Greek: *ta hagia tois hagiois.* Latin: *sancta sanctis.*
[3]   The *diskos* is the Greek equivalent of the paten.
[4]   Cf. CCC, 1328-1332.
[5]   1 Corinthians 10: 16-17.
[6]   1 Corinthians 11:27-29.
[7]   *Didache*, 14:1.

As Catholics, we believe that the recitation of a sincere Act of Contrition outside of Mass absolves one of venial sins. This is also our belief with regard to a sincere participation in the Penitential Act of the Mass (e.g., *Confiteor*, "I confess"). However, any and all mortal or grave sins[8] must be absolved by a priest in the Sacrament of Penance. Thus, for example, in the Nicene Creed, is confessed: "I confess one Baptism for the forgiveness of sins," whereby the link between the Sacraments of Baptism and Penance is implied. The Fathers of the Church often referred to the Sacrament of Penance as a "second baptism," not with water but with the tears of repentance.

The Church's unity and catholicity are underscored in the *Didache* when it describes the Church as meant to be gathered into the Kingdom of Heaven from the ends of the earth, elsewhere referred to as the four winds or four corners of the earth, as grain once scattered on the hillsides is gathered together to form a single loaf of bread, an allusion with clear eucharistic overtones.[9]

This is considered not only an actual truth about the Church at the time, but likewise expressive of an eschatological hope, a prayerful wish for the end times when Christ will return in glory to bring to full glory the Church He founded. In order to make the best preparation possible for the "Second Coming" of the Lord (Greek: *parousia*), the *Didache* stresses the need to live a coherent Christian life.

In doing so, the *Didache*, not unlike the Book of Deuteronomy 11:26-31 and *The Dead Sea Scrolls* of the Essene monks who lived at Qumran near the Dead Sea in Our Lord's time, distinguishes clearly between two ways: the way that leads toward sin and everlasting death, and the way of life based on love of God and neighbor that leads toward holiness and everlasting life. In the *Didache*, we learn what the distinguishing characteristics of "the way of death" are:

> But this is the way of death. First of all, it is evil and filled with a curse: Murders, adulteries, passions, fornications, thefts, idolatries, magic arts, deeds of sorcery, robberies, false testimonies, hypocrisies, duplicities, deceit, haughtiness, wickedness, arrogance, greed, obscene speech, jealousy, boldness, pride, boasting, lack of reverence.

---

8 There are three conditions for a sin to be considered mortal or grave: 1) grave matter; 2) full knowledge of the gravity of the matter; 3) full consent of the will to commit the sin.

9 Pope John Paul II's last encyclical, promulgated for the "Year of the Eucharist" (October 2004-October 2005), was entitled *Ecclesia de Eucharistia* ("The Church from the Eucharist"). The Holy Father's theology also implied that "the Eucharist is from the Church," namely, *Eucharistia de Ecclesia*.

They are persecutors of good people, hating truth and loving false-hood, who are ignorant of the reward of justice, who do not keep watch for good but for evil. Gentleness and patience are far from them, and they love vain things, run after repayment, do not have mercy on the poor, are not troubled over the oppressed and do not recognize their Creator. They are murderers of infants, abortionists of the creation of God; they turn away from the needy and despise the afflicted. They are advocates of the rich, the unjust judges of the poor, persons altogether sinful. May you be delivered, my children, from all of these![10]

Excursus: The Dead Sea Scrolls

The Dead Sea lies between the borders of Israel and Jordan. It is the lowest place on the earth's surface. It is 67 km long, 18 km wide, and 799 m below sea level at its deepest point. The Dead Sea's surface is 394.6 meters or 1269 feet below sea level. Because the Dead Sea, also referred to as the "Salt Sea," contains four times the amount of salt of any of the oceans of the earth, practically no living organism can be found in it; hence the use of the adjective "dead."

The Dead Sea Scrolls were inadvertently discovered by a Bedouin shepherd boy in caves at Qumran near the Dead Sea in 1947 when he threw stones into one of the caves and heard the sound of jars breaking. The scrolls are the old-est copies of the Sacred Scriptures known to mankind thus far, save for some important earlier archeological inscriptions. They number about 1100 docu-ments, plus more than one hundred thousand fragments. They were written in Hebrew, Aramaic and Greek.

They are also astonishing because they were practically perfectly preserved over two millennia in clay jars, having been written on leather parchment made from goat or sheep skins, on papyrus, with one notable exception on copper. The scrolls, which are believed to have been written between 250 B.C. and A.D. 68, contain fragmentary texts of all the Old Testament books, save for the Book of Esther, along with commentaries on other books of the Bible.

Perhaps the most celebrated of the scrolls, kept in Israel's museum known as *The Shrine of the Book*, is the entire text of Isaiah. The Book of Isaiah is considered therefore the oldest manuscript of an Old Testament book that has come down to us. It is dated around 100 B.C.

Contrary to the claims of Dan Brown's *The Da Vinci Code,* the Dead Sea Scrolls do not contain manuscripts of any New Testament texts, nor do they

---

[10] *Didache*, 5.

refer to New Testament personages like Jesus and Mary Magdalene, let alone describing an amorous relationship between the two.

The Essenes were a group of monks, some of whom were celibate, who lived in the desert area of Qumran near the Dead Sea. They are believed to have moved into the desert because they rejected the corruption of the Temple priests and Sadducees, the aristocratic priestly class, who controlled the Temple at Jerusalem in collaboration with the Roman overlords. In order to purify themselves in preparation for the Messiah's coming (sometimes identified with the "Master/Teacher of Righteousness" mentioned in their writings), the Essenes devoted themselves to the so-called "Way of Light" as opposed to "the Way of Darkness."

The Way of Light or Righteousness consisted in a highly ascetical life of prayer, fasting, study and copying of Sacred Scripture, ritual purification, and the sharing of sacred meals. Some scholars argue that John the Baptist may have had contact with the Essenes, may even have been a member himself for a time, and likewise may have served to introduce Jesus to the Essenes, their teachings and ascetical practices.

CHAPTER TWENTY-FOUR
LESSER CHRISTIAN WRITINGS I

The Epistle of Barnabas

Around A.D. 96, a letter surfaced known as the Epistle of Barnabas,[11] attributed falsely (hence, also called "Pseudo-Barnabas"), to one of the Saint Paul's closest missionary companions mentioned frequently in the Acts of the Apostles, who founded the Church at Antioch and preached the Gospel to peoples throughout Asia Minor (modern-day Turkey) from A.D. 44 to A.D. 52. It is an epistle with a strong anti-Jewish polemic because its author criticizes the Jews for having misinterpreted the messianic prophesies of the Old Testament, relying more on the literal rather than the spiritual sense of the text. Nevertheless, this epistle is important for our consideration of the four marks of the Church. For example, concerning the unity of the Church our author writes:

> Do not isolate yourselves, retreating into yourselves as if you have already obtained justification; but rather reunite yourselves together, and of one accord seek that which is useful to all.[12]

In this letter, the Church is described as an assembly of brothers,[13] called to live in unity and fellowship as sons of joy,[14] sons of love and patience,[15] who seek holiness together by virtue of the strength given them by the one Spirit who lavishes upon them a plethora of holy gifts that imbue them with hope for the life on high. With regard to the so-called "Way of Light," the *Epistle of Barnabas* exhorts us:

> Do not doubt whether your prayer will be heard. Do not take the name of the Lord in vain. You will love your neighbor more than your own life. You will not destroy a child by abortion, nor in turn

---

[11] Barnabas is an Aramaic name, meaning "son of encouragement."

[12] *Epistle of Barnabas*, 4:10.

[13] Ibid., 6:16.

[14] Ibid., 7:1.

[15] Ibid., 21:9.

Fourth century terracotta chrismon lamp displaying the superimposed Greek letters Chi (X) and Rho (P), the monogram of Christ. People used clay oil lamps to light their homes and, when decorated with Christian symbols, to refer to Christ as the symbolic light of the world.
Source: Walters Art Museum, Wikimedia.

will you do away with what has been born[16] [...]. You will guard what you have received, neither adding to nor taking away from it. You will hate evil to the end. You will judge justly. You will not foment schism, but you will make peace and bring enemies together. You will confess your sins. You will not come to prayer with an evil conscience.[17]

The Shepherd of Hermas

Another significant piece of early Christian literature that deserves our attention is the document known as *The Shepherd of Hermas.*[18]

This text was composed about one hundred and ten years after Our Lord's death and resurrection. It was one of the non-biblical texts most cited by Fathers of the Church, like Irenaeus of Lyons and Clement of Alexandria, as well as by such early Christian writers as Origen of Alexandria and Tertullian of Carthage. It is believed to have been written by the brother of a Pope, Pius I, whose brother was Hermas.

In the archives of the University of Michigan, fragments of *The Shepherd of Hermas* are found written in Greek on papyrus scrolls, dating back to the second and third centuries. However, the largest portion of this ancient text is contained in the fourth-century *Codex Sinaiticus* (Codex of Sinai), an invaluable manuscript of the canon or official list of books recognized as Sacred Scripture, housed in the British Museum in London, England. There also exists a second-century version of *The Shepherd of Hermas,* written in Latin that is kept at Karlsruhe in Germany.

Many believe that Hermas was, in fact, an actual person who in this text recounts how having fallen asleep on a journey to Cumae,[19] he wakes up to find

---

[16]   Here the author refers to the evil of infanticide. Cf. CCC, 2268.
[17]   *Epistle of Barnabas*, 19:1-3, 8-12.
[18]   This work is occasionally referred to as *The Pastor of Hermas.*
[19]   Cumae was a city near Naples regarded by the ancient Romans as the shrine of the most

standing before him his old matron, Roda, who is apparently dead and appearing to him from beyond the grave. Roda then takes it upon herself to castigate Hermas for a grave sin that he had committed and for which he still needs to do penance. Hermas, in turn, has a second vision of another old matron. This time the old matron is said to symbolize the Church. The old matron appears to be decked out in multi-colored vesture; she reprimands Hermas, and thereby other Christians, for not having afforded their children a decent or adequate Christian education.

The woman, symbolic of the Church, appears several more times, for a total of five visions, to offer instruction to Hermas. She teaches him that the life of the Church, likened to a tower, must be based on solid foundations, which are the Sacraments of Christian Initiation, especially Baptism.

Furthermore, the old matron exhorts Hermas, and so too us, to edify or build up the Church by practicing the virtues of knowledge, purity of life, simplicity, sexual continence or chastity, and charity. Without these virtues, the Christian like Hermas will fall into sin and will not be capable of withstanding persecution from within the Church or from outside her confines.

The old matron reveals to Hermas in a prophetic, almost charismatic fashion, that such persecution can only be avoided by positively practicing such virtues and by engaging in strict penitential exercises.

The Shepherd of Hermas concludes with a vision to Hermas of an angel disguised as a shepherd (hence, the name of the work), in which he describes for the young Christian the august duty of bringing to Pope Saint Clement I a list of twelve precepts (several already mentioned) that ought to govern Christian living. After this, ten similes, based on Our Lord's parables in the Gospels, are revealed to Hermas; these similes are meant to shed light on the meaning of the previous visions and list of twelve precepts.

This fantastic story becomes the basis for a *vademecum* (handbook), dealing with sin and penance in the life of several early Christian communities. Sin is the cause of disunity while penance, accompanied by God's grace and a life of virtue, is the primary means of restoring unity. Here, perhaps it would be helpful to recall some brief passages of *The Shepherd of Hermas* to illustrate the points we have just made:

---

important sibyl—an idol (statue) of a pagan prophetess. The pagan Romans consulted sibyls in much the same manner as the ancient Greeks went to Delphi to receive oracles from the statue of Apollo, the pagan god of the sun and music (culture). In ancient mythology the god Apollo is seen as the opposite of the god Bacchus (Dionysus), the pagan god of wine and revelry.

> When the Church of God will be one body, one soul, one mind, one charity, then the Son of God will exult and be glad.[20]

Again, we learn that:

> Men who are arid and have become solitary, not being united to the servants of God, but living in isolation, ruin their own souls.[21]

Finally, *The Shepherd of Hermas* exhorts us:

> I say to all of you Christians, to have simplicity, neither to be mindful of offenses received, nor to persist in your maliciousness or in the remembrance of the bitterness of offenses, but rather become each one of you one spirit, so that every damaging division may be mitigated and taken from you.[22]

Athenagoras of Athens

Around A.D. 163, a significant work by a Christian philosopher from Athens, known as Athenagoras, was composed. He wrote two key works. The first was an apologetical work addressed to Emperors Lucius Aurelius Commodus (reigned 161-180) and Marcus Aurelius (reigned 180-192), entitled *Supplication on Behalf of the Christians,* in which Athenagoras sets out to dispel many of the false notions about Christianity that the majority of pagans held and brandished as weapons against its fundamental truthfulness. Athenagoras argues that the pagan Greek philosophers Euripides and Plato were monotheists, thus serving as a *praeparatio evangelica* ("a preparation for receiving the Gospel").

Athenagoras defends Christians against the absurd accusation of atheism since they worship the One True God, Father, Son and Holy Spirit, and derive their unity from this self-same source.

A second work of Athenagoras is known by its Latin title, *De Resurrectione Mortuorum* (On the Resurrection of the Dead). In the Apostles' Creed, we profess our faith in *the resurrection of the body and life everlasting.* In the Nicene Creed, the believer declares:

> I look forward to the resurrection of the dead and the life of the world to come.

---

20   *The Shepherd of Hermas*, 9: 18, 4.
21   Ibid., 9: 26, 3.
22   Ibid., 9:31, 3-4.

Death, for Athenagoras, is merely the temporary interruption of the union of body and soul. Athenagoras firmly believes that if the soul has an inherent principle of immortality, so too does the body, for a man cannot be completely himself if he is not reconstituted in the after-life as a being with an immortal body and soul. This is why the great medieval philosopher and theologian Thomas Aquinas could state in his *Summa contra Gentiles* (Summa against the Gentiles—On the Truth of the Catholic Faith) that, without his body, Thomas could not possibly be considered Thomas as God had meant him to be.

Consequently, Athenagoras' apologetical work is important for our theme because by defending the Christian belief in the resurrection of the body, based on his philosophical/theological vision of man as a body-soul composite, he also upheld the doctrine of the Church as the communion of saints, for all the saints are alive with God in Christ Jesus, the Head of the Mystical Body.

Tatian

One of the most controversial of early Christian writers was a man by the name of Tatian. He was a disciple of Saint Justin Martyr, one of the Church's earliest and greatest apologists. Tatian was born in Syria, studied under Justin in Rome, and focused his harsh polemical apologetics on the Greeks whom he resented in a way his master could hardly have imagined.

According to Tatian's *Discourse to the Greeks*, pagan Greek civilization, including its pantheon of philosophers, was inferior to what he termed sarcastically the "barbarian" philosophy of Christianity, which God had established in order to purify the old world order created by the Greeks. Tatian was not afraid of asserting that Christ had come not to bring peace but a spiritual sword, dividing the corrupt ways of the pagans from the pristine ways of true Christians.

After the death of Justin Martyr in A.D. 167, however, Tatian carried his vehement opposition to pagan culture to an extreme when he began to follow a regimen of strict asceticism, known also as "encratism,"[23] which betrayed a dangerous dualism between matter and spirit.

Consequently, Tatian began to disparage marriage and procreation as works of the flesh and of the Devil. Once Tatian became so heterodox in his understanding of sexual morality, he broke from communion with Rome. He was so ostracized by the orthodox Christian community that he felt compelled to return home to Syria.

---

[23] This word derives from the Greek *enkrateia*, meaning "self-control," "renunciation," or "ascesis."

Tatian is best known for composing a work entitled *Diatessaron* (literally from the Greek, "through/by means of the four parts"), more commonly referred to in English translation as *The Harmony of the Four Gospels*. This work, perhaps originally written in Syriac around A.D.180, proved invaluable to the life of the early Church, and was even heavily relied upon in the Sacred Liturgy.

Theophilus of Antioch

In A.D. 169, a pagan convert to Catholicism, a priest by the name of Theophilus,[24] was consecrated the seventh bishop of Antioch. Eusebius of Caesarea, a noted Church historian and official biographer of the Emperor Constantine in the fourth century, notes that Theophilus converted to Catholicism precisely when the heretics were spreading seeds of dissent in the field of God's Church. It is believed that Theophilus wrote many important theological treatises, but unfortunately only three apologetical works have survived, all of which were addressed to an erudite pagan man by the name of Autolicus, whom he had tried to convert. Hence, the title of the three books: *Ad Autolicum* (To Autolicus).

Theophilus' apologetic for Christianity is multi-pronged. He tries to convince Autolicus that Christianity is the one, true religion on any number of levels. First, Christianity is the true religion because it is monotheistic and trinitarian. In fact, it is in the writings of Theophilus that the word "Trinity" is first found to describe God's being. Secondly, because Christianity teaches the resurrection of the body as opposed to the Pythagorean notion of the transmigration of souls (an ancient equivalent of reincarnation), and thus the Christian doctrine reassures us that there is direct continuity between our life on earth and our life in Heaven.

Here is a sample of Theophilus' writing about the importance of the Catholic Church as compared to the perilous ecclesial improvisations of the heretics:

> As there are inhabitable islands in the sea which are enriched with good waters, that are fertile and gifted with secure ports and anchors that offer refuge to those who are tossed by the tempests of the sea, so too God has given to the world, which is suspended and agitated by the tempest of sins, assemblies, that is to say, the holy churches in

---

[24] Theophilus derives from two Greek words: *theos* (God) and *philein* (to love). Hence, "God-lover." Cf. Hamell, *Handbook of Patrology*, 43: "St. Theophilus was not a philosopher-apologist, but a man of letters. He possessed an easy and elegant style, and was a writer with personal and original ideas. He was born near the Euphrates, and was of mature age when converted, received a Greek education and had a knowledge of Hebrew."

which the doctrines of the truth dwell and to whose doctrines men make haste as to the good ports of the sea, those men who desire to save themselves by loving the truth and desiring to flee from anger and the judgment of God. And as there are other islands that are rocky and sterile, infested by beasts and uninhabitable, created only for the ruination of navigators and for shipwrecks, on which islands the docking of ships falls apart while those who succeed in hanging to those sinking ships perish, thus there are erroneous doctrines, called heresies, that destroy as many as draw near to them.[25]

---

[25] Theophilus of Antioch, *To Autolicus*, 18.

CHAPTER TWENTY-FIVE:
LESSER CHRISTIAN WRITINGS II

Melito of Sardis

Before Augustine of Hippo in the fourth century dealt with the delicate relationship between the Church (The City of God) and the State (The City of Man), the early Christian writer Melito, Bishop of Sardis[1] in Asia Minor, tried to negotiate a *via media*[2] or political compromise between the Christian religion and Imperial Rome.

The main thrust of his apologetics, of which we have a few fragments thanks to the *Ecclesiastical History* of Eusebius of Caesarea, (biographer of the Emperor Constantine in the fifth century), was to convince the Emperor Marcus Aurelius (A.D. 170) that Christianity was meant to co-exist with the Roman Empire.

How else could one explain the providential occurrence of the birth of Jesus Christ during the reign of the first Roman Emperor Octavian Augustus, whose reign inaugurated a period of world peace known as the *Pax Romana* (The Roman Peace)?

Melito of Sardis, like the historian Eusebius, believed that God in His infinite wisdom and providential love planned that the Roman Empire would become a paradoxical instrument for the spread of Christianity. In due time, history would bear this out. Melito's so-called "political theology" highlights the unity of God's economy or plan for our eternal salvation, which He won for us on Calvary and at the empty tomb.

This leads us to a discussion of Melito's second great theological contribution—his Paschal Homily, excerpts of which are still read in the Liturgy of the Hours on Holy Thursday and Easter Monday.

---

[1] Sardis has been identified as the ancient capital of Lydia mentioned in the Bible. During the seventh and sixth centuries B.C. under the rule of Croesus, Sardis was one of the wealthiest capitals in Asia Minor. One can visit the ruins of Sardis in modern-day Turkey.

[2] "Middle Road."

The immediate context in which to understand Melito's Easter Homilies is the Easter Date Controversy (already explained in previous chapters), a long and often bitter controversy between Rome and the Churches of Asia Minor, also known as the *Quartodecimans* (from the Latin for "fourteenth day").

Prescinding from the details of this controversy, Melito's homilies, a prolonged commentary on the Passover account in Exodus 12, teaches about the unity of the two testaments, for as Saint Augustine would later write:

> The New is hidden in the Old and the Old is revealed in the New.[3]

Melito teaches us that the Jewish Exodus or Passover was fulfilled in Christ's definitive Passover from death to everlasting life, making possible our own participation in the victories of His Paschal Mystery (Our Lord's Death and Resurrection) through Baptism and the reception of the other Sacraments of Christian Initiation.

According to Melito of Sardis, Christian salvation, unity, and freedom are derived primarily from Christ's redemptive sacrifice as the Lamb of God who

---

[3] Cf. CCC 129.

takes away the sins of the world, which is the ultimate paradox in the history of salvation and fulfills all its typologies (e.g., sacrifice of unblemished lambs) in the Old Testament. Melito writes:

> [Christ Jesus] is the one who delivered us from slavery into freedom, from tyranny into an eternal kingdom. He has made us a new priest-hood and a special people forever.[4] He is the Passover of our salva-tion. Although Lord, He clothed Himself with man and suffered on account of him who was suffering, was bound on account of him who was being conquered, was judged on account of the one con-demned, and was buried on account of him who had been buried [...]. "Come, now, all you families of men who have been steeped in sin and receive forgiveness of your sins. For I am your forgiveness, I am the Passover of salvation, I am the Lamb Who was slain for you. I am your ransom, I am your life, I am your Resurrection. I am your Light, your Salvation, your King. I lead you up into the heights of Heaven. I will show you the Eternal Father. I will raise you up by my right hand."[5]

Scholars of early Christian literature underscore the importance of an anony-mous Easter homily (not unlike Melito's Paschal Homily), whose provenance is probably the same as that of Melito's homily, namely, Asia Minor. Most date this text to the second half of the second century A.D. It seems as though the writer of this homily, like Melito of Sardis, had as his immediate context the theological controversy about the date of Easter—a particular concern to the local churches of Asia Minor.

In the introduction to the homily, the author dwells on the spiritual aes-thetics of the Easter celebration. In the main body of the work, our author's focus is brought to bear on typology or how the Passover (Exodus) of the Jews under the leadership of Moses was fulfilled in the Paschal Mystery—the Pas-sion, Death and Resurrection of Jesus the Christ.

Our anonymous Christian writes that Jesus:

> wished to suffer for us, to free us from passion with the Passion.

For the contemporary Catholic, this may bring to mind the vivid and mov-ing portrayal of the Lord's Passion that Mel Gibson gave us in his critically acclaimed film, *The Passion of the Christ*, a film that begins with a quote about the figure of the Suffering Servant from the Book of the Prophet Isaiah:

---

[4]   Cf. Exodus 19:6; 1 Peter 2:9; Revelation 5:10. See also *Lumen Gentium*, 10.

[5]   Melito of Sardis, *Paschal Homily*, 100-103.

He was pierced for our offenses, crushed for our sins. Upon Him was
the chastisement that makes us whole; by His stripes we are healed.[6]

This theology of substitution and atonement[7] hearkens back to the feast of *Yom
Kippur* (Day of Atonement)[8] — the holiest day of the Jewish calendar. On that
day only, the high priest entered the "Holy of Holies" (*Sancta Sanctorum*), in
order to offer sacrifice of incense in atonement for his own sins and those of all
the Chosen People.

On that day alone, the high priest was allowed to pronounce the *tetragram-
maton*, a Greek word referring to "The Four Letters," of *YHWH*,[9] that spell out
in Hebrew the ineffable name of God ("I AM WHO I AM"). This sacred Name
was revealed to Moses at the theophany of the burning bush and is substituted
regularly by Jews in the reading of the Scriptures with other divine names like
Adonai (Lord).

Furthermore, on *Yom Kippur*, the ancient Jews engaged in a sacred ritual — sending out into the wilderness a scapegoat, a goat that symbolically carried off the sins of the priests and all the people. In the New Testament, Christ
Jesus becomes the scapegoat for the entire human race as He substitutes or takes
our place on the Cross.

In Chapter Twenty-Seven, we shall see how this "theology of substitution"
is developed by subsequent Christian thinkers.

Abercius' Epitaph: "The Queen of Christian Inscriptions"

Literature, as such, is not the only witness to Catholic truth in the early
Church. We find at Gerapolis in Phrygia (Asia Minor, now Turkey) perhaps the
most extraordinary Christian funerary inscription (dated to around A.D. 170),
so much so that Christian archeologists have called it the *Queen of Christian
Inscriptions.*

---

[6] Isaiah 53:5.

[7] This word is comprised of several English words: "at-one-ment," which means to bring
about a state of oneness.

[8] *Yom Kippur* literally translated from Hebrew means "Day of Covering." The Hebrew word
kippah (from *kipporet*) refers to the "head covering" that observant Jewish men wear as a
sign of reverence for God who is utterly transcendent. In other words, the *kippah*, also called
yarlmaka in Yiddish, reminds the observant Jewish man of the infinite abyss between God
and himself, a mortal creature. Catholic priests and bishops adopted this head covering for
practical and ceremonial purposes. In Italian this head covering is called a *zucchetto* and in
English a skull-cap.

[9] Recall that the Hebrew language has no vowels, only consonants. Vowel signs were eventually added to aid in pronunciation.

It is known as the epitaph of Abercius, Bishop of Gerapolis, who died when he was seventy-two years old.

What makes this funerary epitaph so significant? Its significance is both archeological and theological. The inscription, written during the persecution of the Roman Emperor Marcus Aurelius, is cryptic in nature insofar as it is covered with Christian symbols that would not have been easily decoded by the pagans of the time.

There is a depiction of a shepherd and his flock that refers to Christ the Good Shepherd and the one sheepfold of His Church, a portion of which had been entrusted to Bishop Abercius. The fish is an ubiquitous symbol of Jesus in the Christian catacombs.[10] The picture of loaves of bread and a cup of wine is an allusion to the Eucharist, the source and summit (*fons et culmen*) of the Church's communion.[11]

The inscription itself testifies to Abercius' own discipleship under a shepherd of the Church, probably a bishop, who handed on to him the apostolic Faith. Abercius says this shepherd (bishop) sent him to Rome, to the center of the Catholic Church, and from there he became familiar with fellow disciples in many different countries throughout the Middle East, even past the Euphrates River (modern-day Syria/Iraq). No matter where Abercius traveled, he was blessed to share the fellowship of his brothers and sisters in Christ by partaking of a common Eucharistic Banquet.

Thus, we find that Abercius bears strong testimony to the belief of the early Christians in: the four marks of the Church (a doctrine centered on belief in the primacy of Rome), the Real Presence of Our Lord in the Mystery of the Eucharist, the veneration due to the Blessed Virgin Mary, Mother of the Church, and prayer for the dead who are part of the Communion of Saints.

The Octavian of Minucius Felix

A gem of early Christian literature bears the title *The Octavian of Minucius Felix*. How does one explain this title? Marcus Minucius Felix was born at the beginning of the second century A.D. at Cirta in what is today Algeria in North Africa.

---

[10] The Greek word for fish is *ichthus*. Among the early Christians the fish was a symbol of Jesus. The Greek word was an acronym which spelled out **Iesuos Christos Theou Uios Soter** (Jesus Christ, Son of God, Savior).

[11] A floor mosaic of loaves and fishes decorates the site of the multiplication of the loaves and fishes in the city of Tagbha in the Holy Land. Cf. Matthew 14:13-21, 15: 32-39; Mark 6: 30-44, 8:1-10; Luke 9:10-17; John 6: 1-15, 21:1-14.

He was educated at Rome where he was a successful lawyer, becoming a convert from paganism to Catholic Christianity as a young adult. Around A.D. 175, he wrote a splendid apologetical work that takes the form of a dialogue, dedicated to a close friend by the name of Octavian Januarius, one of the dialogue's principal interlocutors, and to another, Caecilius Natalis.

It is important to note here in relation to our understanding of the Church as a holy communion that there existed among the early Christians, especially in the face of persecution by the pagan Roman state, a most admirable solidarity.

About the virtue of solidarity among the early Christians (as underscored in the friendship between Minucius Felix and Octavius Januarius), the following commentary is helpful:

Fragment of a Dead Sea scroll.
Source: Berthold Werner, Wikimedia.

> There was a rather delightful tradition in ancient theories of friendship, according to which a friend was, in a sense, a second self—a sort of extension of one's own soul. A Christian writer of the second century with the marvelous name of Marcus Minucius Felix used this idea when he spoke of a dead friend, Octavius. Such was his closeness to his friend, he wrote, that when he remembered him it seemed like he was not simply remembering the past but actually revisiting it; they had been so familiar that you would have thought they had one mind between

them. And Christians talked about their community in the same way.[12]

Minucius Felix wrote his apologetical dialogue in response to the calumnious claims about Christian doctrine and devotion that Octavian had imbibed from various circles of anti-Christian philosophical schools and sects. Minucius Felix cleverly uses a refined Christian philosophy to show the compatibility of faith and reason and, even more specifically, the truth of the Cross as God's ultimate, providential paradox that confounds the wisdom of the world.

From the following statement of Minucius Felix we can deduce his belief in the unity of the Church based on his acceptance of oneness as one of the many attributes of God in which we participate to varying degrees. Minucius writes:

> We (Christians) are easily recognizable because of the sign of our innocence and modesty: given that we so much love each other, because we have never learned to hate. Therefore, we call each other brothers because we are sons of the one God, we participate in the same faith, we are heirs of the same future hopes.[13]

Epistle to Diognetus: "The Pearl of Christian Antiquity"

Writing in perhaps the second half of the second century A.D., one of the earliest apologists of Catholic Christianity wrote the anonymous *Epistle to Diognetus*,[14] in which he defends Christian comportment against the erroneous aspersions of the Roman persecutors.[15] He asserts that by accepting persecution, the Christians prove themselves to be steadfastly one in faith, hope and charity, a true fellowship of saints destined to live for all eternity in the City of God (Heaven).

This work gives evidence of the four marks of the Church in several ways. The author posits the origins of the Church in the unity of the Trinity, most

---

[12]   Hill, *What Has Christianity Ever Done for Us?*, 109.

[13]   *The Octavian of Minucius Felix*, 31.

[14]   The *Epistle to Diognetus* has been called "the pearl of Christian antiquity" and could be more properly considered an apologetical treatise, rather than an epistle.

[15]   It is interesting and ironic to note that some scholars believed that the Diognetus of this work was the Diognetus who had been the teacher of the stoic philosopher and Roman Emperor, Marcus Aurelius who, despite his erudition (see his work *Meditationes*, "The Meditations"), was responsible for several cruel persecutions of Christians. On the Capitoline Hill of Rome stands a copy of the oldest equestrian bronze statue from the Roman period, which is believed to be the bearded Emperor Marcus Aurelius riding gallantly on his horse, situated in the middle of a grand piazza designed by Michelangelo.

especially in the actions of Christ in the Gospels.[16] The author also unabashedly defends the veracity of the Christian religion against all others, based on the exemplary holiness that Christians demonstrate, even upon the verge of being martyred.[17]

He argues that, despite constant persecution, the Church continues to expand throughout the Roman Empire; hence, her universal or catholic appeal.[18] The work underscores the Church's apostolic roots by contrasting her teachings anchored in Divine Revelation with the sophist musings of so many self-contradictory philosophical groups in vogue at the time.[19]

Finally, the anonymous author offers us this moving description of his fellow Christians—whose very demographic make-up is proof of their "catholicity," "universality," and extraordinary *humanitas* (humanity):

> Christians are not distinguished from other people, neither by origin, by language nor by mode of dress. They do not live in their own cities nor do they have their own language, nor indeed do they live any special life style. They live in their own countries, but as foreigners; every foreign land is their homeland, and their homeland is as a foreign country. They live their lives on earth, but are citizens of Heaven. They obey the laws of the land, but by the tenor of their lives, they live above the law. They love everyone, but are persecuted by all. They are unknown and condemned; they are put to death and gain life. They are poor and yet make many rich. They are dishonored, and yet gain glory through dishonor. They are attacked by Jews as aliens, and are persecuted by Greeks; yet those who hate them cannot give any reason for their hostility. To put it simply, the soul is to the body as Christians are to the world [...]. The soul is in the body but is not of the body; Christians are in the world, but not of the world.[20]

Hippolytus of Rome: The Early Christian Liturgy

We now turn our attention to the life and writings of a Greek-speaking priest of the Diocese of Rome by the name of Hippolytus, who lived in the second and third centuries A.D.

---

[16] *Epistle to Diognetus*, 5-6.
[17] Ibid., 7:7.
[18] Ibid., 7:7-8.
[19] Ibid., 8:2-4.
[20] Ibid., 6:1, 8.

Hippolytus was a moral rigorist, especially about the rules governing Catholic marriage. In the early part of the third century, he went over the line on these disciplinary matters and started a schism, breaking from communion with Pope Saint Callistus I, who reigned from A.D. 217-222. Thus, in A.D. 217, Hippolytus became the first anti-pope in history.

Providentially, he was able to be fully reconciled with the Church before dying in exile on the Mediterranean's second largest island, Sardinia, although in those days it was considered a rather remote place in the world and infamous for having mines in which Roman prisoners would be sent to do forced labor.

Most ironically, the man who had become the first anti-pope was exiled together with Pope Pontianus according to the imperial edict of Maximus Thracian in A.D. 235. In that same year or perhaps in the following, Hippolytus died. The present liturgical calendar for the Roman Rite celebrates the optional memorial of the martyrs Pope Pontian and Hippolytus, on August 13.

Whether or not Hippolytus was actually murdered while in exile is historically doubtful; nevertheless the early Christians clearly considered Hippolytus a martyr in the traditional sense. Not long after his death, the lay faithful brought the remains of Hippolytus back to Rome and buried them in the catacombs along the Via Tiburtina, an ancient consular road that can still be traveled upon today.

The catacombs on the Via Tiburtina were named after Hippolytus as we can also find in Rome today on the Via Appia,[21] the Catacombs of Saint Callistus, named after his one-time nemesis.

In the Catacombs of Saint Callistus, the remains of the martyred bodies of Saints Peter, Paul and Cecilia were at one time preserved. Pope Saint Damasus I, who had a tremendous devotion to the martyrs, also dedicated a chapel to the pope-martyrs of the third century, who were buried in the chapel or in the surrounding area inside. In these same catacombs, one finds depictions of the Sacraments of Baptism and the Holy Eucharist. In the case of the Sacrament of Baptism, a fisherman is shown casting his net into the water, calling to mind the words of Jesus: "Follow me, and I will make you fishers of men" (Mark 1:17). In the depiction of the Sacrament of the Holy Eucharist, one notices on the left side a plate of fish, an early symbol of Jesus.

---

[21]   The Via Appia was a consular road, lined with the funerary monuments of Roman noble men that connected Rome to the southern Adriatic port of Brundisium, known today as the Italian city of Brindisi. This palm-laden city is located in the region of Puglia (Apulia in Latin and in English). It is an important port of commercial trade and tourism between the western and eastern portions of the Mediterranean because of its proximity to the Balkan countries of Albania and Greece, as well as to Turkey.

In 1551 in those same catacombs was found a list of Hippolytus' writings carved onto a marble statue that represents Hippolytus seated on an episcopal (pontifical) throne or *cathedra*, reminding us that he had been declared a bishop by his schismatic sect as well as a pretender to the throne of Peter. Most scholars agree that not all of the works listed on the statue are, in fact, original compositions of Hippolytus.

At the entrance to the Vatican Library is found a marble episcopal chair or cathedra that has inscribed upon it a calendar giving the date of Easter during the time of Hippolytus of Rome.

Hippolytus' most famous work, and the one that most directly touches upon the question of the Church's four indelible marks, is known as the *Apostolic Tradition*, probably written about A. D. 218. Even if Hippolytus may have been of Middle Eastern origins, scholars are fairly sure that he lived most of his adult life in Rome, and that it was from the Eternal City that he wrote the majority of his works.[22]

The *Apostolic Tradition* of Hippolytus of Rome is so important because it is one of the oldest liturgical books that we possess from the Early Church. The prayers we find in it give us a good indication of what the Liturgy of Rome was like at the beginning of the third century. The Eucharistic Prayer (*anaphora* is the preferred term for that prayer in Greek) that Hippolytus presents, containing the words of consecration, is the oldest extant prayer of its kind. As a matter of fact, the ancient Church of Abyssinia (Ethiopia) still makes use of Hippolytus' Eucharistic Prayer, and a modified version of it was adopted as the Second Eucharistic Prayer with its own preface for the Roman Liturgy following the reforms of the Second Vatican Council.

The *Apostolic Tradition* deals with many important issues that affect the way we understand the Church as one, holy, catholic and apostolic, the last term already highlighted in the title of the document. It deals with the structure of the Church's hierarchy and the structure of the catechumenate or what we refer to today as the *Rite of Christian Initiation of Adults* (RCIA).

---

[22] The works of Hippolytus of Rome not dealt with here are the following: *Philosophoumena*, in which Hippolytus identifies and confutes certain strains of Greek "philosophy" in Christian theology, for example, Gnosticism, as the root cause of all heresies; *De Christo et Antichristo* ("On Christ and the Anti-Christ"); *Commentary on the Book of Daniel*; *Chronicon*, a fragmentary work in which Hippolytus "chronicles" world events from the creation of the world to A.D. 234 and tries to convince his readers that the Second Coming of Our Lord or Parousia was not imminent; and *Concerning Easter*, a work that is no longer extant.

One of the most intriguing aspects of the work is the fact that it reports the ancient rite of Baptism as it was celebrated in the Church of Rome in the third century A.D. The Baptismal Creed, to which we have all become accustomed even as we pray the Apostles' Creed, has a tripartite structure, meaning that the Creed was broken down into three questions, addressed to the catechumen or candidate that dealt respectively with the three Persons of the Blessed Trinity.

It seems that this Trinitarian structure of the Baptismal Creed made its appearance in the middle of the second century A.D. Saint Justin Martyr refers to this form of the Baptismal Creed on numerous occasions in his writings. It is also mentioned in the so-called *Apostolic Constitutions*, an anonymous work of the third century that contains catechetical and liturgical information strikingly similar to the information we find in Hippolytus' *Apostolic Tradition*.

Scenes from the Life of St. Augustine: The Saint Baptized by St. Ambrose, *Nicoló di Pietro, c. 1400.*

Hippolytus provides us with the following rubrics for the celebration of Baptism:

> The person to be baptized goes down into the water and the one who is baptizing places his hand on the candidate's head saying: "Do you believe in God the Father Almighty?" And the one being baptized responds: "I believe." Then [the minister] baptizes [immerses] for the first time, holding his hand on the head of the candidate. Afterwards he says: "Do you believe in Jesus Christ, the Son of God, who was born through the work of the Holy Spirit and from the Virgin Mary, who died, was buried, rose on the third day, ascended into Heaven, is seated at the right hand of the Father and will come to judge the living and the dead?" The candidate responds: "I believe." And the minister baptizes the candidate a second time. Then he questions the candidate again: "Do you believe in the Holy Spirit, in the holy church, in the resurrection of the flesh?" And the candidate to be baptized will say: "I believe." And the minister baptizes the candidate a third time.[23]

The Roman Baptismal Liturgy at the beginning of the third century reveals that the pastoral offices of deacon, priest and bishop were all exercised in a single baptism. The candidate would renounce Satan and receive a pre-baptismal exorcism and anointing by a priest. The candidate would then descend naked into the waters of the baptismal font in order to be baptized, immersed three times by a deacon, as the candidate made his three-fold profession of faith. Thus, the candidate died to sin and was buried with his old sinful self to rise up and live the new and everlasting life of the Gospel in conformity with the righteousness of Christ Jesus, the New, Second or Better Adam.

At the conclusion of the immersion process, the candidate would come out of the font, receive post-baptismal anointing from a priest, be clothed, and then led in procession by the priest into the church. We recall that most ancient churches were constructed with the baptistry as a separate building. The prototype of all baptistries in the West perhaps is an honor belonging to the Basilica of Saint John Lateran in Rome.

Once inside the church, the neophyte (newly baptized person) would receive the imposition of hands from the bishop. As the bishop made the sign of the cross on the forehead of the baptized individual, he would pray that the

---

[23]   Hippolytus of Rome, *Apostolic Tradition*, 21, 12-18.

Holy Spirit seal the gift of Baptism just received.[24] The new member of the Church was then admitted to the Eucharistic Sacrifice and Banquet.

Having received the Body and Blood of the Lord, the new member was also given a cup of milk mixed with honey—symbols in the Old Testament of the Promised Land of Canaan, a country flowing with milk from the cows of Bashan grazing on the northern plains of Israel (e.g., the city of Dan) and with honey extracted from the bees thriving in the arid climate of the southern territory of Judah (e.g., the city of Beersheba). In the case of Baptism, the milk and honey were meant to symbolize the abundant goodness and sweetness of the Lord, His saving grace, and the Heavenly Food He was preparing for all those who believe in Him. Thus, this simple but suggestive rite of the Sacraments of Christian Initiation pointed to the fulfillment of happiness in the Promised Land of Heaven.

Likewise, Hippolytus lays out a theology of the Holy Eucharist that is thoroughly Catholic, precisely because it is the fruit of the Apostolic Tradition. In doing so, he presents us with ancient forms of prayers for the laying on of hands and the ordination of deacons, priests and bishops, consecratory prayers that highlight the continuity between the priesthood of the Old and New Testaments.

In the prayer of consecration for a bishop, Hippolytus underscores how as a successor of the Apostles, the bishop's role is one of manifesting the holiness of the Church through his episcopal life and ministry, that is to say, through the witness of his own personal sanctity that should flow from the constant contact he has with the sacred mysteries he celebrates:

> Grant, O Father, who know the secrets of hearts, to this your servant, whom you have chosen for the episcopate, to feed your holy flock and to exercise his sovereign priesthood without stain of sin, serving you day and night; to render his service propitiously in your sight and to offer the oblations of your holy Church; to be able to remit sins, in virtue of the Spirit of the High Priesthood according to your command; to distribute his functions according to your will; to loose every bond, in virtue of the power you gave to the apostles; to be pleasing to you on account on his meekness and purity of heart, offering to you a sweet-

---

[24]   This ritual action of signing or sealing the candidate both in the Eastern and Western Churches is the essential form of administering the Sacrament of Confirmation, known in the East as the Sacrament of Chrismation. In the East, priests and bishops are the ordinary ministers of the sacrament, while in the West the ordinary minister is the bishop. In the West, the authority to confirm may be delegated by the bishop to a priest, for instance, in the case of receiving adult converts.

smelling oblation through your beloved Son, Jesus Christ. Through Him you have glory, power and honor, Father, Son and Holy Spirit, now and forever unto ages of ages. Amen.[25]

Furthermore, Hippolytus treats of the Christian feast or banquet known as the *agape* (Greek: "sacrificial love") that preceded the celebration of the Eucharist in apostolic times and abuses of which had already occurred in the first century A.D.—a constant thorn in the side of Saint Paul as he sought to evangelize, for example, the nascent Christian community at Corinth.

In addition, one finds in the *Apostolic Tradition* interesting descriptions of the discipline of third-century Roman Christians with regard to prayer and fasting. Hippolytus exhorts Christians to make frequent, reverent use of the Sign of the Cross:

> Seek in every circumstance to sign yourselves, in a worthy manner on the forehead. This sign of the Passion is a secure means against the Devil, as long as you make it in a spirit of faith and not to be ostentatious, knowing that by doing so you are protecting yourselves as with a shield.[26]

In the Eucharistic Prayer, after the words of consecration, Hippolytus has the priest address the Father so that He might send the Holy Spirit to transform the congregation of believers as He has already sent the Holy Spirit to transform the gifts of bread and wine into the Body and Blood of the Lord Jesus Christ. This prayer, found in most Eucharistic Prayers, is sometimes referred to as a "second epiclesis," complementing the epiclesis that immediately precedes the consecration or, in the case of the Byzantine liturgies that follows the consecration.

The word *epiclesis* is derived from the Greek, meaning "to call down upon." This "second epiclesis" of Hippolytus' Eucharistic Prayer (*anaphora*) refers to the marks of the Church's holiness and unity. He writes:

> Make holy, therefore, these gifts, we pray and send forth your Spirit onto the offering of your holy Church, to gather together into one those who receive Holy Communion, to fill them with the Holy Spirit, in order to strengthen their faith in the truth.[27]

---

[25] Hippolytus of Rome, *Apostolic Tradition*, 3.
[26] Ibid., 36.
[27] Ibid., 4.

In the Second Eucharistic Prayer of the modern Roman Rite, the "first epiclesis" reads:

> You are indeed Holy, O Lord, the fount of all holiness. Make holy, therefore, these gifts, we pray, by sending down your Spirit upon them like the dewfall, so that they may become for us the Body and Blood of our Lord Jesus Christ.

In the Second Eucharistic Prayer, the "second epiclesis" reads:

> Humbly we pray that, partaking of the Body and Blood of Christ, we may be gathered into one by the Holy Spirit.

CHAPTER TWENTY-SIX:
THE *APOSTOLIC CONSTITUTIONS*

"The Law of Praying Is the Law of Believing"[1]

The *Apostolic Constitutions* is an anonymous work, a compilation of ecclesiastical laws probably composed in Constantinople but compiled in Syria in the latter half of the fourth century. In fact, the author of these laws may not have been an orthodox Christian in good standing with Rome but a follower of Arius, who was a heretical priest from Alexandria, Egypt, who stripped Jesus of His co-equal divinity with the Eternal Father.

The *Apostolic Constitutions* are more properly referred to as *The Ordinances of the Holy Apostles through Clement.* It is a work comprised of eight chapters. The seventh chapter deals with the so-called "Apostolic Canons," that most likely had been added to the original composition at a later date.

As has already been noted concerning the writings of Hippolytus of Rome, most especially his *Apostolic Tradition,* one also finds similarities between the content of the *Apostolic Constitutions* and the *Didache,* or "Teaching of the Twelve Apostles." The *Apostolic Constitutions* succeeds in highlighting the four marks of the Church.

For instance, we find therein a litany composed for the celebration of the Eucharistic Sacrifice. This litany is similar to the litanies that dot the landscape of the Byzantine liturgies and what our Anglican (Episcopalian) brothers and sisters have adopted in the Book of Common Prayer as the "Bidding Prayers."

Likewise, it can be considered a precursor of the Prayer of the Faithful (General Intercessions) that was first solemnized as a rite of the Good Friday Liturgy and restored to the Roman Rite by the Second Vatican Council as an option meant to conclude the Liturgy of the Word (in the Missal of Pope Paul VI). It reads in part:

---

[1]   Latin: *Lex orandi, lex credendi.*

We beseech You, O Lord, for your holy Church, that she might reach
from one end of the world to another [...]. We pray for the universal
episcopate, that transmits faithfully the word of truth [...]. We present to you this offering for all the saints [...]. We present to you this
offering for this people, so that it may become the praise of Christ,
a royal priesthood, a holy nation [...]. We pray [...] for those who
are outside the Church and for those who are lost, so that you might
lead them back to goodness and placate their fury [...]. Finally we
praise you for those who are absent for a legitimate reason, that you
might keep them in piety and gather them into the Kingdom of your
Christ, God of every creature visible and invisible and our King;
keep them from falling, keep them without fault and without stain.[2]

Furthermore, the *Apostolic Constitutions* relates a prayer of thanksgiving
that emphasizes how the oneness and holiness of the Church's various members
from highest to lowest are gifts resulting from communion with the three Persons of the Blessed Trinity:

Sanctify your people, protect virgins, maintain spouses in fidelity,
give strength to those who have embraced chastity, make children
to increase, confirm neophytes, teach catechumens and render them
worthy of initiation; and then reunite us all in the Kingdom of
Heaven, in Christ Jesus, Our Lord. To Him, as to you, and the Holy
Spirit, be glory, honor and veneration for ever. Amen.[3]

---

[2] *Apostolic Constitutions*, 8: 12, 40-51.
[3] Ibid., 8: 15, 2-5.

PART VI

Chapters Twenty-Seven to Thirty continue to explore early Christian writings on certain essential Catholic doctrines, namely atonement for sin, the Petrine primacy, episcopal authority and ecclesial communion and charity.

Chapter Twenty-Seven:
A Theory of Atonement

Divine Substitution and Atonement

At this point in our patristic reflections, we can consider certain doctrines by means of an historical overview. The theology of divine substitution and atonement advanced by certain Fathers of the Church was also popular with later Christian writers like Saint Anselm of Canterbury in the eleventh century.

Saint Anselm argued that since the breach in the covenant between God and man caused by the fall of Adam (original sin) was infinite, only the God-Man as the "Great Bridge-Builder" (*Pontifex Maximus*) could repair it. No merely human act, not even the death of the Blessed Virgin Mary, would have sufficed in God's sight to make the atonement or satisfaction required by the infinite offense caused Him by our first parents. In other words, from Anselm's perspective, God's infinite justice[1] had to be given its due, something that only He Himself could accomplish.

The Catechism of the Catholic Church teaches:

> It is this love "to the end"[2] that confers on Christ's sacrifice its value as redemption and reparation, as atonement and satisfaction. He knew and loved us all when He offered His life. Now "the love of Christ controls us, because we are convinced that one has died for all; therefore all have died."[3] No man, not even the holiest, was ever able to take on himself the sins of all men and offer himself as a sacrifice for all. The existence in Christ of the divine person of the Son, who at once surpasses and embraces all human persons and

---

[1] The cardinal virtue of justice means to give to each person, but, above all, to God, what is owed or due by right. Justice is meant to be equal for everyone. Hence, allegorical statues of justice, often seen outside court houses, depict a blindfolded woman. God is justice *par excellence* because, as the Bible teaches, He is no respecter of persons. Cf. Leviticus 19:15, Colossians 4:1.

[2] John 13:1.

[3] 2 Corinthians 5:14.

The Crucifixion, *by Duccio di Buoninsegna, 14th century.*

constitutes Himself as the Head of all mankind, makes possible the redemptive sacrifice *for all*.[4]

An anonymous Christian writer of the second century says that the Lord Jesus overcame *death with His Death*,[5] for our death would not have been sufficient in procuring eternal salvation for all those subject to it. And so, before dying on the Cross, our ancient author notes, Jesus instituted a new Passover meal fulfilling all others, the Eucharistic Sacrifice, in which sacrificial meal He gave us *immortal life with invisible food*.[6]

Our author goes on to describe how Jesus the New Adam[7] substituted the tree of Adam's disobedience in the Garden of Eden with the tree of the Cross. Adam and Eve ate of the tree of the knowledge of good and evil in the middle of the garden and in disobeying God's strict injunction incurred His wrath; they were forced to flee the Garden as the original harmony of their relationship with God, each other and creation was disrupted — but not irreparably damaged.

Our Lord, dying between two thieves (the middle place being the place of honor),[8] rewards with eternal life those who partake of the immortal wisdom He offers through the Gospel. The tree of the Cross[9] bears much fruit because of Him who hung upon it. The tree of the Cross also fulfills the Old Testament typology of Jacob's ladder that reached from Heaven to earth.[10]

Praying in the Garden of Gethsemane,[11] Jesus gave proof of His full humanity by expressing deep sentiments of anguish before the prospect of death.

In Saint Thomas More's masterpiece, *The Sadness of Christ*, written while imprisoned in the Tower of London by King Henry VIII, the soon-to-be martyr argued that human anguish or anxiety in the face of torture and impending death was anything but abnormal for man; nor did it indicate pusillanimity in a man's character. On the contrary, the great English statesman[12] writes that Our

---

[4] CCC, 616.

[5] In Preface I of Easter the priest prays: "For He is the true Lamb who has taken away the sins of the world; by dying He destroyed our death, and by rising, restored our life."

[6] Anonymous Author of the Second Century, *Homily on Easter*, 49-55.

[7] Cf. CCC, 411: "The Christian tradition sees in this passage [Gen 3:15] an announcement of the 'New Adam' who, because He 'became obedient unto death, even death on a cross' [Phil 2:8], makes amends superabundantly for the disobedience of Adam."

[8] Cf. Matthew 27:38.

[9] Cf. 1 Peter 2:24; Matthew 26: 42.

[10] Cf. CCC, 618. Here, the Catechism cites St. Rose of Lima: "Apart from the cross there is no other ladder by which we may get to heaven."

[11] Gethsemane, meaning from Hebrew, "oil press," is located on the Mt. of Olives. In the Garden of Gethsemane there are olive trees whose roots are two thousand years old.

[12] Thomas More was Lord Chancellor of England during the reign of King Henry VIII, who

Lord's righteous fear is ultimately resolved in full submission of His will to that of the Heavenly Father.

Christ triumphs through His Agony in the Garden[13] in preparation for His greater triumph on the third day in the Garden of the Resurrection. It is precisely in those two gardens that the Lord Jesus brings about a new creation, surpassing the beauty and harmony of the first creation in the Garden of Eden.

The Crowning with Thorns[14] is reflected on by our second-century homilist as Christ's willingness to be crowned not so much with thorns from a prickly plant but with the thorns of the multitude of our sins from the first man to the last to be created.

On Golgotha or Calvary (The Place of the Skull),[15] our author interprets Jesus' being stripped of his garments[16] as a sign of Christ's indomitable will.

What is meant by this expression? The author means that Jesus, though man, fully subject to pain and suffering, would not allow His tribulations to drive a wedge between Himself and His heavenly Father. In other words, no amount of suffering, not even the cruel scourging He endured, could conquer His will since it was so perfectly in harmony with the will of the Father for our salvation.

As Jesus hung dead upon the Cross, a soldier[17] pierced His side, causing blood and water to flow out.[18] Many Fathers of the Church have seen in this

---

had him executed when Thomas refused to sign an oath swearing allegiance to Henry as Supreme Head of the Church of England. One of St. Thomas More's most famous quotes is: "I am the King's good servant, but God's first."

[13] First Sorrowful Mystery of the Holy Rosary.

[14] Third Sorrowful Mystery of the Holy Rosary.

[15] Often crucifixes have a skull placed at the feet of Our Lord. According to tradition, this skull is that of Adam. Certain artists depict the Most Precious Blood of Jesus dripping off the Body of Christ and from the wood of the Cross in order to cleanse Adam's skull, that is, to redeem Adam and every man, who is a son of Adam, from sin. Another tradition holds that the creation of Adam and the crucifixion of Jesus took place in the same exact place, perhaps even on the same day centuries apart.

[16] Tenth Station of the Cross.

[17] According to tradition, the soldier who pierced Christ's side was named Longinus, usually depicted as bearing his long spear. A statue of Longinus, with the related relic of the spear, is in St. Peter's Basilica, situated near the baldacchino or canopy that adorns the main papal altar. Longinus is said to have converted from paganism to Christianity when the blood and water that flowed out of Jesus' pierced side fell upon his face and garments, with one pious legend asserting that the Precious Blood healed his one blind eye. Another tradition identifies Longinus with the Roman soldier who in Mark 15:39 exclaims at the foot of the Cross: "Truly this man was the Son of God."

[18] Cf. John 19:31-37.

action a certain symbolism, the water representing the Sacrament of Baptism[19] and the blood representing the Sacrament of the Holy Eucharist.

Fathers of the Church, like Ambrose and Augustine, compared the creation of Eve from the side of the sleeping Adam to the creation of the Church, Christ's mystical and spotless bride, from His side as He slept the sleep of death on the Cross.[20]

Here, our anonymous writer from the second century offers his own interpretation:

> The Lord wanted to destroy the work of the woman and to counter her who at the beginning had come from the side of Adam, as a carrier of death. He opened His sacred breast, and from it flowed blood and water, complete signs of the spiritual and mystical marriage, of adoption and regeneration. It has been written that "He will baptize you with the Holy Spirit and fire" (Matthew 3:11); here, water as Baptism in the Holy Spirit, the blood as Baptism in fire.[21]

In comparing and contrasting the figures of the two thieves crucified with Jesus, our writer compares and contrasts two types of personalities, two sets of moral values.

The good thief, later known in tradition as Saint Dismas who, according to the wit and wisdom of the Venerable Fulton J. Sheen, *stole heaven*, is a man who is grateful for the opportunity to repent of his sins and who shows *pity on his Sovereign*, who has been innocently condemned.

The bad thief, on the other hand, is impervious to the suffering of the Messiah and unrepentant of the sins for which he was justly condemned. He shows neither gratitude nor piety.

These external attitudes, reflected in their respective dialogues with the Crucified Savior, are matched by interior dispositions. Our anonymous homilist writes:

> They are also a sign of two sentiments of the soul: one of them is converted from his old sins, strips himself naked before his Sovereign and thus obtains mercy and a reward, through doing penance. The other one has no excuse, because he does not want to change, and remains a thief until the end.[22]

---

[19] Cf. CCC, 694.

[20] Cf. CCC, 766. See also, *Lumen Gentium*, 3; *Sacrosanctum Concilium*, 5.

[21] As cited in Claire Russell, *Glimpses of the Church Fathers*, 46.

[22] Russell, *Glimpses of the Church Fathers*, 46.

The Crucifixion of Our Lord had tumultuous consequences for all mankind and indeed for the whole of creation. No one and no thing remained indifferent, out of reach of the tremendous impact that the death of God in Christ had on the universe He Himself had created, and now redeemed and sanctified.

Our homilist notes the earthquake, the darkening of the sun and the Temple veil being torn in two from top to bottom,[23] as examples of the powerful changing force of the death of the Lord of the Universe, the Eternal and Great High Priest.

Above all, the crucifixion of Christ[24] and the breathing forth of His spirit[25] in commendation of His soul to the Father occurred because Satan, the archenemy of the great militia, [had been] laid low.

And then, on the third day, the day of His Resurrection, the homilist remarks:

> while the waters were disturbed and stirred up by apprehension of fear, when the divine spirit joined up again, immediately the universe found its stability again, almost totally enlivened, consolidated and with a new spirit.[26]

---

[23]   Cf. Mark 15:38.

[24]   Cf. Matthew 27: 32-44; Mark 15:21-32; Luke 23:26-43; John 19: 17-30.

[25]   Cf. John 19:30.

[26]   As found in Russell, *Glimpses of the Church Fathers*, 47.

Chapter Twenty-Eight:
Petrine Primacy

Pope Saint Clement of Rome in his late first-century *Letter to the Corinthians* admonishes the local Christian community not to support a group of their younger members who had banded together to undermine the authority of their local presbyters (elders) or priests. Clement writes in reaction to the schismatic tensions rising up within the Christian community at Corinth by exhorting the true believers to band together for a very different purpose, the unity of the Church:

> To what purpose are those quarrels, ill tempers, dissensions, schisms and warfare among you? Do we not have one God and one Christ and one Spirit of charity which has been poured out on us, and one calling in Christ? To what purpose are we pulling apart and tearing asunder the members of Christ? Why do we rise up against our own body and come to such a state of madness as to forget that we are members of one another? Be mindful of the words of Jesus, Our Lord. For He said: "Woe to that man. It would be better for him for a millstone to be bound on him and to be cast into the sea than to lead astray one of my chosen ones."[1]

Thus, Pope Clement's intervention from Rome in the local affairs of the Church at Corinth constitutes him the first patristic writer to inculcate belief in the primacy of the See of Rome in relation to the universal Church. In his *Letter to the Corinthians*, Pope Clement writes:

> You will please us greatly if, being obedient to the things which we have written through the Holy Spirit, you will root out the wicked passion of jealousy, in accord with our call for peace and concord.[2]

Pier Franco Beatrice comments thus about Saint Clement's Letter to the Corinthians:

---

[1] Clement of Rome, *Letter to the Corinthians*, 46:5-47:4.
[2] Clement of Rome, *Letter to the Corinthians*, 63.

Christ Handing the Keys to St. Peter, *Perugino, 1482.*

In this letter, there appears for the first time in history the manifesta-
tion of an awareness of the "Roman Primacy" based on the authority of the founding Apostles, Peter and Paul. With his summons to
amendment and penance, to bending "the knee of the heart," Clement aims at restoring the damaged authority of the local hierarchy.
The hierarchy constitutes the foundation and the guarantee of the
peace and harmony of the members who make up the Church, the
true Body of Christ. The intensive use of the Sacred Scriptures is
intended to show how much hatred has injured humanity and, to
the contrary, what benefits the concord willed by the Creator pro-
ducers.[3]

---

[3]   Beatrice, *Introduction to the Fathers of the Church,* 20.

Excursus: The Donatist Controversy

Before Saint Augustine of Hippo entered into controversy with the schismatic group known as the Donatists, Bishop Optatus of Milevis confronted the Donatist bishop of Carthage, Parmenian. Optatus had written a seven-volume work, entitled *The True Church*. In this work, Optatus refutes the idea that Donatist schismatic churches can be considered "true churches," not merely because they failed to maintain communion with the local bishop but also because their link with the "chair of Peter" had been severed. Optatus bases his arguments on the actual letters of communion which were shared among all the bishops in communion with Rome and with one another; these have their equivalent today in the papal mandate necessary for the licit consecration of bishops.

Besides emphasizing communion with the Bishop of Rome as an outward sign of the Church's indelible mark of apostolicity, Optatus also focuses on the catholicity of the Church which the Donatists deny because of their arrogant claim that the true Church existed only where their sect was present. In his ongoing debate with the Donatists, Optatus makes several important theological distinctions that Saint Augustine would later develop. Optatus teaches that the efficacy of the sacraments depends on the sanctity of God as their author and not on the sanctity of the individual minister who celebrates them. The Donatists pointed out that such a teaching actually vindicated the validity of their sacraments!

CHAPTER TWENTY-NINE:
EPISCOPAL AUTHORITY

Fathers of the Church like Saint Ignatius of Antioch, writing in the second century A.D., held that schismatics (those who had broken from communion with the See of Rome) were ineligible to "inherit the Kingdom of God." Furthermore, Ignatius notes as a matter of widely-known fact and practice the three-tiered hierarchy of bishop, priest and deacon.

In Ignatius' seventh and last letter (addressed to Church of Smyrna), he exhorts:

> Pay attention to the bishop, if you would have God pay attention to you. I offer myself up for those who obey the bishops, priests and deacons.

Ignatius adds that he wants to follow the path of martyrdom trod by the bishops, priests and deacons: "May it be my lot to be with them in God!"

Ignatius then turns his attention once again to his readers and urges them to cultivate the virtue of loyalty and fidelity to their religious superiors, so as to avoid at all cost heresy, schism, or worse, apostasy.

He writes:

> Toil and train together, run and suffer together, rest and rise at the same time, as God's stewards, assistants and servants. Please the leader under whom you serve, for from him you receive your pay. May none of you turn out a deserter! Let your Baptism be ever your shield, your faith a helmet, your charity a spear, your patience a panoply. Let your works be deposits, so that you may receive the sum that is due to you. In humility be patient with one another, as God is with you.[1]

Blessed John Henry Newman once remarked:

---

[1]   Ignatius of Antioch, *Letter to the Smyrnaeans*, 1-6.

The whole system of Catholic doctrines may be discovered at least in outline, not to say in parts filled up, in the course of [Ignatius'] seven epistles.[2]

Beatrice reflects on Ignatius' theological contributions about the Church's unity, especially as they are revealed in the seven letters he addressed to the churches of Asia Minor as he made his way from Syria to Rome to be devoured by wild beasts in the circus:

Against those who were sowing discord in the Christian communities, Ignatius vigorously and repeatedly reaffirms the fundamental and irreplaceable role of the bishop, the sign of unity of the local church and the one who fosters the holiness of its members. Ignatius is the first Christian theologian to have worked out a strongly defined doctrine on the role and significance of the bishop in the Christian community. He is the first theorist of the "monarchical" episcopate.[3]

Regarding Church unity, Ignatius wrote:

Faith is the beginning and love is the end.

As for the Church of Rome, he states in his *Letter to the Romans* that she *presides in charity* over all other local churches.

Furthermore, he counseled Christians: We ought to regard the bishop as the Lord Himself, because the local bishop is meant to safeguard the rule of faith.

In his *Letter to the Ephesians*, Ignatius of Antioch, relying on the metaphor of musical harmony, extols the role of the bishop in the life of the universal and local churches:

It is fitting in every respect to glorify Jesus Christ who glorified you, so that drawn up into one obedience and subjected to the bishop and to the presbyterate you may be made holy in every way [...]. For Jesus Christ, our unwavering life, is the mind of the Father, just as the bishops, who have been established to the boundaries of the world, are the mind of Jesus Christ. For which reason it is fitting for you to be in accord with the mind of the bishop, as indeed you are. Your presbyterate, in keeping with its name, is worthy of God and

---

[2] Beatrice, *Introduction to the Fathers of the Church*, 25.
[3] Ibid.

has thus been in harmony with the bishop as strings with a lyre. On account of this, by your oneness of mind and your concord in love Jesus Christ is being hymned. May each one of you become a chorus! Since you are in concord in your oneness of mind and have taken up the melody of God in unity, may you sing in one voice to the Father through Jesus Christ, in order that He may hear you and recognize you through your good works as members of His Son [...]. It is thus useful for you to be always in irreproachable unity, so that you may always participate in God. If I in a brief time have entered into such fellowship, which is not human but spiritual, with your bishop, how much more do I consider you blessed who are so closely united to him as is the Church to Jesus Christ and Jesus Christ to the Father, so that everything may be in concord unity. Let no one be deceived. Unless one is within the sanctuary,[4] he is deprived of the bread of God. If the prayer of two people possesses such strength, how much more does that of the bishop and of the entire church?[5]

No Unity, No Sacraments

Cyprian of Carthage, Bishop of Carthage in North Africa and martyr there in A.D. 258, took a rigorous position when it came to those Gnostics who believed that they could be saved without submitting to legitimate Church authority. He firmly believed that Jesus had established the one chair of the episcopal office in which all twelve Apostles shared authority, with the primacy given over by Our Lord to Peter.[6]

---

[4]   Here, St. Ignatius uses figurative speech to get across his point that no one should have access to Holy Communion who does not maintain communion with the Catholic Church. Some have misinterpreted Ignatius' words in an overly literalistic sense to suggest that lay people should enter the sanctuary to receive Holy Communion. This practice, as well as the practice of having the laity gather around the altar for the Eucharistic Prayer as though they were concelebrants, is strictly forbidden by the liturgical law of the Catholic Church.

[5]   Ignatius of Antioch, *Letter to the Ephesians*, 2:2-5:2.

[6]   Although the power to bind and loose was given to all the Apostles, the keys to the Kingdom of Heaven were entrusted only to Peter—one of the scriptural bases for the doctrine of Petrine Primacy. Cf. Matthew 16:18-19; 18:18.

Therefore, schismatics who broke from union with the local bishop endangered their immortal souls. In his work *De Ecclesiae Catholicae Unitate* ("On the Unity of the Catholic Church"), Cyprian claimed that schismatics and heretics could not administer valid sacraments, even the Sacrament of Baptism, which is referred to as the door to all the other sacraments.[7]

Because Cyprian envisions the unity of the Church as a consequence of her communion with the three Persons of the Blessed Trinity, the act of schism is considered reprehensible not only since it is an attack on the Church—a divine institution—but even more fundamentally an attack on God Himself.

---

[7]   See CCC, 1213: "Holy Baptism is the basis of the whole Christian life, the gateway to life in the Spirit (*vitae spiritualis ianua*) and the door which gives access to the other sacraments."

CHAPTER THIRTY:
ECCLESIAL COMMUNION AND CHARITY

Justin's First Apology

Justin Martyr, in his *Dialogue with Trypho the Jew*, explained that whosoever adhered to whatever is honorable and good in the universe, nature, or pre-Christian philosophy, as well as in the Old Testament, would be eligible for resurrection unto eternal life on the Last Day. In describing the ancient liturgy, Justin relates the theology of Eucharistic communion to Christian charity as that virtue that should be its primary fruit. In his First Apology, Justin exhorts:

> At the end [of the Liturgy], those who possess goods and who have the good will [to donate them] give spontaneously that which they want and the collection is then handed over to the one who presides [priest/bishop], who will aid the orphans, the widows, those who find themselves in difficulty because of illness or for another reason, prisoners and strangers passing through: he [priest/bishop], in brief, succors all who are in difficulty.[1]

Tertullian's Ecclesiology

The early Christian writer Tertullian (c. A.D. 160-225), a most formidable apologist of the booming Christian Church in North Africa (Carthage), displayed an insightful ecclesiology. Because of the tight-knit, communal nature of the Church's identity and life, Tertullian speaks of his membership in the Church in the first person plural ("we"), rather than in the first person singular ("I"). For example, he writes:

> We are a united body from the bond of our piety, from the unity of our discipline, and from the pact of our hope.[2]

Relying on Pauline theology, Tertullian makes frequent use of concepts like "body," "spouse," "virgin," "mother" in reference to the Church. For Tertullian,

---

[1] Justin Martyr, *First Apology*, 67.
[2] Tertullian of Carthage, *Apology* 39:1.

the Church is never more the mother of Christians than when she generates them as children of God at the baptismal font.[3] So convinced is Tertullian about the importance of safeguarding the unity of Baptism as a sacrament administered by the orthodox body of believers in the Catholic Church that he considers all baptisms performed outside the Catholic Church to be false, that is to say, invalid (a position ultimately not adopted by the Church).[4]

In Tertullian's thought, the integrity of the Sacrament of Baptism in the Catholic Church is carefully linked to the Church's unity and apostolicity. Tertullian highlights the mark of the Church's unity when he describes the Church as not only the Mystical Body of Christ but also as the earthly image of Trinitarian communion. Tertullian writes:

> Since where there are the three, Father, Son and Holy Spirit, there one finds the Church that is the body of the three.[5]

Tertullian underscores the Church's mark of apostolicity remarking:

> That which the churches have received from the Apostles, the Apostles received from Christ, and Christ from God [the Father].[6]

Tertullian was no coward when it came to defending the Church against her fiercest enemies in the Roman Empire:

> We are but of yesterday and we have filled all you have — cities, islands, forts, towns, assembly halls, even military camps, tribes, town councils, the palace, the senate, and forum. We have left you nothing but the temples.

Again, the witty and outspoken apologist Tertullian takes up the sword of the tongue to defend a persecuted Christianity:

> If the Tiber rises too high or the Nile too low, if the sky remains closed or the earth moves, if plague or famine come, the cry is: "The Christians to the lion. What, all of them to a single lion?"[7]

Elsewhere, Tertullian discusses how Christians are in fact woven into the fabric of the pagan society in which they live yet remain distinct for their

---

3   Tertullian of Carthage, *On Baptism*, 20.
4   Ibid., 15.
5   Ibid., 6:2.
6   Tertullian of Carthage, *On the Prescription [Against] Heretics*, 21:3.
7   Tertullian of Carthage, *Apology*, 40.

unwillingness to commit the idolatrous acts that the pagans were trying to force upon them.

In effect, Tertullian's rhetoric is meant to highlight the normalcy of Christian living whose internal unity is based on faith and not merely on custom. Tertullian writes:

> We live with you, we have the same food, the same clothes, the same things, the same way of life. We are not Brahmans [...]. At this time we live with you, frequenting the plazas, the butcher shop, the roads, the taverns, the shops, the stalls, the markets, exercising all the other commercial activity. With you we sail and serve as soldiers [...].[8]

In the pagan environment in which Christians were then living, Tertullian is swift to exhort his fellow believers to be counter-cultural, united in certain practices that defied the attempts of the Roman persecutors to divide them. Although they could not marry in public, they considered their consent as binding before God and before one another, sometimes seeking out the secret blessing of a Catholic bishop.

Christian Marriage

Tertullian writes about the unity of the spouses in Holy Matrimony in his treatise, *Ad Uxorem* ("To His Wife"):

> How can one describe the happiness of this matrimony that the Church approves, that the oblation [the Eucharistic Sacrifice] confirms, that the blessing [of the bishop] seals, that the angels recognize, that the Father ratifies?[9]

Remaining in the realm of Christian ethics and morality, Tertullian strictly prohibits Christians from engaging in the barbarous pagan acts of divorce, polygamy and abortion. He recommends that a Christian not marry a pagan, lest there be division in the family over the fundamental issues of God and the religion He established.

Interestingly enough, Tertullian sees the threat of disunity in the Christian family as involving the education of Christian children in pagan, public schools. He states that even though Christian children may have no other recourse for their education but to attend the pagan, public schools because of the open

---

[8]   Ibid., 42, 1-3.
[9]   Tertullian of Carthage, *To His Wife*, 2:6.

persecution, it is nevertheless incumbent on Christian parents to provide an alternative Christian education for their children at home.

Overall, Tertullian strove to defend Christian solidarity as a visible expression of the Church's four marks, especially unity and holiness. Jonathan Hill notes:

> A contemporary of Minucius Felix, the first great Latin theologian Tertullian wrote his famous *Apology* to attack the slanders that were spread by the opponents of the Christians, and to present their way of life and thought in a favorable way. According to him, the pagans would comment, "See how they love one another!" in amazement. They could not understand why Christians called each other "brother," when they were not brothers. Tertullian commented that, having been born out of the same ignorance and come to the same knowledge of the one Heavenly Father, Christians had more right to

The Seven Works of Mercy: To Feed the Hungry
Carolo da Camerino, c. 1400. Vatican Museums.

regard each other as brothers than those who were related only by
blood ties. The Christians did not deny each other anything, and
they shared everything in common: indeed, they could be said to
have possessed a single mind and soul, uniting them all.[10]

Tertullian, in his major treatise, *De Praescriptione Hereticorum* (On the Prescription [Against] Heretics), defends: the four marks of the Church as linked
to the Church's doctrine of the divine institution of the Church on the foundation stones of the twelve Apostles; apostolic succession; and the communion of
the local churches with the Catholic Church, which alone dispenses the fullness
of truth and whose main episcopal see is the Diocese of Rome, founded by the
Apostles Peter and Paul. Tertullian writes:

> Our Lord Jesus Christ, as long as He was on the earth, Himself
> declared what He was, what He had been, what will of the Father
> He was administering and what He was establishing to be done by
> men. He did this either openly before the people or separately before
> His disciples, from whom He elected as intimate companions twelve
> chosen ones who were to instruct the nations. Then, since one of
> them had been removed, as He was returning to His Father after
> the Resurrection He ordered the remaining eleven to go and teach
> all nations, baptizing them in the Name of the Father, the Son and
> the Holy Spirit. Once Matthias had been added by lot as the twelfth
> in the place of Judas according to the authority of the prophecy in
> David's Psalm,[11] and once they had received the promised power of
> the Holy Spirit for working miracles and for preaching, the Apos-
> tles—the name means "those who have been sent"—immediately
> proclaimed the faith in Jesus Christ and established churches, begin-
> ning in Judea. They then set out into the rest of the world and pro-
> claimed the same teaching of the same faith to the nations. In like
> manner they founded churches in every city, from which the scion
> of the faith and the seeds of doctrine were transplanted daily in other
> churches so that the church comes into existence. For this reason, as
> offspring of the apostolic churches, these churches are themselves
> considered apostolic. Every race must be judged according to its ori-
> gins. Therefore, of so many and such great churches there is one
> which is the first, founded by the Apostles, from which the rest are
> derived. Thus all are first and all are apostolic since all are one. The
> communion of peace, the title of fraternity and the bonds of hos-
> pitality bear witness to this unity. No motive governs these rights

---

[10] Hill, *What Has Christianity Ever Done for Us?*, 109.
[11] Cf. Acts 1:15-26; Psalm 69:26. See also Psalm 109:8.

other than the one tradition of the same sacred bond. What did they preach? That is, what did Christ reveal to them? I would prescribe that this must be proved in no other manner than by the same churches which these very Apostles founded, who preached to them either *viva voce*,[12] as they say, or subsequently by letters. At some time the Lord said plainly, "I have many things still to say to you, but you are not able to bear them now." Yet He added, "When the Spirit of Truth will have come, He will lead you to all truth" (John 16:12-13). He showed that those whom He promised were going to obtain "all truth" through the Spirit of Truth were ignorant of nothing. Indeed, He fulfilled His promise, as the Acts of the Apostles prove when they speak of the descent of the Holy Spirit.[13]

---

[12]   This Latin expression literally means "by means of a live voice," that is, in person.
[13]   Tertullian of Carthage, *On the Prescription [Against] Heretics*, 20:1-9; 21:3; 22:8-10.

PART VII

Chapter Thirty-One serves as the capstone for the entire book, much as Chapter Eight on "Mary in the Mystery of Christ and the Church" served as the capstone of the Second Vatican Council's Dogmatic Constitution on the Church, Lumen Gentium. *This chapter is focused on Patristic Marian doctrine and devotion, including two of the most venerable Marian prayers in our Christian patrimony: the Sub Tuum Praesidium and the "Akathist" Hymn.*

CHAPTER FORTY-FIVE:
THE MARIOLOGY OF THE FATHERS

The Fathers of the Church took the Sacred Scriptures as their starting point for speaking about Mary. They referred to Mary initially as a bulwark of an orthodox Christology (e.g., Council of Ephesus in A.D. 431).

The Fathers also referred to Mary's cooperation in the divine economy or plan of salvation in order to clarify the salvific mission of the Church.

What factors contributed to the development of Mariology in the Early Church?

1. The development of symbols of faith, such as the Apostles' Creed.

2. The development of the canon of Sacred Scripture, that is, the list of officially recognized books of the Old and New Testaments.

3. The contribution of the Apocryphal Gospels.

4. The formation of theological and catechetical schools, like those at Alexandria, Antioch, and Jerusalem.

5. The confrontation between the old pagan culture and the Judeo-Christian culture.

6. The syncretism of the Gnostic systems that prided themselves on dualism, Docetism and adoptionism, which ended up downplaying or denying the fullness of the human nature and/or divine nature in the one divine Person of Christ.

7. The soteriological implications of the Gnostic heresies.

The Divine Maternity of Mary

Ignatius was the first Father of the Church to speak of Mary in a direct fashion. The main foundation of his Mariology is his understanding of Pauline theology.

The letters or epistles of Saint Ignatius contain invaluable insights into his theology, not to mention his Mariology.

He insists on the true motherhood (divine maternity) of Mary as the guarantee of the historical and soteriological reality of Our Lord's Incarnation. Ignatius emphasized the doctrine of the virginal conception of Jesus in his *Letter to the Smyrnaeans*. Ignatius explains that Jesus was of the royal stock of David conceived by the power of the Holy Spirit and born of the Virgin Mary:

> You are firmly convinced about Our Lord, who is truly of the race of David according to the flesh, Son of God according to the will and power of God, truly born of a virgin [...]. He was truly nailed to a tree for us in the flesh under Pontius Pilate [...]. He truly suffered, as He is also truly risen.[1]

Ignatius underscores the significance of God's economy of salvation which alone makes sense out of the miracle (mystery) of the virginal conception, the Incarnation and Paschal Mystery and defeats the wily plans of the Devil for our ruination. Ignatius writes in his *Letter to the Ephesians*:

> Mary's virginity and giving birth, and even the Lord's death escaped the notice of the prince of this world: these three mysteries worthy of proclamation were accomplished in God's silence.[2]

Ignatius highlights the unity of the Christ-event, so that the life and ministry of Jesus, the Word-Made-Flesh, is completely united to His origins in the virginal womb of Mary. To say that Jesus comes from God and from Mary is not a contradiction. Consequently, the Lord God Who is impassible according to His divine essence, becomes one capable of and even subject to suffering according to the mystery of the Incarnation and that of the Cross.

The Virginal Conception of Jesus

Justin wrote two apologies (defenses) of Christianity to the Roman emperors of his time; he also crafted an important *Dialogue with Trypho*, a contemporary Jewish thinker. In that dialogue, Justin plays the part of a Christian philosopher of the Word Incarnate whose coming, he declares emphatically, has fulfilled the Law and the Prophets.

Justin's *Dialogue with Trypho* is a response to the question: "Why did God become man?" An essential part of Justin's apology is one that affirms that

---

[1]   Ignatius of Antioch, *Letter to the Smyrnaeans*, 19:1; cf. CCC, 498.
[2]   Ignatius of Antioch, *Letter to the Ephesians*, 19:1; cf. CCC, 498.

Mary's virginal conception is not an example of mythological *parthenogenesis*, a term used to describe the physical union of virgins and pagan gods or heroes in Greek and Roman mythology.

Justin underscores how the Incarnation is the product of neither myth nor chance but the direct result of God's providential plan of salvation in the fullness of time.

To the pagans, Justin seeks to demonstrate that the Incarnate Word, Christ Jesus, is the fulfillment of every philosophy. All men have seeds of the Logos (God's Word or Reason) who, because of the coming of the Logos Incarnate, now have the possibility of achieving full illumination and, therefore, eternal salvation.

To the Jews, Justin seeks to demonstrate that the Incarnate Word is the fulfillment of all the Old Testament prophecies. Of course, among those prophecies are those concerning the virginal conception, such as Genesis 49:10-11; Isaiah 7:14; 53:8; Daniel 2:34; 7:13.

According to Justin, the virginal conception is a mystery of faith that acts as a motive of credibility in the unique divine origins of Christ and Christianity. Justin explains that Our Lord's birth from the Virgin Mary is a testimony to His historicity and to the reality of His Sacred Humanity.

Why did God will that the Second Person of the Blessed Trinity, His Only-Begotten Son, be conceived and born of the Virgin Mary? Because an integral part of His salvific plan is the reversal of the Fall and its evil effects brought about by the obedience of Christ the New Adam and Mary the New Eve.

Justin compares and contrasts Eve and Mary as two virgins who heard two different words and therefore produced two contrary effects, namely, death and life, respectively. The disobedience of the Virgin Eve in response to the deceptive message of the serpent (Satan) is contrasted strongly with the obedience of the Virgin Mary in response to the joyful message of the Archangel Gabriel at the moment of the Annunciation.

Thus Eve and Mary are presented by Justin Martyr as being responsible, respectively, for the fall and restoration of mankind in subordination to the first and last Adams.

Justin explains his theology of Mary the New Eve in his *Dialogue with Trypho*—here cited from John Henry Cardinal Newman's apologetical masterpiece, *Letter to Pusey*:

We know that He before all creatures proceeded from the Father by His power and will [...]. And by means of the Virgin became man, that by what way the disobedience arising from the serpent had its beginning, by that way also it might have an undoing. For Eve, being a virgin and undefiled, conceiving the word that was from the serpent, brought forth disobedience and death; but the Virgin Mary, taking faith and joy, when the Angel told her the good tidings, that the Spirit of the Lord should come upon her and the power of the Highest over-shadow her, and therefore the Holy One that was born of her was the Son of God, answered: "Be it done to me according to thy word."[3]

Mary, the New Eve

Irenaeus is sometimes referred to as the "Father of Mariology" since he had one of the most developed understandings of Mary among the earliest Fathers of the Church.

He produced a five-volume work, *Against Heresies*, as well as a brief work, entitled *The Demonstration of the Apostolic Preaching.*

Irenaeus wrote primarily to confute the Gnostic heretics. His main perspec-tive was that of the economy, plan or history of salvation. Irenaeus teaches that since there is only one Son of God Incarnate there must be only one salvific economy, one history of salvation, one faith, one Church, one Divine Revela-tion, one sacramental life, and one hierarchy with apostolic succession, most especially in the Chair of Peter.

For Saint Irenaeus, the Virgin Mother of God, Mary of Nazareth, has a special, indeed a unique, role to play in the economy of salvation that gravitates around her vocation as the New Eve.

Mary the New Eve cooperates with Christ the New Adam in the divine plan to recapitulate all things in Christ by the power of the Holy Spirit to the glory of God the Father. There takes place a wonderful exchange at the moment of the Incarnation (the Annunciation) when God assumes a human nature and we become partakers in the divine life, which is effected through Baptism and the other sacraments.

Irenaeus explains that just as the first Adam was taken from a virgin earth, so too the New Adam is conceived and born of the Virgin Mary. Indeed, Mary transmitted to the Second Person of the Trinity Incarnate all of the substance

---

[3]   Justin Martyr, *Dialogue with Trypho*, 100, as cited in John Henry Newman's *Difficulties of Anglicans*, 2: 33.

Byzantine mosaic of Madonna and Child found in the remains of the former Hagia Sophia Basilica, Istanbul. Source: Phi-Gastrein, Wikimedia.

of the Sacred Humanity He assumed and consubstantially united to His one Divine Person as the primary instrument of our salvation.

Irenaeus concludes that Christ is the New Adam because unlike the first Adam he did not fall into disobedience when tempted by Satan, God's Adversary. Based on this antithetical parallelism between Adam and Christ—already developed in Saint Paul's writings[4]—Saint Irenaeus develops the antithetical parallelism between Eve and Mary. This antithetical parallelism is explained thus: As Eve was a "cause of death" (*causa mortis*) because of her disobedience, so Mary became the "cause of salvation" (*causa salutis*) because of her obedience.

The Catechism twice cites Irenaeus in this regard:

> As Saint Irenaeus says: Being obedient she became the cause of salvation for herself and for the whole human race [...]. The knot of Eve's disobedience was untied by Mary's obedience: what the virgin Eve bound through her disbelief, Mary loosened by her faith.[5]

We can remark with Irenaeus that the virginal conception of Jesus prophesied in Isaiah 7:14 is a divine sign for the whole human family that Emmanuel, God-with-us, is the universal Redeemer/Savior.

Irenaeus' Mariology affords us a keen understanding of Our Blessed Mother as the New Eve, to whom he also refers as *Advocata Evae* (Advocate of Eve), and the *Causa Salutis* (Cause of Salvation).

Irenaeus explains that Mary's obedience loosed the knot of Eve's disobedience; that as Eve consented to the word of a fallen angel (Satan) for our ruin, Mary consented to the word of the Archangel Gabriel for our recapitulation by Christ, together with all things, at the end of time to the glory of God the Father. The Bishop of Lyons writes:

> As the human race was made a slave of death because of a virgin (Eve), by means of a virgin (Mary) it obtained salvation. Above and beyond an exact judgment was placed in contrast to the disobedience of one virgin (Eve) the obedience of another virgin (Mary). Moreover, the sin of the firstborn (Adam) and the cunning of the serpent (the Devil) were conquered by the simplicity of a dove, and the chains with which we were bound to death were broken.[6]

Mary, the Hinge of Salvation

Tertullian ardently defended orthodox Christology and Mariology against the rantings of the Gnostic heretics. He defended as part of the nucleus of the Christian creed the doctrines of the virginal conception and, therefore, divine maternity of Mary. As part of his defense of the mystery of the Incarnation and

---

[4] Cf. Romans 5:1; 1 Corinthians 15.
[5] CCC, 494.
[6] CCC, 494. Cf. Irenaeus of Lyons, *Adversus Haereses*, 5: 19, 1.

of Mary's real cooperation in that mystery, (against the Gnostics) Tertullian gave us the pithy expression: *caro cardo salutis* (the flesh is the hinge of salvation).

However, Tertullian insisted that even though Mary was a virgin in conceiving Our Lord, she was not a virgin in giving birth to Him. Tertullian makes this assertion primarily because the Gnostics, in certain instances, maintained that Jesus came into this world passing through Mary as water passes through a tube.

Tertullian rejected this image which was intended to undermine belief in the reality of Jesus' birth, one that would have brought Him into direct contact with the material world. For the Gnostics the material world, human nature, human flesh and human sexuality were all considered corrupt realities.

Of course, Tertullian's position is not reflective of the overall Apostolic Tradition that upholds Mary's perpetual virginity *ante partum, in partu, post partum* (before the birth, during the birth, after the birth), an expression cherished by Fathers of the Church like Augustine.

Although the doctrine of Mary's perpetual virginity was never solemnly defined as dogma *ex cathedra Petri* (from the chair of Peter), as were the doctrines of Mary's Immaculate Conception and bodily Assumption, the Lateran Synod (which was a local and not an ecumenical council) held in A.D. 649, is noteworthy for having provided the ancient Church with an avid defense of this doctrine held from apostolic times—one of Mary's oldest titles being *Aeiparthenos* (Ever-Virgin).[7]

We should remark that Tertullian's exegesis of certain passages of Sacred Scripture dealing with Our Lady contrasts with the Gnostic interpretation. For example, in Mark 3:33 and Matthew 12:48, the Gnostics believed that Jesus was repudiating Mary's role for some sort of lack of faith. Tertullian, commenting on these same texts together with Luke 11:27-28, concluded quite the contrary—that Jesus used those occasions for highlighting Mary's role of perfect discipleship that went far beyond her mere physical ties to Him in order to create an even more intimate bond with the Savior.

Cardinal Newman was particularly impressed with Tertullian's understanding of the Scriptures in terms of the parallel between Christ and Adam and, by extension, between Eve and Mary, showing how these comparisons form the basis of the economy of salvation.

To understand Tertullian's views about the Virgin, it is helpful to summarize his thought about Mary's relation to the most convincing proof of Our

---

[7] Cf. CCC, 499.

Lord's Incarnation. Tertullian logically argues that the reality of Christ's Sacred Humanity is, first and foremost, to be derived from the fact that the Son of God was born of a woman.

Tertullian relates that Mary is a descendant of the great patriarchs and prophets of Israel, tracing her genealogy back to the messianic line of David; she is likewise a daughter of Eve, a true descendant of Adam. Thus, the Virgin Mary guarantees Christ's entrance into humanity and it is His Sacred Humanity assumed from her body which is the primary instrument of our salvation. Hence, Tertullian's famous adage, *caro cardo salutis* (the flesh is the hinge of salvation). If this is true, then it follows that Mary's giving birth to Our Lord according to the flesh constitutes her the primary human "cooperatrix" in the work of our salvation.

According to Tertullian, by His Incarnation Christ transfigures man, so that he might ever more resemble his Creator as he did before the Fall and therefore, with body and soul, come to share in the full benefits of the Resurrection, arriving at complete restoration to God's image and likeness on the Last Day.[8]

The rival operation of the Devil, as Tertullian sees it, is one that contributes to the deformation of man, the disfigurement of God's image and likeness. Christ's coming as Man from the Virgin Mary defeats the wily plan, aimed at death and destruction of mankind's harmony, while the economy or plan of God ultimately succeeds because it is based on the principles of life and unity as Christ's Incarnation effects a recapitulation of the human condition. This recapitulation of which Tertullian speaks is more or less the one first laid down in the Epistles of Saint Paul.

In this process of recapitulation, as Tertullian envisions it, the cooperation of the Virgin Mary is willed in a particular way, so that mankind is made whole and, at the same time, the female sex is restored to its proper dignity in God's image and likeness. In this way, Mary's cooperation in the work of salvation as the New Eve is not limited to a general representation of humanity but also acquires a particular significance in that she also represents womankind.

---

[8]   Cf. Benedict XVI, *The Fathers*, 50: "In his famous affirmation according to which our soul 'is *naturally* Christian,' Tertullian evokes the perennial continuity between authentic human values and Christian ones. Also, in his other reflection borrowed directly from the Gospel, according to which 'the Christian cannot hate, not even his enemies,' is found the unavoidable moral resolve, the choice of faith which proposes 'non-violence' as the rule of life. Indeed, no one can escape the dramatic aptness of this teaching, also in light of the heated debate on religion."

Mary, the Incorruptible Ark of the Covenant

A priest of the Diocese of Rome, Hippolytus was a great exegete, historian and controversialist. To Hippolytus is ascribed the celebrated work, *The Apostolic Tradition* (*Traditio Apostolica*). In this work, Hippolytus describes the traditions, most especially the liturgical traditions, of the Diocese of Rome in the second century, which may have been also the traditions of the Church of Alexandria in Egypt.

Of particular importance is Hippolytus' description of the Eucharistic Liturgy, with special emphasis on the Eucharistic Prayer (Greek: *anaphora*). In a homily on the Paschal Supper, Hippolytus focuses on Mary as a key figure in the divine project of salvation that culminates in the Incarnation and Paschal Mystery of the God-Man.

Hippolytus, in grand style, asks some beautiful rhetorical questions, such as:

> Tell me, O Blessed Mary, what was it that you conceived in your womb? What was it that you were bearing in your virginal womb?

He responds in short order:

> He was the Only-Begotten Word of God who, descended from the heavens upon you, was being formed in your womb as a first-born man, because the Only-Begotten Son, the Word of God manifested Himself united to the Only-Begotten man.[9]

Hippolytus emphasizes the eternal generation of the Son of God in the bosom of the Father and the temporal generation of the Son of God in the virginal womb of Mary.

He refers to Mary using adjectives such as "blessed" and "holy." He speaks of her as "the incorruptible ark." In his *Commentaries on the Canticle of Canticles* (Song of Songs), Hippolytus reflects on Mary as the chaste spouse enamored of the Bridegroom, who is Christ.

Mary, Model of the Church

Clement of Alexandria was a very educated man who had a profound knowledge of the Christian Faith and of the Hellenistic-Roman cultures with which he sought to interface, both at a philosophical and theological level. His most important work is called *Stromata* (in Greek, literally, "things left lying around" or "miscellany").

---

[9] Hippolytus of Rome, *Homily on the Paschal Supper*, IV. 14.2.

Clement argued that true knowledge or *gnosis* (Greek: knowledge) is not Gnostic, that is to say, true knowledge does not pertain to a sect of men and women who claimed to have received secret divine revelations into which they alone had been initiated through a series of rites.

Rather, true knowledge according to Clement of Alexandria derives from knowledge of the mystery of Christ the *Logos* or "Word" Incarnate through whom, as Saint Paul already teaches in his Epistles to the Colossians and the Ephesians, all the universe is created, sustained, redeemed, sanctified and ultimately recapitulated.

Clement tries to exhort his pagan audience to give up their pagan ways (e.g., participation in the gladiatorial games, especially on Sundays) in order to emphasize the centrality of Christ and His worship.

He makes reference to the Blessed Virgin Mary in two places in his works where he highlights Mary as the Virgin-Mother figure of the Church who is the spiritual mother of all men. He writes of the Church nourishing her children with the pure milk of God's Word and with the sacraments, most especially with the Eucharist, the Bread of Everlasting Life.

From the early Christian writers (all before the close of the third century), we find the strong and impressive foundations of a Mariology that would develop even more in the ensuing generations of Christian reflection on the place of Mary in the economy of salvation. History reveals, then, that Mariology is by no means an "add-on" to Christian doctrine or a medieval "accretion."

Origen's Marian Apologetic and Spirituality

Origen was arguably the greatest theologian of his age, certainly the greatest biblical exegete, and one of the Church's finest apologists. The focus of his theology was Christ the Incarnate Word (*Logos*). Origen underscores how Our Lord's Incarnation aimed at our deification, our conformity to God in Christ Jesus and through the power of the Holy Spirit. Given Origen's focus on the mystery of the Incarnation, he also emphasizes the cooperation of the Virgin-Mother, Mary.

Origen's Mariology is characterized by an emphasis on the virginal conception of Jesus, the divine maternity of Mary, and her perpetual virginity. Concerning the virginal conception, he writes to the pagan philosopher Celsus to defend the virginal conception against the accusation that it was a myth, like the pagan notion of *parthenogenesis*, whereby Olympian gods, quite anthropomorphic in nature, ravished and sometimes even raped mortal maidens in order to sire children by them.

Origen defends Mary's virginity by offering ample commentary on the historicity of Mary as the Virgin of Nazareth in light of scriptural prophecies like Isaiah 7:14. The virginal conception is a work of God, and not of man, a true miracle wrought by the power of the Holy Spirit. Thus it cannot be argued that God's birth from a woman was unworthy of God, as Celsus and others argued. Nor is there any credibility to Celsus' fantastic claim that Mary had been raped by a Roman soldier named Pantera.

Concerning the divine maternity of Mary, the only testimony to Origen's belief comes from an historian by the name of Sozomenos (fifth century), who says that Origen defended the title of *Theotokos*, which already had a widespread use in Egypt in the second and third centuries, long before Nestorius would oppose its use as Patriarch of Constantinople in the fifth century.

Concerning the perpetual virginity of Mary, Origen realizes that the doctrine is a popular belief among the lay faithful (*sensus fidelium*), recognizing that its popularity is due to a certain extent to the spreading of apocryphal gospels. He writes:

> According to those who believe in a healthy way, no one outside of Jesus is the Son of Mary.

In this way, Origen professed the Church's perennial belief that Mary was *aeiparthenos*, the venerable Greek term for "ever-virgin."

Origen holds that the so-called "brothers and sisters" of Jesus mentioned in the New Testament were sons of the widower Joseph. Origen finds it almost repugnant to suggest that Mary, having conceived and given birth to the Incarnate Word by the power of the Holy Spirit, would ever have had any other creature take up its abode in her virginal womb. Along these lines, Origen proposes Mary as the model of feminine virginity, while Jesus remains the primary model of male virginity.

Origen depicts a Gospel portrait of Mary. He highlights Mary's pilgrimage of faith as she precedes the Church, which follows her example in meeting the Word Incarnate and knowing Him through faith, so as to welcome Him in the sacraments and to incarnate Him in the holiness of their lives.

The grace-filled events of Mary's life are meant to designate her as the model of the Church, the Spotless Bride forever in search of a more intimate and perfect union with Christ, the Bridegroom. Origen comes to these conclusions by means of a profound exegesis of the Canticle of Canticles, for which he wrote one of the most significant commentaries among the early Christian writers. Likewise, Origen reflects on Mary's singular chastity in his *Commentaries on the Gospel of Matthew*:

> I believe conveniently that the first-fruits of the chaste purity of men is Jesus, and that of women, Mary: it would not in fact be pious to ascribe to another woman if not to Mary the first-fruits of virginity.[10]

Origen proposes that the Gospel portrait of Mary be regarded as consisting of two types of integrated pilgrimages: "a pilgrimage of faith" and "a pilgrimage of love."

Origen delineates Mary's pilgrimage of faith in the following manner. The Virgin contemplates the mystery of the Incarnation by reflecting on the fulfillment of the Old Testament in the Christ-Event. Mary knew the Law, was holy, and knew well the divine prophecies through her daily meditation. Despite her profound contemplation of the mystery of the Word Incarnate, it was difficult at times for Mary to understand the teachings and behavior of her Divine Son, such as when she and Joseph, filled with anxiety, searched for the Child Jesus (he had been lost three days), finally finding Him among the doctors of the Law in the Temple at Jerusalem.

The Wedding Feast at Cana, *St. John the Baptist Church, Pijnacker, Netherlands. Source: Hpruxpbvm, Wikipedia.*

---

[10]   Origen of Alexandria, *Commentaries on the Gospel according to Matthew*, 10:17.

For Origen, the perplexed reaction of Joseph and Mary on that occasion proved that they both needed to make a pilgrimage of faith. In other words, only perfect knowledge (reserved to God alone) can make for perfect faith, as Origen reflects.

With regard to the prophecy of Simeon at Our Lord's Presentation in the Temple, Origen equates the sword prophesied by Simeon with the scandal of the Cross, which would create in Mary certain doubts, especially when she would think of the Crucified One as the innocent fruit of her virginal womb, once over-shadowed by the Holy Spirit at the Annunciation. According to Origen,

> If the Virgin did not experience scandal during the Passion of the Lord, Jesus did not die for our sins.[11]

Origen, like numerous theologians before and after him, found it difficult to maintain Mary's absolute sinlessness while also affirming the universality of sin and the need to recognize Jesus as Universal Redeemer.

Lacking the insights of later theologians, such as John Duns Scotus and John Henry Cardinal Newman, Origen insisted that Mary had to lack in some thing, in some area of her life, in a particular virtue (e.g., faith) in order to be redeemed by Christ. Origen writes:

> What is one to think then? That while the Apostles remained scan-dalized by the Cross, that the Mother of the Lord had been immune from scandal?[12]

For Origen, Mary's pilgrimage of faith was truly tested by doubt and uncertainty. Only in his later exegesis does he come to understand that Mary stood solid in her faith at the foot of the Cross.

Origen describes Mary's pilgrimage of love as proof that the Virgin Mary is the model of the spiritual and apostolic [mission-minded] believer. In this way, Origen reflects on Mary's visitation to the house of Zechariah and Elizabeth, and on her proclamation of the *Magnificat*, her canticle of praise sung by the Church each day at Vespers.

At the Visitation, Mary appears in the horizontal dimension of love, dem-onstrating clearly her love of neighbor that flows from her vertical love of God. Mary makes haste to the house of Elizabeth under the constant impulse of the Holy Spirit. Mary's going up to the house of Elizabeth over the hills of Judea

---

[11] Origen of Alexandria, *Homilies on Luke*, 17: 6-7.
[12] Ibid.

corresponds, according to Origen, to a type of spiritual ascent toward divine realities, the apex of spiritual perfection.

Mary's voice praising God in the *Magnificat* expresses her greatness in the sight of God's greatness; her voice becomes a voice of evangelization, the voice of Christ the Incarnate Word filled with the inspirations of the Holy Spirit.

Final Patristic Thoughts on Mary

Aristide of Athens (second century) wrote an apologetical work addressed to the Emperor Hadrian in which he declares:

> that God descended from Heaven and took flesh from a Jewish virgin; and dwelt in a daughter of man, the Son of God.[13]

Melito of Sardis (d. ca. 180) in his *Paschal Homily*, written in Greek on papyrus discovered in the late twentieth century, describes Mary as the *beautiful lamb* whose purity and innocence in the mystery of the Incarnation (Annunciation) made possible the generation of Christ Jesus the sacrificial Lamb of God immolated for our salvation.[14]

Cyprian of Carthage (d. 258), Novatian of Rome (d. circa 258), Lactantius (d. 317) and Victorinus of Pettau (d. 384) write of Jesus as being *apator* (without a father) according to His Humanity and *ametor* (without a mother) according to His Divinity.

These notions are enshrined in the Niceno-Constantinopolitan Creed where we profess that Jesus is:

> God from God, Light from Light, true God from true God, begotten, not made, consubstantial with Father; through Him all things were made [...].

Methodius of Olympus or Philippi (d. 311), in his work *The Banquet of the Ten Virgins*, praises virginity, making Mary the node that links the virginal cortege of the Old Testament from Abel to the New Testament figure of John the Baptist, the friend of the Bridegroom, for she is the figure of the Church as Virgin-Mother.

Alexander of Alexandria (d. 328) was the first Christian author to use the title *Theotokos*[15] in writing and to propose Mary as a model of Christian vir-

---

[13]   Aristide of Athens, *Apologia*, 2:6.
[14]   Melito of Sardis, *Epistle*, 70.
[15]   Cf. Pelikan, *Mary Through the Centuries*, 57: "The origins of the title Mother of God are obscure. In spite of the diligence of Hugo Rahner and others, there is no altogether incontestable evidence that it was used before the fourth century, despite Newman's categorical claim

ginity. Consecrated virginity, we should recall, became quite popular with the early Christians during periods when they were not being severely persecuted, especially after the legalization of Christianity under the Emperor Constantine with the Edict of Milan in A.D. 313. Consecrated virginity came to be known as a type of spiritual or white martyrdom because of the enormous sacrifices it encompasses.

Eusebius of Caesaraea (d. 340) asserted that not only Joseph but Mary also was a descendant of David, so as to prove that Jesus was the Messiah, the Son of David not only according to the Law of Moses but also according to the flesh.[16]

The most famous work of Cyril of Jerusalem (d. 347) is his *Catechetical Instructions*. Saint Cyril defends the virginal conception and divine maternity of Mary against the heretical sect known as the Manicheans, followers of Manes. They claimed that God would have rendered Himself impure if he had become man, passing through the maternal womb, considered by them to be the most unclean place of the human body. Cyril responds vehemently to defend the Church's orthodox position:

> He who in forming man touched his limbs, and did not dishonor Himself, would He suffer dishonor in forming for Himself the Sacred Flesh, the veil of His Divinity?[17]

Consequently, in response to the Manichean heresy and other subsequent heresies related to it, Cyril, like Gregory of Nazianzen and Hilary of Poitiers, insists that Mary's sanctification, the sanctification of her body, took place at the moment of the Annunciation when she was overshadowed by the Holy Spirit. On the whole, however, the Catholic Church believed from time immemorial, despite the contrary opinions of certain Fathers of the Church, that Mary was sanctified, indeed was "all-holy" (Greek: *panaghia*) from the first moment of her Immaculate Conception in the womb of her saintly mother Anne.[18]

Athanasius of Alexandria (d. 373) defends the integrity of the mystery of

that 'the title *Theotokos*, Mother of God, was familiar to Christians from primitive times.' What is clear is that the first completely authenticated instances of the use of this title came from the city of Athanasius, Alexandria. Alexander, his patron and immediate predecessor as bishop there, referred to Mary as Theotokos in his encyclical of circa 319 about the heresy of Arius. From various evidence including the taunts of Julian the Apostate from a few decades later about the term Theotokos [...] it seems reasonable to conclude that the title already enjoyed widespread acceptance in the piety of the faithful at Alexandria and beyond."

[16] Eusebius of Caesarea, *Questions on the Gospel Addressed to Stephen*, 1-9.

[17] Cyril of Jerusalem, *Catechetical Instructions*, 12:24.

[18] The feast of Mary's conception from St. Anne is celebrated in the Byzantine Rite on Dec. 9. In the Roman Rite the Solemnity of the Immaculate Conception is observed on Dec. 8.

the Incarnation by defending the integrity of Mary's own humanity. He writes:

> Mary is, in fact, our sister, because we are all sons and daughters of
> Adam [...]. Only concerning the Son of Mary is it written: And the
> Word became flesh.[19]

It seems as though the first Marian homily, which we have in the Coptic language, ought to be attributed to Saint Athanasius. It is a commentary on the Annunciation, Visitation and Nativity of Our Lord. He writes, for example:

> Truly your soul magnifies the Lord and your spirit exults in God
> your Savior: in the future for all eternity every generation will praise
> you [...]. Adam praises you, calling you "mother of all the living."
> Moses praises you, contemplating you as the ark of the new cove-
> nant, from every side covered with gold. David acclaims you blessed,
> declaring you "city of the Great King," "city of the God of heavenly
> hosts." Also in the future all human generations will praise you.[20]

Ephrem the Syrian, deacon (d. 373), was a pioneer in Mariology, being the first theologian to put into poetic verse (using the Syriac language, which is similar to the Aramaic language spoken by Our Lord in the first century) lullabies placed on the gentle lips of Mary and addressed to her infant Son lying in a cradle. These poetic lullabies are an expression of Mary's profound adoration of her Divine Son, her Infant Savior and ours, too. Ephrem muses:

> Whoever gave in a solitary fashion to conceive and give to the light
> of day He who is together one and many, little and great, completely
> present in me and completely present everywhere? The day in which
> Gabriel entered toward my poor self, in an instant he made me Lady
> (Queen) and handmaiden. Therefore, I am the handmaiden of your
> Divinity, but also mother of your Humanity, O My Lord and My
> Son![21]

In appreciation of Saint Ephrem's deeply poetic and theological writings, he earned the epithet, "Harp of the Spirit."

Basil the Great (d. 379), one of the three Cappadocian Fathers, had his finger on the pulse of the *sensus fidelium*, that is, he understood the faith-intuitions of the People of God. Thus, in commenting on the Infancy Narrative of Mat-

---

[19] Athanasius of Alexandria, *Letter to Epitetus*. Cf. *Patrologia Greca* 26: 1051-1070.

[20] Athanasius of Alexandria, *Homily on the Holy Virgin Mother of God*. Cf. *Le Muséon* 71 [1958] 209-239.

[21] Ephrem the Syrian, *Hymns on the Nativity of the Lord*, 5:19-20.

thew, Basil explains that the Evangelist's use of the word "until" in 1:25 does not necessarily imply that Mary had other children after Jesus. Therefore, Jesus is in fact both Mary's First-Born Son and her Only-Begotten Son. By this form of exegesis, Basil defends the doctrine of Mary's perpetual virginity.[22]

Gregory of Nazianzus (d. 394), the best friend of Basil the Great, anathematizes anyone who would deny the doctrine of the divine maternity of Mary. He boldly states that the person who denies this doctrine is devoid of God Himself.[23]

Gregory of Nyssa (d. 394), the brother of Basil the Great, and part of the trio known as the Cappadocian Fathers, lauds Mary's Viginity having inexorably united her to God. Gregory is exuberant in his praise of Mary's virginity:

> O blessed womb, which by means of its inexpressable purity took to itself that which is the greatest good of the soul! In all other human beings, indeed, [...] a pure spirit may welcome the presence of the Holy Spirit: here instead is the flesh that becomes the dwelling place of the Holy Spirit![24]

Maximus of Turin (d. circa 400) in his sermons highlights parallels such as the virginal and fruitful womb of Mary with the baptismal font of the Church, and the virginal womb of Mary with the never-occupied (virginal) tomb of Our Lord's Resurrection.

Epiphanius of Salamis (d. 403) writes against the Collyridians, a group made up mostly of women who literally worshipped Mary by bringing her cakes and breads (thus giving them their name in Greek):

> One need not honor the saints more than their due, rather one should honor their Lord [...]. Mary's body was certainly holy, I confess, but she was not a goddess [...]. One honors therefore Mary, but one adores the Father, the Son and the Holy Spirit. May no one adore Mary![25]

Regarding the end of Mary's earthly course, Epiphanius of Salamis offers us the first documented testimony, affirming that we do not know how Mary went from earth to Heaven—whether she died or did not die a physical death; whether she died a natural death or like a martyr. Epiphanius explains:

---

[22] See Basil the Great, *Homily on the Nativity of the Lord*, 5. Cf. *Patrologia Greca*, 31: 1468.
[23] See Gregory of Nazianzus, *Letter 101 to Cledonius*. Cf. *Patrologia Greca*, 37:177.
[24] Gregory of Nyssa, *Homily on the Nativity of the Lord*. Cf. *Patrologia Greca*, 46: 1141.
[25] Epiphanius of Salamis, *Against the Heresies*, 79:4,7.

Madonna of Monteluce, *Raphael/Penne/Romano, c. 1500 AD. Vatican Museums, Rome.*

If the Holy Virgin died a natural death and was buried, truly honorable is her dormition ("falling asleep"), her crown is her virginity. If, on the other hand, she was killed, as it is written, "A sword shall pierce your soul" (Luke 2:35), her glory would be among the martyrs, and blessed her body from which arose the light of the world. But she could have also remained alive: God in fact can do whatever He wants. However it might be, no one ever knew how Mary ended her life on earth.[26]

Severian of Gabala (d. 408) taught that Mary, unlike Eve, did not experience pain in giving birth, for the joy announced by the Angel Gabriel to Mary at the moment of the Incarnation exempted her from this particular curse that Eve had incurred as a result of her disobedience in the Garden of Eden.[27] Severian expressed his devotion to Mary, defending her maternal and heavenly intercession on our behalf. He says that if faithful women of the Old Testament like Deborah and Gael could be alive in God's presence and considered victorious on account of their cooperation in the economy of salvation, then how much more so the Virgin Mary through whom Christ came into the world to conquer sin and death.[28]

Jerome (d. circa 419/420), writing to defend the doctrine of the perpetual virginity of Mary against the heretic Helvidius, states:

> You say that Mary did not remain a virgin; but I vindicate for myself greater things, affirming that also Joseph was a virgin for Mary's sake, so that from a virginal matrimony would be born a virginal Son.[29]

Teotecnos of Livia (beginning of the sixth century) is the first Christian author we know to mention the idea of assumption in connection with Our Lady. He accepts apocryphal elements with discretion, but offers biblical and theological motivations for them, demonstrating the full conformity of the way of the Mother with the way of the Son, who died, rose again and ascended into glory, body and soul.

Ildephonsus of Toledo (d. 667), in his writings on several occasions, prays to Mary, asking her to obtain for him spiritual graces, calling her "Lady" and consecrating himself to her as a slave (servant).

Germanus of Constantinople (d. 733) defends the use of icons in Marian devotion as a safeguard of the full doctrine concerning the Lord's Incarnation;

---

[26] Epiphanius of Salamis, *Against the Heresies*, 78:11.
[27] See Severian of Gabala, *Homily on the Creation of the World*. Cf. *Patrologia Greca*, 56:497.
[28] See Severian of Gabala, *Homily on the Legislator*. Cf. *Patrologia Greca*, 56:409-410.
[29] Jerome, *Against Helvidius*, 19.

he emphasizes the power of Mary as Mediatrix of all grace; all who invoke her are protected by her in body and soul, in the present life and in the life of the world to come, even on Judgment Day.

John Damascene (d. 749) writes:

> Why was the Virgin [Mary] born of a sterile mother? [...]. I have another reason, higher and more divine. Nature in fact yields the way to grace and trembling it stops, incapable of proceeding. When in fact the Mother of God was about to be conceived by Anne, nature dared not come before grace, and thus remained without fruit until grace had produced its fruit.[30]

As we conclude our overview of the principal Marian doctrines in the writings of the Fathers of the Church, it should be clear that those teachings do not stem from the Middle Ages or even the nineteenth and twentieth centuries, as some non-Catholic critics assert. Indeed, they come from the earliest years of development in Christian theology, forged by thinkers still living in proximity to the apostolic era.

The Oldest Marian Prayer

The *Sub Tuum Praesidium* is the oldest extant Marian prayer, dating from the third century. The Greek text of this prayer is found on an Egyptian papyrus scroll in the Library of John Ryland in Manchester, England. It was found for the first time in Latin in the *Liber Responsorialis*, attributed to Pope Saint Gregory the Great (fifth century). It is also found in the Latin Antiphonary of Compiègne, dating to the ninth century. The *Sub Tuum Praesidium* most likely does not derive from a liturgical context since liturgical prayers in the ancient Church were, for the most part, directed to one or more Persons of the Trinity, and not to any of the saints, including Mary.

Nevertheless, this beautiful Marian prayer attests to the Marian devotion of the People of God already prior to the Third Ecumenical Council held at Ephesus (Asia Minor, now Turkey) in A.D. 431. At that Council, the teachings of Nestorius, Patriarch of Constantinople, were condemned since he claimed that one could only rightly refer to Mary as the Christ-bearer (*Christotokos*), not as the God-bearer (*Theotokos*). The Council Fathers, led by Saint Cyril of Alexandria (Patriarch of Alexandria in Egypt), distinguished the true doctrine that Mary was the Mother of the Incarnate Word of God from the false belief that she was to be considered the Mother of the eternal, divine Essence.

---

[30] John Damascene, *Homily on the Nativity of Mary*, 2.

This prayer is a summary of key Marian doctrines: it expresses the Church's belief in Mary's maternal intercession (mediation) and protection; her divine motherhood; her perpetual virginity; her outstanding holiness and blessedness in the communion of saints.

It reads in Latin:

> *Sub tuum praesidium confugimus, Sancta Dei Genetrix, nostras deprecationes ne despicias in necessitatibus, sed a periculis cunctis libera nos semper, Virgo, gloriosa et benedicta.* (Under your protection we take refuge, O Holy Mother of God; do not despise our petitions in [our] necessities, but free us always from all dangers, O glorious and blessed Virgin.)

The Akathist Hymn

Bearing in mind the wisdom of the Latin adage, *lex orandi, lex credendi* (the law of praying is the law of believing), let us conclude our reflections on Mary and the Fathers by examining briefly one of the greatest and most ancient of Marian hymns.

The hymn is known by the Greek title *Akáthistos*, or in English, *Akathist*. The Akathist, from the Greek, means "without a chair" or, more colloquially speaking, "not sitting," since the clergy and lay faithful prayed this prayer standing erect.

The Akathist is the only hymn of the Byzantine Liturgy whose text has never been altered in fifteen centuries. It has ecumenical appeal insofar as it has been prayed in common, especially on the Saturdays of Lent, by Eastern Christians, both Catholic and Orthodox, from time immemorial. So beloved is this Marian hymn that for centuries Eastern monks throughout the world have chosen to have the sacred events, narrated in its stanzas, depicted in art covering entire walls of their monastic churches and chapels.

This hymn was probably composed no later than the first half of the sixth century A.D. Its author or authors are anonymous, though it has sometimes been attributed to great hymnologists like Romanus the Melodist (or Singer), so called because his compositions were renowned for their poetic superiority; he also provided profound Mariological insights.

Certainly, its roots go much deeper, its theology and spirituality reflective of the earliest Fathers of the Church. Perhaps one can already discover the doctrinal and devotional roots of the Akathist prayer in the panegyrics addressed to Mary by Saint Cyril of Alexandria, Father of the Church, at the Council of Ephesus in A.D. 431. We recall here that Cyril, Patriarch of Alexandria in Egypt, was the driving force in defending the divinity of Christ and the divine motherhood of Mary against the teachings of Nestorius, Patriarch of Constantinople. The Alexandrian praises Mary thus:

> We hail thee, O Mary, Mother of God, O venerable mistress of the whole earth, inextinguishable lamp, crown of virginity, scepter of orthodoxy, indissoluble temple, mother and virgin. Hail, who in thy holy and virginal womb contained the uncontainable. Through thee was the Trinity sanctified; through thee did the Cross come to be honored and adored throughout the earth; through thee Heaven exults; through thee angels and archangels rejoice; through thee demons are cast out; through thee fallen man is raised up to the heavens; through thee the whole world, a slave to idolatry, came to the knowledge of the truth; through thee there is holy baptism for those who believe, through thee the oil of exultation; through thee are all the churches on earth founded; through thee the peoples come to conversion; through thee the prophets prophesied; through thee the Apostles announced salvation to the nations; through thee the dead rise, and kings reign.[31]

Here is an excerpt of the Akathist hymn, taken from the first of its twelve Byzantine chants:

> An Archangel was sent from Heaven to greet the Mother of God, and as he saw You assuming a body at the sound of his bodiless voice, O Lord, he stood rapt in amazement and cried out to her in these words:
>
> Hail, Thee through whom joy will shine forth;
>
> Hail, Thee through whom the curse will disappear!
>
> Hail, O Restoration of the fallen Adam;
>
> Hail, O Redemption of the tears of Eve!
>
> Hail, O Peak above the reach of human thought;
>
> Hail, O Depth even beyond the sight of angels!
>
> Hail, Thee who have become a kingly Throne;
>
> Hail, Thee who carry Him who carries all!

---

[31] As found in *Patrologia Greca* 77: 991-996.

Hail, O Star who manifest the Sun;

Hail, O Womb of the divine Incarnation;

Hail, Thee through whom the Creator becomes a Babe!

Hail, O Bride and Maiden ever-pure!

CONCLUSION

Our journey together has been under the banner of "The Faith of the Early Church."

The basic definition of faith is derived from the Epistle to the Hebrews 11:1, "Now faith is the assurance of things hoped for, the conviction of things not seen." Saint Paul instructs us to "hold fast to the mystery of the faith with a clear conscience" (1 Timothy 3:9). The Apostle to the Gentiles also refers to "the Deposit of Faith" (1 Timothy 6:20) — the title of the papal letter introducing the Catechism of the Catholic Church in 1992.

The Magisterium, that is, the bishops in communion with the Pope, has been entrusted with safeguarding and handing on faithfully from one generation to the next, "the faith once and for all handed down to the saints" (Jude 3). Saint Augustine of Hippo exhorted: "Believe that you may understand" (*crede ut intellegas*). Likewise, the Doctor of Grace encouraged us to "understand that you may believe" (*intellege ut credas*). Saint Anselm of Canterbury, Benedictine monk and Doctor of the Church in the twelfth century, coined the expression, *fides quaerens intellectum* (faith seeking understanding).

A fundamental distinction in theology is one between *fides quae creditur* (faith which is believed) and *fides qua creditur* (faith by which one believes). The objective content of an individual's faith is important, but so too is a person's subjective act of faith. Blessed John Henry Newman, in his *Grammar of Assent*, distinguished between a "notional faith" and a "real faith." "Notional faith" involves intellectual assent to theological propositions, to Divine Revelation as contained in Sacred Scripture and in Sacred Tradition, whether transmitted in writing or in oral statements. "Real faith" means believing in God as the direct and ultimate object of our faith; entrusting our entire life to Him, body, mind, soul and spirit. In other words, there is a difference between believing truths about God and having a personal faith relationship with Him. The two are not contradictory or mutually exclusive. Rather, they are complementary just as "faith and reason" are complementary, as we are reminded in Pope John Paul II's encyclical, *Fides et Ratio*. We must remember that Jesus taught that not everyone who called Him, "Lord, Lord," would enter the Kingdom of Heaven. Furthermore, even the demons whom Jesus cast out sometimes confessed His Divinity. Therefore, a profession of faith with our lips does not suffice; we must believe in word and in deed. Faith is man's most reasonable act, for who better deserves our faith than the God, "who can neither deceive nor be deceived," as we pray in the traditional Act of Faith?

Therefore, we are challenged not only to understand our Catholic Faith in greater depth, but also to share it effectively with others that they too may believe in the fullness of truth and thus share the fullness of our joy in Christ Jesus, the Way, the Truth and the Life. While faith is a theological virtue (the gift of God through Baptism), it is also an act of man's coop-eration with the grace of the Triune God. Per-haps, as we reflect on the nature of faith, we can also achieve a greater awareness of how the doctrines we believe are meant to be lived out in our daily lives and especially celebrated in the Sacred Lit-urgy, above all, in the Holy Sacrifice of the Mass.

This book has endeavored to identify the apostolic foundations of the Catholic Faith in the writings of the Fathers of the Church and in the prac-tices of the early Christians. Furthermore, we hope that readers will have grown in their appreciation of how the Cath-olic and Apostolic Faith taught by the Fathers is, first and foremost, firmly established in the teachings of the Sacred Scriptures and, then, how that has been faithfully transmitted from age to age by the Church's Magisterium. Indeed, we are confident that the Faith of the Early Church is the most credible and ancient form of Christianity. That said, it is now our solemn duty to engage in the art of apologetics and in the new evangelization, so that our ancient Faith will become the pride, the joy and the salvation of all peoples in this Third Christian Millennium.

EPILOGUE

Having completed our study of the Faith of the Early Church with the guidance of the Fathers of the Church, I would like to call the attention of our readers to the illustration that graces the book's cover. All should recognize the Altar of the Chair in St. Peter's Basilica as one of the greatest achievements of Western art—the masterpiece of the incomparable Baroque Italian sculptor, Gianlorenzo Bernini (1598-1680), who was responsible for the bronze baldacchino over Saint Peter's high altar as well as the two distinctive semi-circular arms of Saint Peter's colonnade. Those arms represent the loving embrace of Holy Mother Church that she extends to all humanity and, in a special way, to the saints and sinners who flock to Saint Peter's Square.

Bernini's Altar of the Chair, like the *Confessio* above Saint Peter's tomb, is the culmination of any visit to the Vatican Basilica. It was once believed that Peter's original chair (throne) was located within Bernini's gilt bronze sculpture. Now historians maintain that the present chair was the gift of Charles the Bald to Pope John VIII in 875.

Nevertheless, the symbolism of the chair remains the same—a very ancient symbol of teaching authority. Indeed, Our Lord Himself mentions the "chair of Moses" which the Pharisees and Scribes occupied as teachers of Israel. Jesus sat down to teach the crowds during the Sermon on the Mount, often called "The Magna Charta of Christianity." Bishops may, in fact, teach while remaining seated, and the English word "cathedral" comes originally from Greek through the Latin word *cathedra*, meaning "seat" or "chair."

Peter's teaching office, symbolized by the Altar of the Chair, has been handed on to each Pope who, as the Successor of Peter and Bishop of Rome, is the visible head and chief shepherd of the Universal Church. The pilgrim to the Eternal City of Rome, entering Saint Peter's Square and Basilica, ventures into the perennial and pulsating heart of the Church, whose four distinguishing characteristics (indeed, indelible marks!) are oneness, holiness, catholicity and apostolicity. In approaching the Vatican Basilica, believer and unbeliever alike comes to the place on earth that most fully expresses the Church's Magisterium, the living teaching office of the world's bishops in communion with the Pope.

This communion is wonderfully encapsulated in the depiction of the four great Fathers and Doctors of the Church whose statues surround the Altar of the Chair. There we are greeted by two Western Fathers (Saints **Augustine** and **Ambrose,** wearing miters) and two Eastern Fathers (Saints **Athanasius** and **John Chrysostom,** with heads uncovered). These noble and graceful figures underscore the unity and diversity of the Catholic Church and recall her mission, "ever ancient and ever new," to teach, sanctify and govern. This is a timeless and inestimable mission: one that is both ethereal, supported symbolically by the angels hovering on the clouds of heaven, and one that is firmly rooted in our earthly, human experience.

Near the Altar of the Chair is an inscription in Greek and Latin that proclaims: "O Pastor of the Church, you feed all Christ's lambs and sheep," reminiscent of Jesus' words to Simon Peter in John 21:15-19; and "Feed my lambs. . . . Tend my sheep. . . . Feed my sheep." The Fathers and Doctors of the Church beckon us to respond courageously, wholeheartedly and unreservedly to the urgent demand to preach the Gospel, advancing the "New Evangelization" in every generation.

The alabaster dove depicted above the Altar of the Chair is also a Bernini masterpiece. It represents the Holy Spirit, the Third Person of the Blessed Trinity, who is "the soul of the Church." The Holy Spirit inculcates the belief that the Church's authority to teach in Jesus' Name is an inspired grace of God, the true charism and gift of the self-same Spirit. Without the Holy Spirit's activity, the Church could never accomplish her mission of cooperating in the divine and providential plan for the salvation and unity of the human race. The Holy Spirit likewise leads the Church into the fullness of truth according to Our Lord's promise to the Apostles gathered in the Cenacle for the Last Supper. It was into that same Upper Room that the Holy Spirit descended upon the Apostles as tongues of fire on the Feast of Pentecost, emboldening those first bishops and priests to preach the saving Gospel in the footsteps of their Master, Jesus of Nazareth.

Christ the Lord, Incarnate, Crucified, Risen and Ascended into Heaven, has not abandoned us to carry out the work of evangelization on our own. He sends His Holy Spirit to guide and inspire us as our Second Advocate and Consoler, whom we profess in the Nicene Constantinopolitan Creed to be "the Lord and Giver of Life."

The Fathers of the Church, as Bernini sculpted them, do not sustain the Altar of the Chair in any strenuous fashion; they do not strain or struggle as does the mythological Titan Atlas, who shoulders the world, and whose punitive labor is famously depicted in a bronze statue sculpted by Lee Lawrie (1937) located in Rockefeller Center, across the street from Saint Patrick's Cathedral in New York City. Rather, the Altar of the Chair is effortlessly borne aloft by the powers of Heaven, God's holy angels, reminding us that the Catholic Church, though a profoundly human institution, is ultimately of divine origin and inspiration, for she is the Bride of Christ and His Mystical Body.

Gazing at our cover art, perhaps we can draw a breath of inspiration from the patristic insights of the Dominican theologian Father Aidan Nichols, who summarizes the import of the Fathers of the Church for the life of the Church in every time and place.

> The age of the Fathers, then, was the moment when the apostolic teaching was given an exact form, partly with a view to excluding interpretations of it to be felt at variance with the basic thrust of Jesus' teaching and significance.
>
> The Fathers determined the fundamentals of Christian faith, the basic dogmas about God, Christ and salvation. They forged for the future the elements of a whole Christian language.
>
> To think of a Church without Athanasius' work in establishing the divinity of Christ, Basil's activity in affirming the Godhead of the Holy Spirit, or Augustine's achievements in determining the independent and sovereign activity of God's grace, is to imagine a Church quite different in credal structure from the Church to which Catholic Christians in fact belong. The same is true of the liturgical life of the Church [....] Again, the fixing of the canon of Scripture is an achievement of the patristic Church [...].
>
> Indeed, in the patristic reception of the scriptural revelation all subsequent tradition thus crystallized transmits itself in tradition—not only in the Creeds, the liturgy, and the canon of Scripture but also iconography and hagiography, those beautiful expressions of the sense of the faithful, as well as the institutional forms of councils and the primatial ministry of the Roman bishop in his teaching office—all emerged in this decisive moment.[1]

---

1 Aidan Nichols, *Epiphany: A Theological Introduction to Catholicism* (Collegeville, Minnesota: Liturgical Press, 1996), 53f.

Suggested Further Reading

Achtemeier, Paul J. (General Editor). *Harper's Bible Dictionary.* San Francisco: Harper, 1985.

Akin, Jimmy. *The Fathers Know Best: Your Essential Guide to the Teachings of the Early Church.* San Diego: Catholic Answers, 2010.

Alexander, Pat (Editor). *The Lion Concise Bible Encyclopedia.* Herts (England): Lion Publishing, 1980.

Alexander, Pat and David (Editors). *Zondervan Handbook to the Bible.* Grand Rapids, Michigan: Zondervan, 2002.

Aquilina, Mike. *The Fathers of the Church: An Introduction to the First Christian Teachers.* Huntington, Indiana: Our Sunday Visitor Press, 2006.

_____. *The Way of the Fathers: Praying with the Early Christians.* Huntington, Indiana: Our Sunday Visitor Press, 2000.

Athanasius, St. *On the Incarnation. Crestwood,* New York: St. Vladimir's Seminary Press, 1989.

Bainton, Roland. *Christianity.* Boston: Houghton Mifflin, 1992.

Beatrice, Pier Franco. *Introduction to the Fathers of the Church.* Vicenza (Italy): Edizioni Istituto San Gaetano, 1987.

Benedict XVI, Pope. *The Fathers.* Huntington, Indiana: Our Sunday Visitor Press, 2008.

Benestad, J. Brian. *Classical Christianity and the Political Order.* Lanham, Maryland: Rowman & Littlefield, 1996.

Bettenson, Henry (Editor). *Documents of the Christian Church* (second edition). New York: Oxford University Press, 1967.

Brandmüller, Walter. *Light and Shadows: Church History amid Faith, Fact and Legend.* San Francisco: Ignatius Press, 2009.

Brown, Peter. *Augustine of Hippo: A Biography.* Berkley: University of California Press, 1975.

Brox, Norbert. *A Concise History of the Early Church*. New York: Continuum Press, 1995.

Chadwick, Henry. *The Early Church*. New York: Penguin Books, 1967.

Chrysostom, St. John. *Six Books on the Priesthood*. Crestwood, New York: St. Vladimir's Seminary Press, 1984.

Church, F. Forrester and Mulry, Terrence J. *The Macmillan Book of Earliest Christian Prayers*. New York: Macmillan Publishers, 1988.

Cowie, L. W. and Gummer, John Selwyn. *The Christian Calendar*. Springfield, Massachusetts: G & C Merriam Co., 1974.

Cunliffe-Jones, Hubert. *A History of Christian Doctrine*. Edinburgh (Scotland): T & T Clark, 1978.

Cyril of Jerusalem, St. *Lectures on the Christian Sacraments*. Crestwood, New York: St. Vladimir's Seminary Press, 1986.

D'Epiro, Peter and Pinkowish, Mary Desmond. *What Are the Seven Wonders of the World?* New York: Anchor Books, 1998.

Douglas, J. D. (General Editor). *Dictionary of the Christian Church* (revised edition). Grand Rapids, Michigan: Zondervan, 1978.

Dulles, Avery. *A History of Apologetics*. San Francisco: Ignatius Press, 2005.

Eusebius. *The History of the Church*. New York: Dorset Press, 1965.

Ferguson, Everett. *Backgrounds of Early Christianity*. Grand Rapids, Michigan: Eerdmans Publishing Co., 1987.

Freeman, Charles. *A New History of Early Christianity*. New Haven: Yale University Press, 2009.

Gambero, Luigi. *Mary and the Fathers of the Church: The Blessed Virgin Mary in Patristic Thought*. San Francisco: Ignatius Press, 1999.

Glazier, Michael and Hellwig, Monika. *The Modern Catholic Encyclopedia* (revised and expanded edition). Collegeville, Minnesota: Liturgical Press, 2004.

Guy, Laurie. *Introducing Early Christianity: A Topical Survey of Its Life, Beliefs and Practices*. Downers Grove, Illinois: InterVarsity Press, 2004.

Hamell, Patrick J. *Handbook of Patrology: A Concise, Authoritative Guide to the Life and Works of the Fathers of the Church*. New York: Alba House, 1991.

Healey, Charles J. *Christian Spirituality: An Introduction to the Heritage*. Staten Island, New York: Alba House, 1999.

Hill, Jonathan. *Zondervan Handbook to the History of Christianity*. Grand Rapids, Michigan: Zondervan, 2006.

Hill, Nathan. *What Has Christianity Ever Done for Us? How It Shaped the Modern World*. Downers Grove, Illinois: InterVarsity Press, 2005.

Hitchcock, James. *History of the Catholic Church: From the Apostolic Age to the Third Millennium*. San Francisco: Ignatius Press, 2012.

Johnson, Paul. *A History of Christianity*. New York: Simon & Schuster, 2005.

Jurgens, William A. *The Faith of the Early Fathers* (3 volumes). Collegeville, Minnesota: Liturgical Press, 1970-1979.

Kelly, J.N.D. *Early Christian Creeds* (third edition). Essex (England): Longman Group, 1972.

Kelly, Joseph F. *The World of the Early Christians: Message of the Fathers of the Church*. Collegeville, Minnesota: Liturgical Press, 1997.

Korn, Frank J. *The Tiber Ran Red: The Age of the Roman Martyrs*. Boston: St. Paul's Books and Media, 1989.

Lane, Tony. *The Lion Concise Book of Christian Thought*. Herts (England): Lion Publishing, 1984.

Lietzmann, Hans. *A History of the Early Church* (two volumes). Cambridge (England): James Clarke & Co., 1993.

Lowden, John. *Early Christian & Byzantine Art*. London: Phaidon Press, Ltd., 1997.

de Lubac, Henri. *The Christian Faith*. San Francisco: Ignatius Press, 1986.

MacCulloch, Diarmaid. *Christianity: The First Three Thousand Years*. New York: Viking, 2010.

McGinn, Bernard and John Meyendorff and Jean Leclercq (Editors.). *Christian Spirituality: Origins to the Twelfth Century*. New York: Crossroad, 1985.

McManners, John (Editor). *The Oxford History of Christianity.* New York: Oxford University Press, 1990.

de Margerie, Bertrand. *An Introduction to the History of Exegesis: The Greek Fathers* (Volume I). Petersham, Massachusetts: St. Bede's Publications, 1993.

——————. *An Introduction to the History of Exegesis: The Latin Fathers* (Volume II). Petersham, Massachusetts: St. Bede's Publications, 1995.

——————. *An Introduction to the History of Exegesis: Saint Augustine* (Volume III). Petersham, Massachusetts: St. Bede's Publications, 1991.

Metzger, Marcel. *History of the Liturgy: The Major Stages.* Collegeville, Minnesota: Liturgical Press, 1997.

Mullin, Robert Bruce. *A Short World History of Christianity.* Louisville, Kentucky: Westminster John Knox Press, 2008.

Mursell, Gordon (Editor). *The Story of Christian Spirituality: Two Thousand Years, From East to West.* Minneapolis: Fortress Press, 2001.

Neuner, J. and Dupuis, J. *The Christian Faith in the Doctrinal Documents of the Catholic Church* (revised edition). New York: Alba House, 1982.

Newman, John Henry. *The Church of the Fathers.* Notre Dame: Notre Dame University Press, 2002.

——————. *Select Treatises of Saint Athanasius in Controversy with the Arians* (two volumes). Westminster, Maryland: Christian Classics, n.d.

Nichols, Aidan. *Epiphany: A Theological Introduction to Catholicism.* Collegeville, Minnesota: Liturgical Press, 1996.

O'Collins, Gerald and Farrugia, Edward G. *A Concise Dictionary of Theology.* Mahwah, New Jersey: Paulist Press, 2000.

O'Grady, Desmond. *Caesar, Christ, and Constantine: A History of the Early Church in Rome.* Huntington, Indiana: Our Sunday Visitor Press, 1991.

Olsen, Glenn W. *Beginning at Jerusalem: Five Reflections on the History of the Church.* San Francisco: Ignatius Press, 2004.

Payne, Robert. *The Fathers of the Eastern Church.* New York: Dorset Press, 1985.

_____. *The Fathers of the Western Church*. New York: Dorset Press, 1971.

Pelikan, Jaroslav. *Jesus through the Centuries: His Place in the History of Culture*. New York: Harper and Row, 1985.

_____. *Mary through the Centuries: Her Place in the History of Culture*. New Haven: Yale University Press, 1996.

Quasten, Johannes. *Patrology* (four volumes). Westminster, Maryland: Christian Classics, 1986-1988.

Rubin, Miri. *Mother of God: A History of the Virgin Mary*. New Haven: Yale University Press, 2009.

Russell, Claire. *Glimpses of the Church Fathers*. New York: Scepter Press, 1994.

Sokolowski, Robert. *The God of Faith and Reason: Foundations of Christian Theology*. Washington, D.C.: Catholic University of America Press, 1995.

Stark, Rodney. *Cities of God: The Real Story of How Christianity Became an Urban Movement and Conquered Rome*. New York: HarperCollins, 2007.

_____. *The Rise of Christianity: How the Obscure, Marginal Jesus Movement Became the Dominant Religious Force in the Western World in a Few Centuries*. New York: HarperCollins, 1997.

_____. *The Triumph of Christianity: How the Jesus Movement Became the World's Largest Religion*. New York: HarperCollins, 2012.

Studer, Basil. *Trinity and Incarnation: The Faith of the Early Church*. Edinburgh (Scotland): T & T Clark, 1993.

Taft, Robert. *The Liturgy of the Hours in East and West*. Collegeville, Minnesota: Liturgical Press, 1986.

Toal, M. F. *The Sunday Sermons of the Great Fathers* (four volumes). Swedesboro, New Jersey: Preservation Press, 1996.

Verbraken, Patrick. *The Beginnings of the Church*. New York: Paulist Press, 1968.

von Balthasar, Hans Urs. *Credo: Meditations on the Apostles' Creed*. Edinburgh (Scotland): T & T Clark, 1990.

Ware, Timothy. *The Orthodox Church (new edition)*. New York: Penguin Books, 1997.

Wegman, Herman. *Christian Worship in East and West: A Study Guide to Liturgical History*. New York: Pueblo Publishing Co., 1985.

Whitehead, Kenneth D. *One, Holy, Catholic and Apostolic*. San Francisco: Ignatius Press, 2000.

Wilkin, Robert Louis. *The Spirit of Early Christian Thought*. New Haven: Yale University Press, 2003.

Willis, John R. *The Teachings of the Church Fathers*. San Francisco: Ignatius Press, 2002.

BIBLICAL APOLOGETICAL INDEX

Abortion: The deliberate termination of the life of a pre-born baby at any stage of his or her development is a direct violation of the Fifth Commandment: "Thou Shalt Not Kill!"

A Catholic who has or procures an abortion is automatically excommunicated.

Cf. Gen 1:26-27; Ex 20:13; 2 Mac 7:22-23; Jb 12:10; Ps 51:7; 82:3-4; 139:13-15; Prov 24:11; Is 44:2; Jer 1:5; 7:6; Mt 18:1-6; 19:13-15; Lk 1:15, 41-44; Acts 17:28; Gal 1:15; 1 Jn 3:15.

CCC 362-368, 2270-2275, 2319, 2322-2323.

Following the principle that all human life is sacred from conception to natural death, the Church also condemns the evils of embryonic stem cell research, infanticide and all forms of abortifacients. Cf. Pope John Paul II's Encyclical *Evangelium Vitae* (1995).

Abstinence: A form of self-control and self-denial.

Sexual abstinence is known as continence. The Church requires sexual continence of all those not living in a lawful, valid marriage.

Abstinence from meat is mandatory for Catholics on the Fridays of Lent, Ash Wednesday, Good Friday, and all other Fridays of the year. Weekly Friday Abstinence may be substituted with another suitable penance, if permitted by the regional episcopal conference.

Adultery: Marital infidelity arising from lustful desires (concupiscence) entertained in a person's heart. Cf. Ex 20:14; Deut 5:18; Mt 5:27-30. CCC 1646, 1756, 1856, 1858, 2336, 2364-2365, 2380-2381, 2397, 2400.

Almsgiving: Giving alms to the poor, prayer and fasting are the main pillars of Christian piety; they are strongly recommended during Lent.

Cf. Lev 16:29-34; Jgs 20:26; 1 Kgs 21:9,12,27; Ezr 8:23; Neh 1:4; 9:1; Est 4:15-16; 9:31; Bar 1:5-6; Is 58:1-2; Jer 14:12; Dan 9:3; Jl 1:14; 2:12-17; Jon 14:23; Zec 8:19; Mt 4:1-11; 6:1-4, 16-18; 9:14-15; Mk 2:18-20; Lk 2:37; 4:1-13; 5:33-35; 18:12; Acts 13:2-3; 14:23; 27:9.

CCC 538-540, 566, 1095, 1430-1439, 1460, 1490, 1969, 2043, 2447, 2462.

Altar: Gen 12:7f; 13:18: 26:25; 33:19-20; 35:1-7; Ex 20:24-26; 21:12-14; 27:1-8; 29:12; 30:10; Jgs 6:19-24; 1 Sam 14:35; 1 Kgs 3:4; 8:62-64; 2 Chr 4:1; 26:16-20; 29:18-36; 35:7-18; Ezr 3:1-6; 1 Mac 4:44-59; Ps 26:6; 84:4; 118:27; 17:1; Mt 5:23-24; 23:18-20; Lk 1:11; Heb 13:10; Jas 2:21; Rev 6:9-11; 8:3-5; 9:13.

The altar of the Lord's Eucharistic Sacrifice is venerated as a symbol of Christ's Body and His empty tomb. From time immemorial, the relics of martyrs were placed in the altar to symbolize the link between the deaths of martyrs and the Lord's sacrificial death on the Cross.

Anointing of the Sick: Mt 10:1; Mk 6:13; Rom 8:17; Col 1:24; Jas 5:14-16.

Apostolic Authority: Mt 18:17; Lk 10:16.

Apostolic Succession: Mt 3:3-15; 10:5ff; 16:16-18; 18:18; 28:16-20; Jn 21:15-19; Acts 1:15-26; 2 Tim 1:6; Ti 1:4-6.

Apostolic Tradition: 1 Cor 11:2, 23; 2 Thes 2:15; 3:6; 2 Tim 2:2; Heb 13:7.

> Jesus condemned hypocritical traditions (Mt 15:6, 8-9), but upheld the Pharisees' teaching authority (Mt 23:3).

Ashes: A sacramental derived from the blessed palm or olive branches burned after Palm Sunday.

> On Ash Wednesday, the beginning of Lent in the Roman Rite, ashes are imposed on the head or forehead as a reminder of our human mortality and repentance.
>
> Cf. Gen 3:19; 37:34; 44:13; Jgs 11:35; 1 Sam 4:12; 2 Sam 1:2; 11; 13:31; 1 Kgs 21:27; 2 Kgs 2:12; 5:7-8; 6:30; 11:14; 22:11; 2 Chr 23:13; 34:19, 27; Est 4:1-8; Ps 51:3-5,9,11-12; 102:10; Is 58:5; 61:2-3; Jer 6:26; 25:34; 36:24; Ez 26:16; Dan 9:3; Jl 2:12-13; Jon 3:6-10; Mt 11:21; Lk 10:13.

Assumption/Queenship of Mary: Gen 5:24; Deut 34:6; 2 Kgs 1:1-12; Ps 45:13ff; 132:8; Sg 3:6; 4:86ff; 6:9; Mt 17:3-4; Mk 9:4-5; Lk 1:41,44; 9:30,33; 12:1ff.

> Pope Pius XII defined the dogma of the Assumption (1950). The question of Mary's death is open to theological speculation. Eastern Fathers, Mary's "Dormition" or "Falling Asleep" (Greek: *Koimesis*); Western Fathers, Mary's Assumption.

Baptism: Necessary for salvation (Jn 3:3,5; 22-23). The Apostles are commissioned to baptize using the Trinitarian formula (Mt 28:18-20; Mk 16:15-20); Baptism imparts the forgiveness of sins and the Holy Spirit (Acts 2:38, 41; 8:38; 9:18; 10:44-49; 11:1-18); incorporates into the Paschal Mystery and spiritually regenerates (Rom 6:3-4; Ti 3:5); fulfills the type of Noah's ark by which men are saved (1 Pt 3:18-22).

> Infant Baptism: Mt 19:13-15; Mk 10:13-16; Lk 18:15-16; Col 2:11-12; Acts 2:38-39; 16:15, 33; 1 Cor 1:16.

Binding and Loosing: Rabbinical power to impose or lift excommunications, and to offer authoritative interpretation of God's Word. Jesus grants this power to all the Apostles, especially to Peter (Mt 16:19; 18:18).

Baptism of Blood: Received by a "martyr" (from the Greek word for "witness") who gives up his or her life in defense of the Faith without Baptism.

Baptism of Desire: Received by a catechumen (one preparing for Christian Initiation) or other sincere persons who would have desired Baptism explicitly if they had known of its necessity, but who die without Baptism.

> Babies who die without Baptism are entrusted to God's mercy in the hope of their eternal salvation.
>
> Cf. CCC 1257-1261.

Blessings: Gen 9:26; 12:2-3; 24:60; 27:33; 47:7; 48:20; Ex 18:10; Num 6:22-26; 23:20; Deut 7:13-14; 28:2-6; Ru 4:14; 1 Sam 25:33; 2 Sam 14:22; 21:3; Ps 68:19; 103:1-2; 109:28; Is 8:21; 61:9; Prov 5:18; Mt 5:3-11; 21:9; 23:39; 24:46; 26:26-30; Mk 11:9-10; 14:22-26; Lk 10:23; 11:27-28; 14:15; 22:14-20; 24:50; 1 Cor 10: 14-22; 11:23-34.

> According to biblical theology, to bless God is to praise Him. The Hebrew

word "*berakah*" means "blessing." In the Ordinary Form of the Roman Rite, the priest prays Jewish prayers of *berakah* at the Preparation of the Gifts (Offertory).

To bless persons, places and objects serves to set them apart for a special purpose, especially in the context of the Sacred Liturgy. For Catholics, the blessing of the priest imparted at the conclusion of Mass, sacramental absolution, and the Rite of Benediction with the Blessed Sacrament are among the most solemn blessings received on a regular basis.

"Born Again": To be baptized is to be "born again" or "born from above" (Greek: *anothen*, Jn 3:1-21).

Candles/Torches/Lamps: Ex 25:6, 31-40; 28:20-21; Jgs 7:16; Jb 18:5; Ps 119:105; Prov 13:9; Is 42:3; Zec 4:2; Mt 5:14-16; 6:22-23; 25:1-13; Jn 1:4-5, 7-9; 3:19; 8:12; 9:5; 11:9-10; 12:35-36, 46; 18:3; 2 Cor 3:7-18; Eph 5:6-14; 1 Pt 2:9; 2 Pt 1:19; 1 Jn 1:5-10; 2:7-11; Rev 4:5; 12:1.

Celibacy: Jesus and Paul as celibates commended celibacy for the sake of the Kingdom of Heaven (Mt 19:12, 29-30; 22:30; 1 Cor 7:7-9). Although the Apostles were married (Mt 8:14-15; Mk 1:29-31) neither their wives, nor their children are mentioned as accompanying them once they left everything to follow Jesus.

Church/Divine Institution: Mt 16:18; Acts 9:4-5; Gal 1:13; Col 1:18; 1 Tim 3:15.

Confirmation: Acts 8:4-25; 19:5-6; 2 Cor 1:21-22; Eph 1:13-14; Heb 6:1-3.

Contraception, Artificial: Means used to frustrate deliberately the unitive and procreative purposes of sexual intercourse. The use of contraception prohibits a full "gift of self" between spouses.

In the ancient world, the pagans made recourse to "*magikoi*" (magicians) and "*pharmakoi*" (sorcerers) who employed a variety of drugs (potions) some of which were intended to prevent pregnancy (cf. Gal 5:20; Rev 9:21; 18:23; 21:8; 22:15).

Cf. Gen 1:27-28; 9:1; 17:6, 20; 28:3; 38:9-10; Ex 23:26; Lev 7:14; Deut 7:14; 28:18; 1 Sam 1:4-16; Tob 6:17; 8:7-9; Ps 127:3-5; 128:3; Prov 17:6; 30:16; Jb 15:34; 1 Cor 7:5.

CCC 1652-1654, 2249, 2349, 2352, 2366-2379, 2398-2399.

Origen: "Christians marry, as do others, and they have children. They do not stifle their offspring."

Augustine: "Marital relations even with a lawful wife, are unlawful and degrading when the conception of a child is deliberately frustrated."

G. K. Chesterton commented that advocates of artificial birth control "want fewer births and no control."

Instead of having recourse to artificial contraception, the Catholic Church encourages couples to practice responsible parenthood through natural family planning (NFP).

Cf. Pope Paul VI's Encyclical *Humanae Vitae* (1968).

Creed: A formal profession or fixed statement of faith like the Apostles Creed and Nicene-Constantinopolitan Creed.

The Nicene-Constantinopolitan Creed, which we sing or recite on Sundays and other solemnities, was formulated at the First Council of Nicea (325) and the First Council of Constantinople (381).

Cf. Mt 28:19; Rom 10:9; 1 Cor 15:3ff; 2 Cor 13:13; Phil 2:11. CCC 194-195. Pope Paul VI's "The Credo of the People of God" (1968).

Cross, Sign of the: By the second century A.D., Christians were accustomed to making the sign of the cross as part of their daily devotion. Doing so in the Name of the Persons of the Blessed Trinity while using holy water allows us to recall the principal Christian doctrines of the Trinity, Incarnation and Redemption, as well as our Baptism.

Crucifix: A cross with a fixed image of Jesus' crucified body.

Our Lord's crucifixion fulfilled certain Old Testament prophecies (cf. Zec 12:10; Jn 19:37). A powerful theology of the Cross is developed in the New Testament, especially in the writings of St. Paul.

Cf. Mt 16:24-25; Acts 2:23-24,36-39; Rom 6:1-12; 1 Cor 1:17-25; 2 Cor 1:5-7; 13:14; Gal 2:19-20; 3:1; 5:24; 6:14; Phil 2:8-11; 3:18; Col 1:19-20,24; 2:13-15; Heb 12:2.

At first, the early Christians, who were still suffering fierce persecution, did not use the cross as a symbol of devotion because they regarded it as a pagan symbol, an instrument of ignominious torture and shame. Eventually, however, the Christians began to feel more comfortable in depicting Jesus Crucified. A door panel, carved out of cypress wood, on the Basilica of Santa Sabina in Rome (5th c.) is the first known depiction of Jesus' Crucifixion.

Some Protestants reject the use of a crucifix, claiming that it is inappropriate in the light of the Resurrection. However, one needs to recall that when the Risen Lord appeared to the Apostles in the Upper Room He showed them precisely His pierced hands and side and the Book of Revelation refers often to the Lamb who was slain in the present tense.

Cf. Jn 20:19-22; Mt 10:38; 16:24; 28:19; Mk 8:34; 10:21; Lk 9:23; 14:27; Acts 2:38; 1 Cor 1:18; Gal 6:14; 1 Thes 5:9; Rev 7:1-3; 9:4; 14:1.

Dead, Prayer for the: 2 Mac 12:39-40; 2 Tim 1:16-18.

Degrees of Sin/Venial Sin/Mortal Sin: Lev 4:27; 5:20-24; 18-20; Mt 5:22-26; 12:37; 16:27; Lk 12:47-48; Rom 2:5-13; 1 Cor 3:11-15; 6:9-10; Gal 5:19-21; Eph 5:5; 1 Pt 1:17; 1 Jn 5:16-17; Rev 22:12.

Deposit of Faith (*Depositum Fidei*): Rom 1:16; 1 Tim 1:10b-11.

Divorce-Remarriage: Gen 1:26-31; 2:18-25; 17:15-21; 21:12-20; 21:10-14; Jgs 8:31; Sg 8:7; Mal 2:14-16; Mt 5:31-32; 19:1-9; Mk 10:2-11; Lk 16:18; Rom 7:2-3; 1 Cor 7:1-24, 39; Gal 4:21-31; Eph 5:2, 21-33; Heb 13:4; 1 Pt 3:1-9. Cf. CCC 1534-1535, 1601-1666, especially 1629, 1650-1651, 2382-2386.

Eucharist: Types are the sacrifices of Abel, Abraham and Melchizedech (Roman Canon). The prophet Malachi predicted that from the rising of the sun to its setting pure sacrifices would be offered to the glory of God's Name (Mal 1:11; Third Eucharistic Prayer).

Jesus' miracle at Cana and the multiplication of the loaves and fish prefigured the miracle of transubstantiation (Mt 14:13-21; 15:32-39; Mk 6:30-44; 8:1-10; Lk 9:10-17; Jn 2:1-11; Jn 6:1-14).

In the Bread of Life Discourse (Jn 6) the Greek verb "*trogein*" (to gnaw) is used rather than the verb "*phagein*" (to eat) to underscore the literalism of Jesus' teaching.

Jesus' words were understood literally. Many disciples left His company thinking His words too hard to bear (Jn 6:30-50). He does not dissuade them (Jn 6:51-59).

Jesus used sacrificial language when He instituted the Eucharist at the Last Supper (Passover Meal) on Holy Thursday in anticipation of His sacrificial death on Good Friday (Mt 26:26-30; Mk 14:22-26; Lk 22:15-20; 1 Cor 11:23-25).

Jesus is really present in the Eucharist: "This is My Body," "This is My Blood," not "This is a symbol of My Body/My Blood" (Mt 26:26,28; Mk 14:22,24; Lk 22:19,20).

When Jesus broke the bread for the disciples on the road to Emmaus, they immediately recognized Him and He vanished (Lk 24:13-25).

The Apostles celebrated the Eucharist, termed "the breaking of the bread," (Acts 2:42).

Paul taught that to receive the Body and Blood of the Lord unworthily without a prior examination of conscience is to sin against Christ and His Body, the Church (1 Cor 11:27). To drink from the cup is to participate in the Blood of Christ (1 Cor 10:16). To eat the broken bread is to participate in the Body of Christ (1 Cor 10:16).

The Eucharistic Banquet anticipates the eschatological banquet (Mt 26:29; Mk 14:5; Lk 22:18; Rev 19:9).

Euthanasia: Literally, from the Greek meaning: "good death" – euphemistically known as "mercy killing." The deliberate termination of the life of the handicapped, the sick and the dying is a direct violation of the Fifth Commandment, "Thou Shalt Not Kill!"

Cf. Gen 2:7; Ex 23:7; Deut 32:39; Jb 12:10; 33:4; Ps 139:16; Mt 5:21; Acts 17:25; 1 Cor 6:19; Gal 2:20.   CCC 2261-2269, 2276-2283, 2320, 2324-2325.

Evangelical Counsels: Traditionally, they are three: (1) Poverty: (Mt 5:3; Mk 10:21; Lk 6:20); (2) Chastity: (Mt 19:2; 1 Cor 7:25); (3) Obedience: (Mt 12:48-49; Mk 3:35).

These are called "counsels" because they are not obligatory for all states of life. Men and women in consecrated life profess religious vows to observe the evangelical counsels.

"Faith Alone" (Sola Fide): Works are necessary for salvation (Jas 2:14-26).

Fasting: An ancient practice found in many religions. The Judaeo-Christian practice is rooted in scriptural texts like Jl 2:12-18 and Mt 6:1-6, 16-18, read as the First Reading and Gospel on Ash Wednesday.

A fast consists in one full meal with two smaller meals that taken together do not equal another full meal.

Fasting is required of Catholics of the Roman Rite on Ash Wednesday and Good Friday.

Father as a title: "Call No Man Father" (Mt 23:9): Jesus' injunction excludes putting any human creature on God the Father's level. It does not forbid calling

human beings "father" in a literal/figurative sense (Mt 1:2; 3:9; 10:37; Mk
·   10:29; Lk 16:24, 30; Jn 8:39; Acts 4:25; 7:2; Rom 4:11-18; 9:10; 1 Cor
     4:15; Eph 6:2; 1 Pt 5:13; Jas 2:21).

Fornication: Refers to engaging in sexual intercourse outside marriage. The word is
     derived from the Greek word "*porneia*." Hence, the word "pornography."
     Cf. Ex 20:17; Mt 5:8, 28; 1 Cor 6:16-18; Gal 5:13-26; Eph 2:3; 4:19; 5:5;
     Col 3:5; 1 Jn 2:16.   Pope John Paul II's "Theology of the Body."

Genuflection/Kneeling: 2 Chr 6:12-13; Ps 95:6-7; Mt 2:11; 8:2; 9:18; 15:25; 20:20; Lk
     24:52; Jn 9:38; Rev 5:8.
     Catholics genuflect before the Most Blessed Sacrament, for private prayer,
     and at various times during Holy Mass (e.g., the Eucharistic Prayer).

Holy Water: Ex 23:25; 40:12; Lev 14:5-7; Num 5:17; 8:7; 2 Kgs 5:1-14; Ps 1:1-3; Is
     12:3; 55:1; Mt 3:13-17; Jn 7:37-39; Eph 5:25-27; Rev 21:6; 22:1-2, 17.
     Holy water is a sacramental used to sprinkle people, places and objects
     to claim them for God and to ward off the presence of the Evil One.
     Customarily, it is used to make the Sign of the Cross upon entering and
     leaving a Catholic church.
     Holy water derives its theological significance from the Blessing of Baptismal
     Water and the Renewal of Baptismal Promises celebrated during the Easter
     Season.
     A priest may bless the Sunday Mass congregation during the "*Asperges*" or
     "*Vidi Aquam*" Sprinkling Rite.
     Cf. CCC 1667-1673, 1677-1678.

Homosexual Activity: The sexual complementarity of a man and a woman is an
     integral part of God's original design for His creation and the sacred
     institution of marriage (Gen 1:27-28; 2:18-24; Prov 30:19).
     Homosexual acts are intrinsically disordered and immoral (Gen 19:1-29;
     Rom 1:24-27; 1 Cor 6:10; 1 Tim 1:10).
     While the precise origins of same-sex attraction are unknown, the Church
     distinguishes a disordered homosexual orientation from homosexual acts,
     exhorting us to love and respect homosexual persons, but to condone neither
     their homosexual acts nor life-styles. Homosexual persons are encouraged to
     accept their same-sex attraction as a cross to be carried with dignity.
     With the help of prayer, sacramental grace, and Christian fellowship, persons
     with same-sex attraction should strive to be chaste and modest.
     Same-sex unions and same-sex marriage are clearly contrary to the natural
     law and divine moral law.
     Cf. CCC 369-372, 383, 1605, 2331-2363, 2392-2396, 2520-2527, 2529-
     2533.

Images/Statues/Icons: The First Commandment forbids the worship of graven images
     (Ex 20:4; Deut 4:15-18). Nevertheless, God does not altogether forbid the
     use of images (Ex 25:10-22, 33-36; 26:1; Num 21:9; 1 Kgs 6:23-7:51; 2 Chr
     3:10-4:22).
     John Damascene defended the use of icons. The honor paid to an icon passes
     from the image to the reality represented. We venerate but do not worship
     flags, monuments, photos, etc.

Immaculate Conception: Luke uses Greek word "*kecharitomene*," a perfect passive participle, to signify that Mary was "full of grace" before consenting to the Angel's message (Lk 1:28).

The Bible teaches that "all men have sinned and fall short of God's glory" (Rom 3:23). However, the word "all" (Greek: *pas*) does not preclude exceptions (compare Ps 14:3 & Ps 15:2). Mary is an exception to the rule of Original Sin. Cf. Sg 4:7.

In the *Protoevangelium* ("First Gospel," Gen 3:15) God promised that the future Mother of the Messiah would be at "enmity" with Satan.

The Fathers of the Church dubbed Mary the "New Eve" because of her sinless obedience as contrasted with Eve's sinful rebellion.

The Early Christians venerated Mary as "all-holy" (Greek: *panagia*).

Augustine: "On account of the Lord's honor" (*propter honorem Domini*) there should be no mention of sin regarding Mary.

An authentic development of doctrine (Newman) took place in the Catholic Church under the ongoing guidance of the Holy Spirit (Jn 14:16) so that Pope Pius IX defined the Immaculate Conception as a dogma (1854).

The dogma states that at the moment of Mary's conception God preserved her from Original Sin in view of Our Lord's Death and Resurrection. Thus, God prepared a sinless mother for His sinless Son.

Anselm of Canterbury: To be preserved from sin is a more excellent form of redemption than being purified from sin; it was appropriate for God to create His own mother without sin.

Eadmer of Canterbury: Compared Mary's sinless conception to how a chestnut emerges unharmed from its thorny surroundings.

Mary's Immaculate Conception is analogous to preventive medicine as distinct from curative medicine. Similarly, it is better to be prevented from falling into a ditch than to be rescued from one.

Mary is not exempt from salvation. In her canticle of praise (*Magnificat*), Mary recognized God as her Savior (Lk 1:47) even as He recognized her "lowliness" (Greek: *tapeinosis*, Lk 1:48).

Mary was saved not due to her own merits but by a "prevenient grace" (Duns Scotus), so that she could play an unique role in salvation history.

Holy Orders: Mt 10:1-5ff; Mk 3:13-19; Lk 9:1-6; Lk 22:19-20; Jn 20:19-23; 1 Cor 11:23-25; Acts 13:1-3; 14:23; Rom 15:16; 1 Tim 1:18; 3:1-13; 4:14; 5:22; 2 Tim 1:6-7; Ti 1:6-7; Jas 5:14-15.

Incense: Ex 25:6; Lk 1:8-20; Eph 5:2; Rev 8:3-5.

Incense symbolizes our prayers rising to God as a sweet-smelling oblation. Incense is also used in the Sacred Liturgy as a sign of reverence for the sacredness of persons and objects – the priest offering Holy Mass; the priestly people of the Eucharistic Assembly; the Book of the Gospels; and the Eucharistic gifts of bread and wine, as well as those elements become the Body and Blood of the Lord.

Indulgences: The Church uses the power of the keys to grant a partial or plenary remission of the temporary punishment due to sin to appease God's infinite justice. Indulgences can be applied to oneself or to another person.

Job offered sacrifices to atone for his sons' sins (Jb 1:5). David was forgiven adultery and murder, but still had to do penance (2 Sam 12:13-14). Paul ordered that a man be excommunicated so that his soul might be saved on the day of the Lord (1 Cor 5:1-5).

Intercessory Role of Saints/Angels: The dead Onias and Jeremiah prayed for the living (2 Mac 15:11, 14). God of the living not the dead (Mk 12:27). Those who die in the Lord are spiritually alive (Eph 2:4-7). The Communion of Saints in Heaven constitutes "a great cloud of witnesses" (Heb 12:1). Angels guard us and receive the prayers of the saints on earth (Tob 5:10; Mt 18:10; Rev 8:3-5).

The intercession of angels/saints does not obstruct/detract from the unique mediation of Christ Jesus because their mediation is subordinate to His and its efficacy depends entirely on the omnipotent, divine will.

Jesus as the God-Man is indeed the "One Mediator between God and man" (1 Tim 2:5). Paul uses the Greek word "*henos*" (one), not "*monos*" (only), to describe Jesus' mediation. Thus, Paul does not exclude lesser forms of mediation.

The saints are our heroes in the faith (Sir 44:1-15). We venerate their memory by imitating their holiness (Heb 6:11-12; 13:7). If we who are sinners can pray for each other, then surely the saints in Heaven and the souls in Purgatory can pray for us.

Cf. Tob 12:12-14; Lk 16:19-31; Rev 5:6-8; 6:9-11.

Laying on of Hands: Num 27:23; Deut 34:9; Acts 6:1-6; 8:17; 19:6; 13:3; 1 Tim 4:14; 5:22; 2 Tim 1:6).

Litanies: Ps 118:1-4; 136:1-26.

Magisterium: The living teaching office of the college of bishops in communion with the Pope.

Cf. "Apostolic Authority."

Matrimony: Gen 1:27-28; 2:21-24; 4:1-2, 25; Lev 18:1ff; Deut 5:21; Mt 5:31-32; 19:1-12; 22:2-14; 25:1-13; Mk 10:11-12; Lk 16:18; Jn 2:1-11; 1 Cor 7:10ff; Eph 5:21-33.

Marian Devotion (Lk 1:48): Mary exhibited reasoned faith and Elizabeth praised it (Lk 2:19,51; 1:42,45). Jesus did not rebuke Mary as lacking faith (Mk 3:31-35; Lk 11:27-28) but, as Augustine pointed out, that she was more blessed for her discipleship of faith than for her divine maternity.

Marian Doctrine:

Divine Maternity (Lk 1:43; cf. 2 Sam 6:9; Gal 4:4): The Fathers of the Church refer to Mary as "*Theotokos*" (God-bearer), a title vindicated at the Council of Ephesus in 431.

Mary's Intercessory Power: Mary fulfills the role of "queen-mother" (Hebrew: *gebirah*) who intercedes with the king on behalf of His royal subjects (1 Kgs 2:19-20). Mary intervenes at Cana prompting Jesus to perform His first sign (Jn 2:1-11).

Mary/Meeting Tent: Lk 1:35.

Mary/Ark of the Covenant: Compare Lk 1:39-45 & 2 Sam 6. As King David danced for joy before the ark of the Lord, so John the Baptist leaped in his mother's womb when Mary's greeting reached Elizabeth's ears. Perpetual Virginity of Mary: Jesus alone is called "the Son of Mary" (Mk 6:3). The brethren of Jesus are referred to as the sons of Mary the wife of Cleophas (Mt 13:55; Mk 15:40) or as the sons of the "other Mary" (Mt 28:1; Jn 19:25). Cf. also: Assumption; Immaculate Conception.

There is no separate word in Aramaic/Hebrew for cousins or other close relatives, so according to Semitic custom they are called brothers and sisters (Gen 14:14; 1 Chr 23:21-22).

If Jesus in fact had biological brothers and sisters, He would not have entrusted Mary to John (Jn 19:26-27).

The Fathers of the Church and the Lateran Synod of 649 taught that Mary was "ever-virgin" (*aeiparthenos*) having remained a virgin "before Jesus' birth, during His birth, and after His birth," (*ante partum, in partu, post partum*). Cf. Sg 4:12.

Certain Fathers taught that the brothers and sisters of Jesus may have been Joseph's adopted children (*Protoevangelium of James*) or children from a previous marriage of his.

Jerome maintained that Joseph remained a virgin to respect Mary's own vow of virginity implied in her response to the Angel Gabriel (Lk 1:34).

John Chrysostom explains that the use of "until" in Mt 1:25 affirms Mary's virginity and does not imply any change after Jesus' birth. See the use of "until" in Gen 8:6-7; Ps 110:1; Mt 28:20; 1 Cor 15:25.

Mt 1:25 and Lk 2:7 refer to Jesus as Mary's "first-born son." This is a Jewish legal term designating the privileges of the first male child who opened the womb and therefore was consecrated to the Lord. It does not indicate that a couple had other children (Ex 13:2). Cf also: Assumption, Immaculate Conception.

Novena: Nine days of prayer in imitation of Mary and the Apostles who awaited the coming of the Holy Spirit (Acts 1:13-14).

"Once Saved, Always Saved": Salvation begins at Baptism and the believer must work out his salvation with fear and trembling, persevering until the end to achieve definitive salvation (Jn 8:31; Rom 2:7; Phil 1:6; 2:12; Col 1:23; 1 Tim 4:16; Rev 2:7).

Penance, Sacrament of: Mt 16:19; 18:15-20; Lk 15:1-32; Jn 20:19-23; 1 Cor 5:1-13; 2 Cor 2:5-11.

Petrine Primacy: Peter is one of three Apostles in Jesus' inner circle (Mt 17:1-13; Mk 9:2-8; 13:3; Lk 9:28-36); the first named in the lists of the Apostles (Mt 10:1-4; Mk 3:16-19; Lk 6:14-16; Acts 1:13); acts as spokesman for the Twelve (Mt 17:1-13; Mk 10:28-30; Acts 1:15-26; 5:29; 15:6-12); Jesus ordered Peter to pay the tax for them both (Mt 17:26); Jesus taught from Peter's boat; hence the expression the "barque of Peter" referring to the Pope's supreme teaching authority (Lk 5:3); Peter decided matters at the Council of Jerusalem (Acts 15:7,12); chose the method for electing Judas' successor in the Apostolic College (Acts 1:15-26); was the first Apostle to enter the empty tomb (Jn 20:6); encounter the Risen Christ (Lk 24:34; 1 Cor 15:5); address the Jewish leaders (Acts 4:8-9); preach the Gospel and work a miracle on Pentecost (Acts 2:14; 3:1-10); bring the Gospel to the Gentiles (Acts 10); the only Apostle to raise a person from the dead (Acts 9:36-43); when Peter's shadow fell upon the sick they were cured, hence, the origin of the expression "*sub umbra Petri*," (under the shadow of Peter); in his presence alone were a man and woman struck dead for lying to the Holy Spirit (Acts 5:1-11).

Jesus changed Peter's name. In the Bible to change a person's name signified to change a person's identity and mission: so Abram became Abraham; Jacob (Israel); Saul (Paul); and Simon (Peter); (Mt 16:18; Mk 3:16; Lk 6:14; Jn 1:42).

Divinely inspired, Peter confessed Jesus' divine and messianic identity. Jesus responded by blessing Peter and instituting His Church, built on Peter and his rock-solid confession of faith (Mt 16:17).

The Evangelist changed the Greek word from "*petra*" to "*petros*" to respect Peter's masculinity. However, in Aramaic, the word "*kephas*" (*cephas*) would remain the same in both instances: "You are Peter [*kephas*] and upon this [*kephas*] I will build My Church." It is clear, therefore, that Jesus built His Church on the rock who is Peter.

It is fitting that Jesus spoke those words against the backdrop of the massive rock formation at Caesarea Philippi, in an area once dedicated to Pan, the pagan god of shepherds.

Peter alone is entrusted with the keys of the Kingdom. The symbolism of the keys can be understood against the background of Is 22:20-22 in which King Hezekiah made Eliakim his prime minister, giving him keys as a symbol of his new authority.

The Pope is the Successor of Peter. He exercises the power of the keys when he teaches infallibly on matters of faith and morals "from the chair of Peter" (*ex cathedra Petri*). He cannot err in his teaching because of Jesus' promise that the gates of hell will never prevail against the Church (Mt 16:18).

Jesus prayed for Peter that his faith would never fail. Peter having repented of his denial was tasked with strengthening the faith of his brethren (Lk 22:32).

Peter reversed his three-fold denial with a three-fold confession after the Resurrection. Consequently, Peter was made Christ's Vicar on earth, the chief visible shepherd of the Church (Jn 21:15-19).

Origen of Alexandria, Hilary of Poitiers and Jerome explain that Jesus called Peter "Satan" (Mt 16:21-23) because his misplaced compassion was an obstacle to the Cross, but that Peter was not Satan in a literal sense, for he had already confessed Jesus' Divinity, thus becoming the rock on which the Lord intended to build His Church (Mt 16:13).

Paul chided Peter for hypocrisy, not heresy (Gal 2:11).

Ambrose: "*Ubi Petrus, ibi ecclesia*" ("Where Peter is, there is the Church").

Augustine: "*Roma locuta est, causa finita est*" ("Rome has spoken, the case is closed").

The Bishops at the Council of Chalcedon (451): "Peter has spoken through [Pope] Leo."

Private Interpretation of Scripture: 2 Pt 1:20-21.

Purgatory: Mal 3:2-3; 2 Mac 12: 38-46; Mt 5:26, 12:32; 1 Cor 3:11-15; Heb 12:14, 23, 29; Rev 21:27.

Relics: Gen 50:25-26; 2 Kgs 2:15; 13:20-21; Acts 19:11-12.

Rosary: **Joyful Mysteries**: Annunciation (Lk 1:26-38); Visitation (Lk 1:39-56); Nativity (Mt 1:18-25; Lk 1:26-38); Presentation in the Temple (Lk 2:22-40); Finding in the Temple (Lk 41-52). **Sorrowful Mysteries**: Agony in the Garden (Mt 26:36-46; Mk 14:32-42; Lk 22:40-46); Scourging at the pillar (Mt 26:67-68; Mk 14:65; Jn 18:22-24); Crowning with thorns (Mt 27:27-31; Mk 15:16-20; Lk 23:11; Jn 19:2-3); Carrying the cross (Mt 27:31-32; Mk 15:20-23; Lk 23:26-32; Jn 19:17); Crucifixion (Mt 27:32-44; Mk 15:22-32; Lk 23:33-39; Jn 19:17-30). **Glorious Mysteries**: Resurrection (Mt 28:1-10; Mk 16:1-8; Lk 24:1-12; Jn 20:1-10); Ascension (Lk 24:50-53; Acts 1:6-11); Descent of the Holy Spirit (Acts 2:1-13); Assumption of Mary (Rev 12:1-17); Coronation of Mary (Rev 12:1). **Luminous Mysteries**: Baptism of the Lord (Mt 3:13-17; Mk 1:9-11; Lk 3:21-22); Wedding Feast at Cana (Jn 2:1-11); Proclamation of the Kingdom of God and Call to Repentance (Mt 4:12-17; Mk 1:14-15; Lk 4:14-15); Transfiguration (Mt 17:1-13; Mk 9:2-10; Lk 9:28-36; 2 Pt 1:17-18); Institution of the Holy Eucharist (Mt 26:17-29; Mk 14:22-25; Lk 22:17-19; 1 Cor 10:16; 11:23-26).

Tradition holds that Mary entrusted the Rosary to St. Dominic of Guzman as a particular tool to overcome the Albigensian heresy. The Dominican, Alain de la Roche, popularized it.

Blessed Bartolo Longo is known as "The Apostle of the Rosary," describing it as a "sweet chain linking us to God." After Mass and the Liturgy of the Hours, the Rosary holds pride of place in the Catholic spiritual life.

Sacramentals: Mk 5:28-29; 6:56; 7:33-34; 8:23; Jn 9:6

Sola Scriptura ("Bible Alone"): "All [not only!] Scripture is inspired by God," (2 Tim 3:16-17).

Stations of the Cross: The early Christians made pilgrimages to the Holy Land, especially during Holy Week, to retrace the steps of Our Lord during His Passion in the holy city of Jerusalem. A nun by the name of Egeria (Aetheria or Etheria, A.D. 381-384) wrote an account of her three-year pilgrimage to the Holy Land. Her descriptions of the liturgical events of Holy Week in fourth-century Palestine are invaluable.

For those unable to make a pilgrimage to the Holy Land, a venerable custom arose throughout Europe (c. A.D. 1300) of setting up depictions of the "*Via Crucis*" ("Way of the Cross") both outdoors and along the walls of churches, as we see often today. There are fourteen traditional Stations of the Cross.

True Cross, Relic of the: St. Helena, the Mother of the Emperor Constantine, made a pilgrimage to the Holy Land in the fourth century A.D. She found three mounds on Calvary and ordered that a gravely ill man be placed on top of the middle mound; the man was instantly cured. St. Helena then had the true Cross of Our Lord excavated and transported, along with other relics of the Passion, to Rome. Constantine built a home for Helena next to the

Basilica of Santa Croce in Gerusalemme because she wanted to live as close as possible to the chapel containing the relics of the Lord's Passion.

"Vain Repetition": Jesus did not condemn repetition, but deemed it "vain" when men's hearts are hypocritical (Mt 6:7). The repetition of a word in Hebrew expresses the superlative form or emphasis (Is 6:3; Jn 3:3, 5). Jesus prayed the same prayer three times in the Garden of Gethsemane (Mt 26:36-46; Mk 14:32-42, especially v. 39).

Vestments, Priestly: Ex 28:1-43.

The vestments of Catholic priests are based on the garments worn by the priests of the Old Testament and those of the ancient Romans.

For a fuller presentation of the preceding topics and others, consult the following works:

Mike Aquilina, *The Way of the Fathers: Praying with the Early Christians* (Our Sunday Visitor Publishing Division, 2000).

Dave Armstrong, *Bible Proofs for Catholic Truths: A Source Book for Apologists and Inquirers* (Sophia Institute Press, 2009).

_____, *A Biblical Defense of Catholicism* (Sophia Institute Press, 2003).

_____, *The Catholic Verses: 95 Bible Passages that Confound Protestants* (Sophia Institute Press, 2004).

_____, *More Biblical Evidence for Catholicism: A Companion to A Biblical Defense of Catholicism* (self-published, 2007).

_____, *The One-Minute Apologist: Essential Catholic Replies to Over Sixty Common Protestant Claims* (Sophia Institute Press, 2007).

The Church's Confession of Faith: A Catholic Catechism for Adults (Ignatius Press and Communio Books, 1989).

The Didache Bible, with Commentaries Based on the Catechism of the Catholic Church (Ignatius Bible Edition/RSV Translation Catholic Edition) (Ignatius Press & Midwest Theological Forum, 2014).

Robert J. Fox, *Protestant Fundamentalism and the Born Again Catholic* (Fatima Family Apostolate, 1991).

Scott Hahn, *Reasons to Believe: How to Understand, Explain and Defend the Catholic Faith* (Doubleday, 2007).

John Hardon, S.J., *The Catholic Catechism: A Contemporary Catechism of the Teachings of the Catholic Church* (Doubleday, 1981). Karl Keating, *Catholicism and Fundamentalism: The Attacks on "Romanism" by "Bible Christians"* (Ignatius Press, 1988).

Ian Ker, *Mere Catholicism* (Emmaus Road Publishing, 2006).

Peter Klein, *The Catholic Source Book: A Comprehensive Collection of Information about the Catholic Church* (Harcourt Religion Publishers, 2000).

Peter Kreeft, *Fundamentals of the Faith: Essays in Christian Apologetics* (Ignatius Press, 1988).

_____ & Ronald K. Tacelli, *Handbook of Christian Apologetics* (Inter Varsity Press, 1994).

Al Kresta, *Why do Catholics Genuflect? And Answers to Other Puzzling Questions about the Catholic Church* (Servant Publications, 2001).

Xavier Léon-Dufour, *Dictionary of Biblical Theology* (Harper San Francisco Publishers, 1995).

Dwight Longenecker, *Christianity Pure and Simple* (Sophia Institute Press, 2005).

Diarmuid MacCulloch, *Christianity: The First Three Thousand Years* (Viking, 2010).

_____, *More Christianity: Finding the Fullness of the Faith* [Expanded Revised Edition] (Ignatius Press, 2010).

Patrick Madrid, *Where is That in the Bible?* (Our Sunday Visitor Publishing Division, 2001).

_____, *Why Is That in Tradition?* (Our Sunday Visitor Publishing Division, 2002).

Frederick W. Marks, *A Brief for Belief: The Case for Catholicism* (Queenship Publishing Company, 1999).

_____, *Think and Believe* (Emmaus Road Publishing, 2012).

New American Bible: The Catholic Study Bible, edited by Donald Senior, John J. Collins and Mary Ann Getty [Second Edition] (Oxford University Press, 2011).

Aidan Nichols, O.P., *Epiphany: A Theological Introduction to Catholicism* (The Liturgical Press, 1996).

John Francis Noll, revised by Albert J, Nevins, M.M., *Father Smith Instructs Jackson* (Our Sunday Visitor Inc, 1981).

Ludwig Ott, *Fundamentals of Catholic Dogma* (Tan Books, 1974).

Jaroslav Pelikan, *Whose Bible Is It?* (Penguin Books, 2005).

Francis Ripley, *This is the Faith: A Complete Explanation of the Catholic Faith* [Third Edition] (Tan Books and Publishers, Inc, 2002).

Mario P. Romero, *Unabridged Christianity: Biblical Answers to Common Questions about the Roman Catholic Faith* (Queenship Publishing Company, 1999).

Jeffrey Burton Russell, *Exposing Myths about Christianity: A Guide to Answering 145 Viral Lies and Legends* (Inter Varsity Press, 2012).

James V. Schall, S.J. *Reasonable Pleasures: The Strange Coherences of Catholicism* (Ignatius Press, 2013).

The Scripture Source Book (Our Sunday Visitor Curriculum Division, 2008).

Mark Shea, *By What Authority: An Evangelical Discovers Catholic Tradition* [Revised and Expanded Edition] (Ignatius Press, 2013).

_____. *Making Senses Out of Scripture: Reading the Bible as the First Christians Did* (Basilica Press, 1999).

Michael Sheehan, *Apologetics and Catholic Doctrine*, edited and revised by Peter Joseph [Sixth Edition] (The Saint Austin Press, 2001)

Alan Schreck, *Basics of the Faith: A Catholic Catechism* (Servant Books, 1988).

_____, *Catholic and Christian: An Explanation of Commonly Misunderstood Catholic Beliefs* (Servant Books, 1984).

James Socias, *Introduction to Catholicism for Adults* (Midwest Theological Forum, 2012).

Carl J. Sommer, *We Look for a Kingdom: The Everyday Lifes of the Early Christians* (Ignatius, 2007).

Peter M. J. Stravinskas, *The Bible and the Mass* [Fourth Edition] (Newman House Press, 2014).

_____, *The Catholic Church and the Bible* [Third Edition] (Newman House Press, 2014).

_____, *The Catholic Response* [Revised and Updated] (Our Sunday Visitor Publishing Division, 2001).

United States Catholic Catechism for Adults (United States Conference of Catholic Bishops, 2006).

Milton Walsh, *Into All Truth: What Catholics Believe and Why* (Ignatius Press, 2013).

Donald W. Wuerl, Ronald Lawler, O.F.M. Cap., Thomas C. Lawler, *The Teaching of Christ: A Catholic Catechism for Adults* [Fourth Edition] (Our Sunday Visitor Publishing Division, 1995).

Topical Index

Abercius (epitaph), 245-246
Academy, of Plato, 130
Acta Martyrum (Acts of the Martyrs), 122
Adoptionism, 20
aeiparthenos (ever-virgin: Mary), 293
Agatho, Pope St., 81, 83
Akathist Hymn, vi, 303-304
Albigensianism, 13, 25-26
Alexander of Alexandria, 36, 41, 296, 297
Alexander the Great, 68, 130, 216
Alexandrian Canon, 216-217
Alexandrian School (High Christology), 27, 71, 75, 156, 171, 173, 203
Ambrose of Milan, 3, 8, 17, 201-202, 252, 265
Anacletus, Pope St., 103, 121-122
analogia fidei (analogy of faith), 79
Anaphora, 251, 255, 291
Andrew of Crete, 89
Angels, 6, 149, 165, 237, 288 (Satan), 301
Annunciation, the, 6, 52, 67, 149, 161, 285-286, 295, 297-298
Anointing of the Sick (sacrament), 253
Anselm of Canterbury, St., 261, 306
Anthony of Egypt, 38, 202
Antiochean School (Low Christology), 27, 65, 158
Antoninus Pius, Emperor, 131
Apocrypha, the, 214
apocryphal gospels, 17, 293
Apollinarius, 51-52, 72
apologetics, 38, 113, 125, 130, 133, 140, 147, 169, 239, 242, 307
apostasy, 10, 23, 147, 187, 271
Apostolic Fathers, 109
Apostolic Tradition, 3, 121, 125, 139-140, 157, 178, 219, 230, 251-255, 257, 289-291
Apostolic Succession, 103, 109, 138, 143, 223, 278, 286
Apostolic Constitutions, 252, 257-258
Arcadius, Emperor, 3
Arianism (Arians), 34-35, 38, 40-41, 53
Aristeas, 216-217
Aristide of Athens, 296
Aristophanes, 221
Arius of Alexandria, 34, 36, 38, 40-46, 72, 125, 257
Artemis (Diana), 60, 68

ABOUT THE AUTHOR

The Reverend Nicholas L. Gregoris was born on July 26, 1972 in the Borough of Manhattan, New York City. He attended parochial elementary and secondary schools in the Archdiocese of New York, graduating from Saint Peter's Boys' High School in 1989.

An alumnus of the Pontifical North American College in Rome, Father Gregoris was ordained a priest on May 26, 1997.

He studied at Saint John's University and the Marian Library/International Marian Research Institute at the University of Dayton before earning a Bachelor's degree in Classical Languages from Seton Hall University; a Bachelor's degree in Sacred Theology from the Pontifical Gregorian University; and a

Licentiate and a Doctorate in Sacred Theology, both from the Pontifical Theological Faculty Marianum.

His doctoral thesis on the Mariology of John Henry Newman entailed research at Oxford University, the Birmingham Oratory and the Friends of Newman centers in Rome and Littlemore. That thesis was subsequently published under the title of *The Daughter of Eve Unfallen: Mary in the Theology and Spirituality of John Henry Newman* (Newman House Press, 2003).

Father Gregoris has taught on the faculty of the Pontifical College Josephinum and served as the first full-time chaplain of Wyoming Catholic College. He is fluent in several languages and has translated works for the Vatican and the United States Conference of Catholic Bishops.

He has published numerous articles for the Catholic press and has made guest appearances on the EWTN and Relevant Radio. He has been accredited to the Vatican Press Corps, most notably for the Great Jubilee Year 2000 and the Extraordinary Synod of Bishops on the Family in 2014.

Father Gregoris is the co-founder of the Priestly Society of Blessed John Henry Newman and Newman House Press. He currently serves as the managing editor of *The Catholic Response* magazine and resides at Newman House in Ocean County, New Jersey.